Hippeastrum

Royal Horticultural Society Plant Collector Guide

Hippeastrum

the gardener's amaryllis

Veronica M. Read

Timber Press
Portland • Cambridge

ROYAL HORTICULTURAL SOCIETY

Plates and Figures

John Bryan, F.I. Horticultural Consultant, California, United States—Plates 2-4, 9-1.
Jane Edwards, Paulton, Somerset, Great Britain—Plates 8-1, 8-2.
Chris Ireland-Jones, Avon Bulbs, Somerset, Great Britain—Plate 1-11.
Richard Maguire, Maguire's Hippeastrum Farm, Queensland, Australia—
Plates 3-6, 3-10, 3-13, 7-1.
S&O Mathews Photography, Isle of Wight, Great Britain—Plate 1-10.
Isamu Miyake, Miyake Nursery Ltd, Chiba-kon, Japan—
Plates 4-2, 4-3, 6-4 to 6-7, 7-2, 7-3.
Cathy Osselton, Testcentrum voor Siergewassen B.V., Hillegom, The Netherlands—
Plates 6-8 to 6-13.
Alun R. Rees, Horticulture Consultant, Sussex, Great Britain—Figure 8-1.
Royal Botanic Gardens, Kew Library, Surrey, Great Britain—
Plates 1-2, 1-7, 2-2, 2-3, 2-5 to 2-7.
Royal Horticultural Society Lindley Library, London, Great Britain—
Plates 1-1, 1-3 to 1-6, 1-8, 1-12, 2-1, 3-1.
Ian Woolley, Wembley, Middlesex, Great Britain—
Plates 1-9, 3-2 to 3-5, 3-7 to 3-9, 3-11, 3-12, 4-1, 4-4 to 4-15, 5-1 to 5-5, 6-1 to 6-3, 6-14 to 6-26, 7-4 to 7-14, 8-3 to 8-9, 9-2 to 9-6, 11-1 to 11-13.

Published in association with the Royal Horticultural Society in 2004 by

Timber Press, Inc.
The Haseltine Building
133 S.W. Second Avenue, Suite 450
Portland, Oregon 97204-3527, U.S.A.

Timber Press
2 Station Road
Swavesey
Cambridge CB4 5QJ, U.K.

Design by Dick Malt
Printed through Colorcraft Ltd., Hong Kong

Library of Congress Cataloging-in-Publication Data
Read, Veronica M.
Hippeastrum : the gardener's amaryllis / Veronica M. Read.
p. cm. – (Royal Horticultural Society plant collector guide)
Includes bibliographical references (p.).
ISBN 0-88192-639-6 (hardcover)
1. Hippeastrum. 2. Amaryllis (Genus) I. Title. II. Series.

SB413.A5R43 2004 635.9′3434–dc22 2003019953

A catalog record of this book is available from the British Library.

Contents

Foreword by Professor Peter R. Crane 7
Preface 9
Acknowledgments 13

Chapter 1 *Amaryllis* or *Hippeastrum*? 15
Chapter 2 Species 29
Chapter 3 Large-Flowering Singles 41
Chapter 4 Smaller Flowering Hybrids 81
Chapter 5 Yellow Hippeastrums 97
Chapter 6 Modern Hybrids 107
Chapter 7 Doubles 133
Chapter 8 Structure and Development 159
Chapter 9 Growers' Guide to Cultivating Better Hippeastrums 179
Chapter 10 Commercial Breeding and Production 201
Chapter 11 Propagation 219
Chapter 12 Pests and Diseases 235

Appendix: Further Information on the Hybrid Lists in Chapters 3 to 7 257
Glossary 265
Bibliography 270
Index 284

Color plates follow page 96

To the late Malcolm Norris, former director of the Institute for Local Government Studies, Birmingham University (Great Britain), with fondest love and heartfelt thanks for encouraging me in all my academic activities and being such a wonderful friend and mentor.

Foreword

Veronica Read is one of a distinctive breed of British horticulturists and one who makes this nation of plant lovers rather special. She is hooked on *Hippeastrum*—amaryllis to most people. The Royal Botanic Gardens, Kew, first made contact with Veronica in 1998, when she visited in a professional capacity to talk about National Vocational Qualifications. Soon, however, she mentioned her personal interest in *Hippeastrum* and such was her enthusiasm that we started to listen. Initially, she convinced us to look at this group of spectacular bulbs in terms of their occasional inclusion in glasshouse displays, but then these ideas grew into what became the very first of a now-established series of seasonal festivals at Kew. Thus, in the spring of 1999, the north end of the Princess of Wales Conservatory was filled with an astonishing array of new and striking *Hippeastrum* cultivars, selected and sourced with Veronica's help and supported by local business. Even though some of Kew's traditional visitors might have been a little taken aback by the bold style of this display, many, we know, went to the Kew Shop and other outlets to buy their own giant bulbs and impress their friends.

Veronica has a passion for hippeastrums which is infectious and unstoppable. Her work at Royal Horticultural Society shows at Westminster and through the National Council for the Conservation of Plants and Gardens has made hippeastrums more popular than ever before. This has in part been fuelled by the development of new hybrids and strains that she has helped introduce from Holland, the United States and other countries. Even though her resources have always been limited and cultivating these plants is not always plain sailing, she has not paused to promote them. The present book is a well-deserved triumph and one that can only increase the interest in these magnificent subtropical bulbs, with their capacity to brighten our houses and conservatories during the dull days of northern winters. The book's comprehensive treatment and excellent photographs add much to our understanding of the diversity of hybrids and cultivars now available, not to mention the potential for creating more with a wider range of natural species entering cultivation. I can guarantee that the Kew will not be the only botanical garden to use displays of *Hippeastrum* in future years.

Peter R. Crane, FRS,
Director, Royal Botanic Gardens, Kew

Preface

My interest in hippeastrums began following a visit to the Keukenhof (Lisse, The Netherlands) in May 1993 where I saw a splendid display of hybrids. I was immediately fascinated by the plant's beauty and diversity and decided to learn everything I could about the plant and cultivate as many different hybrids as possible.

No authoritative text existed and no British university, botanical or horticultural establishment was able to answer satisfactorily my increasingly complex queries. In 1996, the Institute for Horticultural Plant Breeding in Wageningen (The Netherlands) put me in touch with Marko Penning of Penning Breeding B.V. (Honselersdijk, The Netherlands). At last I had found someone who was able and willing to help me. Thanks to Marko Penning and Joop Doorduin (*Hippeastrum* researcher at the Research Station for Floriculture and Glasshouse Vegetables, Naaldwijk, The Netherlands), I was finally able to advance my research into the plant. Cytogenetics tuition under the guidance of Dr. Peter Brandham at the Jodrell Laboratories, Royal Botanic Gardens Kew in the late 1990s opened my eyes still further to the wonders of *Hippeastrum*.

After I became the National Plant Collection Holder of *Hippeastrum* of the National Council for the Conservation of Plants and Gardens (NCCPG) in 1998, my research activities intensified and led to publications and features in national and international horticultural journals and gardening magazines. I organized shows and festivals in my South Harrow flat and exhibited at the Royal Horticultural Society shows at Westminster where I introduced new American, Dutch, Japanese and South African hybrids and invited comments on these new types. These were occasions of great color and considerable enjoyment. Talks and lectures to horticultural societies and gardening clubs generated further interest and, judging from the numerous queries and correspondence I received from gardeners requesting detailed advice on how to successfully cultivate and propagate the plant and obtain new varieties, a book dedicated to *Hippeastrum* was urgently needed.

Hippeastrum: *The Gardener's Amaryllis* focuses upon the development, cultivation and propagation of hybrid *Hippeastrum* and *H. papilio.* Few details are available on the species and therefore information is limited to those used in hybridization since the 18th century. Many species have exacting cultural requirements making them unsuitable for home cultivation in the Northern Hemisphere and until 2003, only *H. papilio* remained commercially available.

Most hybrids are quick and easy to grow, making them ideal plants for beginners and more experienced gardeners, young and old alike. They make wonderful indoor pot plants and cut flowers for domestic and commercial environments and superb patio and garden bedding plants in frost-free climates. Plants with large flowers look spectacular in large, formal cut flower arrangements and mass indoor and outdoor plantings; smaller, more delicate examples make splendid decorations for the windowsill; coffee, dining room and bedside tables; and the office. Whatever the plant size and end use, the brilliant flower colors add great sparkle which is particularly welcome on dark, gloomy winter days.

This book would not have been possible without the tireless support of Ian Woolley and his wife, Betty. Ian has been photographer to the National Plant Collection of *Hippeastrum* since 1997 and has captured every hybrid in the Collection on film in its various stages of development—from newly purchased bulb to the harvesting of seeds and propagation by seed, offsets, chipping and twin scaling. I now have an extensive and valuable collection of slides which have become an integral part of the Collection, an excellent teaching tool and a wonderful reminder of the plants I have grown over the years. Looking at the slides always gives me the greatest pleasure and I am delighted to be able to include so many them in the book. Thank you very much indeed, Ian and Betty, for all your help, support and friendship which are greatly appreciated.

In 2002, I was fortunate to meet artist Jane Edwards who agreed to paint three recent acquisitions to the National Plant Collection of Hippeastrum. The resulting bulb studies of 'Flamengo', 'Reggae' and 'Tango' were particularly exquisite and I am thrilled to include two of them in the book. These, together with photographs of paintings of some of the finest species and hybrid *Hippeastrum* and *Amaryllis belladonna* by leading 19th- and 20th-century artists, highlight the plant's remarkable diversity and outstanding beauty.

I hope this book will inspire you to cultivate hippeastrums and start your own collection. May I wish you every success in growing the plant and may it give you as much pleasure as it has given me for a decade.

Acknowledgments

I wish to thank Richard Maguire (Maguire's Hippeastrum Farm, Woombye, Queensland, Australia), Antonio F. C. Tombolato (Agronômico Institute at Campinas, Brazil), Chris Ireland-Jones (manager, Avon Bulbs, Somerset, Great Britain), Dennis Wilson (Isle of Wight, Great Britain), S. K. Datta (National Botanical Research Institute, Lucknow, India), Hugh Povey (European sales specialist, Agrexco Agricultural Export Company), Azriel Assaf (general manager, Amaryllis Nurseries, Kibbutz Saad, Israel), Isamu Miyake (director, Miyake Nursery, Chiba-kon, Japan), Andre Barnhoorn (Barnhoorn Hippeastrum Breeding B.V., Noordwijkerhout, The Netherlands), Cathy Osselton (Testcentrum voor Siergewassen B.V., Hillegom, The Netherlands), Marko Penning (Penning Breeding B.V., Honselersdijk, The Netherlands), Justin Bowles (Port Elizabeth, South Africa), Floris Barnhoorn (managing director, Hadeco Pty Ltd, Maraisburg, South Africa), Jerry Charpentier (Florida, United States), John W. Deme (California, United States), John L. Doran (California, United States) and Alan Meerow (Florida, United States) for advice and information on breeding, cultivation and propagation and for commenting on the draft chapters.

I wish to thank Joost Barendrecht (Permanent Expert to the Raad voor het Kwekersrecht for Ornamentals and Fruit Crops, Wageningen, The Netherlands) for advising on Plant Breeders' Rights; Johan van Scheepen (senior taxonomist and senior registrar) and Saskia Bodegom (taxonomist and registrar) of Royal General Bulbgrowers' Association (Koninklijke Algemeene Vereeniging voor Bloembollencultuur; KAVB), Hillegom, The Netherlands, for advising on *Hippeastrum* registration.

I express sincere thanks to Sir Peter Smithers (Vico Morcote, Switzerland) and Charles Hardman (California, United States) for facilitating contacts with breeders and growers. Thanks to Barbara Boyd (XStream Corporation, United States) who downloaded all the chapters for review by

John E. Bryan (horticultural consultant, California, United States). I am most grateful to Barbara and John for their valuable help and advice. Heartfelt thanks are extended to Alun R. Rees (horticultural consultant, Sussex, Great Britain) for advising on plant physiology and commenting on the draft chapter.

I gratefully acknowledge the assistance of staff and volunteers of the Barbican Library, City of London, and the libraries of the Royal Horticultural Society London and the Royal Botanic Gardens Kew. In particular I extend heartfelt thanks and appreciation to Jennifer Vine (picture librarian) and Brent Elliot (librarian) of the Royal Horticultural Society Lindley Library and Marilyn Ward (illustrations curator) of the Library, Royal Botanic Gardens Kew for arranging the photography of paintings and giving permission for them to appear in the book. Thanks are extended to S&O Mathews Photography, Yarmouth, Isle of Wight, which kindly lent the slide of *Amaryllis* seeds for the book.

My thanks to John Lonsdale (head of public programs and curatorial support), Phil Griffiths (displays co-ordinator, Great Glasshouses and Training Section) and Martin Staniforth (practical training co-ordinator, Great Glasshouses and Training Section) of Royal Botanic Gardens Kew; Jim Gardiner (curator), Nick Morgan (superintendent) and Andrew Halstead (senior entomologist) of the Royal Horticultural Society Garden Wisley for advising on potting mixes, pests and diseases, and for providing me with facilities to carry out hot water treatment of bulbs in the National Plant Collection of *Hippeastrum*.

Grateful thanks and appreciation are extended to Sheila Thompson and Rodney Lay who translated Dutch articles and to Cathy Anderson, Sher Baloch, Kevin Bassil, William Blacklock, Sheila Davies, Marianne Foo, Carol Foreman, Pat Fray, Dennis Fulwood, Lina Mehta, John Parrick, Ruth Rees, David Sitch, Enid Taylor, Stam Taylor, Dennis Wilson and Stu Wilson for reading and commenting on the draft chapters.

To all, my sincere thanks and appreciation for your help.

Chapter 1
Amaryllis or *Hippeastrum*?

The true identities of the South African *Amaryllis belladonna* Linnaeus and South American Hippeastrum Herbert have attracted the attention of eminent European and North American botanists and taxonomists since their introduction into European cultivation in the mid 18th century. These scientists sought to clarify a highly complex and confusing situation surrounding the legitimacy of names by presenting and interpreting evidence in different ways to support their own point of view.

Chapter 1 reviews taxonomic developments since 1753 and attempts to clarify the confusion that continues to exist even today. It concludes with a description of *Amaryllis belladonna* and *Worsleya rayneri* (more commonly known as the blue amaryllis). Species used in *Hippeastrum* hybridization since the 18th century are described in Chapter 2.

History

1689–1804

The origins of the *Amaryllis/Hippeastrum* naming mystery can be traced to the first edition of Carolus Linnaeus' *Species Plantarum* (1753) in which he listed *A. belladonna* as one of 9 species within the genus *Amaryllis*. Linnaeus considered the specific name particularly appropriate in view of the plant's outstanding beauty. (The other 8 species were *A. atamasco*, *A. formosissima*, *A. guttata*, *A. longifolia*, *A. lutea*, *A. orientalis*, *A. sarniensis* and *A. zeylanica*, all of which have been renamed and subsequently classified into other genera.)

Previously, in *Hortus Cliffortianus* (1738), Linnaeus had referred to *Amaryllis belladonna* as *A. equestris* (now recognized as *Hippeastrum equestre* Herbert), originating from the West Indies and South America.

Other sources also referred to *A. belladonna* as a South American species. Much later Hamilton P. Traub (1954), former editor of the journal of the American Amaryllis Society (known first as *Plant Life*, then *Herbertia*), referred to the plant's hollow scape, a significant feature of *Hippeastrum*, compared to the solid scape of the South African species.

During the 1760s it became apparent to other botanists that at least 2 species other than *Amaryllis equestris* were being cultivated and described under the name *A. belladonna*—a tall, floriferous, autumn-flowering pink from South Africa and a shorter, less floriferous, spring-blooming red from the Caribbean. The latter, known in England as Mexican lily or *Lilium reginae* was referred to by Linnaeus as *A. reginae* in the 10th edition of *Systema Naturae* (1759).

By the 1780s, several distinguished botanists, including John Miller and Charles L'Héritier referred to the South African species as *Amaryllis belladonna* (Plate 1-1) and the spring-flowering red as *A. reginae* which Linnaeus had referred to as *A. belladonna*, also known as Barbados amaryllis, was named *A. equestris* in the first edition of Aiton's *Hortus Kewensis* (1789) and subsequently illustrated in *Curtis's Botanical Magazine* (tab. 305, 1795) and reproduced here (Plate 1-2). The short-flowered red plant remained as *A. reginae* (*Botanical Magazine*, tab. 453, 1799) (see Plate 1-3), while the Cape plant was referred to as *A. belladonna* (*Botanical Magazine*, tab. 733, 1804). At this time, however, confusion still surrounded the plant's origin and some sources referred to it as possibly originating from Brazil.

1805–1920

Two British botanists, Dean William Herbert (1778–1847) and John Gilbert Baker (1834–1920), dominated developments during the 19th and early 20th centuries.

Dean William Herbert

Herbert carried out extensive research into the Amaryllidaceae in the early 19th century. He hybridized extensively using many different species including the South African *Amaryllis belladonna* and several South American species—*Hippeastrum aulicum* (Plate 1-4), *H. calyptratum* (Plate 1-5), *H. equestre* (Plate 1-2), *H. psittacinum* (Plate 1-6), *H. reginae* (Plate 1-3), *H. solandriflorum* (Plate 1-7) and *H. vittatum* (Plate 1-8)—making discoveries, considered by some, to be way ahead of his time. He recorded and illustrated the differences in structure and development of flowers, foliage, fruit and seed of the South African and South American species, as well as other plants in the Amaryllidaceae, publishing his findings in *Curtis's Botanical Magazine, Botanical Register* and *Transactions of the Horticultural Society of London* in the 1820s and 1830s.

Herbert observed significant differences in the characteristics of seed capsules and their contents (number of seeds, shape, size, color and texture) between the South African and South American species. The South American species were genetically incompatible, unlike the South African *Amaryllis belladonna* which crossed freely with other South African members such as *Nerine* and *Brunsvigia*. Based on these differences, Herbert separated the South African and South American species and placed them in separate genera. *Amaryllis belladonna* was retained as *Amaryllis* and the South American species were categorized as *Hippeastrum* or Knight's star lily. *Amaryllis equestris* and *A. reginae* were reclassified as *Hippeastrum equestre* and *H. reginae* respectively.

Herbert then placed the 8 original *Amaryllis* species mentioned by Linnaeus into the following genera: *Ammocharis*, *Boophone*, *Brunsvigia*, *Nerine*, *Oporanthus*, *Sprekelia* and *Zephyranthes*.

Features of *Hippeastrum*

In addition to the hippeastrum's hollow scape and its 3-celled capsule which contains up to 40 or more flat, black, D- or discoid-shaped seeds (Plate 1-9), Herbert identified the following features which distinguished *Hippeastrum* from *Amaryllis* (*belladonna*): tepal tubes of different lengths and widths, tepals of different shapes and sizes on the same flower and among different species, and individual filaments of different lengths. Bristles were present at the base of the throat in some species. One or more scapes appeared simultaneously or consecutively at different times of the year. Hippeastrum seed capsules burst only when the seeds had ripened fully. Between 2 and 4 linear or lorate leaves developed either at the same time as the scape or following flowering. Most species had umbels of between 2 and 6 flowers, although recent discoveries have shown some, such as *H. fosteri*, to have up to 15 flowers.

Herbert's categorization was not immediately accepted by leading taxonomists, among them John Lindley, editor of the *Botanical Register*, and Sir Joseph D. Hooker. Eventually the new taxonomy was accepted and, for the next 100 years, was recognized in publications connected with the South

American species. It seemed that the identities of the South African and South American species had been finally decided and the matter closed; however, as events subsequently showed, this was not the case.

John Gilbert Baker

Baker's contribution to our understanding of the genus *Hippeastrum* was to devise a classification based on floral and foliage characteristics for all members of the Amaryllidaceae. In "A New Key to the Genera of Amaryllidaceae" (1878a) he divided the family into tribes, subtribes and genera. *Amaryllis* and *Hippeastrum* were separate genera in the tribe Amaryllideae. *Amaryllis* was described as monotypic and *A. blanda* as a variety of *A. belladonna.*

Baker regarded *Hippeastrum* as having great horticultural interest. In "An Enumeration and Classification of the Species of *Hippeastrum*" (1878b) he published details of the 47 known species, classifying them according to the number and shape of their flowers and leaves. He described *Hippeastrum* as being entirely confined to tropical and warm temperate America and differing from *Amaryllis* only by its seeds. *Amaryllis* seeds were few, large and bulbous (Plate 1-10) and were similar to *Clivia*, *Crinum* and *Hymenocallis.* Baker likened the numerous, dark, flat seeds of *Hippeastrum* to those of *Pancratium*, *Pyrolirion* and *Zephyranthes.*

Baker (1878b) originally placed *Hippeastrum* species into 9 subgenera but in 1888 (*Handbook of the Amaryllideae*) reclassified 38 species into 7 subgenera—*Habranthus* (Herbert), *Phycella* (Lindley), *Rhodophiala* (C. Presl), *Macropodastrum*, *Omphalissa* (Salisbury), *Aschamia* (Salisbury) and *Lais* (Salisbury)—based on leaf shape (linear or lorate), shape and size of perianth and individual tepals (openly or narrowly funneled), shape and size of tepal tube (long or short, closed or not closed in at the throat), type of stigma (trifid or capitate) and number of flowers per umbel (1–6).

1921–1990

Fresh controversies erupted in 1938 and resurfaced periodically until the mid 1980s. American botanists including J. C. Uphof, Hamilton P. Traub and Harold N. Moldenke, with William Louis Tjaden of Welling, Kent, Great Britain, endeavored to reinstate *Amaryllis* for the South American *Hippeastrum*, *A. belladonna* for the West Indian *H. equestre* and *Callicore rosea* for the South African *A. belladonna* (Uphof 1938; Traub 1954, 1958,

1970; Traub and Moldenke 1949; Tjaden 1981a, 1981b). An opposing group of eminent botanists led by J. R. Sealy (1939) and including J. E. Dandy, J. Ardagh, S. Savage, T. A. Sprague and F. R. Fosberg, refuted Uphof's claims and developed a compelling case for retaining the name *A. belladonna* for the Cape plant.

Subsequent attempts to have the South African and South American species reclassified failed, although a body of resistance remained. Traub and others refused to accept the decision taken by the Committee of the 7th International Congress in 1954 that the name *Amaryllis belladonna* be retained for the South African species and the name *Hippeastrum* be applied to the South American species. These individuals were in the minority, however, and today *A. belladonna* and *Hippeastrum* have been retained and generally adopted.

Hamilton P. Traub

Traub classified the 95 genera and 5 bigeneric hybrids which comprised the family Amaryllidaceae into 23 tribes. All South American *Hippeastrum* were reclassified as *Amaryllis* within the tribe Amarylleae in *Genera of Amaryllidaceae* (1963). Traub divided the genus into the following subgenera—*Macropodastrum*, *Lais*, *Amaryllis*, *Omphalissa* and *Sealyana* and distributed the 55 species according to their floral and foliage characteristics. *Hippeastrum equestre* was restored to its original name—*A. belladonna. Worsleya rayneri* (formerly *Amaryllis procera* and subsequently *Hippeastrum procerum*) was assigned its own genus within the Amarylleae.

The South African *Amaryllis belladonna* was classified within the subgenus *Coburgia* within the genus *Brunsvigia* which was part of the tribe Crineae. This reclassification added further confusion to an already messy situation.

Descriptions of *Hippeastrum* are given in Traub's *Amaryllis Manual* (1958) and have also been published in *Plant Life* since 1933.

Modern Descriptions of *Amaryllis* and *Hippeastrum*

The *New RHS Dictionary of Gardening* (1992) refers to the Amaryllidaceae having about 70 genera and 1390 species and describes *Amaryllis belladonna* and *Hippeastrum* as follows:

> *Amaryllis belladonna.* 1 species, a bulbous perennial herb. Leaves to 20 in.

(50 cm), hysteranthous, several in 2 ranks, strap-shaped, narrowing slightly toward base, somewhat concave above, keeled beneath toward base, glabrous, glossy, mid green, rather fleshy. Scape to 24 in. (60 cm) stout, flushed red-purple. Flowers sweetly scented, short-stalked, 6 or more in an umbel subtended by 2 large, equal spathes which enclose the whole umbel in bud, perianth 2.5–4 in. (6–10 cm), purple-pink to pink, often white toward base, rarely entirely white, tube ca. 0.5 in. (1 cm), funnelform, somewhat bilaterally symmetric, lobes 6, spreading, oblanceolate, acute, the inner 3 with a small, hairy, inward-pointing appendage just below apex; style and stamens deflexed, then curving upwards towards apex; stamens 6; ovary 3-celled. Fruit a few-seeded capsule. Late summer–autumn. South Africa.

Hippeastrum. About 80 species of perennial herbs. Bulb tunicate. Leaves basal, linear or strap-shaped. Flowering stems stout, leafless, hollow; flowers of cultivated kinds large and showy, 2 to several held horizontally or drooping in an umbel, umbel subtended by 2 large, equal free spathes persisting in flower; perianth tube often long, dilating at the throat, throat often closed or with scales or a corona, perianth lobes 6, erect, spreading, the inner 3 sometimes narrower than the others, white, red or orange-pink to deep crimson or striped combinations of these colors; filaments 6, often with small scales in between. Fruit a 3-valved capsule; seeds black, flattened or compressed. Americas.

This source does not reflect the significant developments which have taken place in *Hippeastrum* breeding since the mid 1990s resulting in new hybrid groups and an expanded color range (see Chapters 4–7 inclusive).

1991–Present

Despite the extensive media coverage given to *Hippeastrum* in some Western European countries and in the United States since 1997, many breeders, growers, exporters, retailers and consumers continue to refer to the plant as an "amaryllis." Efforts to encourage use of the plant's correct name—"hippeastrum"— have been supported on many fronts including British national television and radio, articles in British and international horticultural journals and gardening magazines. Shows and displays at the home of the NCCPG National Plant Collection of *Hippeastrum* in South

Harrow (Great Britain); Royal Botanic Gardens, Kew (Great Britain); Royal Horticultural Society London Shows (Great Britain); and at the Keukenhof, Lisse (The Netherlands) continue to spread the word in an attempt to convince more people of the plant's correct identity.

Amaryllis belladonna

Origins

Amaryllis belladonna, also known as March lily, belladonna lily, Jersey lily and naked ladies, is one of the most spectacular plants in the Amaryllidaceae (Plate 1-1). In 1714 it was already being cultivated in Italy where it was commonly known as *Donna bella*, and by the mid 18th century it was being cultivated in England where it became a popular garden plant.

The monotypic *Amaryllis* has been crossed with other members of the Amaryllidaceae resulting in a range of intergeneric hybrids which include ×*Amarcrinum memoria-corsii* 'Howardii' (*Amaryllis belladonna* × *Crinum moorei*) and ×*Amarine tubergenii* (*Amaryllis belladonna* × *Nerine bowdenii*) (Plate 1-11).

Breeding Developments

Opportunities for creating hybrids in colors other than pink have proved limited. During the 1970s, hybrids in various shades of pink were offered by the Dutch bulb firm van Tubergen. These were named after South African towns and included 'Kimberley', 'Bloemfontein', 'Jagerfontein', 'Johannesburg' and 'Windhoek'.

At the close of the 20th century, Avon Bulbs, Somerset (Great Britain), created their Galaxy group based on the progeny of the Tubergen plants. Up to 10, sweet-scented blooms in delightful shades of pink were borne on tall, leafless scapes in shades of olive to brown, even deep red-purple. Individual flowers remained fresh for up to 2 weeks. During the coming years, the company plans to expand the color range to include hybrids in all shades of pink to pearl white by involving existing named clones.

Geography and Climate

Amaryllis belladonna originates from the Cape Province of South Africa which includes the Cape Peninsula. The area displays amazing diversity in its topography, soil and climate. Rain falls during the winter months (May to September) followed by hot, dry summers (November to March) accompanied by strong winds. In spring, the days lengthen; soils are still damp from the winter rains and temperatures begin to rise. The first rains arrive in early autumn (usually in mid-April) while the soil and air are still warm. Although the Cape flora is most spectacular in spring, the sight of *A. belladonna* blooming in March and April in Southern Hemisphere countries is a wonderful sight.

Floral and Foliage Characteristics

Amaryllis belladonna bears up to 12 funnel-shaped blooms per scape with a scent reminiscent of pear drops, in shades of pink (deep, rose-red to almost white), borne on 24 in. (60 cm) or more tall, solid, purple, leafless scapes from mature bulbs 16 in. (40 cm) or more circumference. Flowers measuring 3.5–5 in. (9–13 cm) diameter consist of a short tube terminating in 6 irregularly shaped tepals with reflexed tips. Clumps of bright green, narrow, strap-shaped leaves up to 24 in. (60 cm) long and 1.4 in. (3.5 cm) wide appear in early winter in Northern Hemisphere countries (November–December), long after the flowers have faded. They continue to develop throughout the spring (March–May), before turning yellow and dying back in early summer (end June–early July). Each flower may produce up to 20, large, fleshy, bulb-shaped seeds which are pomegranate pink when ripe.

Cultivation

Like many other members of the Amaryllidaceae, *Amaryllis belladonna* requires a fertile, well-drained sandy soil, enriched with organic matter. Bulbs are best planted at the foot of a sunny wall, out of the wind and protected from summer showers. In the mild climate of South-West England, plants do not usually require protection during the winter. In cooler climates, however, bulbs will require some frost protection under glass or tunnels to keep them drier, as well as less cold.

Like *Hippeastrum*, *Amaryllis belladonna* has specific cultural requirements which must be satisfied if the plant is to bloom each year. Once the leaves start to die back (normally end June in the Northern Hemisphere), it is essential the bulbs remain warm and are allowed to dry out slowly throughout the summer until fresh scapes appear in late summer to early autumn (August to October).

Although I have been growing *Amaryllis* hybrids since 1999, I had no success in flowering them until 2003. In previous years, thick clumps of glossy, bright green, strap-shaped leaves would emerge during September and October, reach maturity the following spring, and wither and die during June. No scapes followed in early autumn. This was hardly surprising since spells of cool, wet weather, sometimes accompanied by hail stones during July and August with ground frosts by night towards the end of August, are characteristics of the British summer and can prevent *Amaryllis* bulbs from having an uninterrupted and essential summer baking.

Summer 2003 was exceptionally hot, dry and sunny in South East England. Temperatures reached an unprecedented 37°F (100°C) in South Harrow in mid August and only a few degrees lower inside my house. Such conditions were ideal for flowering the *Amaryllis.* During the third week of August, with no rain imminent, I watered my tubs of *Amaryllis* bulbs to prevent their roots from drying out. Within 24 hours I was thrilled to see a purple-red scape emerging from one of my Galaxy hybrids. Nine days later the glossy green spathe leaves parted on the 25 in. (63 cm) tall scape, revealing 8, almost luminous pink buds. Over the next 5 to 7 days all the buds matured into deliciously perfumed, funnel-shaped blooms with reflexed tepal tips and purple-brown ovaries and pedicles, creating a marvelous display.

Rains fell at the end of the month, accompanied by temperatures of 21–25°F (70–77°C) but sometimes several degrees hotter in South Harrow. Less than 24 hours later, *Amaryllis* 'Johannesburg' put forward a purple scape and, in early September, the deep pink blooms provided a wonderful splash of color among the greenery on my patio. Further scapes appeared that month, resulting in a succession of gloriously fragrant pink blooms. Gardeners marveled at their beauty and fragrance and were finally convinced that *Amaryllis* and *Hippeastrum* are two different genera.

Propagation

Amaryllis belladonna can be propagated by seed and division. Growing from seed is slow, taking 4 to 5 years before the plant reaches maturity and flowers. A quicker method is to divide clumps of mature bulbs in late summer as the flower buds emerge from the soil. Root disturbance will be minimal at this time and, providing the bulbs are replanted immediately into fresh soil and given sufficient nutrition, they should recover without difficulty.

Worsleya rayneri

Origins

This magnificent and stately plant was discovered in the early 1860s by Joseph Libon, a French explorer, growing in the Organ mountains, west of Rio de Janeiro (Brazil). Originally classified as *Amaryllis gigantea* because of its large size, it was later reclassified as *A. procera* (synonym *Hippeastrum procerum*). This name could not be sustained because another plant existed with the same name but which is now known as *Crinum erubescens* Aiton.

Today, the plant has been reclassified as *Worsleya* in honor of Arthington Worsley (1861–1943) who traveled extensively to Central and South American before settling in Isleworth, Middlesex (Great Britain). It remains the only member of the genus and owes its species name, *W. rayneri*, to John F. Rayner of Uxbridge, Middlesex (Great Britain), who obtained flowers from the plant in 1870 (Plate 1-12). The reclassification is based on following characteristics which set *Worsleya rayneri* apart from *Hippeastrum* and *Amaryllis belladonna*: florets are enclosed by 4 spathe leaves; D-shaped seeds vary in thickness between the curved and straight edges; the embryo occupies most of the seed; seeds pods have thick, fleshy walls; seeds are too heavy at 0.3 oz. (7.5 grams) per 100 for wind dispersal, they take up to 2 months to disperse, up to 10 weeks to germinate and remain viable for more than 12 months; bulb necks up to 36 in. (90 cm) long; saber-shaped leaves hang vertically; and basic chromosome number is x = 21. Table 1-1 highlights the features of *Amaryllis belladonna*, *Hippeastrum* and *Worsleya rayneri*.

Despite its botanical name, *Worsleya rayneri* continues to be referred to as the blue amaryllis, causing considerable confusion among gardeners who believe a deep blue *Amaryllis* actually exists. The plant is neither an *Amaryllis*, nor is it blue, but ranges from pale mauve to intense bluish mauve with a white base.

No species of *Hippeastrum* or any other related species have been found to grow close to *Worsleya rayneri* in nature and almost all attempts to cross *W. rayneri* with *Hippeastrum* species have proved unsuccessful. Fertile seeds and seedlings, however, have been obtained after self-pollination.

Table 1-1. Features of *Amaryllis, Hippeastrum* and *Worsleya.*

Feature	*Amaryllis*	*Hippeastrum*	*Worsleya*
Number of species	One (*Amaryllis belladonna*)	Approximately 50–70, although some sources refer to up to 85 species	One (*Worsleya rayneri*)
Place of origin	South Africa	South America	Brazil
Chromosome number	X = 11. Crosses freely with other members of the Amaryllidaceae including Crinum, Nerine and Brunsvigia	X = 11. Generally incompatible with other members of the Amaryllidaceae	X = 21. Incompatible with other members of the Amaryllidaceae
Evergreen or deciduous	Deciduous	Evergreen and deciduous, depending on species	Evergreen
Flowering period	Late summer to autumn	Spring, summer, autumn and winter according to species. Some species flower twice a year	Summer to early autumn
Bulb neck	Approximately 1 in. (2.5 cm) tall	From 0.5 to 36 in. (1–90 cm) tall depending on the species	Up to 36 in. (90 cm) tall
Scape	Solid, purple, up to 38 in. (96 cm) tall	Hollow, green, brown, gray or purple, up to 36 in. (90 cm) tall according to species	Hollow, green, up to 66 in. (167 cm) tall
Flowers per umbel	Usually 6 or more, strongly scented flowers	Usually 2–6 but up to 15 flowers in some species, scented or scentless according to the species	Usually 4–8, scentless flowers
Flower color	Shades of pink from deep rose-red to almost white	Red, pink, orange, yellow, green, cream and white; mono	Pale mauve to intense bluish mauve

Table 1-1 *(continued)*

Feature	*Amaryllis*	*Hippeastrum*	*Worsleya*
Flower color continued		and bicolored; striped, streaked, speckled or freckled	
Flower shape	Funnel shaped	Various, including Leopoldii, Reginae, trumpet and Cybister shaped	Funnel shaped
Tepals	6 similar in shape and size	6 similar or different shapes and sizes, according to species	6 overlapping tepals; inner 3 are slightly narrower than the outer 3
Spathe leaves	2	2	4
Tepal tube	Short	Varying lengths and widths according to individual species	Short
Foliage	Clumps of narrow, strap-shaped upright, bright green, glossy leaves, up to 24 in. (60 cm) tall	2–4 linear or lorate, horizontal or upright in various shades of green, glossy or matt, silky or leathery, up to 36 in.(90 cm) tall according to species	Clumps of up to 20 saber-shaped, pendant, dull emerald green leaves with transparent, whitish to pink edges and a glaucous, waxy layer, up to 36 in. (90 cm) tall
Seeds	About 20 bulb-shaped, pomegranate-colored, fleshy seeds per capsule	About 30–45 flat, black D- or discoid-shaped seeds per capsule, dominated by a band of tissuelike paper surrounding the hard raised portion in the center (the embryo)	About 45 jet black D-shaped seeds per capsule varying in thickness between the curved and straight edges, embryo occupies most of the seed
Germination	About 56 days	Usually within 2–15 days	Up to 70 days

Geography and Climate

The plant inhabits rocky crevices almost devoid of soil, containing only decaying grass and leaves, and narrow ledges less than 12 in. (30 cm) wide on the face of the steep, soft porous granite cliffs of the Organ Mountains, Brazil, some 3000–4000 ft. (914–1219 m) above sea level. The cliffs are exposed to scorching sun; fierce, cold winds and torrential rain, and temperatures sometimes approach freezing during midwinter (July in the Southern Hemisphere). Each morning the plants are drenched with dew and moisture which evaporates quickly as the temperatures rise. The dense clusters of *Worsleya rayneri* receive no protection from any vegetation but are cooled by constant air currents (*Gardeners' Chronicle*, May 1929).

Floral and Foliage Characteristics

Mature bulbs may measure up to 25 in. (63 cm) circumference and reach 60 in. (150 cm) tall, of which 36 in. (90 cm) is occupied by the bulb's neck. Up to 20 emerald-green, sickle-shaped leaves with a glaucous, waxy layer reach 36 in. (90 cm) long, extend from the neck of the bulb and hang verti cally over the rock face, reaching the ground below.

An umbel of 4–8 funnel-shaped, scentless flowers, each measuring approximately 5 in. (13 cm) diameter, appears in midsummer to early autumn (January–March in the Southern Hemisphere) borne on hollow, leafless, stout scapes which reach up to 66 in. (167 cm) tall. Although a single scape per year is usual, large, well-established bulbs may produce 2 or 3 scapes annually.

Conclusion

Much work remains to be done to convince gardeners and those involved in the bulb, potted plant and cut flower industry of the hippeastrum's true worth. It is hoped that the following chapters will help dispel any lingering uncertainties and stimulate a desire to learn more about this most fascinating plant that is so quick and easy to grow.

Chapter 2
Species

Hippeastrum is one of the most diverse and exotic members of the Amaryllidaceae. A few species originate from Mexico and the West Indies, but most come from Brazil, Bolivia, Chile, Peru and Argentina. Many more species have entered European and North American cultivation since the introduction of *H. reginae* and *H. vittatum* into Great Britain in 1728 and 1769 respectively. Collectors assigned names to their latest discoveries, unaware that some of them already existed, resulting in a number of species being known by more than one name. Several smaller flowering species have been reclassified as *Habranthus*, *Lycoris*, *Phycella*, *Rhodophiala*, *Sprekelia formosissima*, *Vallota*, *Worsleya* and *Zephyranthes*.

Modern sources refer to between 50 and 85 species. Despite numerous appeals to organizations and individuals having extensive species collections for material for the National Plant Collection of *Hippeastrum* and for research purposes, none have been forthcoming, thus making it difficult to confirm the veracity of species nomenclature currently in use. Chapter 2 highlights the diversity of the species and many of those used to create the earliest hybrids, as well as those being used by 21st-century American, Brazilian, Dutch, Japanese and South African breeders.

Geography and Climate

Habitats and climates are as varied as the plants themselves. *Hippeastrum elegans* grows in grassy meadows where conditions are warm and humid; other species grow by the side of rivers, while *H. angustifolium* inhabits muddy swamps. *Hippeastrum reticulatum* prefers cool, moist and shady conditions, while *H. reginae* is found in soil high in organic matter. *Hippeastrum aulicum* inhabits shady areas and has been found growing in the crotches of trees. *Hippeastrum striatum* grows in the open, in shade as well as in full sun, in acid red clay where early morning temperatures can fall to near freezing occasionally during the winter. Some species inhabit dense Brazilian rain forests where conditions are cool and moist, with around 60–160 in. (1600–4000 mm) of rainfall per year, dense morning and evening fogs and little temperature variation throughout the year (59–70°F or 15–21°C). Vegetation is thick and luscious, and species grow among bromeliads and orchids or, in the case of *H. calyptratum*, cling epiphytically to tree trunks.

Hippeastrum leopoldii, *H. pardinum*, *H. reginae* and *H. vittatum* inhabit the lightly forested Bolivian slopes at 2000–6000 ft. (610–1830 m) where conditions are cool and shady. The ground is covered with a litter of rocks, twigs and leaves, and regular night rains during the spring follow a short dry season.

Hippeastrum cybister, *H. evansiae*, *H. fosteri* and *H. parodii* grow in mountainous areas where conditions are harsh and inhospitable. Temperatures during the summer soar above 100°F (38°C) and fall below freezing during the winter with frosts and heavy snowfalls in some areas. If it were not for their upright position and bluish cast, the leaves of *H. parodii* would be quickly burnt. The entire year's rainfall of 6 in. (15 cm) falls during 2–3 months, resulting in all external growth being completed during this period. Other species send forth scapes following snow melts as moisture trickles to the bulbs situated below the level of frost penetration.

Some plants cling to steep, bare, rocky slopes where soil is almost nonexistent. Others grow among vegetation and bushes or near other plants where dark gray, sandy soils low in organic content are barely moist. *Hippeastrum psittacinum* grows on steep bare rocks, as well as at the base of cliffs which are covered with a thin layer of moss that becomes wet with dew each night and, at certain times of the year, from fog condensation.

Flower and Foliage Development

Most species produce 2–4 blooms per scape while some are more floriferous. Among the latter are *Hippeastrum angustifolium* with up to 9 blooms per scape, *H. cybister* with 4–6, *H. fosteri* with up to 15 and *H. stylosum* with up to 8. Most species flower once a year, but a few bloom twice, including *H. calyptratum* in midsummer and early winter and *H. papilio* in spring and sometimes also autumn. *Hippeastrum correiense*, *H. cybister*, *H. elegans*, *H. equestre*, *H. evansiae*, *H. immaculatum*, *H. lapacense*, *H. papilio*, *H. pardinum*, *H. psittacinum*, *H. reginae* and *H. vittatum* are spring-flowering. *Hippeastrum fosteri* blooms in summer, *H. reticulatum* in autumn, and *H. aulicum* in winter. Many species are deciduous, *H. aglaiae* and *H. striatum* are evergreen, while *H. aulicum* and *H. calyptratum* are epiphytic.

The flowers of some species have short tepal tubes with flat, wide-open faces and tepals of almost equal size. Two examples are *Hippeastrum leopoldii* (Plate 2-1) and *H. pardinum* (Plate 2-2). The flowers of others including *H. brasilianum*, *H. elegans*, *H. fragrantissimum*, *H. immaculatum* and *H. parodii* are trumpet-shaped with long, slender tubes and frilly edged tepals resembling Easter lilies (*Lilium longiflorum*). In between these extremes are numerous permutations. *Hippeastrum bukasovii*, *H. cybister* (Plate 2-3), *H. evansiae* and *H. papilio* (Plate 2-4) look more like exotic birds or insects. *Hippeastrum brasilianum*, *H. fragrantissimum*, *H. immaculatum* and *H. vittatum* are fragrant, making them particularly attractive to modern-day breeders. Scapes vary in color, width and length; *H. cybister*, for example, has tinges of purple towards the base. Some species, such as *H. hugoi* and *H. reginae*, develop leaves that reach 16–24 in. (40–60 cm) long and 1.4–2 in. (3.5–5 cm) wide when mature. Most develop foliage after flowering but sometimes leaves are present with the flowers, as in *H. stylosum* (Plate 2-5).

With a basic complement of 11 chromosomes, most species are diploid with a somatic chromosome number of $2n = 22$. Some triploid ($3n = 33$), tetraploid ($4n = 44$), pentaploid ($5n = 55$) and hexaploid ($6n = 66$) species have also been discovered.

Most flowers come in shades of orange or red, as exemplified by *Hippeastrum aulicum*, *H. equestre*, *H. reginae* and *H. reticulatum*. Other flower colors occur. *Hippeastrum fosteri* is a delightful pink; *H. calyptratum*, green; *H. aglaiae* and *H. parodii*, pale yellow; and *H. fragrantissimum* and *H. immaculatum* are pure white. Some flowers are single-toned, others feature 2 or more colors. The flowers of *H. elegans* var. *ambiguum* are white and rose, those of *H. leopoldii* purple rose and creamy white, while those of *H. papilio* are greenish white and burgundy. Streaks (*H. papilio*; *H. psittacinum*, Plate 1-6), stripes (*H. elegans* var. *ambiguum*), netting (*H. reticulatum*, Plate 2-6), spots (*H. lapacense*, *H. pardinum*), flecks, colored edgings and/or irregular patches of color may be combined to produce stunning effects. Patterns vary from simple to highly complex. Many flowers, such as *H. equestre* and *H. vittatum* have a green throat, which varies from bright to dark green and is sometimes lined with a band of red or dark pink dots. Some of the larger, brightly colored species have a regal aspect while the smaller, dainty pastels and trumpet species appear particularly elegant and have a unique charm.

Of more than 50 species introduced into Europe by the mid to late 19th century, less than 20 formed the basis of the early hybrids. These included *Hippeastrum aulicum*, *H. calyptratum*, *H. correiense*, *H. elegans*, *H. equestre* (Plate 1-2), *H. leopoldii*, *H. pardinum*, *H. psittacinum*, *H. reginae*, *H. reticulatum*, *H. striatum*, *H. stylosum* and *H. vittatum*.

The discovery of new species including *Hippeastrum brasilianum*, *H. cybister*, *H. evansiae*, *H. elegans* var. *ambiguum*, *H. fosteri*, *H. fragrantissimum*, *H. immaculatum*, *H. lapacense*, *H. papilio*, *H. parodii*, *H. reticulatum* var. *striatifolium* and *H. ambiguum* var. *tweedianum* created new and exciting possibilities for late 20th-century breeders, resulting in the development of new hybrid groups by the end of the century (see Chapter 6).

Following is a list of the species used for hybridization in chronological order by year they were introduced to European gardens or first described. Descriptions of the species can be found at the end of this chapter.

1728,	*H. reginae* Herbert
1769,	*H. vittatum* Herbert
1777,	*H. reticulatum* Herbert
1778,	*H. equestre* Herbert
1783,	*H. striatum* Lamarck
1814,	*H. psittacinum* Herbert
1815,	*H. elegans* Sprengel
1816,	*H. calyptratum* Herbert
1819,	*H. aulicum* Herbert
1821,	*H. stylosum* Herbert
ca. 1830s,	*H. correiense* Bury
1837,	*H. elegans* var. *ambiguum* Hooker
1837,	H. *ambiguum* var. *tweedianum* Herbert
1840,	*H. cybister* Bentham & Hooker f.
1867,	*H. pardinum* Lemaire
1867,	*H. leopoldii* J. A. Hort
1927,	*H. immaculatum* Traub & Moldenke
1941,	*H. aglaiae* Castellanos
1951,	*H. fosteri* Traub

1956, *H. evansiae* Traub & Nelson
1959, *H. fragrantissimum* Cárdenas
1967, *H. papilio* Ravenna
1969, *H. parodii* A. T. Hunziker & Cocucci
ca. 1972, *H. lapacense* Cárdenas
1973, *H. brasilianum* Traub & J. L. Doran

Cultivating Species

Cultivating species calls for a detailed knowledge and understanding of their strict requirements, such as temperature, humidity, moisture, nutrition, growth and dormancy periods. Although some species are more tolerant to slight variations, others may not survive if their cultural needs are not completely met and still others may fail to grow. Their susceptibility to pest and disease attack is probably another reason why so few species have entered commercial production and become generally available.

Most deciduous, mainly spring-flowering species lose their leaves in winter and require a dry, cool period (also known as ripening) of between 4 and 6 months if they are to flower the following season. They can be easily stored in their pots in cool, dry temperatures at a minimum of around 46°F (8°C) until new growth appears, such temperatures being essential to maintain dormancy for the required period. Although a few deciduous species are from arid, mountainous regions, the majority require warmth and humidity in summer. If these conditions are absent, the plants become prone to fungal infection by *Stagonospora curtisii* and can be severely crippled and disfigured, although usually not killed. Generally, some artificial heat will be required, particularly in spring and early summer when night temperatures are still relatively low.

The evergreen species retain some leaves all year, but it is a mistake to try to keep them actively growing in unsuitable cooler conditions. Usually growth will slow to a halt for a few weeks over midwinter and again during mid to late summer. During these inactive, almost dormant periods, it is advisable to allow plants to dry out completely between watering. Growth in *Hippeastrum mandonii*, *H. papilio* and *H. rutilum* slows dramatically during mid to late summer when watering should cease for 6–8 weeks. New growth appears in the autumn with flowers in midautumn to early winter. *Hippeastrum rutilum* can usually be relied upon to flower a second time in early spring.

Hippeastrum aulicum will grow until early winter. Watering should then cease for 6 weeks and recommence in mid to late winter or when new growth becomes obvious. Blooms normally follow shortly afterwards. Most evergreen species grow continuously in warmer parts of North America and bloom without a dormant period, providing light and temperatures are suitable. In areas less conducive to optimal growth and performance, including some northern European countries where lighting is poor and temperatures low, cultivating species is more difficult. Flowering is often unreliable and unpredictable.

A few evergreen species prefer some shade and cooler temperatures, including those mentioned above. They are probably the most suitable species for growing in more northerly latitudes. *Hippeastrum papilio*, in particular, can be grown outside and then brought indoors when frost threatens.

Although several species, mainly evergreen, have been grown in Great Britain since the early 18th century, relatively little is known about their cultivation. The majority require additional heat, light and glass protection and are therefore unsuitable for inexperienced growers.

An Uncertain Future

Rapidly changing environmental, economic, political and social climates are already having an adverse effect on some species, making their long-term survival in the wild precarious. Botanical gardens, scientific research establishments and organizations and individuals concerned with plant conservation will play an increasingly important role if many species are to survive into the next century.

Species Descriptions

H. aglaiae Castellanos

Date: 1941.

Synonym: *Amaryllis aglaiae.*

Location: Argentina, Bolivia.

Description: 2–3 delicate, funnel-shaped, greenish yellow blooms per scape 20–20.5 in. (50–51 cm) tall.

H. ambiguum var. tweedianum Herbert

Date: 1837.

Synonym: *Hippeastrum vittatum* var. *tweedianum.*

Location: Bolivia, Brazil, Peru.

Description: 2 white blooms with red stripes per scape 14–16 in. (35–40 cm) tall.

H. aulicum Herbert

Date: 1819.

Synonyms: *Amaryllis aulica, A. robusta, A. rougieri, A. tettauii, Aulica latifolia, Aulica platypetala, Aulica striata, Hippeastrum heuserianum, H. robustum, Omphalissa aulica, Trisacarpis rubra.*

Location: Central Brazil to Paraguay.

Description: 2–4 long-lasting crimson blooms per scape, with purple reticulations and a bright green throat.

H. brasilianum Traub & J. L. Doran

Date: 1973.

Synonym: *Amaryllis brasiliana.*

Location: Brazil.

Description: 2–4 pure-white blooms per scape 31 in. (80 cm) tall.

H. calyptratum Herbert

Date: 1816.

Synonyms: *Amaryllis calyptrata, A. flavovirens, A. fulvovirens, A. unguiculata, A. viridorchida, Omphalissa calyptrata, Trisacarpis falcata.*

Location: Brazil.

Description: 2–3 bright green blooms per scape 24 in. (60 cm) tall with a light pink stigma and pungent aroma. The flowers point in opposite directions and have excessively long, pale pink filaments that reach 6 in. (15 cm) long when fully extended.

H. correiense Bury

Date: ca.1830s.

Synonyms: *Amaryllis aulica* var. *glaucophylla, A. correiensis, A. gardneri, A. organensis, Hippeastrum gardneri, H. organense.*

Location: South Brazil.

Description: 2 crimson, spring-flowering blooms per scape 18 in. (45 cm) tall.

H. *cybister* Bentham & Hooker f.

Date: 1840.

Synonyms: *Hippeastrum anomalum, Sprekelia cybister.*

Location: Bolivia, Brazil.

Description: 4–6 crimson blooms tinged with green per scape 24 in. (60 cm) or more tall.

H. *elegans* Sprengel

Date: 1815.

Synonyms: *Amaryllis elegans, A. longiflora, A. solandriflora, Hippeastrum solandriflorum.*

Location: Brazil to Guiana, Columbia, Venezuela.

Description: 2–4 slightly fragrant, greenish white, trumpet-shaped blooms per scape 24 in. (60 cm) tall.

H. *elegans* var. *ambiguum* Hooker

Date: 1837.

Synonyms: *Amaryllis ambigua, A. solandriflora* var. *conspicua, Hippeastrum ambiguum.*

Location: Peru.

Description: 5 white and rose-striped blooms per scape.

H. *equestre* Herbert

Date: 1778.

Synonyms: *Amaryllis belladonna, A. brasiliensis, A. dubia, A. equestris, A. punicea, A. roezlii, Aschamia equestris, Hippeastrum puniceum, H. purpureum, H. pyrrochroum, H. spathaceum.*

Location: Bolivia, Brazil, Chile, Mexico, West Indies.

Description: 2–4 scarlet blooms per scape 12 in. (30 cm) or more tall which have an attractive yellow-green throat. A scarlet semi or fully double form—*H. equestre* forma *albertii*—was used to create some of the earliest American doubles.

H. *evansiae* Traub & Nelson

Date: 1956.

Synonym: *Amaryllis evansiae.*

Location: Bolivia.

Description: 2–3 open-faced, spidery blooms per scape; pale yellow, green and pastel colored forms exist that tend to fade with age.

H. fosteri **Traub**

Date: 1951.

Synonym: *Amaryllis fosteri.*

Location: East Brazil.

Description: Up to 15 china-rose/salmon-pink blooms per scape 36 in. (90 cm) tall.

H. fragrantissimum **Cárdenas**

Date: 1959.

Synonym: *Amaryllis fragrantissima.*

Location: Bolivia.

Description: 2 pure-white, trumpet-shaped blooms per scape 12–16 in. (30–40 cm) tall.

H. immaculatum **Traub & Moldenke**

Date: 1927.

Synonyms: *Amaryllis candida, Hippeastrum candidum.*

Location: Argentina, Bolivia, Peru.

Description: 6–9 pure-white, trumpet-shaped blooms per scape 20–27 in. (50–70 cm) tall which have a 3.5–4 in. (9–10 cm) long greenish tepal tube.

H. lapacense **Cárdenas**

Date: ca. 1972.

Synonym: *Amaryllis lapacensis.*

Location: Bolivia.

Description: 2 green and red spotted blooms per scape; similar to *H. pardinum.*

H. leopoldii **J. A. Hort**

Date: 1867.

Synonym: *Amaryllis leopoldii.*

Location: Bolivia, Peru.

Description: 2 purple-rose and creamy white blooms per scape 24 in. (60 cm) tall with a greenish white throat.

***H. papilio* Ravenna**

Date: 1967.

Synonym: *Amaryllis papilio.*

Location: Brazil.

Description: 2 and occasionally 3 greenish white blooms per scape 18–20 in. (45–50 cm) tall which are streaked and edged with dark red.

Comment: Some botanists question the veracity of *H. papilio* as a distinct species due to its similarity to *H. psittacinum* and the considerable variation among the flowers of *H. papilio*. The *H. papilio* plant commercially available today is evergreen, unlike the original deciduous *H. papilio* discovered by John L. Doran.

***H. pardinum* Lemaire**

Date: 1867.

Synonym: *Amaryllis pardina.*

Location: Bolivia, Peru.

Description: Usually 2 flesh-colored, flat-faced blooms per scape 16–18 in. (40–45 cm) tall which are covered with vermilion dots. The bright green throat has a purplish band at the base.

***H. parodii* A. T. Hunziker & Cocucci**

Date: 1969.

Synonym: *Amaryllis parodii.*

Location: North Argentina, Bolivia.

Description: 4–6 pale yellow-green blooms per scape.

***H. psittacinum* Herbert**

Date: 1814.

Synonyms: *Amaryllis illustris, A. psittacina, Ashamia psittacina, Leopoldiia illustris, Trisacarpis psittacina.*

Location: South Brazil.

Description: 2–4 apple-green blooms per scape 24–36 in. (60–90 cm) tall which are edged and streaked with burgundy.

H. reginae **Herbert**

Date: 1728.

Synonyms: *Amaryllis reginae, A. spectabilis, Aschamia reginae, Hippeastrum africanum, H. pronum, H. regium, H. spectabilis, H. stenopetalum.*

Location: Bolivia, Brazil, Mexico, Peru, Venezuela, West Central Africa, West Indies.

Description: 2–4 bright red, slightly drooping blooms per scape 12–20 in. (30–50 cm) tall with a large greenish-white star at the base of the throat.

H. reticulatum **Herbert**

Date: 1777.

Synonyms: *Amaryllis agatha, A. carolinae, A. praeclara, A. principis, A. reticulata, Coburgia reticulata, Eusarcops reticulata, Leopoldiia principis, Leopoldia reticulata.*

Location: South and East Brazil.

Description: 4–6 mauve-red blooms per scape 12–15 in. (30–38 cm) tall, reticulated in deeper shades of mauve.

H. striatum **Lamarck**

Date: 1783.

Synonyms: *Amaryllis glaucescens, A. miniata, A. rutila, A. rutilans, A. striata, A. subbarbata, Lais crocata, Lais fulgida, Hippeastrum bahiense, H. brasiliense, H. bulbulosum* var. *rutilum, H. glaucescens, H. latifolium, H. martianum, H. proliferum, H. rutilum, H. simsianum, H. unguiculatum.*

Location: South Brazil.

Description: Exists in several colors such as var. *crocatum*, var. *acuminatum* and var. *fulgidum*. 2–4, bright crimson blooms per scape 24–27 in. (60–70 cm) tall.

H. stylosum **Herbert**

Date: 1821.

Synonyms: *Amaryllis maranensis, A. staminea, A. stylosa.*

Location: East coast of South America to Brazil and French Guiana.

Description: 3–8 salmon or light red blooms per scape 20–24 in. (50–60 cm) tall.

H. vittatum Herbert

Date: 1769.

Synonyms: *Amaryllis lineata, A. superba, A. vittata, Chonais vittata.*

Location: Brazil, Peru.

Description: 2–6 large, white and red striped, moderately fragrant blooms per scape 36 in. (90cm) tall with an intense green throat.

Chapter 3

Large-Flowering Singles

Earliest developments in *Hippeastrum* hybridization can be traced to the mid 18th century with the introduction of *H. reginae* and *H. vittatum* into European cultivation. Mr Johnson, generally acknowledged to be an English watchmaker from Prescot, Lancashire (Great Britain), He crossed these species to produce *H.* 'Johnsonii' (Plate 3-1) which was subsequently used to create further hybrids in the early 19th century. Arthington Worsley of Isleworth (Middlesex, Great Britain) writing in the *American Amaryllis Society Year-Book* (1935) has since cast doubt on the identity of the plant which was being cultivated in the early 20th century as it differed substantially from the original hybrid of that name.

Interest in the *Hippeastrum* burgeoned throughout the 19th and 20th centuries as more species became available to European breeders. Great Britain and The Netherlands became leading centers during the 19th century with France, Belgium and Germany playing lesser roles. British breeders ranked among the finest in the world and won many gold medals for their exhibits at the Royal Horticultural Society's (RHS) London and Chelsea Flower Shows between the two world wars. Outstanding creations were submitted to the Floral Committee of the RHS for consideration and many received a First Class Certificate or an Award of Merit. Dutch breeders also recognized the outstanding quality of some British breeders' work and some were particularly keen to obtain hybrids from James Veitch and Sons (London) and Messrs Robert P. Ker and Sons (Liverpool) to improve their own stock.

The two world wars wrought havoc upon *Hippeastrum* hybridization programs in France and Germany. In England, fuel costs and shortages resulted in the abandonment of many fine collections such as the Bodnant, Dell, Rothschild, and Westonbirt collections, together with the loss of considerable knowledge and expertise. Despite initial interruptions, the Dutch *Hippeastrum* industry made a full recovery and by 1950 had become re-established and today remains the major center of breeding in Western Europe.

By the end of the 20th century, exciting developments were also taking place in the United States, Australia, Brazil, India, Japan and South Africa. Unfortunately, export and quarantine regulations, high transportation costs, domination by Dutch and South African hybrids and the need for new cultivars to satisfy stringent requirements contributed to many hybrids not entering commercial production. Apart from certain introductions of the American Meyer hybrids (see Chapter 6), it would appear that other early 21st-century American hybrids did not have the requisite qualities.

We will never know the exact number of hybrids that have been created since 1799, due partly to the lack of information regarding the achievements of 18th-, 19th-, and early 20th-century breeders. The *Catalog of Hybrid Amaryllis Cultivars 1799 to Dec. 31, 1963* compiled by Hamilton P. Traub, W. R. Ballard, W. D. Morton Jr. and E. F. Authement in 1964 is a useful starting point for understanding developments of the genus. Almost 1000 hybrids are listed, the majority registered since 1940. A brief description is given, but without any illustrations, it is impossible to know what most of these hybrids looked like, since very few remain commercially available today.

Another useful publication is *The Alphabetical List of Amaryllis (Hippeastrum) Cultivars in Cultivation in The Netherlands* (Stuurman 1980) published by the Royal General Bulbgrowers' Association (KAVB). It describes more than 200 large and small Dutch and South African hybrids which were in Dutch cultivation during the late 1970s and early 80s. Many early 20th-century hybrids had already been discontinued and were therefore not included.

Reports in 19th- and 20th-century British journals and magazines including *Botanical Register*, *Curtis's Botanical Magazine*, *Gardeners' Chronicle*, *Gardeners' Magazine*, *Gardening World*, *Journal of the Royal Horticultural Society* (later *The Garden*) and *Transactions of the Royal Horticultural Society* also provide valuable information about breeders and their award-winning hybrids. Exquisite black-and-white line drawings in *Journal of the Royal Horticultural Society* and color plates in *Curtis's Botanical Magazine*, among others, provide a useful insight into the shape and design of the flower.

Modern computer technologies have resulted in the production of full color catalogs and brochures and the development of web sites which include descriptions and photographs of breeders, growers and exporters' assortments. Award-winning hybrids and forthcoming introductions are highlighted and some sites also include cultural tips for successful cultivation.

Other useful sources are the lists maintained by national and European authorities of hybrids which have been granted Plant Breeders' Rights and of hybrids registered by the International Cultivar Registration Authority (ICRA), Hillegom, The Netherlands. It has proved difficult to obtain essential information from the ICRA and in some cases, its accuracy is questionable. Further information about the processes involved in registering a new hybrid and obtaining Plant Breeders' Rights is given in the Appendix.

This chapter begins by summarizing the outstanding hybrids created by leading 19th- and early 20th-century European breeders before 1950. Features of Australian, Dutch and South African large-flowering singles that have been developed since 1951 are then discussed, together with my observations and experiences of having grown these plants since the mid 1990s. Comments from visitors to my shows and festivals are also included, where appropriate. The lack of information regarding the activities of some American breeders has meant that it has not been possible to include these developments. Brief descriptions of each hybrid appear at the end of the chapter.

Hybridization in the 19th and Early 20th Centuries

Botanists and explorers played a key role throughout the 19th century in discovering new species which breeders then used to create new hybrid groups. The discoveries of the British explorer Richard William Pearce (ca. 1838–1867) were particularly significant. During his employment with James Veitch and Sons (London) from 1858 to 1867, he discovered *Hippeastrum leopoldii* (Plate 2-1) and *H. pardinum* (Plate 2-2) while on a visit to Bolivia in 1863. *Hippeastrum leopoldii* was subsequently used to create the first Leopoldii hybrids which, together with the Reginae hybrids, have dominated developments of large-flowered hippeastrums for almost 150 years.

Prior to the development of these hybrid groups, *Hippeastrum* flowers were characterized by their narrow and acuminate tepals, the lowermost tepal being generally regarded as imperfect or, at best, asymmetrical with the others. Some hybrids had very short tepal tubes while others were long and slender and looked like trumpets. The lime green throat—a prominent feature of many species—was considered inferior by some breeders of the era who sought to eradicate it. I have always found it difficult to understand why such an elegant and attractive feature was regarded in this way. Happily, the green throat has now been restored and, judging from the comments of many visitors to my shows since 1999, the public too considers this characteristic to be a particularly endearing feature of the plant.

Leopoldii hybrids are characterized by their short, sometimes almost nonexistent tepal tubes and by usually 4 broad 9–11 in. (23–28 cm) diameter, flat-faced, rounded blooms with overlapping tepals borne on tall, robust scapes. More than any other group, the Leopoldii hybrids exuded an air of grand formality and looked majestic. Early assortments were dominated by flowers in various shades of red, but during the 1950s, the creation of delightful pastel shades and dramatic red and white-striped cultivars heralded a new chapter in *Hippeastrum* breeding which was warmly welcomed by enthusiasts in Europe and the United States. Unfortunately very few remain available today but judging from their names and the brief descriptions and pictures, they must have looked marvelous in mass plantings.

The story of the outstanding achievements of major Western European breeders before 1959 begins with Mr Johnson, who, as previously noted, produced Hippeastrum 'Johnsonii' (*H. reginae* × *H. vittatum*) with red and white flowers in 1799. Dean William Herbert, using *H. reginae*, *H. reticulatum*, *H. striatum*, *H. vittatum* and others, created some of the earliest British hybrids from 1778 to 1847, while in The Netherlands, Jan de Graaff, working with *H. striatum* var. *crocatum*, *H. striatum* var. *fulgidum* and *H. vittatum* from 1797 to 1862, produced *H.* 'Graveana', a hybrid that had significant influence upon the breeding work of his son, Simon Adrianus de Graaff.

The next two outstanding hybrids came from Messrs Garroway and Sons of Great Britain: *Hippeastrum* ×*acramannii* (*H. aulicum* var. *platypetalum* × *H. psittacinum*), produced in 1835, had scarlet and white flowers with deep carmine veins and was followed by *H.* ×*acramannii* 'Pulcherrima' (*H. aulicum* × *H.* 'Johnsonii') in 1850. Meanwhile, Simon Adrianus de Graaff, working in The Netherlands from 1840 to 1911, produced, among others, H. 'Empress of India' (*H. psittacinum* × H. 'Graveana'). This glorious hybrid had bright red blooms with rounded, white banded tepals and heralded the beginning of the large-flowering Reginae hybrids, so-named by the American Amaryllis Society because of the similarity of the flower shape to *H. reginae*. James Douglas referred to the plant as *Lilium reginae* upon its first flowering in Great Britain on 1 March 1728, the birthday of Queen Caroline, wife of George II. Back in Great Britain, B. S. Williams created crimson-flowered *H.* 'Williamsii' in 1862 and a second hybrid, *H.* 'Mrs Garfield' (*H. reticulatum* × *H.* 'Defiance').

Messrs Robert P. Ker & Sons of Great Britain were renowned throughout the world between 1839 and 1910 for their large-flowering hybrids. Outstanding among them were white-flowered *H.* 'Albescens', *H.* 'Midas' and *H.* 'Virgin Queen'; crimson-flowered *H.* 'Black Prince', *H.* 'The Chancellor' and *H.* 'Crimson King'; scarlet-flowered *H.* 'Cynthia', *H.* 'President' and *H.* 'Scarlet Gem'; and red-flowered *H.* 'Lothair' and *H.* 'Mercury'. Multicolored hybrids included *H.* 'Eurydice', *H.* 'Melpomene' and *H.* 'Satura' with white and red flowers.

The prize-winning hybrids of E. H. Krelage had scarlet, crimson, pure white and pink flowers which lacked the green throat considered objectionable by many breeders and growers at that time. Krelage received a Gold Medal in 1898 at the International Horticultural Exhibition in Ghent, Belgium, and the Queen's Large Medal in 1919 at the Haarlem Show in The Netherlands.

The London-based nursery of Messrs James Veitch and Sons was responsible for pioneering the early development of the Leopoldii hybrids involving *Hippeastrum leopoldii*, *H. pardinum* and the finest available Reginae hybrids. The outstanding hybrids included *H.* 'Ambient', with scarlet and white flowers, 1887; *H.* 'Autumn Beauty', pale rose; *H.* 'Crown Princess of Germany', medium white and rose-scarlet, 1886; and scarlet-flowered *H.* 'John Ruskin'. Numerous RHS Gold Medals were awarded to the exhibitor.

Towards the end of the 19th century, the Rothschild Collection at Tring Park, Hertfordshire, Great Britain, under the watchful eye of Edwin Hill, head gardener to Lord Rothschild, achieved considerable recognition for its amazing assortment of brilliant dark scarlet hybrids, very large whites, red-striped cultivars and bright red hybrids with a broad white margin. A report in *Gardeners' Chronicle* in February 1906 refers to a "magnificent show of flowers in Tring Park gardens." During the same period, German Georg Bornemann used British (Messrs Robert Ker and Sons, Veitch and Sons) and Dutch (de Graaff) hybrids to create additional large-flowering hybrids, and Belgian Louis van Houtte used *Hippeastrum aulicum*, *H. psittacinum* and *H. vittatum* to create flowers with pointed tepals, long tubes and a green throat.

C. R. Fielder, gardener to Mrs W. H. Burns of North Mymms Park, Hatfield, Hertfordshire, Great Britain, is credited with creating the first large, pure white Leopoldii hybrid in 1904—*Hippeastrum* 'Snowdon'. Slight green was evidence in the throat.

The Westonbirt Collection was regarded as one of the finest British collections for more than 50 years, and exhibits from the collection received many RHS Gold Medals between 1890 and 1910. Among the outstanding hybrids created by A. Chapman, gardener to Lt. Col. George L. Holford of Westonbirt, Gloucester, are *H.* 'Agamemnon', deep scarlet and white, 1906; *H.* 'Apple Blossom' (almost white with salmon scarlet towards the margins, not the form available today), 1899; *H.* 'Black Beauty' and *H.* 'Black Knight', almost black; *H.* 'Black Prince', dark crimson,1903; *H.* 'Calypso', white with rose veins; *H.* 'Chimborazo', deep crimson, 1897; *H.* 'Duke of York', orange flushed with crimson, 1897; *H.* 'Field Marshal', scarlet, 1906; *H.* 'Marjory', crimson with white veins, 1906; *H.* 'Murillo', crimson maroon, 1899; *H.* 'Pearl Maiden', scarlet and white, 1906; *H.* 'Pink Blossom', rose pink and white, 1925; *H.* 'Robin', scarlet and white, 1899; *H.* 'Virginia', pale pink suffused with red, 1899; and *H.* 'Vulcan', crimson, 1907.

Three Dutch breeders received worldwide recognition for their hybrids and complete our survey of early hybridizers. C. G. van Meeuwen and Sons expanded the range of flower colors in Leopoldii hybrids to include reds, pinks, salmon, orange and pure white. W. S. Warmenhoven created monocolored hybrids described as "large flowers of rounded, ideal shape and dazzling pure colors of many shades, including pure white, clear violet shades, light Havana brown with dark bases, delicate pinks and many others" (Krelage 1938). And around 1940 Ludwig and Company created some of the finest earliest pink and pure white Leopoldii hybrids.

1960–Present

The large-flowering single hippeastrum probably ranks as one of the largest, most flamboyant and popular houseplants available today. Despite the subsequent introduction of doubles and smaller flowering types, large singles remain the favorite of many gardeners in both the Northern and Southern Hemispheres. Each year as new "superior" hybrids are introduced, older "inferior" hybrids are discontinued. While the floral characteristics of some of the new hybrids are definite improvements of earlier creations, this is not always the case. Growers are continually required to review their decisions about which hybrids to maintain, sometimes allowing delightful hybrids to disappear. For this reason it is essential that several bulbs of each cultivar are grown and maintained in the National Plant Collection of *Hippeastrum*.

Occasionally a spectacular new hybrid is launched which generates considerable excitement among *Hippeastrum* enthusiasts eager to acquire that extra special plant for their collections. More often, new hybrids turn out to be mere variations on existing ones and, to the untrained eye, are indistinguishable from them.

Only since the 1990s have many British gardeners been able to purchase hybrids other than *Hippeastrum* 'Red Lion' or *H.* 'Apple Blossom', yet several hundred large-flowering hybrids of Australian, Dutch and South African origin are currently available. Only a tiny fraction ever become widely available and some, such as the Australian hybrids, are only available to those residing in that country. The sheer joy I experience upon receiving a consignment containing the very latest varieties of large singles for the National Plant Collection of Hippeastrum is tremendous, but even more thrilling to me is observing the plant's growth and eventual flowering.

Features of Large-flowering Hybrids

The classification of modern hybrids as "large" refers to the diameter of the flower and not the plant's overall dimensions. Dutch growers consider flowers measuring 6.5 in. (16 cm) diameter or more as large, with some flowers reaching 12 in. (30 cm) across. This one-size-fits-all approach to hybrids may be adequate for most gardeners, but it is woefully inadequate for the dedicated amateur and researcher. Without a photograph and physical description of the plant, the term *large* becomes almost meaningless. Even more absurd for classification purposes is the musical terminology used by the South African company Hadeco (Pty). For example, flowers measuring 6.5 in. (16 cm) diameter or more are classified as Symphony hybrids, a term meaningful only to those familiar with classical musical form. Table 3-1 highlights terminology used by Dutch, Japanese and South African breeders to describe flowers of different widths.

Bulb, Flower and Scape Production of Large-flowering Hybrids

Although some large-flowering hybrids have only 3 or 4 flowers per scape, increasingly many hybrids regularly produce 5 or 6 blooms per scape from

Table 3-1. Classification of Dutch, South African and Japanese hybrids.

Flower diameter	Dutch	South African	Japanese
6.5 in. (16 cm) and above	Large	Symphony	Large
6.0 in. (15 cm)	–	–	Medium
4.5–6.75 in. (12–16 cm)	Midi or medium	–	–
4.0–6.75 in. (10–16 cm)	–	Sonata	–
4.0–4.5 in. (10–12 cm)	Small	–	Mini
2.5–4.0 in. (6–10 cm)	–	Sonatini	–
2.5 in. (6 cm)	–	–	Super mini
Less than 2.5 in. (6 cm)	–	Solo	–

bulbs with a circumference of 11–12 in. (28–30 cm) or more. Furthermore, these bulbs produce 2 scapes and bloom 6–8 weeks after planting when cultivated at 70–72°F (21–22°C). Occasionally a fourth pair of flowers may be present. Larger bulbs not only produce more scapes in the first year after purchase, but they also produce plants with larger overall dimensions.

Some Dutch- and Japanese-bred hybrids grown under commercial conditions reach their maximum circumference of 20 in. (50 cm) after only 3 growing seasons of 8 months each, but such large sizes are unlikely to be achieved from potted bulbs cultivated at home. Unlike many of the large, softer and sometimes watery Dutch bulbs, South African hybrid bulbs are smaller and denser, and usually produce 2 scapes, each bearing 3–6 and occasionally 8 blooms from largest size bulbs.

It is possible for some large-flowering bulbs to maintain a circumference of 12–13 in. (30–33 cm) from one season to the next when cultivated indoors under 600-watt sodium lights for 12–14 hours a day throughout the year, except during the cool period. The scapes of some hybrids reach up to 30 in. (75 cm) tall, but usually are 16–22 in. (40–55 cm) tall. The sodium lights result in shorter, sturdier scapes which do not require staking. Prior to 1999, staking had been a regular activity to prevent spindly, weak scapes from splitting and collapsing. Table 8-1 shows the relationship between the number of scapes, bulb circumference and flower size of modern Dutch and South African hybrids.

Colors and Vase Life of Large-flowering Hybrids

Compared to the mainly single colors available in the early to mid 20th century, early 21st-century gardeners are spoiled for choice. A wondrous assortment of red, orange, salmon, pink, cream, pure white and creamy yellow monocolored and bicolored hybrids are now available. An increasing number combine several colors or shades to produce amazing effects. Breeders are also endeavoring to create hybrids with longer lasting blooms. Today it is possible for some flowers to remain fresh for up to 11 days and even longer when moved to a cooler place at 61°F (16°C).

Leading Reds

Red is synonymous with hippeastrums and remains the most popular color. Young or old, professional or amateur, gardeners' reactions to hippeastrums with their gorgeous velvety or satiny textured tepals and even richer, glossy heart are the same. Whether the flower is a grand, flat-faced Leopoldii hybrid or a more mysterious, hooded variety with pointed tepals, gasps of amazement and delight fill the air as visitors appear momentarily transfixed by the attention-seeking, regal blooms. Unlike many of the pastels which have a delightful lime green throat, most reds remain red throughout, apart from the white- or pink-tipped stigma and yellow pollen grains.

Many fine Leopoldii and Reginae reds were created by Ludwig and Sons, G. C. van Meeuwen and Sons, W. S. Warmenhoven and M. van Waveren during the 1950s and 1960s, but regretfully only *Hippeastrum* 'Red Lion' (1958), *H.* 'Belinda' (1963) and *H.* 'Rotterdam' (1962) remain available today. I was fortunate to grow two other outstanding reds in the late 1990s. *Hippeastrum* 'Scarlet Globe' (Plate 3-2), created by Waveren and Sons in 1962, had a flat face and pale vermilion tepals that reflexed right back, creating an almost rounded appearance and exposing the shiny, blood-red throat. Hippeastrum 'Royal Ruby', from W. S. Warmenhoven in 1959, had tepals with a wonderful vermilion gloss.

It's not difficult to understand why the beautifully proportioned, slightly hooded, velvety blooms and glossy red heart of *Hippeastrum* 'Red Lion' have delighted so many gardeners for almost 50 years. Even newly emerging florets have already acquired their final color and radiate a wonderful glow in the spring sunshine (Plate 8-5). While *H.* 'Red Lion' remains the most popular hippeastrum for bare bulb, pot plant and cut flower sales, breeders are keen to create an improved red to succeed it. Unlike some less popular, older reds which regularly produced 4 blooms per scape, *H.* 'Red Lion' sometimes only produces 3 flowers on the first scape which is considered unacceptable for cut flower sales. However, if *H.* 'Red Lion' is to be toppled, its successor will have to demonstrate significant improvements in bulb growth, flower count, scape length and production, vase life and resistance to certain diseases. Even if a suitable successor does emerge, substantial efforts will be required to convince growers, exporters and consumers of its advantages over *H.* 'Red Lion' and that will not be easy.

Hippeastrum 'Belinda' is even more dramatic than *H.* 'Red Lion' with its large 7 in. (18 cm) diameter berry-red blooms and glossy throat. Very large bulbs with a circumference of 13–14 in. (33–35 cm) have resulted in sturdy, majestic 36 in. (90 cm) tall plants that are almost as heavy as a young child. Transporting *H.* 'Belinda', with 8 mature blooms on tall, robust, bright green scapes and 9 mature, luxuriant, straplike, leathery leaves which were almost the same height, on the London Underground in a carrier bag, was a feat and not to be recommended! Such a spectacle aroused gasps of amazement from fellow travelers, unused to seeing such a magnificent plant which seemed almost as large as its owner. Several staff members assisted me to ensure the plant's safe passage during the London rush hour. Arriving at its destination with no bruising to any of the blooms, the plant remained absolutely splendid for several more days on my office desk.

Hippeastrum 'Rotterdam' remains Warmenhoven's darkest and, in my opinion, most splendid blackcurrant red. Its broad, pointed, hooded blooms release generous quantities of bright yellow pollen, and when the plant is placed next to *H.* 'Yellow Goddess' or *H.* 'Christmas Gift', it looks even more mysterious. The lovely thick, velvety tepals enhance the plant's regal air and, when standing proud on tall, lime green scapes with luxuriant bright green foliage, the effect is almost unbelievable.

Some of the finest reds available today have been created by Marko Penning of Penning Breeding B.V. (Honselersdijk), one of The Netherlands's finest young breeders. *Hippeastrum* 'Parma' (1999) and *H.* 'Benfica' (2001) usually produce 5–6 blooms per scape, unlike *H.* 'Roma' (1993) which usually has only 4 blooms per scape and a tendency to rot after flowering. All three hybrids have a glorious sheen towards the throat and rich velvety tepals. *Hippeastrum* 'Roma' and *H.* 'Parma' make excellent potted plants while *H.* 'Benfica' is cultivated as a cut flower.

Of all large Dutch reds available in 2003, namely, *Hippeastrum* 'Ferrari', *H.* 'Furore', *H.* 'Grand Cru', *H.* 'Liberty' and *H.* 'Red Sensation', *H.* 'Royal Velvet' (Plate 3-3), with its magnificent 8 in. (20 cm), flat-faced, broad, almost blackcurrant blooms, remains my favorite. For several years, the breeder and grower, Berbee and Sons, has mounted a splendid display of *H.* 'Royal Velvet' cut flowers in tall, slender crystal vases at the Keukenhof, Lisse (The Netherlands), where it is greatly admired.

In 1999, I succeeded in securing bulbs of *Hippeastrum* 'Royal Velvet' for the National Plant Collection of *Hippeastrum* and was overawed by the plant's beauty. The blooms appeared almost black when placed next to a snowy white plant. Particularly fascinating were the almost black markings on the tepals, visible only under transmitted light. The result was unbelievable and utterly compelling.

I am also fond of *Hippeastrum* 'Liberty' and, judging by the comments I have received from many British gardeners, so are many others. Its wine-red blooms with their marvelous sheen glisten in the sunlight and its majestic awe is enhanced by mature, upright foliage at the time of flowering which creates a delightful bushy effect.

Since the late 1950s, Hadeco (Pty) has developed many fine reds which are generally characterized by their short tepal tubes; broad, rounded tepals; flat faces and horizontal- or upward-facing blooms. Many have a superb velvet or satin texture and a glorious, glossy heart but, unlike many of the taller-scape Dutch hybrids which naturally bloom in the spring, South African reds are borne on relatively short, stout scapes and naturally flower in autumn and early winter when grown in the Northern Hemisphere. They make marvelous pot plants for the home and add great cheer on dark, gloomy December days. They are quick and easy to grow, the majority flowering after 6–7 weeks when grown under optimum conditions. In some cases they have proved so reliable, it has been possible calculate to within 2 or 3 days, the date when the plants will be fully open. This reliability is a particularly useful trait when cultivating the plants for a show. Many Dutch cultivars are unpredictable, taking up to 10 weeks, sometimes longer, particularly when they have not received the correct preparation prior to sale. Varying amounts of mature foliage may also be present at the time of flowering on the South African hybrids, creating a lovely bushy effect.

After flowering in late autumn or early winter in the Northern Hemisphere in their first year of purchase, some plants rebloom only with difficulty. Providing the plants remain in their pots throughout the following spring, summer and autumn and are watered and fed appropriately, it is easy to achieve repeat blooms each year. All my South African and Brazilian cultivated plants receive the same cool period as for all other hybrids in the National Collection, commencing mid November–early December each year and ending 10 weeks later. What a joy it is to discover plump, juicy green shoots and leaves emerging from the necks of bulbs within just a few hours or days of the cool period having ended when plants are returned to warm, light conditions with 12–14 hours of 600-watt sodium lights per day.

Hippeastrum 'Zanzibar' (1963), one of Hadeco's earliest bright orange-reds, is still available. Its well-proportioned vermilion blooms with a tiny bright green star towards the throat are marvelous looking. When I planted 3 bulbs in a large terracotta planter which was positioned in a corner of my display of South African hybrids at the RHS Westminster Show in November 1999, RHS judges and visitors were almost overwhelmed by the plants' outstanding beauty. Other fine reds available today include *H.* 'Basuto', currant red; *H.* 'Bold Leader', pepper red; *H.* 'Honeymoon', rose red; and 'Miracle', cardinal red. The wide-open, dark, velvety orient-red blooms of *H.* 'Merry Christmas', borne on short, stout scapes with plenty of mature, upright foliage, and the floriferous bright orange-red *H.* 'Double Six', so-named because of the simultaneous appearance of 2 scapes, each bearing 6 blooms, also proved very popular with British gardeners.

For two and a half decades Richard Maguire of Maguire's Hippeastrum Farm in Woombye, Queensland, has produced some of the finest large reds. One of the best of these, *Hippeastrum* 'Tangellino' has dazzlingly beautiful bright orange-red blooms with a marvelous silvery sheen on the outer side (Plate 3-6). Seeing hundreds of *H.* 'Tangellino' plants in full bloom on Maguire's farm in October is an incredible sight and one never forgotten. Although none of Maguire's hybrids are available outside Australia; it is not difficult to imagine how splendid they must look on the patio or as a garden bedding plant.

Pastels

The range of pastel-colored hippeastrums available today remains relatively small. Of the many delightful solid pinks created by Ludwig and Sons (Hillegom) during the 1950s and 1960s, only *Hippeastrum* 'Apple Blossom' (1954) remains in commercial production. Its tall, robust, green scapes; gorgeous pink and white, long-lasting, funnel-shaped blooms; extensive bright green throat which is lined with a ring of red dots and strong bulbs have made it the most popular pink hybrid among commercial and amateur growers. Like its faithful partner *H.* 'Red Lion', the much taller and more robust *H.* 'Apple Blossom' is widely grown for bare bulb sales, pot plant production and as a cut flower. However, the size, quality and vase life of the flowers often fall far short of the larger blooms, so easily achieved under pot plant cultivation.

The only other early Ludwig pink which remains in commercial cultivation is *Hippeastrum* 'Dutch Belle', created in 1953. When shown in April 2000 at my first national *Hippeastrum* Celebration held in South Harrow, Middlesex, its clouds of delicious carmine pink 7.5 in. (19 cm) blooms proved an immediate attraction. *Hippeastrum* 'Beautiful Lady' (Plate 3-7), created by Ludwig in 1963, had exquisitely veined, flat-faced salmon pink blooms which surpassed all other salmon hybrids available at that time including the delicate *H.* 'Rilona' with its frilly edges and light brown throat. The unusual coloring and tall 24–30 in. (60–75 cm) scapes make *H.* 'Rilona' a popular cut flower; however such tall, soft stems collapse easily after only 2 or 3 days and become soggy. Blooms often remain small and pale and frequently fail to open properly, unlike the magnificent large blooms so easily achieved when *H.* 'Rilona' is cultivated as a pot plant.

The range and availability of high-quality cut flower hippeastrums varies considerably in western European countries, as well as among different retail outlets. While it is relatively easy to obtain magnificent cut flowers in Paris and other major European cities, this is not generally the case yet in Great Britain. It is hoped that in the coming years, British wholesalers and retailers will recognize the plant's potential as a superb cut flower, ideal for grand, formal arrangements at hotel receptions and restaurants, cathedrals and many ceremonial occasions. As customers become more discerning, they are likely to insist upon a larger selection of higher quality blooms.

Two of Warmenhoven's surviving pinks are *Hippeastrum* 'Beacon' (1954) and *H.* 'Elvira Aramayo' (1962). *Hippeastrum* 'Beacon' has the most unusual shape and markings with delightful slightly hooded, rectangular blooms whose color is clear vermilion on a salmon-pink background. *Hippeastrum* 'Elvira Aramayo' is particularly robust with tall, thick green scapes and lovely, flat-faced, carmine blooms.

Among van Waveren's pinks only *Hippeastrum* 'Telstar' (1962), with carmine pink flowers, remains available today; it is grown both for bare bulb and cut flower production. More widely known and very popular is the reliable, robust and stunning, frilly edged, long-lasting *H.* 'Orange Sovereign' (1980) which, in my opinion, remains the finest large, deep orange hybrid available today. The well-proportioned, exquisitely veined, long-lasting blooms look marvelous against a backdrop of bright green leathery foliage and never fail to attract attention when shown at my festivals.

Several pinks which appeared in Great Britain for the first time in the late 1990s originated from the Dutch breeder Jac J. Mense. They include *Hippeastrum* 'Angelique', *H.* 'Hercules', *H.* 'Susan', *H.* 'Vera' and *H.* 'Wonderland'. The broad, flat-faced, dusky pink, thick, crepe-textured, silver-frosted blooms of *H.* 'Angelique' appear studded with myriads of tiny diamonds which glisten in the sunlight. Unlike many other Dutch hybrids whose scapes usually reach 21–25 in. (53–63 cm), the stubby scapes of *H.* 'Angelique' often do not exceed 16 in. (40 cm), which can make the plant appear top heavy, particularly when up to 6 large blooms are competing for air space. Plants with short scapes make daily management much easier when cultivated in a home environment and under poor lighting, as they are less likely to topple, providing they are planted in a suitably deep pot. The rose-pink *H.* 'Susan' on a whitish background with lime green throat lined with a ring of red dots is sold under various names, including *H.* 'Rosy Queen' or just *H.* 'Large Pink'. Its flat face and broad, rounded and overlapping petals have a wonderful netted pattern and, being much thinner than those of *H.* 'Angelique', bruise easily when touched.

Most bulbs of *Hippeastrum* 'Wonderland' which I have cultivated have shown a high degree of inconsistency in flower shape and the number and size of individual tepals. Some flowers had only 4 tepals while others had up to 9, often misshapen and sometimes distorted fragments. Such flowers looked rather strange and even grotesque in a few cases. The number of reproductive organs has also been correspondingly reduced or increased with the ratio of one stamen per tepal being maintained. Apart from such abnormalities, some plants have produced perfectly normal rounded blooms which represented a departure from more hooded or triangular hybrids which emerged during the 1980s and early 1990s.

By the end of the 20th century an imaginative assortment of pinks had emerged from Penning Breeding B.V. and T. van Nieuwkerk Amaryllis B.V. Both breeders recognized the need to produce a varied assortment with more unusual shapes and exciting patterns. Penning's *Hippeastrum* 'Amigo' has carmine rose blooms with a faint green star in the center and remains one of the finest solid pinks (Plate 3-4). It proved very popular at the Hippeastrum Celebration (Royal Botanic Gardens, Kew) in April 1999 and looked marvelous beside the flamboyant *H.* 'Mont Blanc'.

Other Penning hybrids which proved very popular among British gardeners are *Hippeastrum* 'Faro' (salmon and pink), *H.* 'Lambada' (rose and white), *H.* 'Nagano' (orange and white), *H.* 'Solomon' (salmon) and *H.* 'Trendsetter' (salmon, pink and white). The long-lasting, funnel-shaped blooms of the floriferous *H.* 'Solomon' have a remarkable charm and elegance enhanced by the lime green throat lined with a ring of dark red dots. The broad, flat-faced blooms of *H.* 'Nagano', with reflexed tips, enable the bright green throat to be fully appreciated. Like all hybrids, but particularly the pastels, *H.* 'Nagano' is light sensitive and becomes an even deeper orange when cultivated under good light conditions.

Hippeastrum 'Trendsetter' is Penning's first salmon-pink in which shades of pink are skillfully combined. Its slightly hooded blooms tend to droop somewhat compared to the flat-faced *H.* 'Faro' with its broader, rounded tepals. Many Penning hybrids are characterized by their high flower count and regularly produce 5–6 blooms per scape and 3 scapes from 13–14 in. (33–35 cm) bulbs. Some have a vase life of 10–11 days per bloom and most flower after 6–7 weeks.

Several of Nieuwkerk's pink hybrids are becoming widely available in Europe and the United States, including *Hippeastrum* 'Exposure', *H.* 'Flavio', *H.* 'Pink Diamond', *H.* 'Pink Impression' and *H.* 'Queen of Hearts'. Some are particularly regal with their broad, triangular or rounded blooms on 21–25 in. (53–63 cm) tall scapes. Some have tepaloids on the upper pair of tepals and most flower 6–8 weeks after planting. Most foliage develops after flowering. Hybrids having particularly tall, stout scapes and longer-lasting blooms are perfectly suited for grand state and civic occasions.

Only since the late 1990s have British gardeners been able to obtain some of the lovely South African pastels from Hadeco (Pty). *Hippeastrum* 'Barotse' and *H.* 'Milady' are pure, solid pinks; *H.* 'Masai', *H.* 'Springtime' and *H.* 'Summertime', among others, combine pink with red and white in varying proportions resulting in some remarkable effects. The floriferous *H.* 'Blushing Bride', Hadeco's oldest surviving pink (1962), has broad, flat-faced, rose-pink blooms, exquisite venation and lime green throat. The smaller, catlike *H.* 'Candy Floss' combines shades of pink and ox-blood red. The tall, elegant *H.* 'Desert Dawn' remains Hadeco's only salmon and, with its gorgeous flat-faced, exquisitely veined, triangular blooms, it remains one of my favorite Hadeco hybrids.

A visit to Maguire's Hippeastrum Farm reveals the finest collection of pastels available today. Maguire has always had a particular affinity with pink hippeastrums, evident from the several hundreds he has created since the 1970s. The distinctive shapes, patterns and color combinations of his plants separate them from the more predictable, more ordinary Dutch and South African hybrids. *Hippeastrum* 'Brevney', *H.* 'Harbour Lights', *H.* 'Kaitlin', *H.* 'Maguire's Envy' and *H.* 'Queen of the Nile' are very popular with Australian gardeners. They are quick and easy to flower, usually producing 4 blooms per scape and reaching 12–20 in. (30–50 cm) tall.

Whites

Creating a large pure white hybrid, devoid of the red or pink speckles or flushes which characterized many early large whites, presented breeders with an exciting challenge in the early 20th century. Today several outstanding pure white Australian and cream and snow white Dutch and South African hybrids are available. Some make wonderful cut flowers, others make stunning pot plants, particularly when placed next to a dark red. I find the vivid green throat and gently undulating, frilly tepals of *Hippeastrum* 'Athene' and *H.* 'Christmas Gift' particularly fascinating. These 2 snow whites are slower growing, taking up to 10 weeks from planting to flowering; however, the extra wait becomes worthwhile when the flowers finally open.

Hippeastrum 'Mont Blanc' remains the largest Dutch cream with 5–6 long-lasting blooms per scape from large 13–14 in. (33–35 cm) circumference bulbs. Its tall, stout scapes and high flower count make it a popular cut flower. *Hippeastrum* 'Intokazi' and *H.* 'Wedding Dance', two Hadeco (Pty) snow whites, are particularly lovely and become even whiter with age. The tepal tips reflex back as the flowers mature, creating a distinctly rounded appearance. *Hippeastrum* 'Intokazi' has marvelous glistening properties; its tepals appear to be covered with tiny diamonds.

Picotee hybrids

During the 1950s and early 1960s, the Dutch firm Ludwig and Company developed several medium and large whites edged with red. Among these were *Hippeastrum* 'Dutch Doll', *H.* 'Picotee' and *H.* 'Red Lining'; however, they all tended to show red flushes or speckles as the flowers aged and the thickness of the red border varied too. During the 1960s the company succeeded in creating *H.* 'Petticoat', a pure white with a thin, conspicuous red edging. Judging from the variation in the size and number of flowers per scape, degree of white, presence of streaks and speckles and the thickness of the red picotee, it would appear that several Dutch hybrids are being sold today, all marketed under the name *H.* 'Picotee'. Most of them have blooms less than 6.5 in. (16 cm) diameter, and therefore this hybrid is included in the list of small-flowering hybrids in Chapter 4. Many of these bulbs are slower growing compared to other small and medium-flowering hybrids. Plants usually bloom during spring and can be slow to root. Like other more difficult hybrids, when a picotee finally reveals its long-lasting, snowy blooms, edged with a pencil-thin red border and lined with a dark green throat, the effect is stunning.

A larger, more recent, easy-to-grow picotee is *Hippeastrum* 'Showmaster' from Penning Breeding B.V. This larger version of *H.* 'Charisma' (see Chapter 4) has glorious bright red and white speckled, hooded blooms with a thick red picotee. The hybrid caused great excitement among British gardeners when it bloomed in the National Collection for the first time in December 2002. Many exquisite and elaborate but easy-to-grow picotee hybrids have been created by Maguire in Australia; these have been made even more beautiful by the delicate red edging.

Striped hybrids

Many bright red-orange hippeastrums are particularly arresting with their bold central white stripes and bright green throat, sometimes lined with a ring of red dots. The arrangement and thickness of the stripes vary among cultivars. Some have delightful feathery venation which softens the overall effect, others have a white star towards the throat. *Hippeastrum* 'Minerva' (1962), *H.* 'Happy Memory' (1980) and *H.* 'Ster van Holland' (1986) remain the most popular and widely available red and white Dutch hybrids.

By the late 1990s many more striped hybrids had become available including *Hippeastrum* 'Cocktail', *H.* 'Coquette' *H.* 'Design' (Plate 3-11), *H.* 'Happiness', *H.* 'Hermitage', *H.* 'Mambo', *H.* 'Prelude', *H.* 'Razzle Dazzle', *H.* 'Stargazer' and *H.* 'Sydney'. Some had better-proportioned blooms than others. Shapes varied from round (*H.* 'Design'), to square, rectangular, triangular or hooded (*H.* 'Pizzazz', *H.* 'Razzle Dazzle').

Two of my favorites are *Hippeastrum* 'Carnival' and *H.* 'Pizzazz'. The slightly looser constructed scarlet, orange and snow-white jolly blooms of *H.* 'Carnival' with a thick white edging have proved popular with visitors to my shows. *Hippeastrum* 'Pizzazz' (Plate 3-12) is smaller and more formal with vivid red and white stripes combined with a snow white edging. Mature, upright foliage present at the time of flowering makes it an outstanding pot plant for the home and well-suited for mass indoor plantings.

Flower Shapes, Patterns and Textures of Large-flowering Hybrids

Earlier 20th-century assortments lacked the variety of shapes and patterns now available. Designs are becoming more intricate with streaks, stripes, spots, flecks, speckles and colored edgings featuring among many late 20th- and early 21st-century hybrids. Plants with more complex designs are more interesting, particularly those with more intricate venation and color combinations. The lovely lime green throat has always had considerable appeal for me, adding an extra dimension to any hybrid.

While Dutch breeders used to cater to customers preferring round-faced blooms, experience has shown that gardeners are more concerned with the overall effect and desire a well-proportioned flower. Today round, rectangular, triangular and star-faced hybrids have become widely available and appear plain when placed next to the smaller, exotic, wispy Cybisters and elegant Trumpets which are gradually becoming available (see Chapter 6).

Compared to the Dutch selection, Maguire's assortment is far more varied. Particularly interesting are the elaborate patterned and veined *Hippeastrum* 'June Maree' and *H.* 'Harbour Lights'. Some of the streaked, striped (*H.* 'Kaitlin', *H.* 'Queen of the Nile'), spotted (*H.* 'Maguire's Envy'), flecked, speckled and picotee hybrids (*H.* 'Barbara's Magic', *H.* 'June Maree') are amazing. A few have flowers which are divided into halves horizontally, each segment being a different color (*H.* 'Jennifer Jean'), while others sport attractive star-shapes towards the throat.

Hippeastrum hybrids may have triangular (*H.* 'Tangellino'), star-shaped (*H.* 'June Maree', *H.* 'Harbour Lights') or circular faces. Other hybrids have more open faces with short tepal tubes and broad, rounded, heavily imbricated tepals (*H.* 'Brevney') or broad, slightly pointed tepals (*H.* 'Kaitlin') which reflex at the tips. Some, such as *H.* 'Delicate Damsel', appear majestic, even mysterious with their ruffled-edged tepals which project forwards from slightly longer tepal tubes.

Overall, textures range from thick and velvety with a wonderful sheen to thin with a sumptuous satin complexion. Some tepals have a delightful netted effect, others sparkle in the sunshine as if adorned with minute jewels.

Scape and Foliage Development of Large-flowering Hybrids

A full discussion of variations in scape and foliage development of large-flowering hybrids occurs in Chapter 8. For now, it is sufficient to say that, unlike many smaller flowering hybrids which produce varying amounts of foliage at the time of flowering, many freshly purchased large singles produce little or no foliage in their first season, making particularly tall varieties look rather bare. Some Australian hybrids produce 3–5 leaves at the time of flowering; others develop smooth, green, upright mature leaves after flowering which reach 18 in. (45 cm) long and 3 in. (7.5 cm) wide.

Offset Production of Large-flowering Hybrids

Offset production varies according to cultivar, with some producing only 1 or 2 offsets each year or every 5 years while others produce many more and in some cases, up to 30–35 offsets in only 18 months! Newly purchased bulbs have sometimes had any offsets removed by the grower—a fresh indentation above the basal plate indicates this. Some mature bulbs will show evidence of offsets beneath the papery outer layers while others may have already emerged from old leaf bases. See Chapter 9 for the best time to remove offsets from the parent bulb.

Conclusion

Since 1800, several thousand large-flowering hybrids have been created but only a tiny fraction have entered production and become commercially available. Over 100 hybrids are currently available; some combine innovative shapes with intricate patterns and exciting color combinations, others are less imaginative. With such a fantastic choice, this is the perfect time for hippeastrum enthusiasts to establish their own collections and participate in the exciting changes taking place. Days are long gone when only a handful of large reds was available and one can only speculate as to what color combinations and patterns will be available 50 years from now.

For an explanation of the classification categories used in the descriptions that follow and for details of hybrid registration or the granting of Plant Breeders' Rights, see the Appendix.

Red Large Singles

'Basuto'

Breeder: Harry Deleeuw Ltd (South Africa); Date of Registration: 1977; Classification: Reginae (4b).

Description: Usually 4 upward facing, currant-red blooms 7.5 in. (19 cm) diameter per scape 18.75 in. (47 cm) tall.

'Belinda'

Breeder: G. C. van Meeuwen and Sons (The Netherlands); Date of Registration: 1963; Classification: Leopoldii (5a).

Description: Usually 3–4 blood-red to raspberry-red blooms 7 in. (18 cm) diameter per scape 16–18 in. (40–45 cm) tall. A particularly robust and dramatic hippeastrum.

'Benfica'

Breeder: Penning Breeding B.V. (The Netherlands); Plant Breeders' Rights: 2001; Classification: (Large-flowering).

Description: Usually 5–6 dark red blooms 7.5–8 in. (19–20 cm) diameter per scape 19–21 in. (48–53 cm) tall.

'Bold Leader'

Breeder: Harry Deleeuw Ltd (South Africa); Date of Registration: 1977; Classification: Leopoldii (5a).

Description: Usually 4–5 well-proportioned, orient-red blooms 6.5 in. (16 cm) diameter per scape 14 in. (35 cm) tall.

'Double Six'

Breeder: Hadeco (Pty) Ltd (South Africa); Plant Breeders' Rights: 1996; Classification: (Large flowering).

Description: Usually 6 orange-red blooms 7.25 in. (18 cm) diameter per scape 14 in. (35 cm) tall with delightful frilly edges.

'Eos'

Breeder: T. van Nieuwkerk Amaryllis (The Netherlands); Plant Breeders' Rights: 1997; Classification: Leopoldii (5b).

Description: Usually 4 bright orange-red, triangular blooms 8–10 in. (20–25 cm) diameter per scape 16–18 in. (40–45 cm) tall.

'Ferrari'

Breeder: Kwekersvereniging Amaryl (The Netherlands); Plant Breeders' Rights: 2001; Classification: Large-flowering.

Description: Usually 4 wine-red, velvety blooms 6–7 in. (15–18 cm) diameter per scape 20 in. (50 cm) tall with a wonderful sheen. Tepaloids are present on the upper pair of tepals.

'Furore'

Breeder: T. van Nieuwkerk Amaryllis B.V. (The Netherlands); Plant Breeders' Rights: 2000; Classification: Leopoldii.

Description: Usually 4–6 wine-red, velvety blooms 8–10 in. (20–25 cm) diameter per scape 20 in. (50 cm) tall.

'Grand Cru'

Breeder: T. van Nieuwkerk Amaryllis B.V. (The Netherlands); Plant Breeders' Rights: 2002; Classification: (Large-flowering).

Description: Usually 4 cherry-red blooms 10 in. (25 cm) diameter per scape 16–18 in. (40–45 cm) tall. Tepaloids are present on the upper pair of tepals.

'Honeymoon'

Breeder: Harry Deleeuw Ltd (South Africa); Date of Registration: 1977; Classification: Leopoldii (5a).

Description: Usually 4 flat, upward-facing, rose-red blooms 8.25 in. (21 cm) per scape 18.75 in. (47 cm) tall.

'Liberty'

Breeder: Jac J. Mense (The Netherlands); Date of Registration: 1980; Classification: Leopoldii (5a).

Description: Usually 4 blood-red blooms 7 in. (18 cm) diameter per scape 21 in. (53 cm) tall which have a glorious velvety, glossy heart. Mature upright foliage is present at the time of flowering.

'Merry Christmas'

Breeder: Hadeco (Pty) Ltd (South Africa); Date of Registration: 1993; Classification: Symphony.

Description: Usually 4 orient-red blooms with a wonderful velvety sheen, 8 in. (20 cm) diameter per scape 12 in. (30 cm) tall. Mature foliage is present at the time of flowering. The luxuriant foliage and shorter scapes contribute to making this an ideal pot plant for the festive season.

'Miracle'

Breeder: Hadeco (Pty) Ltd (South Africa); Date of Registration: 1981; Classification: Symphony.

Description: Usually 4 red, velvety blooms 7.25 in. (18 cm) diameter per scape 16 in. (40 cm) tall with a velvety, glossy heart.

'Parma'

Breeder: Penning Breeding B.V. (The Netherlands); Plant Breeders' Rights: 2001; Classification: Large-flowering.

Description: Usually 5–6 red, velvety blooms 7–8 in. (18–20 cm) diameter per scape 18–21 in. (45–53 cm) tall.

'Red Lion'

Breeder: M. van Waveren (The Netherlands); Date of Registration: 1958; Classification: Leopoldii (5a).

Description: Usually 3–4 dark red, velvety blooms 6.5–7 in. (16–18 cm) diameter per scape 16–18 in. (40–45 cm) tall. Frequently the first scape has only 2 or 3 blooms, followed by a second scape with 4 blooms (Plate 8-5).

'Red Sensation'

Breeder: Jac J. Mense (The Netherlands); Plant Breeders' Rights: 1993; Classification: Reginae (4a).

Description: Usually 4 bright red, free-flowing blooms 6.75 in. (17 cm) diameter per scape 14–18 in. (35–45 cm) tall.

'Roma'

Breeder: Penning Freesia B.V. (The Netherlands); Plant Breeders' Rights: 1993; Classification: Reginae (4a).

Description: Usually 4 dark red blooms 7.5–8 in. (19–20 cm) diameter per scape 20–24 in. (50–60 cm) tall. This cultivar heralded the beginning of a succession of large, velvety reds.

'Rotterdam'

Breeder: W. S. Warmenhoven (The Netherlands); Date of Registration: 1962; Classification: Leopoldii (5a).

Description: Usually 3–4 blackcurrant-red, hooded blooms 7 in. (18 cm) diameter per scape 18–21 in. (45–53 cm) tall which look almost black when the plant is placed next to a snowy white.

'Royal Velvet'

Breeder: Ludwig and Company (The Netherlands); Date of Registration: 1996; Classification: Leopoldii (5a).

Description: Usually 4 purple-red majestic blooms 8.75 in. (22 cm) diameter per scape 21–24 in. (53–60 cm) tall (Plate 3-3).

'Sun Dance'

Breeder: Harry Deleeuw Ltd (South Africa); Date of Registration: 1982; Classification: Symphony.

Description: Usually 4 bright, orange-red blooms 7.25 in. (18 cm) diameter per scape 15 in. (38 cm) tall.

'Zanzibar'

Breeder: Harry Deleeuw Ltd (South Africa); Date of Registration: 1963; Classification: Leopoldii (5a).

Description: Usually 4 vermilion blooms 7.5 in. (19 cm) diameter per scape 16 in. (40 cm) tall with an attractive, greenish center.

Pink Large Singles

'Amigo'

Breeder: Penning Freesia B.V. (The Netherlands); Plant Breeders' Rights: 1994; Classification: Leopoldii.

Description: Usually 4–6 long-lasting, flat-faced, carmine-red blooms 7.5–8 in. (19–20 cm) diameter per scape 18–20 in. (45–50 cm) tall with a faint greenish star towards the center (Plate 3-4).

'Angelique'

Breeder: Jac J. Mense (The Netherlands); Plant Breeders' Rights: 1987; Classification: Large-flowering.

Description: Usually 4–6 flat-faced, wide-open, dusky-pink and white blooms 7.5 in. (19 cm) diameter per scape 12–16 in. (30–40 cm) tall. The thick, crepelike tepals glisten in the sunlight and appear to be studded with tiny diamonds.

'Apple Blossom'

Breeder: Ludwig and Company (The Netherlands); Date of Registration: 1954; Classification: Leopoldii (5a).

Description: Usually 4–6 pale pink and white blooms 6.75–7 in. (17–18 cm) diameter per scape 20 in. (50 cm) tall. A particularly robust hybrid with a delightful lime green throat lined with a ring of red dots. When cultivated under poor lighting, the blooms are almost white.

'Barotse'

Breeder: Harry Deleeuw Ltd (South Africa); Date of Registration: 1969; Classification: Leopoldii (5a).

Description: Usually 4 cherry-red blooms 6.75 in. (17 cm) diameter per scape 18–20 in. (45–50 cm) tall. Mature foliage is present at the time of flowering.

'Bestseller'

Breeder: Jac J. Mense (The Netherlands); Date of Registration: 1980; Classification: Leopoldii (5b).

Description: Usually 4 carmine-pink, hooded blooms 6.75 in. (17 cm) diameter per scape 17 in. (42 cm) tall.

'Blushing Bride'

Breeder: Harry Deleeuw Ltd (South Africa); Date of Registration: 1962; Classification: Leopoldii (5a).

Description: Usually 4–6 flat-faced, rose-madder blooms 6.5–7.5 in. (16–19 cm) diameter per scape 15 in. (38 cm) tall.

'Bolero'

Breeder: Jac J. Mense (The Netherlands); Plant Breeders' Rights: 1993; Classification: Reginae (4a).

Description: Usually 6 rose-pink, flat-faced blooms 8 in. (20 cm) diameter per scape 20–22 in. (50–55 cm) tall.

'Brevney'

Breeder: Maguire's Hippeastrum Farm (Australia); Classification: (Large-flowering).

Description: Usually 4 rose-pink, rounded blooms 7 in. (18 cm) diameter per scape 13 in. (33 cm) tall with a green throat. Foliage is present at the time of flowering.

'Candy Floss'

Breeder: Harry Deleeuw Ltd (South Africa); Date of Registration: 1981; Classification: (Large-flowering).

Description: Usually 4–6 dark, rose-pink, flat-faced blooms 7.5 in. (19 cm) diameter per scape 17 in. (42 cm) tall with a greenish white throat. Foliage is present at the time of flowering (Plate 3-5).

'Dutch Belle'

Breeder: Ludwig and Company (The Netherlands); Date of Registration: 1963; Classification: Reginae (4a).

Description: Usually 3–4 carmine-rose blooms 7.5 in. (19 cm) diameter per scape 18–20 in. (45–50 cm) tall.

'Elvira Aramayo'

Breeder: W. S. Warmenhoven (The Netherlands); Date of Registration: 1962; Classification: Leopoldii (5a).

Description: Usually 4–6 raspberry-red blooms 6.75 in. (17 cm) diameter per scape 18 in. (45 cm) tall.

'Flavio'

Breeder: T. van Nieuwkerk Amaryllis B.V. (The Netherlands); Date of Registration: 1994; Classification: Reginae (4a).

Description: Usually 4 mellow-pink, rounded, flat-faced blooms 8 in. (20 cm) diameter per scape 18–20 in. (45–50 cm) tall.

'Flower Record'

Breeder: T. van Nieuwkerk Amaryllis B.V. (The Netherlands); Date of Registration: 1980; Classification: Leopoldii (5a).

Description: Usually 4–5 pale pink blooms 7 in. (18 cm) diameter per scape 22 in. (55 cm) tall.

'Harbour Lights'

Breeder: Maguire's Hippeastrum Farm (Australia); Classification: (Large-flowering).

Description: Usually 4 pale pink, star-shaped blooms 6 in. (15 cm) diameter per scape 14 in. (36 cm) tall with darker pink shades towards the throat and reflexed tepal tips.

'Hercules'

Breeder: Jac J. Mense (The Netherlands); Date of Registration: 1980; Classification: Leopoldii (5a).

Description: Usually 4 carmine-rose blooms 7.5 in. (19 cm) diameter per scape 19–21 in. (48–53 cm) tall.

'Lilac Wonder'

Breeder: T. van Nieuwkerk Amaryllis (The Netherlands); Date of Registration: 1994; Classification: Leopoldii (5a).

Description: Usually 4 dark pink, broad, flat-faced, rounded blooms 8–10 in. (20–25 cm) diameter per scape 16–19 in. (40–48 cm) tall.

'Milady'

Breeder: Harry Deleeuw Ltd (South Africa); Date of Registration: 1977; Classification: Leopoldii (5b).

Description: Usually 4 rose-pink blooms 6–7 in. (15–18 cm) diameter per scape 18.75 in. (47 cm) tall.

'Springtime'

Breeder: Harry Deleeuw Ltd (South Africa); Date of Registration: 1977; Classification: Leopoldii (5b).

Description: Usually 4–5 soft, rose-pink blooms 7–8 in. (18–20 cm) diameter per scape 18–19 in. (45–48 cm) tall.

'Summertime'

Breeder: Harry Deleeuw Ltd (South Africa); Date of Registration: 1977; Classification: Leopoldii (5a).

Description: Usually 4 rose-pink blooms 7.25 in. (18 cm) diameter per scape 15 in. (38 cm) tall with broad, central white stripes and deeper pink, feathery venation.

'Susan'

Breeder: Jac J. Mense (The Netherlands); Date of Registration: 1980; Classification: Leopoldii (5a).

Description: Usually 4–6 flat, pale, carmine-pink blooms 7 in. (18 cm) diameter per scape 14–16 in. (35–40 cm) tall with a bright green throat lined with a ring of darker pink dots.

'Telstar'

Breeder: M. van Waveren and Sons (The Netherlands): Date of Registration: 1962; Classification: Leopoldii (5a).

Description: Usually 4 carmine-rose blooms 6.75 in. (17 cm) diameter per scape 15.5 in. (39 cm) tall.

'Vera'

Breeder: Jac J. Mense (The Netherlands); Plant Breeders' Rights: 1988; Classification: Large-flowering.

Description: Usually 4 flat-faced, red-pink blooms 6.75–7 in. (17–18 cm) diameter per scape 18–22 in. (45–55 cm) tall.

Orange Large Singles

'Apricot Beauty'

Breeder: T. van Nieuwkerk Amaryllis B.V. (The Netherlands); Classification: (Midi/Large-flowering).

Description: Usually 4 bright orange blooms 8 in. (20 cm) diameter per scape 16–20 in. (40–50 cm) tall.

'Exotica'

Breeder: T. van Nieuwkerk Amaryllis B.V. (The Netherlands); Classification: (Large-flowering).

Description: Usually 3–4 peach/orange blooms 6–8 in. (15–20 cm) diameter per scape 14–16 in. (35–40 cm) tall. The almost translucent blooms have a delicate netted pattern and a small bright green heart making this a truly exotic hybrid.

'Orange Sovereign'

Breeder: M. van Waveren (The Netherlands); Date of Registration: 1980; Classification: Leopoldii (5b).

Description: Usually 4–6 long-lasting, exquisitely veined, bright orange blooms 7–7.5 in. (18–9 cm) diameter per scape 14–16 in. (35–40 cm) tall with frilly edged tepals. A particularly robust hybrid whose beauty is enhanced by the presence of mature foliage at the time of flowering.

'Tangellino'

Breeder: Maguire's Hippeastrum Farm (Australia); Classification: (Large-flowering).

Description: Usually 4 deep orange, flat-faced blooms 7 in. (18 cm) diameter per scape 20 in. (50 cm) tall with delightful silver markings on the outer side of the tepals. A particularly stunning hybrid (Plate 3-6).

Salmon-flowered Large Singles

'Beautiful Lady'

Breeder: Ludwig and Company (The Netherlands); Date of Registration: 1963; Classification: Leopoldii (5a).

Description: Usually 3–4 flat-faced, salmon-orange blooms 10.5 in. (26 cm) diameter per scape 26 in. (66 cm) tall (Plate 3-7).

'Desert Dawn'

Breeder: Harry Deleeuw Ltd (South Africa); Date of Registration: 1977; Classification: Leopoldii (5a).

Description: Usually 3–4 azalea pink blooms 6.75 in. (17 cm) per scape 18 in. (45 cm) tall.

'Desire'

Breeder: Kwekerij De Oudendam B.V. (The Netherlands); Plant Breeders' Rights: 1999; Classification: Large flowering.

Description: Usually 4 delicate, salmon blooms 6.75 in. (17 cm) per scape 18 in. (45 cm) tall. A fine alternative to 'Rilona'.

'Nagano'

Breeder: Penning Freesia B.V. (The Netherlands); Plant Breeders' Rights: 1995; Classification: Leopoldii.

Description: Usually 4–5, long-lasting, salmon-orange blooms 8 in. (20 cm) diameter per scape 18–22 in. (45–55 cm) tall with a white heart (Plate 3-8).

'Rilona'

Breeder: G. C. van Meeuwen (The Netherlands); Date of Registration: 1962; Classification: Leopoldii (5b).

Description: Usually 4–6 shrimp-red blooms 7.5 in. (19 cm) diameter per scape 18–20 in. (45–50 cm) tall.

'Solomon'

Breeder: Penning Freesia (The Netherlands); Plant Breeders' Rights: 1998; Classification: Large-flowering.

Description: Usually 4–6 long-lasting, delicate, salmon blooms 7–7.5 in. (18–19 cm) diameter per scape 18–20 in. (45–50 cm) tall with a lovely lime-green throat lined with a ring of red dots.

White Large Singles

'Athene'

Breeder: Jac J. Mense (The Netherlands); Plant Breeders' Rights: 1993; Classification: Large-flowering.

Description: Usually 4 delicate, snow-white, frilly edged, long-lasting blooms 6.75–7 in. (17–18 cm) diameter per scape 18–20 in. (45–50 cm) tall.

'Christmas Gift'

Breeder: Jac J. Mense (The Netherlands); Plant Breeders' Rights: 1987; Classification: Large-flowering.

Description: Usually 2–4 snow-white, long-lasting, frilly edged blooms 7–7.5 in. (18–19 cm) diameter per scape 18–22 in. (45–55 cm) tall (Plate 3-9).

'Intokazi'

Breeder: Harry Deleeuw Ltd (South Africa); Date of Registration: 1977; Classification: Leopoldii (5a).

Description: Usually 3–4 snow-white blooms 6.75 in. (17 cm) diameter per scape 18 in. (45 cm) tall with petals that are swept back to create a more rounded appearance.

'Ludwig's Dazzler'

Breeder: Ludwig and Company (The Netherlands); Date of Registration: 1957; Classification: Leopoldii (5a).

Description: Usually 4 snow-white, flat-faced blooms 8.5 in. (22 cm) per scape 26 in. (66 cm) tall.

'Matterhorn'

Breeder: Fa. G. van Staalduinen (The Netherlands); Plant Breeders' Rights: 1995; Classification: Leopoldii (5b).

Description: Usually 4–6, snow-white blooms 6.75–7 in. (17–18 cm) diameter per scape 18–22 in. (45–55 cm) tall.

'Vienna'

Breeder: Penning Breeding B.V. (The Netherlands); Plant Breeders' Rights: 2002; Classification: (Large-flowering).

Description: Usually 3–5, snow-white, slightly pointed, wide-open blooms 8 in. (20 cm) diameter per scape 18–22 in. (45–55 cm) tall.

'Wedding Dance'

Breeder: Harry Deleeuw Ltd (South Africa); Date of Registration: 1977; Classification: Leopoldii (5a).

Description: Usually 4, snow-white blooms 7 in. (18 cm) diameter per scape 16 in. (40 cm) tall. As the flowers mature, the tepals reflex back allowing the lovely green heart to become even more noticeable.

Green Large Singles

'Maguire's Envy'

Breeder: Maguire's Hippeastrum Farm (Australia); Classification: (Large-flowering).

Description: Usually 4 pale green blooms 7 in. (18 cm) diameter per scape 15.5 in. (39 cm) tall with numerous pink dots scattered over the broad, slightly pointed, crepe-textured tepals and a lime green throat.

Red Bicolored, Large Singles

'Barbara's Magic'

Breeder: Maguire's Hippeastrum Farm (Australia); Classification: (Large-flowering).

Description: Usually 4 white, star-shaped blooms 5.5 in. (14 cm) diameter per scape 13 in. (33 cm) tall with thin red picotee and dark red throat. Mature foliage is present at the time of flowering (Plate 3-10).

'Carnival'

Breeder: Harry Deleeuw Ltd (South Africa); Date of Registration: 1977; Classification: Leopoldii (5a).

Description: Usually 4–6 frilly edged, bright orange and red blooms 7 in. (18 cm) diameter per scape 18 in. (45 cm) tall rimmed with white. Mature foliage is present at the time of flowering.

'Clown'

Breeder: G. C. van Meeuwen (The Netherlands); Date of Registration: 1980; Classification: Leopoldii (5a).

Description: Usually 4 triangular, mandarin-red and white blooms 8.25 in. (21 cm) diameter per scape 16 in. (40 cm) tall. A robust, dramatic hybrid.

'Cocktail'

Breeder: Harry Deleeuw Ltd (South Africa); Date of Registration: 1977; Classification: Reginae (4a).

Description: Usually 4, signal red and white blooms 7 in. (18 cm) diameter per scape 20 in. (50 cm) tall with a broad, central, white stripe and yellow-green heart which is lined with a ring of red dots.

'Coquette'

Breeder: T. van Nieuwkerk Amaryllis B.V. (The Netherlands); Plant Breeders' Rights: 2001; Classification: (Large-flowering).

Description: Usually 4 flat-faced, wide-open, red and white, flat-faced blooms 8.75–10 in. (22–25 cm) diameter per scape 16–18 in. (40–45 cm) tall.

'Design'

Breeder: Penning Freesia (The Netherlands); Plant Breeders' Rights: 1998; Classification: Large-flowering.

Description: Usually 4–5 scarlet and white blooms 7–7.5 in. (18–19 cm) per scape 18–20 in. (45–50 cm) tall with exquisite venation. Tepaloids are present on the upper pair of tepals (Plate 3-11).

'Happiness'

Breeder: T. van Nieuwkerk Amaryllis B.V. (The Netherlands); Plant Breeders' Rights: 2001; Classification: (Large-flowering).

Description: Usually 4 flat-faced, wide-open, white and red netted blooms 8.75–10 in. (22–25 cm) diameter per scape 16–18 in. (40–45 cm) tall.

'Happy Memory'

Breeder: Ludwig and Company (The Netherlands); Date of Registration: 1980; Classification: Leopoldii (5a).

Description: Usually 4 red and white blooms 7 in. (18 cm) diameter per scape 23.5 in. (59 cm) tall.

'Hermitage'

Breeder: T. van Nieuwkerk Amaryllis (The Netherlands); Plant Breeders' Rights: 1995; Classification: Large flowering.

Description: Usually 4–6 flat-faced, red and white striped blooms 8–10 in. (20–25 cm) diameter per scape 16–20 in. (40–50 cm) tall.

'Jennifer Jean'

Breeder: Maguire's Hippeastrum Farm (Australia); Classification: (Large-flowering).

Description: Usually 4 star-shaped red and white blooms 7.5 in. (19 cm) diameter per scape 13 in. (33 cm) tall. The wide-open, slightly pointed blooms are divided horizontally into halves; the upper portion red, the lower portion white making this a most unusual hybrid.

'June Maree'

Breeder: Maguire's Hippeastrum Farm (Australia); Classification: (Large-flowering).

Description: Usually 4 star-shaped, red and white blooms 7 in. (18 cm) diameter per scape 18 in. (45 cm) tall with a bright red heart and thin red picotee. Mature leaves are present at the time of flowering.

'Mambo'

Breeder: Penning Breeding B.V. (The Netherlands); Plant Breeders' Rights: 2001; Classification: Large-flowering.

Description: Usually 4–6 red and white, flat-faced, exquisitely veined blooms 7.5 in. (19 cm) diameter per scape 14–16 in. (35–40 cm) tall.

'Minerva'

Breeder: G. C. van Meeuwen and Sons (The Netherlands); Date of Registration: 1962; Classification: Leopoldii (5a).

Description: Usually 4 bright red and white, wide-open, flat-faced blooms 7 in. (18 cm) diameter per scape 20 in. (50 cm) tall. The feathery venation goes some way to compensate for the sometimes irregularly shaped, lopsided blooms.

'Pizzazz'

Breeder: Hadeco (Pty) Ltd (South Africa); Date of Registration: 1984; Classification: Symphony.

Description: Usually 5–6 bright red and white, frilly edged, pointed blooms 6.5 in. (16 cm) diameter per scape 14 in. (35 cm) tall edged with white. Mature upright foliage at the time of flowering makes this stunning hybrid extra special (Plate 3-12).

'Prelude'

Breeder: Penning Breeding B.V. (The Netherlands); Plant Breeders' Rights: 2002; Classification: Large-flowering.

Description: Usually 4–5 red and white, flat-faced, rounded blooms 7–7.5 in. (18–19 cm) diameter per scape 18–20 in. (45–50 cm) tall.

'Razzle Dazzle'

Breeder: Hadeco (Pty) Ltd (South Africa); Date of Registration: 1984; Classification: Symphony.

Description: Usually 5–6 red, orange and white blooms 7 in. (18 cm) diameter per scape 14 in. (35 cm) tall. Mature foliage is present at the time of flowering.

'Showmaster'

Breeder: Penning Breeding B.V. (The Netherlands); Plant Breeders' Rights: 2001; Classification: (Large flowering).

Description: Usually 4–5 red and white, pointed blooms 8 in. (20 cm) diameter per scape 22–30 in. or (55–60 cm) tall with a bright green throat lined with a ring of dark red. The exquisite venation and thin red picotee make this a very dramatic hybrid.

'Stargazer'

Breeder: T. van Nieuwkerk Amaryllis B.V. (The Netherlands); Plant Breeders' Rights: 2003; Classification: (Large-flowering).

Description: Usually 4 flat-faced, red and white, wide-open, flat-faced blooms 10 in. (25 cm) diameter per scape 16–20 in. (40–50 cm) tall with a ring of red at the base of the lime green throat.

'Ster van Holland'

Breeder: Jac J. Mense (The Netherlands); Plant Breeders' Rights Expired: 2001; Classification: (Large-flowering).

Description: Usually 4–6 red and white, flat-faced blooms 7–8 in. (18–20 cm) diameter per scape 18–22 in. (45–55 cm) tall. The vibrant blooms with exquisite venation and lime green throat make this a particularly dramatic and popular hybrid.

'Sydney'

Breeder: Kwekersvereniging Amaryl (The Netherlands); Plant Breeders' Rights: 2001; Classification: Large-flowering.

Description: Usually 4–6 stunning, white and red blooms 7 in. (18 cm) diameter per scape 18–20 in. (45–50 cm) tall with a glorious frosting on the inner surface of the flowers. Greatly admired at the Hippeastrum Parade at the Keukenhof, Lisse, in March 2002.

'Toronto'

Breeder: Jac J. Mense (The Netherlands) Plant Breeders' Rights: 1993; Classification: Reginae (4a).

Description: Usually 4 bright red and white, flat-faced blooms 8.25–9 in. (21–23 cm) diameter per scape 20–25.5 in. (50–65 cm) tall.

'Vlammenspel'

Breeder: Kwekersvereniging Amaryl (The Netherlands); Plant Breeders' Rights Expired: 2001; Classification: Large-flowering.

Description: Usually 3–4 red and white blooms 8.25–10 in. (21–25 cm) diameter per scape 22–25.5 in. (55–65 cm) tall with a hint of violet-red towards the throat and a lovely red sheen on either side of the broad white stripes at the base of the throat. Up to 7 days between the opening of the individual pairs of heavily imbricated flowers. A particularly robust hybrid with tepaloids on the upper pair and lowermost tepals.

Orange or Salmon Bicolored, Large Singles

'Charmeur'

Breeder: T. van Nieuwkerk Amaryllis B.V. (The Netherlands); Date of Registration: 1997; Classification: Leopoldii (5b).

Description: Usually 6 orange and white, upward-facing, long-lasting blooms 7.5 in. (19 cm) diameter per scape 16–20 in. (40–50 cm) tall. This lovely robust hybrid with dark green broad foliage looked wonderful in my hippeastrum display at the Royal Horticultural Society show at Westminster in April 1999.

'Flair'

Breeder: T. van Nieuwkerk Amaryllis B.V. (The Netherlands): Classification: (Large-flowering).

Description: Usually 4 salmon-orange and white blooms 8–10 in. (20–25 cm) diameter per scape 18–20 in. (45–50 cm) tall.

Pink Bicolored, Large Singles

'Delicate Damsel'

Breeder: Maguire's Hippeastrum Farm (Australia); Classification: (Large-flowering).

Description: Usually 4 white and pale pink, triangular-shaped blooms 6.75 in. (17 cm) diameter per scape 16 in. (40 cm) tall. The broad, pointed tepals are enhanced further by the deep green throat.

'Exposure'

Breeder: T. van Nieuwkerk Amaryllis B.V. (The Netherlands); Plant Breeders' Rights: 1999; Classification: Midi (Large-flowering).

Description: Usually 4 dark pink and white striped blooms 8–8.75 in. (20–22 cm) diameter per scape 16–20 in. (40–50 cm) tall.

'Faro'

Breeder: Penning Breeding B.V. (The Netherlands); Plant Breeders' Rights: 2002; Classification: Large-flowering.

Description: Usually 4–6 salmon-pink and white, broad, rounded blooms 8.25–8.75 in. (21–22 cm) diameter per scape 18–20 in. (45–50 cm) tall. Delicate shades of salmon pink make this an outstanding addition to Penning's assortment of pink hybrids and a major improvement on the earlier 'Trendsetter'.

'Kaitlin'

Breeder: Maguire's Hippeastrum Farm (Australia); Classification: (Large-flowering).

Description: Usually 4 deep pink and white blooms, 6.75 in. (17 cm) diameter per scape 20 in. (50 cm) tall. The broad, pointed, white-striped tepals reflex at the tips leading to a deep green throat. Mature leaves are present at the time of flowering.

'Lambada'

Breeder: Penning Breeding B.V. (The Netherlands); Plant Breeders' Rights: 2001; Classification: Large-flowering.

Description: Usually 5–6 rose and white, long-lasting blooms 7–7.5 in. (18–19 cm) diameter per scape 18–22 in. (45–55 cm) tall. A particularly beautiful hybrid which has been much admired at my shows.

'Las Vegas'

Breeder: Penning Breeding B.V. (The Netherlands); Plant Breeders' Rights Expired: 2003; Classification: Reginae (4a).

Description: Usually 4 deep pink and white striped, flat-face blooms 8 in. (20 cm) diameter per scape 18–22 in. (45–55 cm) tall. The flowers are often poorly proportioned with a vase life of only 4–5 days.

'Masai'

Breeder: Harry Deleeuw Ltd (South Africa); Date of Registration: 1969; Classification: Leopoldii (5a).

Description: Usually 4 white and red striped blooms 7 in. (18 cm) diameter per scape 18 in. (45 cm) tall. This attractive cultivar reminds me of the markings found on the faces of Kenya's Masai tribesmen.

'Pink Blossom'

Breeder: Penning Breeding B.V. (The Netherlands); Plant Breeders' Rights: 2001; Classification: Large-flowering.

Description: Usually 5–6 pink and white, broad, rounded blooms 8–8.25 in. (20–21 cm) diameter per scape 18–22 in. (45–55 cm) tall. The flowers assume a more rounded appearance as the tepals reflex.

'Pink Diamond'

Breeder: T. van Nieuwkerk Amaryllis B.V. (The Netherlands); Classification: (Large-flowering).

Description: Usually 4 flat-faced, wide-open, dark pink and white triangular blooms 10 in. (25 cm) diameter per scape 16–18 in. (40–45 cm) tall.

'Pink Impression'

Breeder: T. van Nieuwkerk (The Netherlands); Plant Breeders' Rights: 2001; Classification: Large-flowering.

Description: Usually 4 flat-faced, pink and white blooms 8 in. (20 cm) diameter per scape 16 in. (40 cm) tall.

'Queen of Hearts'

Breeder: T. van Nieuwkerk (The Netherlands); Plant Breeders' Rights: 1999; Classification: (Large-flowering).

Description: Usually 4 flat-faced, pink and white blooms 8.75–10 in. (22–25 cm) diameter per scape 14–18 in. (35–45 cm) tall.

'Queen of the Nile'

Breeder: Maguire's Hippeastrum Farm (Australia); Classification: (Large-flowering).

Description: Usually 4 cerise pink and white, star-shaped blooms 7 in. (18 cm) diameter per scape 11 in. (28 cm) tall with a bright greenish yellow throat (Plate 3-13).

'San Remo'

Breeder: Penning Freesia B.V. (The Netherlands); Plant Breeders 'Rights: 1998; Classification: Large-flowering.

Description: Usually 4–6 pale pink, flat-faced blooms 6.75–8 in. (17–20 cm) diameter per scape 16–24 in. (40–60 cm) tall which are suffused with myriad pink dots. The lime-green throat and pink picotee make this a particularly unusual and attractive hybrid.

'Trendsetter'

Breeder: Penning Freesia B.V. (The Netherlands); Plant Breeders' Rights: 1998; Classification: Large-flowering.

Description: Usually 4–5 salmon-pink and white blooms 7.5 in. (19 cm) diameter per scape 16–18 in. (40–45 cm) tall. The broad, pointed tepals project forwards creating a hooded appearance which, combined with the lovely pink shades and lime green throat, make this hybrid so appealing.

'Wonderland'

Breeder: Jac J. Mense (The Netherlands), Plant Breeders' Rights Expired: 2002; Classification: Large-flowering.

Description: Usually 4–6 pale pink and white, rounded blooms 6.5–6.75 in. (16–17 cm) diameter per scape 18–20 in. (45–50 cm) tall. A high proportion of scapes have produced flowers with fewer or more than the usual 6 tepals.

Tricolored Large Singles

'Piquant'

Breeder: Jac Mense (The Netherlands); Date of Registration: 1980; Classification: Leopoldii (5a).

Description: Usually 4–6 salmon, red and white, flat-faced blooms 6.5 in. (16 cm) diameter per scape 16–20 in. (40–50 cm) tall. A stunning hybrid which was greatly admired at the Hippeastrum Celebration (Royal Botanic Gardens, Kew) in April 1999.

Chapter 4

Smaller Flowering Hybrids

Interest in smaller flowering hippeastrums is a relatively new development. Most breeders and growers continue to focus upon the large single hybrids and remain unconvinced of the smaller hybrids' potential. Some, however, recognize and appreciate the special quality of the smaller, more elegant flowering types. As well as expanding their range of conventional flowering types, some Dutch, Japanese, North American and South African breeders are using species extensively to create innovative and exciting new hippeastrums for pot and cut flower production (see Chapter 6).

Since the mid 1990s, an increasing number of retail establishments and mail-order companies have included a few smaller flowering hybrids in their annual assortments. Annual shows organized by the National Plant Collection Holder of Hippeastrum since 2000 and the Hippeastrum Celebration at the Royal Botanic Gardens, Kew, in 1999 helped raise awareness of these dainty types, and by 2003 many British gardeners were keen to obtain bulbs for their own collections.

This chapter explores the development of the conventional smaller flowering hippeastrums since 1940. Plant descriptions are given at the end of the chapter. Development of yellow hippeastrums is discussed in Chapter 5. New American, Brazilian, Dutch and Japanese selections are described in Chapter 6.

1940–1949

Development of smaller flowering hippeastrums began in 1940, when H. Boegschoten, a gardener for Dutch industrialist J. C. Bunge, crossed *Hippeastrum rutilum* with larger hybrids to produce *H.* 'Gracile' (meaning "graceful"). This hybrid was then crossed with *H. rutilum*, producing a race of small, floriferous, velvety red hybrids which were considered particularly suitable as houseplants and cut flowers. Early hybrids displayed the green throat, but Boegschoten eventually succeeded in eliminating this feature which some breeders regarded as undesirable. This resulted in pure red blooms which were admired at shows during the 1940s.

In 1946 Messrs G. C. van Meeuwen and Sons (Heemstede, The Netherlands) acknowledged the significance of Boegschoten's work by naming a small red hybrid after him. Recognizing the plant's commercial potential, the company purchased Boegschoten's entire stock of *Hippeastrum* 'Gracile' with a view to making the hybrid generally available. In December 1952, a small group of Gracilis hybrids, including *H.* 'Ballet', was shown at the Royal Horticultural Society's London show, but sadly they attracted little attention.

S. P. Lancaster of Lucknow (India) was also interested in this form. In 1940, he created *Hippeastrum* 'Mrs Lancaster' which involved *H. stylosum* and *H. reticulatum* var. *striatifolium* in its parentage. *Hippeastrum* 'Mrs Lancaster' had rose red blooms with darker veining and white stripes. It was involved in the parentage of *H.* 'Alipur Beauty', which had carmine pink flowers with white stripes.

1950–1969

Ludwig and Company (Hillegom) dominated developments in the 1950s and 1960s. Their 1951–1952 catalog announced the appearance of "a particularly fine race of miniature *Amaryllis*" and stressed the need to consider the Gracilis hybrid "as a class by itself which has its own special charm." The company considered these dainty types particularly suitable for table decorations.

The 4–6 florets per scape were described as "small and shapely" and measured 3.5–4.5 in. (9–12 cm) diameter. Many had slender, pointed tepals and some reflexed at the tips. Those with frilly edged tepals and longer tepal tubes, such as *Hippeastrum* 'Bianca' (Plate 4-1), resembled small lilies. Others had a looser, less formal appearance. Some had a bright green or white star-shaped throat and long-lasting flowers which remained fresh for up to 14 days if maintained at 61°F (16°C). Some produced foliage at the time of flowering while others, including *H.* 'Bianca' and *H.* 'Voodoo', produced few leaves until flowering had finished.

Cultivars were ranked according to the number of days from planting to flowering: "very early," less than 38 days; "early," 38–42 days; and "half-late," 42–47 days. Most came within the first two categories. They were easy to grow and well suited as a garden border plant. Hybrids with taller scapes of 22–24 in. (55–60 cm), such as *Hippeastrum* 'Carina', *H.* 'Pretty Pal' and *H.* 'Table Decoration, were marketed as cut flowers, Varieties with shorter scapes made attractive table decorations.

By 1969 a range of red, white, picotee and striped hybrids had become available, including *Hippeastrum* 'Constant Comment' (claret), *H.* 'Fire Fly (capsicum red), *H.* 'Little Sweetheart' (salmon-red), *H.* 'Melody Lane' (salmon-orange), *H.* 'Picture' (orient-red), *H.* 'Pixie' (Dutch vermilion), *H.* 'Pretty Pal' (capsicum red and white), *H.* 'Red Man' (scarlet), *H.* 'Rubina' (blood-red), *H.* 'Sparkling Gem' (orient-red), *H.* 'Table Decoration' (pale vermilion) and *H.* 'Twinkling Star' (ivory-white with salmon-pink veins) and 'Voodoo' (scarlet with a white star). Of these early hybrids, only *H.* 'Bianca' (snow white), *H.* 'Carina' (red), *H.* 'Pamela' (capsicum red) and *H.* 'Voodoo' (scarlet with a white star) remain commercially available. All four have proved very popular with British gardeners.

Other Dutch breeders also showed interest in small-flowered hippeastrums. Details of their hybrids can be found in Table 4-1.

1970–2002

By the end of the 20th century, more than 50 new small-flowering American, Brazilian, Dutch, Japanese and South African hybrids had become available. Some made extensive use of species and looked very different from many conventional-shaped hippeastrums.

Classification

Until the late 1990s, small- and medium-flowering hybrids were classified as Trumpet, Reginae, Papilio, Medium, Midi, Small or Miniature according to the shape and size of the flowers. Those classified as Miniatures by the American Amaryllis Society (formerly the registration authority for *Hippeastrum* hybrids) were prefixed with the word "Gracilis" in the *Alphabetical List of Amaryllis (Hippeastrum) Cultivars in Cultivation in The Netherlands* (Stuurman 1980) published by the Royal General Bulbgrowers' Association (KAVB).

Table 4-1. Dutch small-flowering hybrids 1958–1980.

Cultivar name and date of registration (if applicable)	Name of breeder	Flower color	Number of flowers per scape (if known) and flower diameter	Scape length
'Beau Joliat' (1959)	W. S. Warmenhoven	Rosy red	3.5 in. (9 cm)	22 in. (55 cm)
'Christmas Joy' (1959)	W. S. Warmenhoven	Red	3.5 in. (9 cm)	24 in. (60 cm)
'Flower Record' (1959)	W. S. Warmenhoven	Deep scarlet	3 in. (7.5 cm)	23 in. (58 cm)
'House of Orange' (1958)	M. van Waveren & Sons	Flaming orange	3–5 flowers, 2 in. (5 cm)	28 in. (72 cm)
'Pygmee' (1975)	D. J. van Geest	Poppy red	4–5 flowers, 4 in. (10 cm)	14.2 in. (36 cm)
'Red Riding Hood' (1980)	D. J. van Geest	Vermilion	4–5 flowers, 4 in. (10 cm)	12.2 in. (31 cm)
'Star of Bethlehem' (1959)	W. S. Warmenhoven	Salmon pink and white	3.5 in. (9 cm)	24 in. (60 cm)
'Stein's Glory' (1980)	K. G. Stein & Company	Deep orange	3–4 flowers, 4 in. (10 cm)	8 in. (20 cm)

Those hybrids developed after 1980 had abandoned the relationship which had categorized small-flowering hybrids of the 1950s and 1960s. Dutch breeders began to classify hybrids with 4.0–4.5 in. (10–12 cm) diameter blooms as small-flowering while those with slightly larger 4.5–6.5 in. (12–16 cm) diameter blooms which were neither small- nor large-flowering, were termed Midi or Medium-flowering. As of March 2003, this category had not been officially endorsed by the International Cultivar Registration Authority. South African growers continued to use musical terminology to distinguish the different flower sizes: Solo—less than 2.5 in. (6 cm) diameter; Sonatini—2.5–4.0 in. (6–10 cm) diameter; and Sonata—4.0–6.5 in. (10–16 cm) diameter. Japanese breeders referred to their hybrids as Super Mini—2 in. (5 cm) diameter; Mini—4–4.5 in. (10–12 cm) diameter; or Medium—6 in. (15 cm) diameter. Japanese terminology did not always reflect the size of the flower but the plant's overall dimensions including bulb circumference and scape length.

Features of Conventional, Smaller Flowering Hybrids

Most modern smaller flowering hybrids flower within 4–5 weeks after planting and produce 3 scapes, occasionally 4, from largest size bulbs, each scape bearing usually 4–6 and sometimes up to 10 dainty blooms per scape (see Table 8-1 for the relationship between bulb circumference and scape production). Some bulbs reach 17.5 in. (44 cm) circumference after only 3 growing seasons of 8 months each, a size similar to that of many large-flowering hybrid bulbs, while others may not exceed 8 in. (20 cm) circumference.

Flower colors now available include delightful shades of red, orange, salmon, pink, pale yellow and snow white. Many smaller flowering hybrids combine 2 or more colors to produce a stunning effect which is often enhanced by the beautiful lime green throat, a characteristic often absent from bright orange and red monocolored hybrids. Examples of the bicolored hybrids include *Hippeastrum* 'Charisma', *H.* 'Fairytale', *H.* 'Moviestar' and *H.* 'Starlet'. Most reds, including *H.* 'Floris Hekker', *H.* 'Rapido' and *H.* 'Toledo', have a glorious velvety throat and a wonderful sheen.

Vase life varies according to cultivar. Individual flowers remain fresh for up to 11 days, sometimes even longer when cultivated under cooler 61°F (16°C) temperatures.

By the end of the 20th century, breeders were under increasing pressure to create distinctive-shaped small-flowering hybrids with more interesting patterns including streaks, stripes, spots, speckles, flecks and colored edgings (known as picotees). Some had marvelous feathery or netted venation. Those with long, slender tepal tubes and sharply pointed, forward-projecting, silky tepals looked like small lilies. Some had shorter tubes and slightly broader, rounded tepals. Frilly edged tepals that reflexed at the tips created a more rounded appearance, enabled the throat to be seen more clearly and softened the overall appearance, making the plants look even more magical. *Hippeastrum* 'Amico' and *H.* 'Starlet' are two examples of the latter. Some striped hybrids, such as *H.* 'Fairytale', were more formal; others, such as the medium-flowering *H.* 'Yellow Goddess', were more loosely constructed.

The scape length and circumference of smaller flowering hybrids is discussed in Chapter 8. Unlike many large singles and doubles, some small-flowering hybrids display mature foliage at the time of flowering in their first season after purchase and in subsequent seasons, creating a wonderful bushy effect and enhancing the plant's general appearance. Among these bushy plants are *Hippeastrum* 'Fairytale', *H.* 'Floris Hekker', *H.* 'Moviestar' and *H.* 'Toledo'. Mature foliage may reach up to 24 in. (60 cm) tall, sometimes even taller, and up to 1.75 in. (4.5 cm) broad. Leaves come in shades of green from lime to bottle-green, matt or gloss. Some leaves are edged and tipped with attractive shades of chestnut-brown or purple. Pink, red or brown shades are often visible towards the base on the outside of the leaf, matching the lower portion of the scape. Textures range from silky to slightly rubbery, even leathery, as the leaves age and when grown under good lighting.

Important Breeders

Beginning in the mid 1970s, Isamu Miyake of Miyake Nursery, Chiba-kon, Japan, used progeny obtained from Ludwig's *Hippeastrum* 'Firefly' to produce a group of delicate, multiflowering hybrids for cut flower production in a range of styles and colors which became available by the mid 1980s. Each 27–31 in. (70–80 cm) scape carried up to 7 dainty blooms. Two hybrids had 10 delicate, star-shaped, orange and white or red and white blooms per scape. Although they were popular in Japan, they did not become available in The Netherlands due to their small size, Dutch growers being only interested in large-flowering singles. Subsequently, medium-flowering hybrids with up to 8 blooms 6 in. (15 cm) diameter per scape 27–31 in. (70–80 cm) tall have been developed for the cut flower trade which should become available by 2010 (Plates 4-2, 4-3).

In The Netherlands, Penning Breeding B.V. has always been interested in the smaller flowering hybrid. By 2003, several distinctive, small- and medium-flowering hybrids in a range of colors had entered commercial production and become available. They included rich, velvety reds (*Hippeastrum* 'Calimero', *H.* 'Floris Hekker', *H.* 'Rapido' and *H.* 'Toledo'), china pink (*H.* 'Pink Star'), pink and white (*H.* 'Starlet'), vivid red and white (*H.* 'Charisma', *H.* 'Fairytale'), orange and white (H. 'Moviestar') and pale yellow (*H.* 'Yellow Moon'). Many exhibited imaginative and exciting color combinations, interesting shapes, novel designs and exquisite veining. These proved very popular when displayed at the home of the National Plant Collection of *Hippeastrum* and at the Royal Botanic Gardens, Kew.

Apart from the slower-growing exotic *Hippeastrum* 'Charisma', Penning's hybrids were quick and easy to grow, usually flowering 4–5 weeks after planting. Many had 5–6 blooms per scape and usually 3, occasionally 4 scapes in the first season from large 10.5–14.25 in. (26–36 cm) circumference bulbs. Some had attractive red or green-purple scapes and pedicels with luxuriant, mature, upright or fan-shaped foliage at the time of flowering. These created a delightful bushy effect.

Since the early 1990s, Hadeco (Pty) of South Africa has created several exquisite small and medium-flowering hippeastrums for pot plant cultivation. They include some lovely velvety reds (*Hippeastrum* 'Amico', *H.* 'Bambino', *H.* 'Top Choice'), vibrant and dramatic red-orange and whites (*H.* 'Christmas Star, *H.* 'Piccolo') and delicate pinks (*H.* 'Amalfi', *H.* 'Pico Bello'). Relatively small bulbs produce up to 3 scapes, each having 4–8 dainty blooms (see Table 8-1 for details). Taller scape varieties were suitable for cut flowers, while shorter scape hybrids made ideal table displays, particularly when several bulbs were planted in a large pot.

Future for the Conventional, Smaller Flowering Hybrid

Until recently, breeders, growers and exporters considered smaller flowering hybrids as inferior. They received little attention and commanded a lower price at auction. Attitudes are finally changing. If breeders, growers, exporters and wholesalers can be convinced of the role of the smaller flowering hybrids in the hippeastrum portfolio, then this group may prove to be one of the most significant developments in the history of the genus.

For an explanation of the classification categories used in the descriptions that follow and for details of hybrid registration and the granting of Plant Breeders' Rights, see the Appendix.

Red Smaller Hybrids

'Amico'

Breeder: Hadeco (Pty) Ltd (South Africa); Date of Registration: 1998; Classification: Sonatini.

Description: Usually 4 dark red, frilly edged 3.5–4.0 in. (9–10 cm) diameter blooms per scape 16 in. (40 cm) tall with a white-brushed center. Within 2 or 3 days of opening, the tepal tips reflex, creating a more rounded appearance. Usually 2 scapes from 7–8 in. (18–20 cm) circumference and 3 from 9.5–10.5 in. (24–26 cm) circumference bulbs. Normally 3–5 weeks from planting to flowering. Maximum bulb size: 10.5–11 in. (26–28 cm) circumference (Plate 4-4).

'Bambino'

Breeder: Hadeco (Pty) Ltd (South Africa); Plant Breeders' Rights: 1999; Classification: Sonatini.

Description: Usually 4–5 light red, trumpet-shaped blooms 2 in. (5 cm) diameter per scape less than 8.75 in. (22 cm) tall. Dark green, matt foliage with a central keel usually develops after flowering, reaching 24 in. (60 cm) long and 1.5 in. (4 cm) wide when mature. Usually 2 scapes from 6.5–7 in. (16–18 cm) circumference and 3 from 8–9.5 in. (20–24 cm) maximum circumference bulbs. After only 6 weeks at 55°F (13°C), 'Bambino' produced a new shoot, together with a handful of leaves, and it flowered after 21 days.

'Calimero'

Breeder: Penning Breeding B.V. (The Netherlands); Plant Breeders' Rights: 1994; Classification: Small-flowering.

Description: Usually 4–6 bright red, pixielike blooms 4.5–5 in. (12–13 cm) diameter per scape 20–22 in. (50–55 cm) tall. Usually 2 scapes from 8–8.75 in. (20–22 cm) circumference and usually 3 from 11–12 in. (28–30 cm) circumference bulbs. Maximum bulb size: 17.5 in. (44 cm) circumference. Unlike the smaller, more delicate 'Pamela', 'Calimero' has particularly tall, robust scapes which have attractive shades of pink-brown towards the base.

'Carina'

Breeder: Ludwig and Company (The Netherlands); Date of Registration: 1967; Classification: Gracilis.

Description: Usually 6 wine-red with vermilion gloss, frilly edged blooms 4–5 in. (10–13 cm) diameter per scape 20–22 in. (50–55 cm) tall. The exquisitely proportioned blooms with a rich, velvety throat; dark red pedicels; bright green, glossy ovaries and robust, chestnut-brown scapes never fail to command considerable attention.

'Floris Hekker'

Breeder: Penning Breeding B.V. (The Netherlands) Plant Breeders' Rights: 1996; Classification: Leopoldii (Midi).

Description: Usually 5–6 red, velvety, long-lasting blooms 5.5–6 in. (14–15 cm) diameter per scape 12–16 in. (30–40 cm) tall with an even richer, velvety throat. Its speed of growth from planting to flowering (3–5 weeks) with two scapes in bloom simultaneously, followed by a third 10–12 days later; 7–9 glossy green leaves, 8–10.5 in. (20–26 cm) tall and 1.4 in. (3.5 cm) wide at the time of flowering; short, manageable scapes make 'Floris Hekker' an ideal and popular pot plant. Usually 2 scapes from 8.75–9.5 in. (22–24 cm) circumference and 3 from 11–12 in. (28–30 cm) circumference bulbs. Maximum bulb size: 17 in. (44 cm) circumference (Plate 4-5).

'Pamela'

Breeder: Ludwig and Company (The Netherlands); Date of Registration: 1967; Classification: Gracilis.

Description: Usually 4–5 capsicum red, sharply pointed, dainty blooms 3 in. (7.5 cm) diameter per scape 20 in. (50 cm) tall. The flowers have exquisite venation and a satinlike texture. Slender, green scapes are tinged with attractive shades of pink-brown towards the base and up to 6 mature leaves may be present at the time of flowering.

'Rapido'

Breeder: Penning Breeding B.V. (The Netherlands); Plant Breeders' Rights: 2001; Classification: Small-flowering.

Description: 6–9 long-lasting, wine red blooms 4.5 in. (12 cm) diameter per scape 14–20 in. (35–50 cm) tall. Usually 2 scapes from 8–8.5 in. (20–22 cm) circumference and 3 from 12–13 in. (30–33 cm) circumference bulbs. Maximum bulb size: 12–13 in. (30–33 cm) circumference. Usually 2–3 scapes bloom simultaneously, producing a miniature garden of blooms enhanced by the purple-green scapes; bright red, shiny pedicels and dark green, glossy ovaries. Immature leaves with chocolate-colored tips are often present at the time of flowering.

'Toledo'

Breeder: Penning Breeding B.V. (The Netherlands) Plant Breeders' Rights: 2002: Classification: Large-flowering (Small/Midi).

Description: Usually 4 bright red, frilly edged, pointed blooms 3.5–5 in. (9–13 cm) diameter per scape 18–20 in. (45–50 cm) tall. Mature, fan-shaped foliage with an initial silky feel becomes more leathery during the summer and reaches a maximum of 27 in. (70 cm) long, 1.75 in. (4.5 cm) wide with a central keel along the underside of the leaf. Shades of pink-red towards the base of the green-gray scapes intensify in the strong sunlight. Usually 2 scapes from 8.75–9.5 in. (22–24 cm) circumference and 3 from 11–12 in. (28–30 cm) circumference bulbs. Bulbs reach a maximum 14.25–15 in. (36–38 cm) circumference. Bulbs of 'Toledo' are particularly dense and produce robust root systems.

'Top Choice'

Breeder: Hadeco (Pty) Ltd (South Africa); Date of Registration: 2000; Classification: Sonata.

Description: Usually 6–8 bright red, velvety blooms 4 in. (10 cm) diameter per scape 13 in. (33 cm) tall which are similar to 'Floris Hekker'. Fast growing, flowering 4–5 weeks after planting, but unlike its Dutch cousin, most foliage develops after flowering. Usually 1 scape from 7–8 in. (18–20 cm) circumference and 2 from 10.5–11 in. (26–28 cm) maximum circumference bulbs.

Pink Smaller Hybrids

'Amalfi'

Breeder: Hadeco (Pty) Ltd (South Africa); Plant Breeders' Rights: 2002; Classification: Sonata.

Description: Usually 4–5 upward-facing, rose blooms 5 in. (13 cm) diameter per scape 16 in. (40 cm) tall with a white central star. Usually 2 scapes from 8.75–9.5 in. (22–24 cm) circumference and 3 from 11–12 in. (28–30 cm) maximum circumference bulbs.

'Cupido'

Breeder: Hadeco (Pty) Ltd (South Africa); Date of Registration: 1999; Classification: Sonatini.

Description: Usually 3–4 pink and white veined blooms 3.5 in. (9 cm) diameter per scape 11 in. (28 cm) tall. Bulbs reach a maximum 7–8 in. (18–20 cm) circumference. Ideal for planting several bulbs to a pot.

'Donau'

Breeder: L. Berbee and Sons B.V. (The Netherlands); Registered: 1994; Classification: Small-flowering.

Description: Usually 5–6 deep pink blooms 4 in. (10 cm) diameter per scape 20–24 in. (50–60 cm) tall which become almost red when placed in strong sunlight. Up to 9, mature leaves are usually present with the flowers. An unusually tall hybrid which makes a wonderful cut flower.

'Pico Bello'

Breeder: Hadeco (Pty) Ltd (South Africa); First sold: 1999; Classification: Sonata.

Description: Usually 6–8 porcelain-rose blooms 4.25 in. (11 cm) diameter per scape 14 in. (35 cm) tall. Bulbs reach a maximum 9.5–10.5 in. (24–26 cm) circumference.

Orange Smaller Hybrids

'Christmas Star'

Breeder: Hadeco (Pty) Ltd (South Africa); Plant Breeders' Rights: 2003; Classification: Sonata.

Description: Usually 6–8 fiery, orange-red, slightly upward-facing blooms 5 in. (13 cm) diameter per scape 18 in. (45 cm) tall with a pronounced white center. Little or no foliage is present at the time of flowering. Usually 1 scape from 8–9.5 in. (20–24 cm) circumference, 2 from 9.5–10.5 in. (24–26 cm) and 3 from 11–13 in. (28–33 cm) maximum circumference bulbs. This vibrant hippeastrum was greatly admired by visitors to my display of South African hybrids at the RHS London Show in November 1999.

'Moviestar'

Breeder: Penning Breeding B.V. (The Netherlands): Plant Breeders' Rights: 1999; Classification: (Midi).

Description: Usually 4–8 vibrant orange, long-lasting, pointed blooms 4.5–5 in. (12–13 cm) diameter per scape 18–28 in. (45–72 cm) tall with a delightful snow-white star towards the throat. Up to 9, mature, upright, dark green, leathery leaves 16–20 in. (40–50 cm) tall and 1.5 in. (4 cm) wide are usually present with the flowers. Usually 2 scapes from 9.5–10.5 in. (24–26 cm) circumference, 3 from 12–13 in. (30–33 cm) and occasionally 4 from 13 in. (33 cm) circumference bulbs. Three weeks after fertilization, pedicles have increased to 4 in. (10 cm) long and the glossy, dark green seed capsules have reached 4.25 in. (11 cm) circumference (Plate 4-6).

Salmon Smaller Hybrids

'Salmon Pearl'

Breeder: Unknown; Date of Registration: 1997; Classification: Gracilis.

Description: Usually 4–6 frilly edged, long-lasting, salmon blooms 3.5–4.5 in. (9–12 cm) diameter per scape 18–22 in. (45–55 cm) tall. Usually 3–4 scapes from 12–13 in. (30–33 cm) circumference bulbs. Up to 5 mature leaves may be present at the time of flowering. This very dainty and delightful hippeastrum often flowers 3 times a year after the first year of purchase, producing a single scape and 2–4 blooms from tiny bulbs measuring only 6.5–7 in. (16–18 cm) circumference and 3 or 4, tough, dark green leaves. 'Salmon Pearl' only requires 5–6 weeks of lower temperatures before a new scape emerges. Due to its propensity to sprout easily while in storage, 'Salmon Pearl' is likely to be discontinued and replaced by 'Moviestar' in the near future. In the meantime, it remains one of the most charming small-flowering hybrids (Plate 4-7).

White

'Bianca'

Breeder: Ludwig and Company (The Netherlands); Date of Registration: 1967; Classification: Gracilis.

Description: Often incorrectly known as 'Green Goddess', this charming hybrid usually has 3–4, exquisite snow-white, frilly edged, long-lasting, trumpet-shaped blooms 4–5 in. (10–13 cm) diameter per scape 16–18 in. (40–45 cm) tall. The slightly shorter brown scapes enhance the appearance of this very elegant hybrid which regularly flowers 4–5 weeks after planting, with 2 scapes often flowering simultaneously followed by a third 7–10 days later from 11–12 in. (28–30 cm) and 12–13 in. (30–33 cm) circumference bulbs. Leaves usually appear after flowering. 'Bianca' remains one of my favorites, its gorgeous blooms resembling small lilies.

'Picotee'

Breeder: Ludwig and Company (The Netherlands); Date of Registration: 1958; Classification: Leopoldii (5a) (Midi).

Description: Usually 3–4 snow-white blooms 6–6.5 in. (15–16 cm) diameter per scape 18–19 in. (45–48 cm) tall with a delicate red picotee and lime green throat. Foliage develops long after flowering has finished. Usually 2 scapes from 12–13 in. (30–33 cm) circumference bulbs. A particularly slow-growing cultivar but so beautiful, it never fails to attract attention at Easter time.

'White Equester III'

Breeder: W. S. Warmenhoven (The Netherlands); Classification: (Midi).

Description: Usually 5–6 gorgeous snow-white, frilly edged, long-lasting, trumpet blooms 5–6 in. (13–15 cm) diameter per scape 16–18 in. (40–45 cm) tall. Chocolate scapes; red-brown, glossy ovaries and pedicels; and brown-red markings on the outside of the tepal tubes make 'White Equester III' one of my favorite medium-flowering hybrids (Plate 4-8).

Red Bicolored, Smaller Hybrids

'Baby Star'

Breeder: Stapoflor, Lda (The Netherlands); Plant Breeders' Rights: 1991; Classification: Gracilis.

Description: Usually 4–6 frilly edged, scarlet and white blooms 3.75–4.25 in. (9.5–11 cm) diameter per scape 16–24 in. (40–60 cm) tall. Up to 7 mature leaves are often present at the time of flowering. This hybrid has never become widely available in Great Britain but when introduced at the Hippeastrum Celebration (Royal Botanic Gardens, Kew) in April 1999, its wonderful netted effect was greatly admired. 'Baby Star' is particularly light sensitive and produces flowers which are almost pink when grown under poor lighting.

'Charisma'

Breeder: Penning Breeding B.V. (The Netherlands): Plant Breeders' Rights: 1999; Classification: Large flowering (Midi).

Description: Usually 4–5, bright red and white, frilly edged blooms

6–6.5 in. (15–16 cm) diameter per scape 16–21 in. (40–53 cm) tall edged with red. The stout, purple-brown scapes, bright red pedicels and attractive matt green glossy ovaries with darker margins make this one of the most beautiful Dutch picotee hybrids available today. Two weeks after fertilization, the pedicels have increased to 2.5 in. (6 cm) long and the cylindrical-shaped capsules have expanded to 2.5 in. (6 cm). Three weeks later, each locule has acquired its typical bulbous shape and the capsule has increased to around 4.5 in. (12 cm) circumference. The horizontally held blooms have the most wonderful venation, the upper 3 tepals being predominantly red, the lower ones speckled with red on a white background.

'Charisma' is slower growing than some other hybrids, usually flowering 8–9 weeks after planting but taking up to 14 weeks when bulbs are given insufficient cool period at 55°F (13°C) with a gap of up to 6 weeks between the emergence of individual scapes. Usually 2 scapes from 10.5–11 in. (26–28 cm) circumference and 3 from 13–14.25 in. (33–36 cm) circumference bulbs (Plate 4-9).

'Fairytale'

Breeder: Penning Breeding B.V. (The Netherlands): Plant Breeders' Rights: 1998; Classification: Large flowering (Midi).

Description: Usually 4–6 medium-flowering, vivid red and white striped, frilly edged blooms 4–5 in. (10–13 cm) diameter per scape 14–24 in. (35–60 cm) tall. This hybrid never fails to amaze me with its clouds of delicate blooms which have exquisite venation and up to 7 leaves present at the time of flowering. Usually 5–6 weeks from planting to flowering but sometimes less than 4 weeks. Usually 2 scapes from 8.75–9.5 in. (22–24 cm) circumference, 3 from 12–13 in. (30–33 cm) and sometimes 4 from 13–14.25 in. (33–36 cm) circumference bulbs. 'Fairytale' is a particularly robust and reliable hybrid whose overall dimensions bear more relationship to some large hippeastrum (Plate 4-10).

'Piccolo'

Breeder: Hadeco (Pty) Ltd (South Africa): Date of Registration: 2000; Classification: Sonatini.

Description: Usually 4 cerise red and white, pointed, impish blooms 3.75 in. (9.5 cm) diameter per scape 16 in. (40 cm) tall. Little or no foliage is present at the time of flowering. Usually 1 slender scape from 7–8 in (18–20 cm) circumference, 2 from 8–9.5 in. (20–24 cm) and 3 from 9.5–10.5 in. (24–26 cm) circumference bulbs. Ideal for planting several bulbs in a pot.

'Voodoo'

Breeder: Ludwig and Company (The Netherlands); Date of Registration: 1960; Classification: Gracilis.

Description: Often incorrectly known as 'Naughty Lady', this hippeastrum usually produces 3–5 scarlet and white, trumpet-shaped, round-tipped, exquisitely veined blooms 3–3.5 in. (7.5–9 cm) diameter per scape 16–20 in. (40–50 cm) tall, enhanced considerably by the lovely bright yellow and green throat. The red style and filaments gradually become white towards the center of the throat. Usually 6 weeks from planting to flowering. Usually 3 slender, brownish scapes appear in close succession from 12–13 in. (30–33 cm) circumference bulbs with leaves usually developing after flowering (Plate 4-11).

Pink Bicolored, Smaller Hybrids

'Pink Star'

Breeder: Penning Breeding B.V. (The Netherlands); Plant Breeders' Rights: 2001; Classification: Small-flowering.

Description: Usually 4 pink and white, delicate pointed blooms 4–5 in. (10–13 cm) diameter per scape 18–20 in. (45–50 cm) tall. Depending on the period of storage prior to planting and the environmental conditions after planting, 'Pink Star' can be particularly fast-growing, sometimes flowering after only 22 days with around 12 days vase life per scape. Usually 1 scape from 7–8 in. (18–20 cm) circumference, 2 from 9.5–10.5 in. (24–26 cm) circumference and 3 from 11–12 in. (28–30 cm) circumference bulbs. Up to 5 leaves with a lovely silky texture and 6.75–7.5 in. (17–19 cm) long are often present at the time of flowering (Plate 4-12).

'Starlet'

Breeder: Penning Breeding B.V. (The Netherlands); Plant Breeders' Rights: 2002; Classification: Small-flowering.

Description: Usually 4 pink and white blooms 4.25–4.5 in. (11–12 cm) diameter per scape 16–20 in. (40–50 cm) tall with exquisite veining. As the flowers mature on purple-green scapes, so the tepal tips reflex allowing the beautiful lime green throat to be clearly seen and the delightful shades of pink interwoven so skillfully, to be fully admired. Usually 1 scape from 5.5–6.5 in. (14–16 cm) circumference, 2 from 8–8.5 in. (20–22 cm) circumference and 3 from 9.5–10.5 in. (24–26 cm) circumference bulbs (Plate 4-13).

Other Bicolored, Smaller Hybrids

'Ambiance'

Breeder: Fa. G. van Staalduinen (The Netherlands); Plant Breeders' Rights: 1995; Classification: Leopoldii (Midi).

Description: Usually 4–6 cream and carmine red, long-lasting blooms 6–6.5 in. (15–16 cm) diameter per scape 20–24 in. (50–60 cm) tall. This tall, robust hybrid with luxuriant broad leaves bears similarities to many large singles but its slightly smaller, elegant, star-shaped blooms are most appealing. It is a wonderful cut flower and pot plant, particularly when several mature leaves are present at the time of flowering. Usually 3 scapes from 12–13 in. (30–33 cm) circumference bulbs (Plate 4-14).

'Jaguar'

Breeder: Fa. G. van Staalduinen (The Netherlands); Plant Breeders' Rights Expired: 2002; Classification: Small-flowering (Midi).

Description: Usually 4–8 ox-blood red, orange, lime green and cream blooms 4.5–6.5 in. (12–16 cm) diameter per scape 18–24 in. (45–60 cm) tall and 3 scapes from 12–13 in. (30–33 cm) circumference bulbs. The Brazilian *Hippeastrum papilio* is believed to be involved in the parentage of this dramatic, almost catlike hybrid with its exotic shape and markings. 'Jaguar' has always proved very popular with British gardeners at my shows and out of all the smaller flowering hybrids, it remains my favorite. Usually 7–9 weeks from planting to flowering (Plate 4-15).

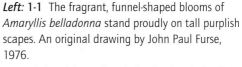

Left: 1-1 The fragrant, funnel-shaped blooms of *Amaryllis belladonna* stand proudly on tall purplish scapes. An original drawing by John Paul Furse, 1976.

By permission of the Royal Horticultural Society Lindley Library.

Above: 1-2 The regal trumpet-shaped blooms of *Hippeastrum* equestre emerge from the erect spathe leaves which some writers have likened to horses' ears. Plate 305 in Curtis's Botanical Magazine 9.

By permission of Royal Botanic Gardens, Kew Library.

Left: 1-3 *Hippeastrum reginae* was one of the parents of the first known recorded hybrid, *H.* 'Johnsonii' (1799). Artist: Priscilla Bury for *Hexandrian Plants*, 1831–1834.

By permission of the Royal Horticultural Society Lindley Library.

Left: **1-4** The unusual shaped blooms and winter-flowering habit of *Hippeastrum aulicum* appealed to Isamu Miyake of Miyake Nursery (Japan) who used it to create delightful autumn-flowering pastels. Artist: M. Hart for *Botanical Register* 6 (1820).

By permission of the Royal Horticultural Society Lindley Library.

Below: **1-5** The twisted, bright green tepals and pink-tipped stigma distinguish *Hippeastrum calyptratum* from all other species. It is being used to create pale green, large-flowering Japanese hybrids. Artist: Sydenham Edwards for *Botanical Register* 2 (1817).

By permission of the Royal Horticultural Society Lindley Library.

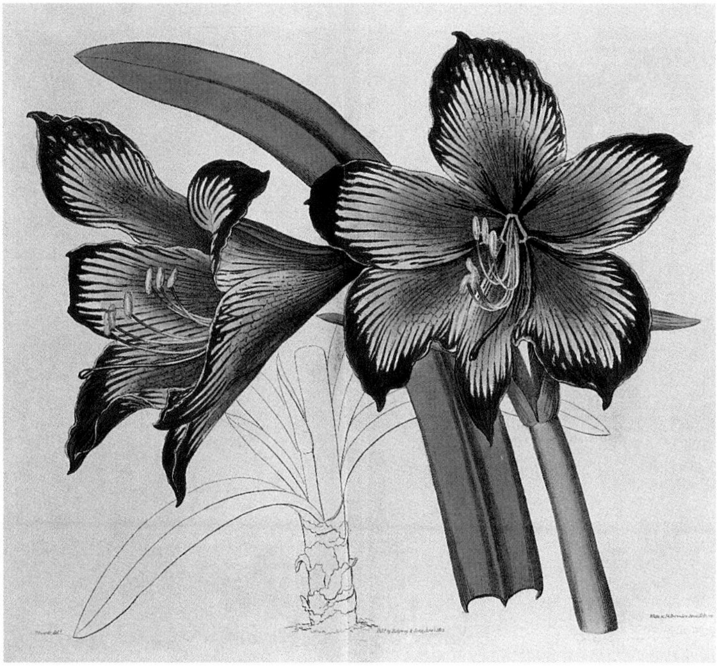

Left: **1-6** The carmine striations of *Hippeastrum psittacinum* look stunning on a lime green background. Artist: Sydenham Edwards for *Botanical Register* 3 (1817).
By permission of the Royal Horticultural Society Lindley Library.

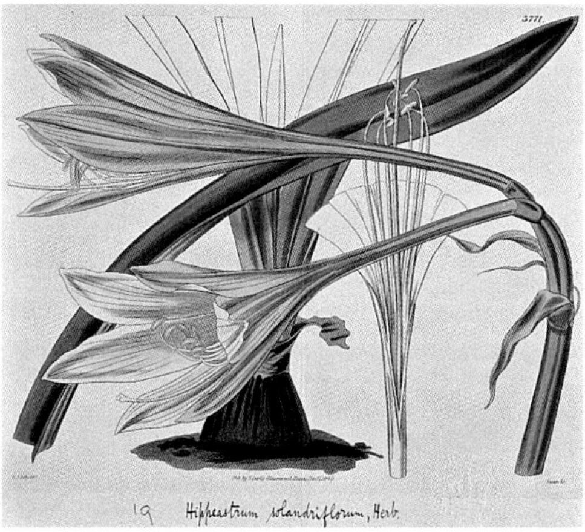

Above: **1-7** The elegant, trumpet-shaped, fragrant, sulfur blooms of *Hippeastrum solandriflorum* make this species particularly attractive to some 21st-century American breeders. Plate 3771 in Curtis's *Botanical Magazine* 6.
By permission of Royal Botanic Gardens, Kew Library.

Below: **1-8** *Hippeastrum vittatum* was the other parent of *H.* 'Johnsonii' created by Mr Johnson of Prescot, Lancashire (Great Britain). Artist: Priscilla Bury for *Hexandrian Plants*, 1831–1834.
By permission of the Royal Horticultural Society Lindley Library.

Above: 1-9 *Hippeastrum* seeds are surrounded by a dark papery band which aids wind dispersal.
Photo by Ian Woolley.

Above: 1-10 The large, fleshy, bulbous seeds of *Amaryllis belladonna* are slow to ripen and germinate.
Photo by S&O Mathews Photography.

Left: 1-12 Also known as the blue amaryllis or empress of Brazil, *Worsleya rayneri* has exotic, funnel-shaped blooms that are more mauve than blue. Artist: Walter Fitch for *Botanical Magazine* 97 (1871).
By permission of the Royal Horticultural Society Lindley Library.

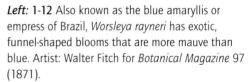

Above: 1-11 The influence of *Nerine bowdenii* is apparent in the delicate cerise pink blooms of × *Amarine tubergenii* (*Amaryllis belladonna* × *N. bowdenii*).
Photo by Chris Ireland-Jones.

Above: 2-1 The robust habit and broad, flat-faced blooms of *Hippeastrum leopoldii* played a major role in the creation of Leopoldii hybrids which have dominated large singles' breeding for almost 150 years. Artist: Worthington Smith for the *Floral Magazine* 9 (1870).

By permission of the Royal Horticultural Society Lindley Library.

Above: 2-2 The exquisite straw-colored, flat, open-faced blooms of *Hippeastrum pardinum* are sprinkled with dots of vermilion. Plate 5645 in Curtis's *Botanical Magazine* 93.

By permission of Royal Botanic Gardens, Kew Library.

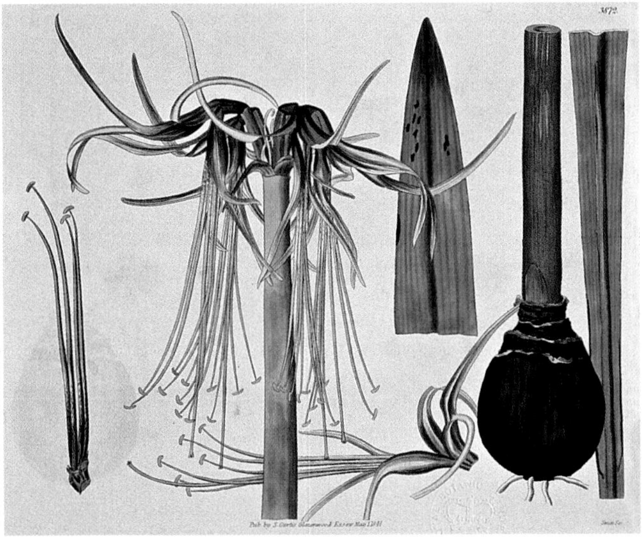

Left: 2-3 Also known as the tumbler sprekelia, the flowers of *Hippeastrum cybister* are dominated by the excessively long filaments and style. Plate 3872 in Curtis's *Botanical Magazine* 67.

By permission of Royal Botanic Gardens, Kew Library.

Above: 2-4 *Hippeastrum papilio* derives its name from the shape of the lower pair of tepals which resembles butterfly wings. Its robust habit makes it a spectacular outdoor bedding and patio plant in frost-free locations.
Photo by John Bryan.

Above: 2-6 *Hippeastrum reticulatum* is also known as the netted-veined amaryllis because of the exquisite reticulations on the trumpet-shaped blooms. Plate 657 in Curtis's *Botanical Magazine* 18.
By permission of Royal Botanic Gardens, Kew Library.

Left: 2-5 Also known as 'long-styled knight's-star lily', the elegant, pointed, salmon and yellow blooms of *Hippeastrum stylosum* are exquisitely veined. Plate 2278 in Curtis's *Botanical Magazine* 49.
By permission of Royal Botanic Gardens, Kew Library.

Etab. Lith. de L. Stroobant, à Gand
A. Verschaffelt, publ.
AMARYLLIS (HIPPEASTRUM ?) ALBERTI. (Laurentius.)
Cuba (Serre-chaude.)

2-7 This bright red, fully double form of *Hippeastrum equestre* was discovered by Albert Wagner in Havana (Cuba) around 1866 and became known as *H. equestre* forma *albertii*. It was used to create some of the earliest American doubles in the 1930s. Plate 498 in *L'Illustration Horticole* 14 (1867).

By permission of Royal Botanic Gardens, Kew Library.

Above: 3-1 *Hippeastrum* 'Johnsonii' is generally regarded as the first recorded hybrid, bred by Mr Johnson of Prescot, Lancashire (Great Britain). Artist: Barbara Cotton for the *Transactions of the Horticultural Society of London* 5 (1824).
By permission of the Royal Horticultural Society Lindley Library.

Above: 3-3 The blackcurrant, velvety flowers of *Hippeastrum* 'Royal Velvet' appear almost black and most mysterious when placed next to a snow white or pale yellow.
Photo by Ian Woolley.

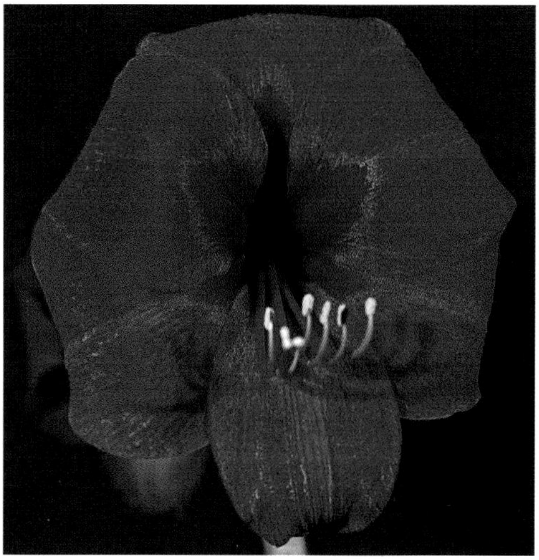

Left: 3-2 The tepals of *Hippeastrum* 'Scarlet Globe' are swept back, creating delightful rounded blooms which have a glorious sheen towards the throat.
Photo by Ian Woolley.

Right: **3-4** *Hippeastrum* 'Amigo' was the first pink to emerge from Penning Breeding B.V. The long-lasting, carmine-rose flowers have a faint greenish star towards the throat.
Photo by Ian Woolley.

Above: **3-6** Hundreds of *Hippeastrum* 'Tangellino' plants in flower on Maguire's Hippeastrum Farm in October are a glorious sight.
Photo by Richard Maguire.

Right: **3-5** Stunning, pink-red veins on a cerise background make *Hippeastrum* 'Candy Floss' appear almost catlike.
Photo by Ian Woolley.

Above: **3-7** The delightful, flat-faced salmon flowers of *Hippeastrum* 'Beautiful Lady' are enhanced by the exquisite venation, making this hybrid one of Ludwig's finest creations.
Photo by Ian Woolley.

Above: **3-8** The tips of the long-lasting flowers of *Hippeastrum* 'Nagano' reflex, allowing the bright green throat to be fully appreciated.
Photo by Ian Woolley.

Right: **3-9** Snow white *Hippeastrum* 'Christmas Gift' has an intense green throat and makes a wonderful Easter pot plant and cut flower.
Photo by Ian Woolley.

Above: **3-10** The red and white star-shaped flowers of *Hippeastrum* 'Barbara's Magic' are enhanced by the fine red picotee and look almost wistful in the bright Australian sunlight.
Photo by Richard Maguire.

Above: **3-11** Tepaloids are present on the upper pair of tepals of the velvety, red and white, flat-faced, award-winning *Hippeastrum* 'Design' from Penning Breeding B.V.
Photo by Ian Woolley.

Above: **3-12** The brilliant red and snow white flowers of *Hippeastrum* 'Pizzazz' are enhanced by the frilly edged tepals. Plenty of upright leaves are usually present at the time of flowering.
Photo by Ian Woolley.

Above: **3-13** The yellowish green throat enhances the dramatic, cerise pink and white blooms of *Hippeastrum* 'Queen of the Nile'.
Photo by Richard Maguire.

Left: 4-1 Snow white, frilly edged *Hippeastrum* 'Bianca' is one of my favorite Gracilis hybrids; its beauty is enhanced by the lovely lime green throat.
Photo by Ian Woolley.

Right: 4-2 A medium-flowering red from Miyake Nursery, Chiba-kon (Japan), raised for cut flower production. Some anthers are yet to split and the white-tipped stigma is yet to ripen.
Photo by Isamu Miyake.

Above: 4-3 Medium-flowering, floriferous, scarlet and white, cut flower from Miyake Nursery, Chiba-kon (Japan).
Photo by Isamu Miyake.

Left: 4-4 The tepal tips of *Hippeastrum* 'Amico' are swept back revealing the lime green throat and attractive cream stripes.
Photo by Ian Woolley.

Left: 4-5 The long-lasting, velvety flowers; short scapes and mature, upright foliage of *Hippeastrum* 'Floris Hekker' made this a popular pot plant in the late 1990s. Although the pollen has been released, the stigma is yet to ripen.
Photo by Ian Woolley.

Above: 4-7 One of the easiest to flower, *Hippeastrum* 'Salmon Pearl' regularly produces scapes three times a year from tiny bulbs.
Photo by Ian Woolley.

Left: 4-6 The orange and white, star-shaped pointed flowers of *Hippeastrum* 'Moviestar' are enhanced by the bright green throat. The spathe leaves of the second scape are beginning to split, revealing florets devoid of their final shape and color.
Photo by Ian Woolley.

Left: **4-8** The chocolate scapes of *Hippeastrum* 'White Equester III' make the long-lasting, snow white, frilly edged blooms appear even whiter.
Photo by Ian Woolley.

Above: **4-9** The stunning red and white speckled flowers and pencil-thin, red picotee of award-winning *Hippeastrum* 'Charisma' make this a very special hybrid from Penning Breeding B.V.
Photo by Ian Woolley.

Above: **4-11** The vivid red and white flowers of *Hippeastrum* 'Voodoo' are enhanced by the feathery venation and yellow-green throat.
Photo by Ian Woolley.

Above left: **4-10** The lowermost tepal of *Hippeastrum* 'Fairytale' is dusted with pollen. The stigma is ripe and ready to receive the pollen grains.
Photo by Ian Woolley.

Left: **4-12** Three scapes of *Hippeastrum* 'Pink Star' develop simultaneously, creating delicious clouds of delicate, pink and white, star-shaped flowers.
Photo by Ian Woolley.

Above: 4-13 Delightful feathery pink and white veins of *Hippeastrum* 'Starlet' lead to the magical, lime green throat, making the flowers appear even more exquisite.
Photo by Ian Woolley.

Above: 4-14 The star-shaped, creamy white flowers of *Hippeastrum* 'Ambiance' with their carmine-red streaks are very special and the tall, robust scapes make the plant an ideal cut flower.
Photo by Ian Woolley.

Above: 4-15 The influence of the Brazilian species *Hippeastrum papilio* can be clearly seen in the exotic, catlike ox-blood red, vivid orange, cream and lime green flowers of *H.* 'Jaguar'.
Photo by Ian Woolley.

Above: **5-2** Long-lasting, frilly edged, creamy yellow trumpets of *Hippeastrum* 'Germa' are enhanced by the lovely, green throat.
Photo by Ian Woolley.

Above: **5-1** Silver-frosted, frilly edged, light-sensitive flowers of *Hippeastrum* 'Green Star' (*H.* 'Yellow Pioneer' × *H. papilio*) flare widely during the brightest part of the day.
Photo by Ian Woolley.

Right: **5-3** The influence of *Hippeastrum* 'Germa' is revealed in the flowers of *H.* 'Yellow Moon', which, unlike the flowers of *H.* 'Germa', become more cream with age.
Photo by Ian Woolley.

Above: **5-4** This dainty Sonatini was one of several yellows on display at Barnhoorn's Open Day in March 2002. It is being considered for cut flower production.
Photo by Ian Woolley.

Left: **5-5** Hornlike projections on the inner and outer tepal surfaces of *Hippeastrum* 'Yellow Goddess' are a prominent feature of this delightful creamy yellow, free-flowing hybrid.
Photo by Ian Woolley.

Above: 6-1 Exquisite, pink and white trumpets of *Hippeastrum* 'Pink Floyd' on tall, slender scapes look magical in the spring sunlight.
Photo by Ian Woolley.

Above: 6-2 The bold venation enhances the beauty of this dainty, bright orange, small-flowering Brazilian hybrid still further.
Photo by Ian Woolley.

Left: 6-3 Dramatic flowers of *Hippeastrum* 'Gilmar' were greatly admired when this Brazilian hybrid was shown in Great Britain for the first time in December 2001.
Photo by Ian Woolley.

Above left: 6-4 Scapes of this elegant, red and white Japanese hybrid emerge from small bulbs which are barely bigger than golf balls!
Photo by Isamu Miyake.

Above: 6-5 Dainty pink and white flowers on striped scapes with variegated foliage add a new dimension to *Hippeastrum* breeding, particularly when cultivated in a wine glass or coffee cup.
Photo by Isamu Miyake.

Left: 6-6 Stunning, red and white blooms of this Japanese Super Mini emerge from tiny 4 in. (10 cm) circumference bulbs, accompanied by broad, rounded foliage, make this hybrid an ideal pot plant for the home and office.
Photo by Isamu Miyake.

Above left: **6-7** The influence of the winter-flowering *Hippeastrum aulicum* is evident in these exotic, upward-facing, autumn-flowering, Japanese hybrids.
Photo by Isamu Miyake.

Below left: **6-8** A selection of Osselton's wispy Star of the Knight and Queen of the Knight hybrids flowering in April 2000.
Photo by Cathy Osselton.

Above right: **6-9** A dainty and delightful, pink and white Star of the Knight hippeastrum from the Osselton nursery.
Photo by Cathy Osselton.

Centre right: **6-10** Wispy, bright red and green flowers make this a splendid addition to the Star of the Knight group.
Photo by Cathy Osselton.

Below right: **6-11** An enchanting pale green Star of the Knight hybrid from the Osselton nursery.
Photo by Cathy Osselton.

Above: 6-14 Delicious clouds of delightful, pixielike orange blooms of *Hippeastrum* 'Supreme Garden' surrounded by luxuriant, silky leaves caused great excitement when launched at my hippeastrum workshop at the Serpentine Gallery (London) on 16 February 2003.
Photo by Ian Woolley.

Above right: 6-12 This stunning Star of the Knight double red hybrid involves a Cybister type in its parentage and is an exciting development in Dutch hippeastrum breeding.
Photo by Cathy Osselton.

Centre right: 6-13 Bright red and white, rounded flowers of this Queen of the Knight hybrid are made even lovelier by the lovely, lime green throat.
Photo by Cathy Osselton.

Right: 6-15 One of Barnhoorn's finest cut flower Sonatini hybrids on display in March 2002. The tiny orange and yellow flowers radiated from tall, slender scapes and remained fresh for 14 days.
Photo by Ian Woolley.

6-16 Wine-red and pale green flowers of *Hippeastrum* 'Reggae' are dominated by the long, creamy white filaments and style. When all flowers are open simultaneously, the effect reminds me of a stork's nest!
Photo by Ian Woolley.

Above: **6-18** Bright green stripes on a cerise pink background make *Hippeastrum* 'Flamengo' a very special Cybister. Prodigious quantities of pollen are released, but the downward sloping stigma is yet to ripen.
Photo by Ian Woolley.

Left: **6-17** Delicate, frilly edged *Hippeastrum* 'Tango' looks even more exquisite when silhouetted against the spring sunlight.
Photo by Ian Woolley.

Right: **6-19** Vibrant orange-brown wispy flowers of *Hippeastrum* 'Merengue' look marvelous on tall, robust scapes in the spring sunshine. Prodigious quantities of nectar ooze along the long filaments.
Photo by Ian Woolley.

Right: 6-20 Snow-white, frilly edged trumpets of *Hippeastrum* 'Amputo' radiate from tall scapes, making this plant a wonderful cut flower.
Photo by Ian Woolley.

Below: 6-21 Myriad red speckles adorn the slender, frilly edged, pale green *Hippeastrum* 'Emerald', which has a delicate red picotee.
Photo by Ian Woolley.

Above left: **6-22** Long filaments of *Hippeastrum* 'Chico' dominate this American Cybister with its reddish brown and pale green, wispy flowers and chestnut scapes.
Photo by Ian Woolley.

Left: **6-23** The delicate, wispy, burgundy-red and pale green *Hippeastrum* 'Lima' was Meyer's first Cybister to become available in the United Kingdom.
Photo by Ian Woolley.

Left: **6-25** The exquisitely curved, red and yellow wispy flowers of *Hippeastrum* 'Ruby Meyer' bear resemblance to *Sprekelia formosissima*, another member of the Amaryllidaceae.
Photo by Ian Woolley.

Opposite: **6-24** Exquisite venation, coupled with a bright green throat make *Hippeastrum* 'Grandeur' a truly wonderful addition to the Meyer portfolio.
Photo by Ian Woolley.

Above right: **6-26** The exquisite flowers of *Hippeastrum* 'Cyber Queen' become more cream and pink with age. This hybrid was the first Cybister to emerge from Penning Breeding B.V. in 2002.
Photo by Ian Woolley.

Above: 7-1 The delightful, peony-shaped pink and white flowers of *Hippeastrum* 'Boysenberry Swirl' are sometimes more semi than true double.
Photo by Richard Maguire.

Right: 7-2 This compact bright red and white Japanese double lacks the petaloid stamens and tepal fragments which can make some doubles appear rather messy.
Photo by Isamu Miyake.

7-3 The two-toned, pink and white, star-shaped flowers of this delicate Japanese double appear on different scapes simultaneously and make a splendid show.
Photo by Isamu Miyake.

Above: 7-4 *Hippeastrum* 'Fanfare' was one of Hadeco's first Sonata doubles to become available in Europe in the late 1990s. The small, bright orange-red wispy semi or fully double flowers proved popular with many British gardeners when shown in Great Britain in 2001.
Photo by Ian Woolley.

Left: 7-5 Robust, reliable and stunning *Hippeastrum* 'Red Peacock' usually lacks reproductive organs but sometimes the remnants of filaments are detected as white streaks along the length of the tepal and at the tepal tips.
Photo by Ian Woolley.

7-6 Long-lasting flowers of *Hippeastrum* 'Salmon Peacock' are often more semi than true double and are enhanced by a background of mature, luxuriant, upright foliage.
Photo by Ian Woolley.

Above: 7-7 Considered by Hadeco as a triple because of its multiple layers of tepals, *Hippeastrum* 'Alfresco' often produces 6–8 flowers per scape from small bulbs. It proved very popular with visitors to my display of South African hybrids at the RHS London Show in November 1999.
Photo by Ian Woolley.

Below: 7-8 A slight fragrance has been detected from the semi-double, creamy, waxen, trumpet flowers of *Hippeastrum* 'Jewel'. Petaloid stamens and other fragmentary pieces form a corona in the center of the flower.
Photo by Ian Woolley.

Above: 7-9 Exquisitely sculptured *Hippeastrum* 'Flaming Peacock' flowers are enhanced by mature upright foliage at the time of flowering and look magical when silhouetted against the sunlight.
Photo by Ian Woolley.

7-10 In the second season, *Hippeastrum* 'Flaming Peacock' flowers were snow white with only a hint of red.
Photo by Ian Woolley.

7-11 Magnificent white, frilly edged tepals of *Hippeastrum* 'Aphrodite' are flushed and edged with pink and enhanced by the lime green throat. The long pedicels and weighty blooms often result in the flowers drooping.
Photo by Ian Woolley.

Left: 7-12 Robust scapes and peony-shaped, cream and pink flowers of *Hippeastrum* 'Nymph' look splendid in large formal, cut flower displays.
Photo by Ian Woolley.

Above: 7-13 Dramatic, orange and white, frilly edged flowers of *Hippeastrum* 'Dancing Queen' tend to droop when mature. Spathe leaves and bracts have become straw-colored and hang limply.
Photo by Ian Woolley.

Right: 7-14 Burgundy-red and white, South African *Hippeastrum* 'Joker' is particularly fast-growing; sometimes flowering only 14–16 days after planting in September in Great Britain.
Photo by Ian Woolley.

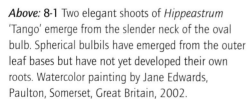

Above: 8-2 Fat purplish scapes of *Hippeastrum* 'Reggae' emerge from the flat, almost spherical bulb which has attractive brown and pink outer leaf bases. Watercolor painting by Jane Edwards, Paulton, Somerset, Great Britain, 2002.

Above: 8-1 Two elegant shoots of *Hippeastrum* 'Tango' emerge from the slender neck of the oval bulb. Spherical bulbils have emerged from the outer leaf bases but have not yet developed their own roots. Watercolor painting by Jane Edwards, Paulton, Somerset, Great Britain, 2002.

Right: 8-3 Inflorescences of *Hippeastrum* 'Amazone' emerge simultaneously from the broad neck of the irregularly shaped bulb with chestnut brown, crispy outer leaf bases.
Photo by Ian Woolley.

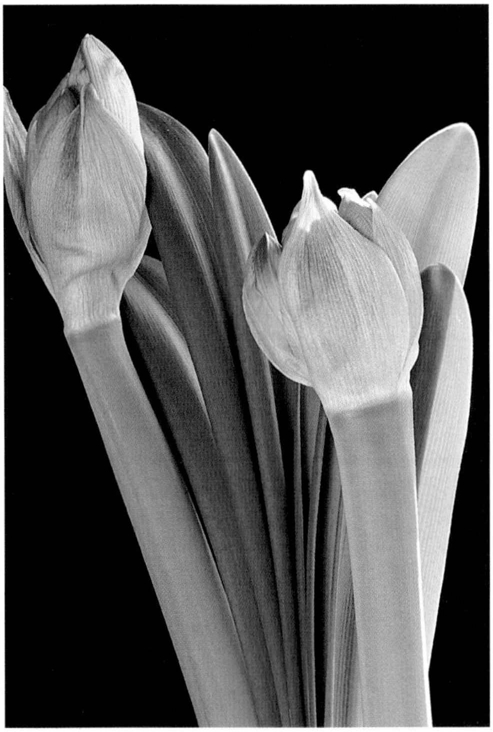

Above: 8-4 Florets of *Hippeastrum* 'Promise' emerge from short, stubby spathe leaves which are already fading and becoming wrinkled.
Photo by Ian Woolley.

Above right: 8-5 Velvety buds of *Hippeastrum* 'Red Lion' emerge from the spathe leaves and within 36 hours have moved into the horizontal position and begin to open. A thin green bract remains upright and the spathe leaves begin to lose their color and wither.
Photo by Ian Woolley.

Right: 8-6 Flowers of *Hippeastrum* 'Chico' have faded and are no longer recognizable. They resemble tissuelike fragments. One flower self-pollinated and a cylindrical dark green capsule has begun to develop.
Photo by Ian Woolley.

Left: **8-9** *Hippeastrum* 'Jewel' is slowly dividing, resulting in two bulbs, each producing scapes and leaves but sharing a basal plate.
Photo by Ian Woolley.

Opposite, above left: **8-7** Within 2–3 days of fertilization, the pedicels rapidly expand in length and width. The tripartite, glossy green capsule expands to accommodate the rapidly developing seeds.
Photo by Ian Woolley.

Opposite, below left: **8-8** Capsules at different stages in their development. One capsule has already split, revealing numerous flat, black seeds neatly stacked in each locule. Most seeds have dispersed within 72 hours, assisted by air currents. Another capsule has lost its former sheen and begins to shrink. A few days later it will become straw-colored and split.
Photo by Ian Woolley.

Above: 9-1 *Hippeastrum* make a wonderful outdoor bedding plant in frost free locations.
Photo by John Bryan.

Right: 9-2 Roots are hydrated for 24 hours before planting by sitting the bulb on top of a jar containing tepid tap water. New branching roots are developing lateral to the basal roots.
Photo by Ian Woolley.

Above: 9-3 Ten offsets clustered around the base of a newly purchased bulb of *Hippeastrum* 'Pink Floyd' have recently emerged from the outer leaf bases. Dead roots can be removed easily, either before or after hydrating the few live, basal roots.
Photo by Ian Woolley.

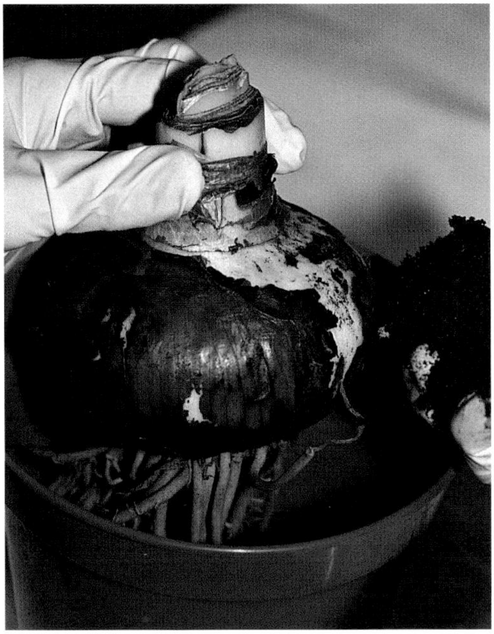

Above: 9-4 After putting mix into the pot, the rooted bulb is lowered gently into the pot until its shoulders are level with the rim of the pot. More mix is added, until two-thirds of the bulb is covered.
Photo by Ian Woolley.

Above right: 9-5 Some newly purchased bulbs may have no roots at the time of planting. In such cases, a mound is formed and the rootless bulb placed on top so that its shoulders are level with the rim of the pot. More mix is added until two-thirds of the bulb is covered.
Photo by Ian Woolley.

Right: 9-6 After planting and adding the label, the bulb is watered with tepid tap water and then placed in a warm light place, a sunny window sill or a shelf above a warm radiator being ideal.
Photo by Ian Woolley.

Above: 11-1 Select a large healthy bulb for chipping or twin scaling.
Photo by Ian Woolley.

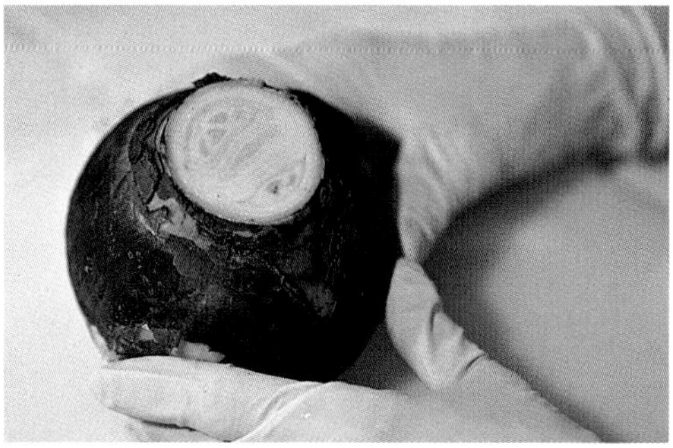

Above: 11-2 The neck is removed, revealing the bulb's sympodial structure. Two inflorescences towards the rim of the bulb are about to emerge. Sap glistens on the cut surface and the bulb becomes sticky and slippery.
Photo by Ian Woolley.

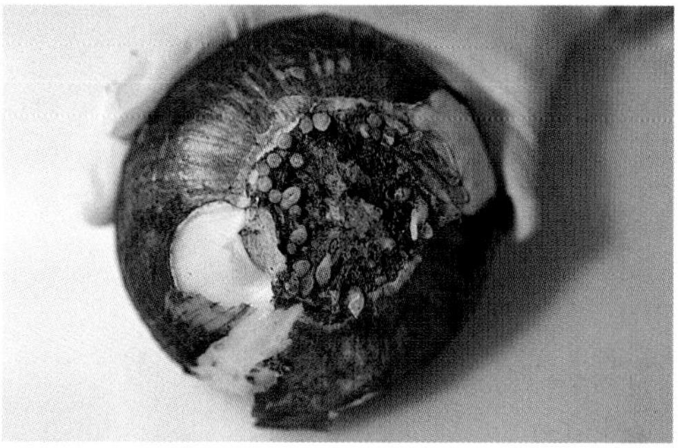

Above: 11-3 The roots are removed with a sharp knife, taking care not to cut or damage the basal plate.
Photo by Ian Woolley.

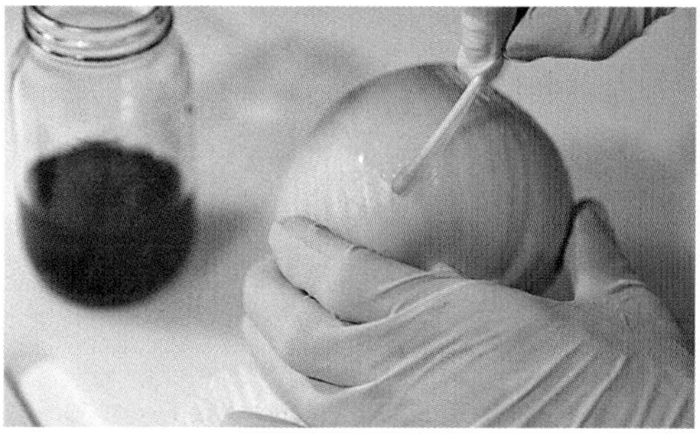

Above: 11-4 The surface of the bulb is swabbed with surgical spirit, including the cut neck, prior to chipping or twin scaling.
Photo by Ian Woolley.

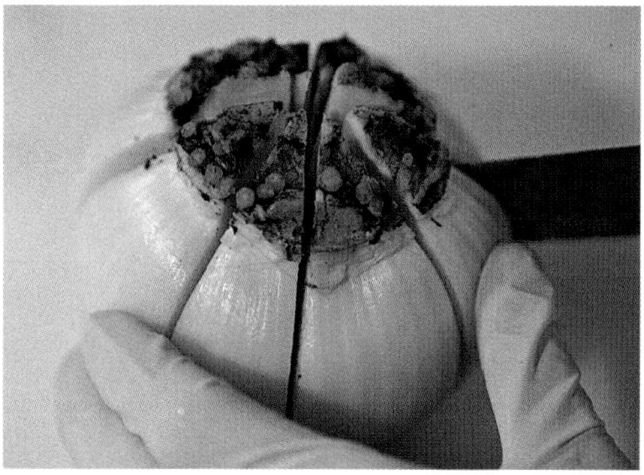

Above: 11-5 A series of vertical cuts are made through the bulb resulting in 8 segments or chips.
Photo by Ian Woolley.

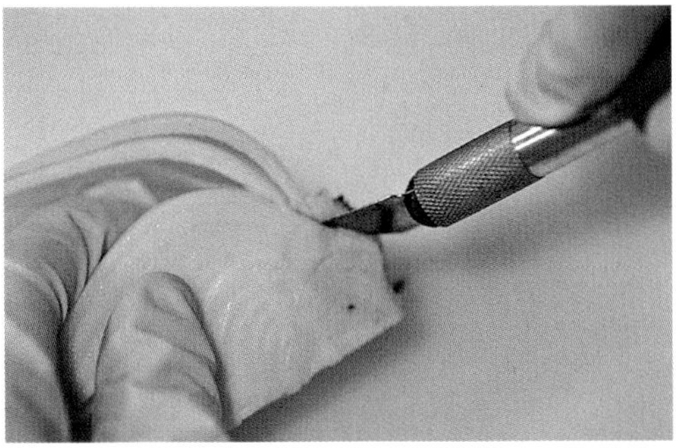

Above: **11-6** Starting from the outside, two adjacent fleshy scales are identified and a vertical cut made through the basal plate, ensuring each twin scale has a piece of basal plate attached.
Photo by Ian Woolley.

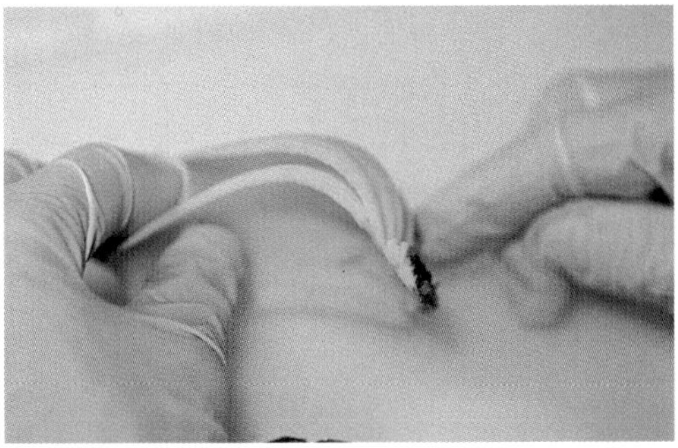

Above: **11-7** The twin scale is now ready for dipping in systemic fungicide.
Photo by Ian Woolley.

Above: **11-8** Immerse chips or twin scales for 30 minutes in a systemic fungicide or dust with green or yellow sulfur to reduce the risk of fungal attack.
Photo by Ian Woolley.

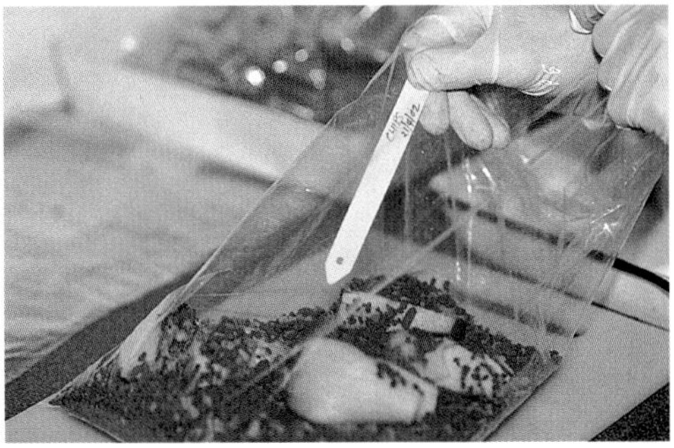

Above: **11-9** Place a prepared label into the bag containing dampened Seramis or moist vermiculite and the chips or twin scales.
Photo by Ian Woolley.

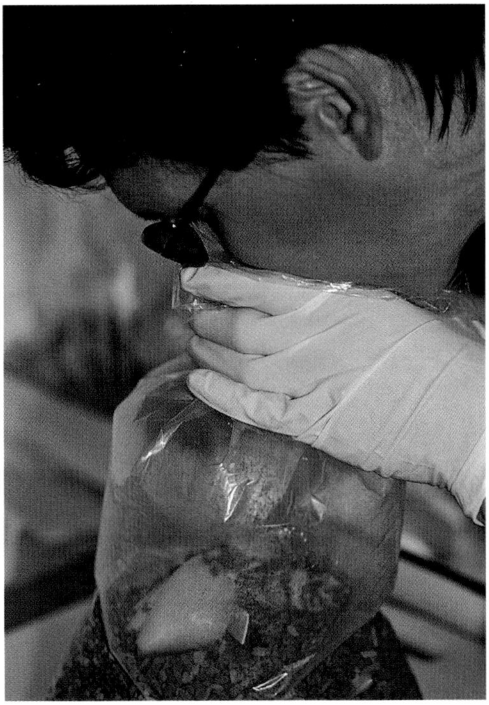

Above: **11-10** Inflate the bag and secure with a tie.
Photo by Ian Woolley.

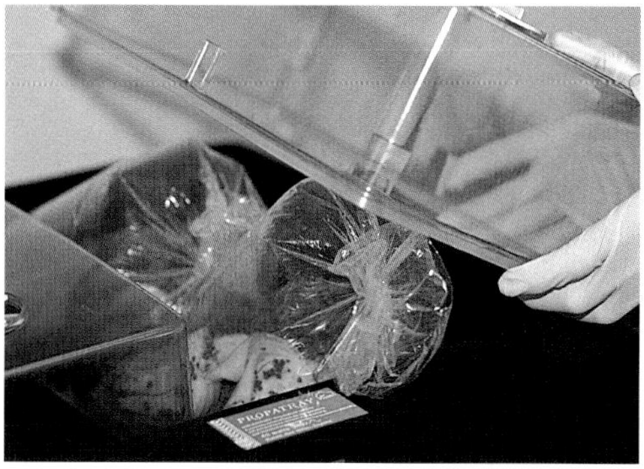

Left: **11-11** Place the inflated bag in the heated propagator and cover with a dark cloth to make sure no light penetrates.
Photo by Ian Woolley.

Left: **11-12** A 12-week-old bulbil from chipping has already developed its first leaves and is ready to be potted up. Basal roots are already beginning to develop.
Photo by Ian Woolley.

Right: **11-13** Seven months after chipping, 4–5 leaves and a robust network of basal and branching roots have developed. The small plant was repotted into a larger, deeper pot, giving greater room for root development and providing stability for the developing leaves.
Photo by Ian Woolley.

Chapter 5

Yellow Hippeastrums

Attempts to create a large, deep yellow hippeastrum have occupied breeders' attentions for more than 50 years. By 2003 only 7 pale yellow hybrids—*Hippeastrum* 'Germa', *H.* 'Lemon Lime', *H.* 'Limone', *H.* 'Moonlight', *H.* 'Yellow Goddess', *H.* 'Yellow Moon', *H.* 'Yellow Pioneer'—had entered commercial production. They varied in their degree of yellow; some were more green or cream than yellow and most faded with age. Pink or red flushes or speckles often became apparent as the flowers matured. Hornlike projections were also apparent on some hybrids, and many displayed a range of cultural problems making them unattractive to most growers. With the exception of *H.* 'Yellow Goddess' and *H.* 'Lemon Lime', most remained exclusive and did not become widely available.

Hippeastrum aglaiae, *H. evansiae* and *H. parodii* formed the basis of the earliest yellows together with white Dutch clones, such as 'Christmas Gift', 'Maria Goretti', 'Nivalis' and 'White Christmas'. *Hippeastrum* anzaldoi, *H. fosteri*, *H. striatum* and *H. papilio* have also been used.

Most breeders have now recognized that the maximum degree of yellowness has been reached for hybrids involving *Hippeastrum aglaiae*, *H. anzaldoi*, *H. evansiae* and *H. parodii*. Thus they are focusing their efforts upon improving cultural characteristics and existing color, and breeding this into large- and small-flowering hybrids for pot plant and cut flower production. This chapter reviews the development of yellow hippeastrums and describes the achievements of leading breeders.

North American Yellows

Breeding yellows has interested several U.S. breeders since the late 1960s, but by the mid 1990s, only 2 hybrids had entered commercial production—

Hippeastrum 'Yellow Pioneer' and *H.* 'Germa'. Research by William D. Bell during the 1970s and 1980s revealed yellow or green pigments which were also present in green-flowered species and those having green or yellow throats. Radiation was used to improve the size, form and depth of yellow hybrids, resulting in chartreuse, primrose yellow, white, cream and pink blooms of various shapes and sizes, many of which displayed pink veins or became cream with age. Some had deep green or yellow-green throats. Three California breeders dominated mid to late 20th-century developments: Charles D. Cothran, John L. Doran and John Cage.

Throughout the 1970s, Charles D. Cothran used *Hippeastrum aglaiae*, *H. evansiae*, *H papilio*, *H. parodii* and *H. striatum* with large Dutch white singles to create yellows having 2–4 blooms per scape. The 5–7 in. (13–18 cm) diameter flowers varied in shape and degree of yellowness. Many became cream with age and exhibited red veins and flushes. In 1973, Cothran placed pollen of *H. papilio* onto *H. evansiae* and other species. Only the *H. evansiae* and *H. papilio* cross succeeded, resulting in 3–4 deep yellow, flat-faced 6 in. (15 cm) diameter blooms with traces of green, dark red veins and a thin red picotee showing the influence of *H. papilio* (Cothran 1979).

In the late 1970s, Cothran produced his 591 series which compared favorably to the earlier 339 and 340 series. Most had 3–4 large 7–8 in. (18–20 cm) diameter, open, flat-faced blooms per scape with overlapping tepals. Some were bright yellow but after 2–3 days, pale pink flushes became evident. They self-crossed and crossed readily with other hybrids producing many seeds.

While Cothran never considered *Hippeastrum* 'Yellow Pioneer' to be his final product, it marked a significant step forward in the evolution of the yellow hippeastrum and became a starting point for further improvements. It was crossed with (*H. evansiae* × *H. papilio*) resulting in a large 7 in. (18 cm) diameter yellow hybrid which lacked the red veins apparent on earlier crossings. Cothran considered this hybrid to be his deepest yellow. Although it was not as robust as *H.* 'Yellow Pioneer', it grew well. Like other American breeders who unsuccessfully sought commercial rewards during the 1980s, Cothran became disillusioned and by the mid 1980s abandoned all further breeding.

Hippeastrum 'Yellow Pioneer' has continued to be crossed with species and various hybrids to create novelties displaying varying degrees of yellowness. Since the early 1990s, Jerry Charpentier of Florida has used *H.* 'Yellow Pioneer' as the seed parent with *H. papilio* pollen, resulting in seedlings of various shades of yellow, red and green and many combining shades of red and green. A particularly fine seedling has been provisionally named *H.* 'Green Star' and entered commercial trials in 2002.

Unlike *Hippeastrum* 'Yellow Pioneer', which has a weak constitution, *H.* 'Green Star' (Plate 5-1) is robust. It also is tolerant of very high and low temperatures and has shown no signs of frost burn. In the United States, it is cultivated outside throughout the year where it is subjected to temperatures in the mid 90°F (34–36°C) during the summer with cool or cold periods and occasional freezing during the winter. Like *H. papilio*, 'Green Star' is evergreen and produces numerous offsets. It regularly puts forth 2–3 scapes each February when cultivated in the USA from largest size 10.5–10.75 in. (26–27 cm) circumference bulbs, each bearing up to 7, usually 4–6 predominantly pale-green blooms 6–7.5 in. (15–19 cm) diameter per scape with bright-green central stripes extending the length of each tepal. The pencil-thin red picotee, carmine streaks, exquisitely ruffled-edged tepals that flare widely by the end of the second day, and the silver frosting effect on the inner side of each tepal, are particularly endearing features. Tepal widths range from 1.5 in. (4.5 cm) of the uppermost tepal to 1 in. (2.5 cm) of the lowermost tepal. When cultivated indoors in Great Britain under 600-watt sodium lights, scapes tinged with reddish brown towards the base, remained short at 11.5 in. (29 cm) in their first year compared to a more usual length of 18.5–22 in. (46–55 cm) when cultivated in Florida. Smooth, silky leaves developed mainly after flowering had finished and eventually reached 26 in. (66 cm) long and 2 in. (5 cm) broad. Plants flowered from small 7 in. (18 cm) circumference bulbs after 26 days of the scape having emerged and individual flowers remained fresh for 4–6 days.

Although little or no yellow is evident in any of the flowers, this remarkable hybrid represents a most fascinating development, its flowers looking unlike any other hippeastrums currently available. *Hippeastrum* 'Green Star' proved a big attraction at my *Hippeastrum* Spring Show in March 2003. Visitors of all ages and backgrounds appreciated its outstanding beauty and often referred to the lovely ruffled edges and pointed tepal tips, the gorgeous sheen and subtle combination of green and carmine, its light and airy appearance and outstanding charm and sheer elegance. It would appear there would be no shortage of British enthusiasts keen to cultivate this hippeastrum were it to become commercially available.

Charpentier undertook further crossings in 1996 and 1999 involving *Hippeastrum* 'Green Star' pollen and *H.* 'Yellow Pioneer'. The result was smaller statured, pale yellow seedlings similar to *H.* 'Yellow Pioneer' and other solid colors, including mint green. *Hippeastrum* 'Windswept' and 'Pastel' showed particular promise and entered commercial trials in 2002. The latter has since been crossed with *H.* 'Green Star' and during the coming years, Charpentier aims to create further yellow and green hippeastrums, as well as a double yellow.

John L. Doran had always been interested in yellow hippeastrums. In the early 1970s he used *Hippeastrum parodii* with *H. aglaiae* and *H. evansiae* to create small, dainty yellows with 6–7 blooms per scape. Crossing *H. parodii* with (*H. evansiae* × (*H. aglaiae* × *H. evansiae*)) resulted in a creamy yellow, frilly edged trumpet—*H.* 'Germa'—which derived its name from "Ger" (Gerald, director of *Floralia*, a Dutch hippeastrum wholesaler) and "Ma" (Margaret, Gerald's wife). *Hippeastrum* 'Germa' was Doran's only yellow to enter commercial production in the early 1990s and remains the deepest yellow available today and my favorite of all the small flowered yellows (Plate 5–2).

Doran's only other registered yellow was *Hippeastrum* 'Mananita' (meaning "break of day") in 1981. Marcia Wilson of the American Amaryllis Society referred to it as being a small, vigorous, spring-flowering Trumpet with 4 yellow blooms 3.5 in. (9 cm) diameter per scape 13 in. (33 cm) tall which was created by crossing 4 unknown yellow species. *Hippeastrum* 'Mananita' has been crossed successfully with several species and hybrids. Unfortunately it has not been possible to obtain any further information about this hybrid.

John Cage, another American breeder, created only one large green-yellow hybrid. *Hippeastrum* 'Irish Summer' (1980) resulted from crossing a seedling of *H.* 'Lime A' with *H.* 'Oasis'. Its slightly fragrant 8–10 in. (20–25 cm) diameter blooms gradually became white as the flower matured. A cross of *H.* 'Irish Summer' and *H.* 'Yellow Pioneer' proved difficult to produce seed. After 40 years of breeding activities, Cage became disillusioned by the lack of commercial success and in the early 1980s abandoned breeding hippeastrums.

Dutch Yellows

Since the 1980s, Agriom B.V., T. Nieuwkerk Amaryllis B.V. and Penning Breeding B.V. have led Dutch developments. Each sought to improve the degree of yellowness and cultural characteristics. By 2003, four pale yellows had entered commercial production—*Hippeastrum* 'Lemon Lime', *H.* 'Limone', *H.* 'Moonlight' and *H.* 'Yellow Moon'. *Hippeastrum* 'Limone' and *H.* 'Moonlight' were the first large yellows since *H.* 'Yellow Pioneer'. Although the flowers were slightly larger than some earlier cultivars and demonstrated cultural improvements, the color was no darker than in existing hybrids.

South African Yellows

Since the mid 1980s, Andre Barnhoorn, formerly of Hadeco (Pty) Ltd (Maraisburg, South Africa) and now working in Noordwijkerhout (The Netherlands), has been using species to develop creamy yellow Sonatini hybrids for cut flower production. Their delicate rounded tepals and 4–6, long-lasting, trumpet-shaped blooms borne on tall, robust scapes make this a particularly exciting development. It is hoped that the best Sonatini hybrids will be available by 2010. Barnhoorn then plans to turn his attention to developing shorter scaped varieties for pot plant production. Barnhoorn's yellow Sonatini hybrids aroused considerable interest among British gardeners in March 2002 who were enthralled by their delicate, dainty, long-lasting blooms, each scape remaining fresh for 14 days (Plate 5-4). See Chapter 6 for further details of Barnhoorn's Sonatini hybrids.

Hadeco (Pty) Ltd continues to breed yellows which they hope to introduce by 2010.

Future for the Yellow Hippeastrum

Yellows remain an unknown quantity, but until significant improvements are made to bulb, root, scape and floral development and offset production, existing hybrids will continue to have commercial value. As gardeners become more aware of yellow hippeastrums and as superior cultivars become available, demand is likely to increase. However, when compared to the large single and other smaller, more floriferous and reliable hybrids, the yellow hippeastrum will remain unattractive to most commercial growers and therefore will remain elusive.

Descriptions

'Germa'

Breeder: John Leonard Doran; Registration: 1995; Classification: Long Trumpet.

Description: Usually 3–5 exquisite, creamy yellow trumpets 4–5 in. (10–13 cm) diameter radiate from tall, slender 18–24 in. (45–60 cm) tall, slightly rubbery, dull-green scapes. The delicate, frilly, pointed tepals have an ivory middle vein, and the plant's beauty is enhanced by the bright green throat. Bulbs reach a maximum 12–13 in. (30–33 cm) circumference with 1 scape from 8 in. (20 cm) circumference, 2 from 10.5–11 in. (26–28 cm) circumference and 3 from 11–12 in. (28–30 cm) circumference bulbs. Leaves typically reach a maximum 16–19 in. (40–48 cm) long and 1.25–1.5 in. (3–4 cm) wide when mature.

Unlike other hybrids which reach maturity after only 2 growing seasons, *Hippeastrum* 'Germa' is much slower and takes at least 3 seasons of 8 months each before the bulbs reach maturity. Newly purchased bulbs may take up to 16 weeks before flowering and in subsequent years, fresh shoots may not appear until spring. The irregularly shaped bulbs with a barely visible neck are prone to fungal attack beneath the persistent crispy brown, outer leaf bases which take up to 18 months before they finally disintegrate. The irregularly shaped, surprisingly tough leaves do not make the beautiful fan shapes created by many other hippeastrums. Instead the more bluntly tipped, matt, dull green, rubbery textured leaves which develop a bluish cast when cultivated under high light are displayed in an irregular fashion. However, unlike the leaves of some other small-flowering hippeastrums, they may remain fresh for up to 16 months, even tolerating the poor light during the cool period. Other problems include poor rooting, high offset production and premature splitting of the spathe leaves revealing tiny, immature, green florets which usually take 10 more days before acquiring their final shape and color.

Prior to repotting all my *Hippeastrum* 'Germa' bulbs in the Kew potting mix in late summer 2002, I had little success in maintaining bulbs from one season to the next. Plants rotted easily after flowering and developed few or no roots. But, the improved aeration and drainage properties of the Kew mix combined with a slow-release fertilizer with trace elements applied at the time of planting, and thereafter fortnightly feeding at half strength with a well-balanced feed containing trace elements; improved watering technique; bottom heat and light from 600-watt sodium lights for 14–16 hours per day throughout the year apart from during the cool period resulted in all plants developing a robust and extensive root system during winter 2002 and spring 2003.

Three weeks after the cool period had ended in February 2003, 3–4 new leaves emerged followed by further new growth in June and July. After 8 weeks of high temperatures that reached 37°F (100°C) in South Harrow in August 2003, a third crop of 3–4 leaves emerged, and by mid September, all my plants had developed 9–11 tough, matt leaves which reached 17.5–18.75 in. (44–47 cm) tall and up to 1.5 in. (4 cm) wide. I had never witnessed such excellent growth before on *Hippeastrum* 'Germa' plants. The bulbs resembled miniature cricket bulbs and by late August 2003, root tips were poking through the drainage holes of 7 in. (18 cm) pots. Several plants produced 2–3 offsets which developed their first leaves throughout summer and autumn 2003.

It always amazes me how such tall scapes can emerge from almost inconspicuous necks of tiny 8 in. (20 cm) circumference bulbs. In April and May of 2003, my plants produced 2 scapes in succession, each bearing 4 gorgeous, creamy yellow, long-lasting trumpets. Contrary to comments made by some Dutch breeders and growers, my experience has shown that *Hippeastrum* 'Germa' is no more difficult to cultivate than other small-flowering hippeastrum.

Some North American and Dutch breeders continue to use *Hippeastrum* 'Germa' to breed deeper, brighter yellows since it remains the deepest yellow hybrid available today. However, its disadvantages make it undesirable for most bulb growers, and thus its long-term future is uncertain.

'Lemon Lime'

Breeder: Agriom B.V.; Plant Breeders Rights: 1993; Classification: Reginae (4b).

Description: Usually 3–4, pale yellow-green, frilly edged blooms 4.25–4.5 in. (11–12 cm) diameter per scape 18–24 in. (45–60 cm) tall with a lime green throat lined with a ring of dark red dots. Hornlike projections are often present on the back of the tepals and numerous tiny pink-brown dots appear on the inner side of the tepals following exposure to the sun. 'Lemon Lime' usually flowers 4–6 weeks after planting and produces

2–3 scapes from 12–13 in. (30–33 cm) circumference bulbs. The tall scapes, which have attractive red-brown shades towards the base, make this hybrid a suitable cut flower. Individual flowers remain fresh for 7–8 days. Clumps of leaves 18–22 in. (45–55 cm) tall and 2–2.5 in. (5–6 cm) wide appear after flowering. A particular disadvantage of 'Lemon Lime' is the high offset production which makes lifting of the parent bulb difficult.

'Limone'

Breeder: T. van Nieuwkerk Amaryllis B.V.; Plant Breeders' Rights: Pending; Classification: Large flowering.

Description: Usually 4 flat-faced, creamy yellow blooms with frilly edged, pointed blooms 8 in. (20 cm) diameter per scape 16–18 in. (40–45 cm) tall. The company is promoting this hybrid as suitable for pot plant and cut flower production.

'Moonlight'

Breeder: Penning Breeding B.V.; Plant Breeders' Rights: 2003; Classification: Large flowering.

Description: Usually 4 creamy yellow, flat-faced, free-flowering blooms 6.75 in. (17 cm) diameter per scape 18–30 in. (45–75 cm) tall. Although hornlike projections are usually absent, the flowers tend to become more cream with age. 'Moonlight' usually flowers 5 weeks after planting, producing 1 scape from 7–8 in. (18–20 cm) circumference, 2 from 9.5–10.5 in. (24–26 cm) circumference and 3 from 12–12.5 in. (30–32 cm) circumference bulbs. Bulbs reach a maximum size of 15–16 in. (38–40 cm) after 3 years when grown under optimal conditions. Mature leaves reach 30 in. (75 cm) long and 2–2.5 in. (5–6 cm) wide and are usually present with the flowers, providing bulbs are given a 10-week preparation at 55°F (13°C). The tall scapes make 'Moonlight' suitable for pot plant and cut flower production, particularly as individual blooms remain fresh for 9–10 days.

'Yellow Goddess'

Breeder: Uncertain, likely to be Dutch or American; Plant Breeders' Rights: 1994; Classification: Reginae (4b).

Description: Usually 3 creamy yellow, loosely constructed, irregularly shaped blooms 5–5.5 in. (13–14 cm) diameter per scape 14–18 in.

(35–45 cm) tall with a delightful green throat. The variously shaped and size tepals can sometimes result in lopsided blooms. Initially the florets are pale green, gradually turning pale yellow. Even before the florets have opened, hornlike projections are visible on the outer side of the tepals. As the flowers open, horns become visible on the inner side which can detract from the plant's overall beauty (Plate 5-5). The number of horns vary among individual flowers with up to 6 outer and 3 inner horns on a single bloom.

Despite such irregularities, 'Yellow Goddess' remains the most reliable of yellows, usually flowering 5–6 weeks after planting. New shoots emerge after a cool period of 6–7 weeks at 55°F (13°C). Often 2–3 slender dull green scapes with attractive shades of brown towards the base appear and develop simultaneously from 9.5–10.5 in. (24–26 cm) circumference bulbs with a clump of 5–6 leaves appearing up to 4 months after flowering. 'Yellow Goddess' produces many bulblets and the absence of new roots at the time of flowering makes the plant liable to collapse at the slightest knock. It is therefore recommended to plant this bulb a little deeper to aid anchorage until new roots develop. After replanting my bulb into the Kew mix in autumn 2002, it developed a robust root system of many new basal roots by the end of the cool period at the beginning of February, thus providing stability for the plant. Up to 7 new leaves developed a week later, followed by two fresh shoots 3–7 days later.

'Yellow Moon'

Breeder: Penning Breeding B.V.; Plant Breeders' Rights: 2002; Classification: Small flowering (Large-flowering).

Description: Usually 3–5 slightly trumpet-shaped, pale yellow blooms 3.5–4.5 in. (9–12 cm) diameter per scape 18–20 in. (45–50 cm) tall. 'Yellow Moon' lacks the pink spots, flushes and horns which develop on some other hybrids and is slightly faster-growing than 'Germa'. Bulbs normally reach 8.75–10.5 in. (22–26 cm) circumference after a 2-year growing cycle, and when cultivated under optimal condition, reach 13–14.25 in. (33–36 cm) circumference after 4 years. 'Yellow Moon' is a slower growing hybrid, usually flowering 8–9 weeks after planting with improved root development compared with 'Germa' and fewer offsets. The influence of 'Germa' is apparent in the shape and color of the throat, but overall the flowers are paler and become cream with age.

'Yellow Moon' usually produces 1 scape from 8–8.75 in. (20–22 cm) circumference, 2–3 from 10.5–11 in. (26–28 cm) circumference and 3 from 11–12 in. (28–30 cm) circumference bulbs. The strong, upright, matt leaves reach 24–27 in. (60–70 cm) long and 1.5–2 in. (4–5 cm) wide. The combination of scape length and 15–17 days vase life per scape make 'Yellow Moon' a suitable cut flower. Although initially slow to root, within 5 months of repotting this bulb into fresh Kew mix, it had developed a robust root system by the end of the cool period (Plate 5-3).

'Yellow Pioneer'

Breeder: Charles D. Cothran; Date of Registration: 1979; Classification: Leopoldii (5b).

Description: It has 3–4 large 7.25 in. (18.5 cm) diameter, pale yellow blooms per scape 18.5 in. (46 cm) tall with 6–9 bright green, 20 in. (50 cm) tall, 1.75 in. (4.5 cm) broad leaves per year. Flowers are held horizontally from 3.25 in. (8 cm) long pedicels and display no signs of red veining or flushes as they age. Many shiny black seeds are obtained from the triangularly lobed capsule. Unlike some other seedlings which take up to 5 years before producing their first scape, 'Yellow Pioneer' reaches maturity in less than 2 years, but like some other yellows it displays poor root growth, has a weak constitution and has never become widely available.

Chapter 6

Modern Hybrids

Developments of new hybrid groups since 1970 owe much to breeders' and geneticists' renewed interest in *Hippeastrum* species and their expeditions to South America during the mid to late 20th century. Explorers included Harry Blossfeld (Brazil), Julio César Vargas Calderón (Peru), Martin Cárdenas (Bolivia), John Leonard Doran (United States), Q. M. Stephen-Hassard (United States), Elbert Hennipman (The Netherlands), Fred Meyer (United States), Pedro Félix Ravenna (Argentina), C. Gomez Ruppel (Argentina) and Thomas W. Whitaker (United States).

The discovery of new species, which included different color forms, as well as increased knowledge of the existing plants acquired from observations in the field and laboratory promoted breeders' enthusiasm to develop new hippeastrums. Other contributing factors were advancements in plant physiology generally and breeding techniques, and the development of rapid multiplication techniques, such as *in vitro* tissue culture.

Some breeders were keen to share their knowledge and plant material with others. They published details of their expeditions and findings in *Plant Life* and other international horticultural publications.

At the beginning of the 21st century, American and Dutch Cybisters (so named because of their similarity to the wispy blooms of *Hippeastrum cybister*) and Trumpets were becoming more widely available and the Dutch Bloeiende Klisters and South African Sonatini hybrids were about to enter commercial production. Some of the most thrilling developments are taking place in Japan involving the breeding of miniature hybrids with spotted scapes and variegated foliage for cultivation in wine glasses and coffee cups. They make splendid coffee table, desk and windowsill decorations and are ideal for the lounge, dining room and office. Pots can be fastened to the kitchen notice board, adding a touch of exotica to the home. Other Japanese developments include autumn-flowering and large-flowering green hybrids.

Classifying these new hippeastrums proved difficult as they did not fit into the existing classification (see Chapter 10 for details). While Japanese breeders referred to their new selections as Super Mini or Mini, reflecting the overall size of the plant, some Dutch breeders considered it inappropriate to categorize their new developments merely according to flower size as it ignored the plant's unique features. Fanciful terminology such as Star of the Knight and Queen of the Knight emerged which evoked images of a bygone chivalrous age.

Chapter 6 describes the features of these new hippeastrums and the research at the Agronômico Institute at Campinas (Brazil) and the National Botanical Research Institute, Lucknow (India), to develop hybrid selections suited to particular environmental and climatic conditions. Individual hybrids are listed at the end of this chapter. Information on conventional small-flowering types can be found in Chapters 4 and 5.

North American Hybrids

Three individuals are responsible for the development of modern hybrids, including Cybisters and Trumpets: John L. Doran, Alan W. Meerow and Fred Meyer.

John Leonard Doran

During the 1960s and 1970s, John Doran traveled to Central and South America, where he made numerous discoveries including *Hippeastrum brasilianum*, *H. candidum*, *H. fosteri*, *H. lapacense* and *H. parodii*. In addition to using *H. aglaiae*, *H. evansiae* and *H. parodii* to breed small-flowered yellows such as *H.* 'Germa' (see Chapter 5), he used *H. ambiguum*, *H. ambiguum* var. *tweedianum*, *H. fosteri* and *H. fragrantissimum* to create pink and white Trumpets. Only *H.* 'Pink Floyd' and the wispy *H.* 'Jungle Star' entered commercial production and remain available. (Although the International Cultivar Registration Authority acknowledges Doran as the breeder of *H.* 'Pink Floyd', Doran himself questions this, and other sources cite Fred Meyer as having created this hybrid. Inquiries have so far failed to establish the correct situation.)

Doran shared his knowledge and experience willingly with others, generously donating pollen, seeds and bulbs to fellow enthusiasts for their own collections and breeding activities. In 1972 the American Amaryllis Society awarded Doran the Herbert Medal in recognition of his work in collecting species and other plants, suitable for cultivation in Southern California.

In late autumn 2002, I acquired several mature, healthy bulbs of *Hippeastrum* 'Pink Floyd' which were from 7.75 in. (19.5 cm) to 8.75 in. (22 cm) circumference. It was difficult to imagine such small bulbs being capable of producing up to 2 scapes, each bearing 3 or 4 exquisite, rose-pink and white-striped trumpets and the loveliest of lime green throats. Particularly striking were the central white stripes on both the inner and outer side of the tepals and the glossy, bright green, slender tepal tubes. Unlike the long pedicels of some Trumpet hybrids, the pedicels of my plants were relatively short and able to support the horizontal blooms. Within 72 hours of emerging from the spathe leaves, the oldest flower had acquired its final shape and color and moved into the horizontal position ready to open. During the night, it began to open, followed by the other flowers at 2- to 3-day intervals, each remaining fresh for around 8 days.

Considering the inherent weaknesses of *Hippeastrum* 'Pink Floyd', establishing and maintaining appropriate nutrient and moisture levels are essential to avoid root burn and possible bulb rot. I have found that the more delicate American hybrids benefit from being kept slightly drier, particularly during the cool period. Using the Kew mix (see Chapter 9) and 12–14 hours of light each day from 600-watt sodium lamps have produced excellent results—much deeper pink flowers and short, firm 10.75–14 in. (27–35 cm) tall scapes. Plants cultivated under poor lighting produced soft 18 in. (45 cm) tall scapes and lanky foliage which collapsed easily.

The presence of numerous offsets with long, slender necks having already emerged or being about to emerge from the dark brown, papery layers of squat, mature bulbs distinguishes *Hippeastrum* 'Pink Floyd' from other American hybrids (Plate 9-3). It was incredible for an 8 in. (20 cm) circumference bulb to be surrounded by 10 offsets of various sizes which, after planting, almost immediately began to produce foliage. Over the next 8 weeks, a forest of slender, pale green leaves developed around the base of the mother bulb which produced 2 magnificent 14 in. (35 cm) scapes, each bearing 4 exquisite trumpets which emerged from bright green, slender, pointed spathe leaves. In common with the majority of Meyer hybrids, bulbs of *H.* 'Pink Floyd' are best planted during February since little external development occurs when bulbs are planted earlier.

Doran's only other hybrid available today is *Hippeastrum* 'Jungle Star'.

I managed to obtain bulbs of this exquisite burgundy red and pale green Papilio hybrid during the late 1990s and was immediately struck by its similarities in coloring and markings to Meyer's *H.* 'Lima'. *Hippeastrum* 'Jungle Star' is more floriferous than *H.* 'Lima', producing 4 or 5 burgundy and pale green blooms per scape from 13–14 in. (33–35 cm) circumference bulbs on thick, majestic 30 in. (75 cm) tall scapes. Such dimensions have more in common with scapes of some large-flowering Dutch singles than with some of the more delicate Cybisters. *Hippeastrum* 'Jungle Star' exudes prodigious quantities of nectar, the globules sliding hesitantly along the long, upturned filaments where they lay suspended for several days before finally dripping onto furniture below. The plump, sharply pointed, sensuous buds are reminiscent of the heads of exotic birds and when they finally open, the effect is pure magic.

Alan W. Meerow

Meerow, a research geneticist and plant taxonomist with the U.S. Department of Agriculture in Miami, Florida, began breeding hippeastrums in 1987 while associated with the University of Florida, initially using *Hippeastrum papilio* and *H. brasilianum*. His objectives were to develop evergreen cultivars with attractive foliage and fragrant flowers of novel form and coloration patterns for pot and landscape use.

Meerow successfully produced reciprocal F_1 progeny between *Hippeastrum papilio* and, respectively, *H. ambiguum* var. *tweedianum*, *H. brasilianum*, *H. lapacense*, *H. pardinum* and *H. reticulatum* var. *striatifolium*. Succeeding generations have introduced old Dutch tetraploid clones into the more novel diploids to create triploid hybrids with more and larger blooms. In 15 years Meerow produced more than 600 carefully documented crosses and developed many interesting hybrid selections. In 1999 the University of Florida released 3 of these with U.S. Patent protection: *H.* 'Bahia', *H.* 'Rio' and *H.* 'Sampa', a semi-dwarf with 6–8 blooms per scape and in some cases up to 10. The cultivars exhibit novel floral coloration patterns and resistance to the fungus *Stagonospora curtisii*. Other hybrids included those with purple shades, fragrant trumpet types, and intense orange miniatures. Meerow is also focusing upon developing a superior commercial yellow variety.

Fred Meyer

Meyer's lifelong passion for unusual plants began in the 1960s and his association with hippeastrums began in the 1970s when he visited Brazil, Chile, Ecuador and Peru in search of new species and those with novel features for his breeding program. Today, he is generally regarded as one of the most significant U.S. breeders of the late 20th century. By the late 1990s, Meyer had amassed a vast collection of material and substantial knowledge and experience of breeding and cultivating the plant. He used many different species with large Dutch singles and *in vitro* techniques, including embryo culture, mutation breeding with colchicine and meristem culture to eliminate viruses, to create new hippeastrums including some that are fragrant.

Meyer's sudden death in May 1999 robbed horticulture of one of its most innovative breeders. It is fortunate that his brother and sister, Thom and Marlene Meyer, are carrying on his work through New World Plant, the commercial vehicle for marketing Meyer's hybrids. A 10-year agreement signed with Berbee and Sons (Hillegom) in the late 1990s is already resulting in a small selection of Cybisters and Trumpets becoming available. In 1999, Meyer was awarded the Herbert Medal in recognition of his achievements in plant breeding and horticulture in general.

Cybisters

By December 2002 nine Cybisters had become commercially available. With their strange shapes; spidery, frilly edged tepals; intricate patterns; exotic color combinations and prodigious quantities of nectar, Meyer's Cybisters were unlike all other hybrid groups. The Cybisters aroused considerable attention when launched at my shows and festivals and at the Hippeastrum Parade at the Keukenhof. Some have delightful, sharply pointed, curvaceous buds which remind me of the heads of newly hatched chicks, and some flowers look more like exotic insects. It was easy to imagine that such buds, along with prodigious quantities of nectar, would make the Cybisters an immediate attraction to any passing insect or bird.

The wonderful shapes and unusual colors of *Hippeastrum* 'Chico' (reddish-brown and pale green), *H.* 'Emerald' (pale green with dots of vermilion and a thin red picotee), *H.* 'Flamengo' (deep pink and green), *H.* 'Lima' (burgundy red and green), *H.* 'Merengue' (orange-brown), *H.* 'Ruby Meyer' (cherry red and yellow) and *H.* 'Reggae' (burgundy red) were widely admired by British gardeners, many unable to believe such plants were hippeastrums. *Hippeastrum* 'Tango' and *H.* 'La Paz' were similar with cherry-red and pale green, frilly edged blooms. For the first time, green featured prominently on the tepals, filaments and styles of several hybrids. The lower 3 tepals of *H.* 'Chico', *H.* 'La Paz', *H.* 'Lima' and *H.* 'Tango' were predominantly or entirely pale green. The lower tepal pair often is divided almost equally lengthwise, the lowermost segment being pale green and the "beard" tepal invariably entirely green.

Scapes came in attractive shades of bright green (*Hippeastrum* 'Emerald'), gray (*H.* 'Lima'), green-gray (*H.* 'Merengue'), gray-brown (*H.* 'Tango'), gray-purple (*H.* 'Tinto'), purple-red (*H.* 'Flamengo', *H.* 'Reggae') and wine-red (*H.* 'Chico'). Pigments are enhanced when plants are cultivated under high light intensities. Floriferous hybrids with tall, robust scapes and long-lasting blooms, such as *H.* 'La Paz', *H.* 'Reggae' and *H.* 'Tango', are well-suited for cut flower production, while shorter scaped, more delicate hybrids, such as *H.* 'Chico' and *H.* 'Ruby Meyer', make exotic pot plants for the home and office, particularly when combined with other plants having luxuriant, glossy green foliage and other ornaments.

Large 12–13 in. (30–33 cm) bulbs like those of *Hippeastrum* 'Merengue' and *H.* 'Tango' usually produced 3, sometimes 4 scapes, with 5–8 flowers per scape, while *H.* 'Reggae' and *H.* 'Flamengo' usually produced only 2 scapes from similar size bulbs, each having 3–5 blooms. *Hippeastrum* 'Chico', *H.* 'Lima' and *H.* 'Ruby Meyer' bloomed from bulbs barely bigger than golf balls! While none of the Cybisters produced the huge bulb sizes associated with some conventional small- and large-flowering hybrids, several reached maximum circumference sizes: 12 in. (30 cm) for *H.* 'Flamengo' and *H.* 'Merengue', 13 in. (34 cm) for H. 'Reggae' and 15 in. (38 cm) for *H.* 'Tango'. Pedicle color ranged from glossy red (*H.* 'Reggae', *H.* 'Tango') to chocolate-brown (*H.* 'Chico', *H.* 'Flamengo') or pale brown (*H.* 'Merengue'), which enhanced the plant's overall appearance.

In the first season after bulb purchase, most leaves develop after flowering. Up to 9 slender, 1–1.5 in. (2.5–3.5 cm) wide, pointed leaves emerge in various hues of green extending up to 27 in. (70 cm) when mature, and make the most attractive fan shapes. Some Cybisters have a slightly rubbery texture (*Hippeastrum* 'Reggae'); others are more silky (*H.* 'Tango' and some leathery *H.* 'Merengue'). Like the leaves of other hybrid hippeastrums, Cybister leaves become tougher during summer. Several leaves are edged and tipped with attractive shades of pink, dark red, purple or chestnut brown and particularly on the outer side towards the base of the leaf (*H.* 'Chico', *H.* 'Flamengo', *H.* 'Merengue', *H.* 'Reggae'). Some have a central keel extending the length of the leaf (*H.* 'Chico', H. 'Merengue', *H.* 'Tango').

Cybisters are generally no more difficult to cultivate than more conventional hybrids, but some are particularly sensitive to viral and fungal attacks and develop few roots until after flowering, making correct cultivation essential. In June and July 2002, all my Cybisters were repotted into the Kew mix (see Chapter 9), fed intensively and given 12–14 hours of light from 600-watt sodium lights. By the end of September, they had developed extensive and robust root networks and mature foliage. A further examination at the end January 2003 prior to ending of the cool period revealed the development of around 20 new basal roots. After the bulbs were returned to the warmth, fresh shoots emerged on *Hippeastrum* 'Merengue', *H.* 'Reggae' and *H.* 'Tango' bulbs within a few days, ahead of more conventional small-flowering hybrids.

Of all Meyer's Cybisters, *Hippeastrum* 'Emerald' is particularly graceful and in 2003 remained the only pale green Cybister. Its elegant, frilly edged tepals appeared even lovelier by the pencil-thin, red picotee and the liberal scattering of dots of vermilion, predominantly on the uppermost and upper pair of tepals. Usually 5–6 blooms emerged on smooth, lime green scapes and remained fresh for up to 10 days when kept at 64°F (18°C), making it a suitable cut flower.

When I flowered *Hippeastrum* 'Ruby Meyer' for the first time in 1999, I was immediately struck by its similarities to *Sprekelia formosissima*, another member of the Amaryllidaceae, in the shape and color of its blooms. Tiny bulbs measuring only 7.5 in. (19 cm) circumference were reluctant to root and produce a single, reddish scape with 4–6 small, cherry-red blooms with a pale yellow, central stripe on the uppermost and upper pair of tepals. Unlike some other Cybisters which have a vase life of 7–8 days and sometimes longer, blooms of *H.* 'Ruby Meyer' remained fresh for only 4–5 days.

The high scape and flower count of *Hippeastrum* 'Merengue' can result in the most amazing spectacle when 16–18 deep orange-brown blooms on 3 scapes struggle to open simultaneously. Even more incredible was the emergence of a fourth scape in the first year after purchase, 14 days after the final flower had faded, bearing 6 blooms! Another feature that provoked much comment at my Hippeastrum Celebrations in March 2002 and 2003 was the excessively long, upward-curving filaments which protruded in all directions, creating a slightly comical effect.

Compared to other Cybisters currently in the National Plant Collection of Hippeastrum 'Merengue' is particularly vigorous. Scapes extended by

2 in. (5 cm) per day and freshly purchased bulbs were usually in full bloom after 4–5 weeks. Existing bulbs grew even faster; some bloomed after only 21 days following 6 weeks at 55°F (13°C) which commenced 1 December 2002.

I first acquired *Hippeastrum* 'Merengue' in 2002 as a potted plant. It was growing in a 5 in. (13 cm) pot in poor quality coir with no added nutrients. The result was short 16 in. (40 cm) scapes and small blooms, making it difficult for me to believe that scapes normally reach 27 in. (70 cm) tall. By the time the plant was in bloom, considerable bulb shrinkage had already occurred. I realized I had a major job on my hands to restore the bulb to its former size and health.

I replanted the bulb into a deeper pot filled with a nutrient-rich mix including a well-balanced slow-release fertilizer containing trace elements. I carefully watered the bulb and regularly applied a complete liquid feed containing trace elements throughout the year, apart from during the cool period. It was hardly surprising that the plant made excellent progress. By January 2003, the dense, firm bulb had almost regained its former size. I was confident the plant would perform well and I was not disappointed. After 21 days the first scape reached 22 in. (55 cm) tall. It was considerably more robust than each of the 4 scapes produced the previous season. A second equally robust scape followed close behind. All the flowers were larger and a much richer orange-brown, partly due to the 600-watt sodium lights but maybe also influenced by the fertilizer. It was also interesting to note that no bulb shrinkage had occurred after the production of such a large first scape. No doubt the presence of a strong root system and a nutrient-rich potting mix had also contributed to such a magnificent display.

Even more dramatic were the burgundy-red, spidery blooms of *Hippeastrum* 'Reggae' borne on tall, robust, purple scapes which looked like a stork's nest on stilts, the twisted tepals reminiscent of twigs.

Hippeastrum 'Chico' was Meyer's wispiest Cybister to become available in Great Britain at the time of this writing, appearing in a few retail outlets in autumn 2002. It produced up to 6 tiny, wispy, reddish brown and pale green blooms per scape which had the longest, upward-curving pale green filaments and style I had ever seen. Flowers could be divided into halves horizontally, the upper half being predominantly red and the lower portion mostly pale green. The uppermost tepal was a delicate shade of red and the uppermost pair had a thin, pale green central stripe on a reddish background. The lower pair was almost equally divided between red on the upper portion and pale green on the lower portion. The lowermost tepal was entirely green with matching filaments, stigma and style. Also remarkable was the way in which the lower pair of tepals remained tightly drawn together throughout the life of the flower.

When I saw *Hippeastrum* 'Chico' displayed at the Keukenhof in 2001 and 2002, I was captivated by its beauty. I obtained bulbs in autumn 2002 and was fascinated to observe every stage in the plant's development and to compare its growth and performance with that of other Cybisters. One flower self-pollinated, resulting in a glossy, dark green, oval-shaped capsule, the pedicel doubling in width and increasing in length from 2 in. (5 cm) to 2.5 in. (6 cm) within 7 days of fertilization. As the blooms began to fade, I resisted the temptation to remove them, preferring to observe their decay. Ten days later the tepals had lost their former shape and color and had become dry and shriveled, resembling tissue paper (Plate 8-6). A few pollen grains were still visible on the anthers, and globules of gluey nectar lay suspended on the withered, threadlike filaments which hung limply, clinging to the style.

Trumpets

Of all Meyer's Trumpets, only *Hippeastrum* 'Amputo' (Plate 6-20) was available by 2003. The dainty, snow-white, frilly edged blooms looked like small lilies. Many gardeners have experienced problems with the bulbs of this hybrid rotting prior to or after flowering. In November 2002 I obtained top-quality bulbs which produced the most spectacular blooms some 11 weeks later followed by clumps of bright green, silky fan-shaped foliage.

In 2001 and 2002 Berbee and Sons mounted splendid displays of *Hippeastrum* 'Amputo' as a cut flower. Scapes reached 24–30 in. (60–75 cm) tall, making this cultivar ideal for large formal displays and perfect for Easter and spring weddings. When cultivated under 600-watt sodium lights, scapes remained short and sturdy, making *H.* 'Amputo' well suited as a pot plant for home and office environments.

A selection of Meyer's Cybisters and Trumpets appear in Plates 6-16 to 6-25 inclusive. Further details of individual hybrids are given at the end of this chapter.

Brazilian Hybrids

Since 1982 Antonio F. C. Tombolato and colleagues at the Floriculture and Ornamental Plants Section of the Horticultural Center of the Agronômico Institute at Campinas (IAC) have been researching the genetic and horticultural aspects of native Brazilian species and commercially available hybrids. This has included surveying a range of species to determine their suitability for hybridization, the ultimate goal being to breed new and superior hippeastrums for cut flower and pot plant production. More than 100 accessions have now been introduced into the IAC collection, most from south, southeast and west central Brazil. A germoplasm bank of Brazilian species and commercial hybrids has been established, and Julie Dutilh of the State University of Campinas (UNICAMP) has carried out taxonomic studies.

The first crossings were made in 1982 initially for cytological studies, but more recently as part of a program of genetic improvement, the emphasis being on exploring Brazilian germoplasm. Crossings between different species have occasionally proved difficult possibly due to the variation in the number of chromosomes, but *in vitro* embryo culture has now enabled researchers to overcome these difficulties

Since 1990, thousands of hybrids have been produced of which more than 600 have been tested and evaluated for commercial production. Several thousand hybrids were waiting to be tested in 2002, but 20 of the finest hybrids had been selected and were undergoing micropropagation at the ClonAgri Laboratory, Arthur Nogueira, SP. In the same year, some cut flower hybrids were tested for post-harvest durability and the capacity of bulbs to survive a minimum of 3 months of cold storage at 41°F (5°C). Results look encouraging and it is hoped that by 2004 or 2005, the first Brazilian-bred hybrids will be commercially available (Plates 6-2, 6-3).

Indian Hybrids

Hippeastrums are popular garden bedding plants, cut flowers and pot plants for the house and veranda in the plains of northern India. Since the 1970s, staff at the National Botanical Research Institute, Lucknow, have undertaken cytogenetics investigations of the species and have researched the suitability of existing Dutch hybrids for cultivation in the Indian plains.

Under the directorship of T. N. Khoshoo, researchers S. K. Datta, V. N. Gupta, M. A. Kher and the late P. Narain made many discoveries which contributed to enhancing the plant's popularity in India. These included propagation by notching, improving the plant's normal vase life and extending the flowering period.

Japanese Hybrids

Since the early 1990s, Isamu Miyake of Miyake Nursery, Chiba-kon, has developed many new small-, medium- and large-flowering hippeastrums for pot plant and cut flower production. Apart from some large- and medium-flowering doubles which became available in Europe and the United States during the 1990s (see Chapter 7), Miyake's hybrids remained virtually unknown outside Japan. It is hoped that Dutch growers will soon be convinced of the potential of these exciting new developments and be persuaded to bring them into commercial production.

Small-flowering hippeastrums cultivated in 4.5–5 in. (12–13 cm) diameter pots have occupied Miyake's attention for more than 10 years. Several are now available in Japan where they are proving popular as home decorations (Plate 6-4). Bulbs measuring 6–8 in. (15–20 cm) circumference are planted either in pots or in flowerbeds during the spring (March–April) and bloom 4–6 weeks later. Largest size bulbs produced 2–3 scapes 10–16 in. (25–40 cm) tall per year, each having 4–6 dainty blooms 4–4.5 in. (10–12 cm) diameter. Between 6 and 10 glossy green leaves 12–20 in. (30–50 cm) long and 1.4 in. (3.5 cm) wide develop mainly after flowering.

Spring-flowering Mini hybrids have many offsets; attractive white, red, bronze and yellow spotted scapes; and green and cream variegated foliage (Plate 6-5). They are cultivated in wine glasses or coffee cups and are almost certain to attract attention. Up to 8 blooms 4–8 in. (10–20 cm) diameter per scape 8–12 in. (20–30 cm) tall in shades of red, white or pink, flowered 30–40 days after planting from tiny bulbs 3 in. (8 cm) circumference. Bulbs reached a maximum 8 in. (20 cm) circumference after 4–5 years. Variegated leaves 8–12 in. (20–30 cm) tall and 0.75–1 in. (2–3 cm) wide appeared with the flowers adding further to their appeal. The proportion of green to cream varied from one season to the next. Cream portions tended to burn easily, making cultivation under partial shade essential.

Spring-flowering Super Mini hybrids were a particularly exciting development (Plate 6-6). Up to 3 scapes 6–8 in. (15–20 cm) tall, each bearing 3–5 miniature blooms 2.5 in. (6 cm) diameter emerged from 4 in. (10 cm) circumference bulbs and flowered in 3.5 in. (9 cm) pots 4–6 weeks later. Hippeastrum 'Red Star' was propagated in 2002 and more colors, including pink will become available in subsequent years. The presence of up to 8 glossy green leaves 7–8 in. (18–20 cm) long and 1.4–1.5 in. (3.5–4 cm) wide at the time of flowering enhanced the overall effect.

Using DNA from 3 species which bloomed at different times, Miyake wanted to breed distinctive characteristics into autumn-flowering hybrids which were absent from spring-flowering types (Plate 6-7). Due to the increasing availability of Southern Hemisphere bulbs, grown in Brazil and South Africa and naturally flowering in autumn (early October), this development has now been suspended.

Miyake's fascination with green-flowered hippeastrums has resulted in 2 large spring- and autumn-flowering green hybrids involving *Hippeastrum calyptratum*, *H. aulicum* and a large white Dutch hybrid. Bulbs reached maturity after 3 years and produced up to 3 scapes per year; the bulbs reached a maximum 10 in. (25 cm) circumference after 4–5 years. Like Miyake's other hybrids, those with green flowers were quick and easy to grow and bloomed 4–6 weeks after planting. A delicate, pale green, spring-flowering hybrid resembled the loosely constructed, free flowing *H.* 'Yellow Goddess' with its exquisite, frilly edged blooms. Up to 5 blooms per scape 27–36 in. (70–90 cm) tall followed the development of 7–10 leaves 27–36 in. (70–90 cm) tall and 1.75–2.25 in. (4.5–5.5 cm) wide. A brighter green, autumn-flowering hybrid showed a strong likeness to *H. calyptratum* (Plate 1-5) in color, shape, position and the number of blooms per scape. Between 5 and 6 leaves 16–20 in. (40–50 cm) tall and 1.25–2 in. (3–4 cm) wide preceded the blooms. Miyake hopes in the future to be able to darken the shade of green still further.

Dutch Hybrids

Cathy Osselton of the Testcentrum voor Siergewassen B.V., Hillegom, has dominated Dutch developments with the introduction of the Star of the Knight, Queen of the Knight, and Knight Garden hybrids. Also making significant contributions to the modern Dutch hybrids are Penning Breeding B.V. and Andre Barnhoorn, formerly with Hadeco (Pty) of South Africa, but now living in Noordwijkerhout, The Netherlands.

Cathy Osselton

Since 1993, Osselton has been involved in creating new hybrid groups using species originally collected by Elbert Hennipman (Bilthoven) and following field research carried out in Bolivia, Argentina, Paraguay and Chile during the 1980s. The results of this work are an assortment of forms, colors and designs which breeders refer to as Star of the Knight, Queen of the Knight and Knight Garden hybrids. It is hoped that by 2005 some will have entered commercial production and become available.

Star of the Knight hybrids were launched at Keukenhof in 1999 and were similar to some of Meyer's Cybisters with their delicate, wispy blooms. They make wonderful stylized cut flower table decorations and appear even more exotic when combined with luxuriant foliage and other materials. By the beginning of the 21st century, red, rose pink, pale green, cream and pure white monocolored and bicolored flowers had begun to emerge together with a magnificent double red Cybister. By 2010 Osselton expects Cybisters in clearly defined colors to be available, including clear white with a red heart, creams, yellow-limes, pinks and reds (Plates 6-8 to 6-12).

Queen of the Knight hybrids are classic medium- to large-flowered hippeastrums. In 1999, Osselton launched 2 Queen of the Knight hybrids—93.068-1 (fuchsia pink) and 93.388-1 (brown). In 2000, several more were introduced including a stunning red and white single with an enchanting lime green throat (Plate 6-13).

The development of small 7–10.5 in. (18–26 cm) circumference bulbs surrounded by 10–22 klisters (a cluster of offsets) of various sizes which remained attached to the parent bulb, was one of the most thrilling developments of the early 21st century. Shorter scaped varieties with a maximum length of 16 in. (40 cm) were ideal for the home, those with taller scapes made ideal patio or garden bedding plants. Known as Knight Garden hybrids, Bloeiende Klister hybrids or simply Klisters, these hybrids are so quick and easy to grow, flowering 3–6 weeks after planting when cultivated at 70–77°F (21–25°C). Usually 2–3 scapes in attractive shades of green-gray, purple or brown with a whitish bloom emerged from the main bulb and 1, sometimes 2, from largest size offsets. Each scape bears 3–6 dainty blooms with narrow pointed or broader, rounded, satin or silky textured tepals. Although 4 blooms per scape were regarded as the minimum for pot plant production, 3 were considered acceptable in view of the large number of scapes. Green leaves were sometimes edged and tipped with delightful shades of chestnut brown. Some hybrids developed plenty of luxuriant leaves simultaneously with the scapes, creating the effect of luscious undergrowth. Others produced little foliage at the time of flowering. The succession of dainty scapes resulted in clouds of glorious blooms which lasted several weeks, creating the appearance of a miniature garden. Although early Klisters were orange and red, Osselton aims to expand the range of flower shapes and colors to include pink, yellow and white in the future.

Penning Breeding B.V.

There appear no limits to the ingenuity of Penning Breeding. Red, pink, salmon, white and picotee Cybisters are expected to become available during the coming years, following *Hippeastrum* 'Cyber Queen', the company's first Cybister hybrid (Plate 6-26). This delightful, wispy, pale pink and white produces some of the thickest, most robust scapes which reach 26.5 in. (68 cm) tall from largest size bulbs of 14 in. (36 cm) circumference. Four scapes emerged in quick succession, each bearing 4 exquisite blooms. Foliage developed 8–10 weeks after the final flower had faded; the leaves reached 27 in. (70 cm) tall and 1.4 in. (3.5 cm) wide.

In January 2003, a marvelous assortment of Cybisters with flowers in shades of red, orange, pink, yellow and cream flowered for the second time at Penning's nursery. I can hardly wait for them to become available as either a pot plant or cut flower. Many of Penning's hybrids have particularly fascinating designs and intriguing color combinations and represent some of the finest development in early 21st-century Dutch breeding.

Andre Barnhoorn

Sonatini hybrids were introduced in the 1980s when Barnhoorn established a breeding program for Hadeco (Pty) to produce hybrids which bloomed from tiny bulbs. The goal was to reduce the costs of transporting bulbs from South Africa to North America, Japan, Scandinavia and Europe.

Hippeastrum 'Veneto', the first Sonatini to emerge, was launched at a Dutch auction in 1994 where it proved an immediate attraction. It usually produces 6 delightful salmon-pink, trumpet-shaped 3 in. (7.5 cm) diameter blooms with a delicate lime green throat on slender scapes 20 in. (50 cm) tall, from tiny 7–8 in. (18–20 cm) maximum circumference bulbs. Most foliage developed after flowering. Although the scapes were too tall for pot plant cultivation, they were ideal as cut flowers. I successfully cultivated bulbs of this hybrid in autumn 1999 and included it as part of my display of South African hybrids at the Royal Horticulture Society's show at London in November 1999. After 48 hours of being subjected to poor lighting at the show, the plant's scapes had become etiolated and were about to collapse. Nevertheless, the delicate blooms were so delightful that many British gardeners were enthralled by their beauty and were enthusiastic to obtain bulbs for their own collections.

The snow-white blooms of *Hippeastrum* 'Swan Lake', Barnhoorn's second Sonatini, proved very popular when the plant was launched in March 2002 at the Keukenhof. During the same month, Barnhoorn invited breeders, growers, researchers and exporters to his open days where thousands of Sonatinis in a kaleidoscope of reds, oranges, salmon, pinks, cream, snow-whites and pale yellows were in bloom after only 6 weeks (Plate 6-15). Row upon row of small plots, divided by narrow paths covered with straw, was densely planted with 50–65 bulbs per approximately 11 square feet (1 square meter). Each plant produced several green scapes which reached up to 27 in. (70 cm) tall and bore up to 8 tiny blooms per scape, each up to 3.25 in. (8 cm) diameter. Typically, however, scapes carried 4–6 blooms and some had 7 blooms. Many flowers resembled miniature Trumpets with their long, slender, tepal tubes which opened to reveal frilly edged blooms with pointed or slightly rounded tepals. Some had exquisite patterns which included spots, flecks or stripes. Some of the finest hybrids were those with a fine red or pink picotee. The sight of the horizontal or slightly drooping blooms swaying gently in the soft breezes was almost overwhelming.

Once back in Great Britain bearing 10 slender stems of some of Barnhoorn's finest creations harvested 26 hours earlier, I carefully removed each scape from its tight scroll of newspaper and placed it into water. The tiny, tightly closed buds began to swell almost immediately and, after 48 hours the oldest flowers had acquired their final color and began to open. During the next 7 days the flowers matured, the cluster remaining fresh for 14 days. Such a good vase life will enable the Sonatini to compete with other popular cut flowers. Up to 12 leaves in shades of green developed after flowering, reaching up to 20 in. (50 cm) tall and 0.75–1.5 in. (2–4 cm) wide.

CHAPTER 6

Future for the Exotics

Developments in hippeastrum breeding at the turn of the 21st century are unparalleled in the plant's history. In frost-free climates, the Klisters will make a superb patio plant and in cooler climates an exotic plant for the office, home or conservatory. The best time to cultivate and flower the Klisters is midspring (May), but with the plant's continuing association with Christmas, bulbs will have to be raised in Southern Hemisphere countries so they can be given the appropriate preparation to ensure spectacular blooms in time for Christmas. The sight of a miniature garden of blooms in midwinter is a thrilling prospect for the pot plant industry.

The Sonatini represents a new concept in cut flower production and has considerable potential. Its long vase life has proved it can compete with other popular, well-established cut flowers. Careful marketing will be essential to convince growers, exporters and consumers of its unique qualities. Barnhoorn is looking to the future when a shorter stemmed Sonatini will be available for pot plant cultivation.

It is regrettable that European growers have, so far, shown no interest in the exotic Japanese novelties. Not everybody likes the large, flamboyant singles and doubles. Research has already shown a growing interest among some European gardeners and particularly among British enthusiasts for the small, floriferous types. It is hoped that attitudes will change and growers and exporters will recognize the benefits of offering customers a greater selection, including the Japanese miniatures.

Much work remains to be accomplished if these new developments are to take their place alongside well-established conventional types of hippeastrums. In some cases, serious cultural problems must be overcome, while in others growers, exporters and consumers must be convinced of the unique qualities of these new hippeastrums. If these difficulties can be resolved, then there is every reason to expect these new hippeastrums will have an exciting and successful future.

For an explanation of the classification categories used in the descriptions that follow and for details of hybrid registration or the granting of Plant Breeders' Rights, see the Appendix.

Red Modern Hybrids

'La Paz'

Breeder: F. Meyer (United States); Plant Breeders' Rights: 2002; Classification: Cybister.

Description: Usually 4–6 cherry red and lime green blooms 3.25–4.75 in. (8–12.5 cm) diameter per scape 22–27 in. (55–70 cm) tall. 'La Paz' shows similarities in coloring and shape to 'Tango'. Vase life is around 8 days per flower. Foliage develops after flowering has finished.

'Lovely Garden'

Breeder: C. Osselton (The Netherlands); Plant Breeders' Rights: 2002; Classification: (Knight Garden or Bloeiende Klisters).

Description: Usually 3–6 bright red, rounded, trumpet shaped, long-lasting blooms 3.25–4 in. (8–10 cm) diameter per scape 10.75–16 in. (27–40 cm) tall from largest size 7–9 in. (18–23 cm) circumference bulbs. The flowers have a glorious velvety sheen on the outside of the tepals with dark green ovaries and attractive reddish brown 1 in. (2.5 cm) pedicels.

Largest size bulbs are surrounded by up to 5 offsets 5.5–7 in. (14–18 cm) circumference which in turn are surrounded by up to 8 smaller 1.25–4 in. (3–10 cm) circumference offsets, making a cluster of 10 or 11 bulbs. The bulbs are slightly smaller and flatter compared to bulbs of 'Supreme Garden' and are prone to fungal attack. Within 3–5 days after planting, the first of 29 scapes with purplish tinges and a whitish bloom had emerged from a clump of bulbs planted in a large plastic container. Four weeks later the first flowers matured, and throughout March I was treated to a wonderful display of exquisite tiny blooms. Largest size bulbs produced 2 or 3 scapes simultaneously while slightly smaller offsets produced 1 or 2 scapes and smallest offsets produced only leaves.

Little foliage developed at the time of flowering, but I expected growth to become vigorous during the summer. By the end of July 2003, few leaves had emerged. I suspected *Fusarium oxysporum* might be the cause of such poor growth. My suspicions were confirmed upon lifting the bulbs and examining them. The fungus had attacked some of the outer leaf bases and bundles of dead basal roots lay in the compost. After removing all traces of diseases, I thoroughly cleaned the bulbs and left them to dry for 72 hours before re-examining them and dusting the surfaces with green sulfur as a precautionary measure against possible further rotting, prior to repotting in fresh Kew mix. Within a month, fresh roots were developing on some of the bulbs and new foliage was appearing. Only time will tell if the bulbs will make a full recovery and produce flowers in 2004.

'Reggae'

Breeder: F. Meyer (United States); Plant Breeders' Rights: 2001; Classification: Cybister.

Description: Usually 4–6 claret-red and pale green, wispy blooms 4–4.5 in. (10–12 cm) diameter per scape 18–24 in. (45–60 cm) tall. Usually 2, occasionally 3, robust, purple-red scapes develop simultaneously or in close succession from 11–12 in. (28–30 cm) circumference bulbs, the twisted, wispy blooms reminiscent of a young child's tousled hair or a bird's nest on stilts. Vase life is around 8 days per flower. Foliage usually develops after flowering has finished (Plates 6-16, 8-2).

'Tango'

Breeder: F. Meyer (United States); Plant Breeders' Rights: 2001; Classification: Cybister.

Description: Usually 4–6 cherry red and pale green, frilly edged blooms 3.25–5 in. (8–13 cm) diameter per scape 18–24 in. (45–60 cm) tall. Vase life is around 8 days per flower. Usually 2 gray-brown scapes from 10.5–11 in. (26–28 cm) circumference and 3, occasionally 4 scapes from 11–12 in. (28–30 cm) circumference bulbs. Usually 6 weeks from planting to flowering. Individual flowers remain fresh for 7–8 days. Up to 9, narrow, slightly silky green leaves with a keel develop after flowering and reach 27 in. (70 cm) tall and 1.4 in. (3.5 cm) wide. Numerous offsets develop around the base of the parent bulb (Plates 6-17, 8-1).

Pink Modern Hybrids

'Flamengo'

Breeder: F. Meyer (United States); Plant Breeders' Rights: 2001; Classification: Cybister.

Description: Usually 4–6 cherry red, hooded blooms 3.25–4 in. (8–10 cm) diameter per scape 12–24 in. (30–60 cm) tall with a thin pale green, central stripe along the length of the upper 3 tepals. Usually 2 purple-red scapes from 9 in. (22 cm.) circumference bulbs and around 8 days vase life per flower. Fresh foliage in delightful purple shades developed prior to or simultaneously with scapes in the second year after purchase, enhancing the plant's overall appearance (Plate 6-18).

'Pink Floyd'

Breeder: J. L. Doran (United States) (?); Date of Registration: 1997; Classification: 1a Elegans.

Description: Usually 3–4 rose-pink, slightly frilly edged, trumpet-shaped blooms 3–3.25 in. (7–8.5 cm) diameter and 5–5.5 in. (13–14 cm) long per scape 10.75–18 in. (27–45 cm) tall with a white central stripe, bright green throat and white-tipped stigma. Rose-pink filaments and styles become white and ultimately pale green towards the throat. Apart from the narrower 0.3 in. (8 mm) diameter lowermost tepal, other tepals are 0.5 in. (1 cm) diameter at the widest part. Tepal tips are slightly rounded and reflex slightly with age. Individual flowers remained fresh for 7–8 days vase life. Several immature, glossy, pale green silky leaves are sometimes present at the time of flowering but most foliage develops after flowering. Usually 1–2 scapes from 7.75–8.75 in. (19.5–22 cm) circumference bulbs and normally 7 weeks from planting to flowering when bulbs are planted mid to late winter (end January–early February) (Plates 6-1, 9-3).

Orange-Brown Modern Hybrids

'Merengue'

Breeder: F. Meyer (United States); Plant Breeders' Rights: 2002; Classification: Cybister.

Description: Usually 4–8 deep orange-brown spidery blooms with a satin texture, 3–4 in. (7–10 cm) diameter per scape 18–27 in. (45–70 cm) tall. Usually 2 robust scapes from 8.75–9 in. (22–23 cm) circumference bulbs, usually 3 and occasionally 4 robust, green-gray scapes with 2.5 in. (6 cm) long, 2.5 in. (6 cm) wide spathe leaves emerging and developing simultaneously or consecutively from 11–12 in. (28–30 cm) circumference bulbs. Results in delirious clouds of blooms with long, upward-curving, orange-brown filaments. The rich orange-brown sheen towards the throat, bright green stripes on the outside of each tepal, pale brown pedicels 1 in. (2.5 cm) long and the even deeper brown, velvety throat make this a truly wonderful and most exotic plant. Vase life is 7–8 days per flower. Throughout summer 2003, bright green, leathery foliage with a steep keel developed which reached 26 in. (66 cm) tall and 1.4 in. (3.5 cm) wide (Plate 6-19).

'Supreme Garden'

Breeder: C. Osselton (The Netherlands); Plant Breeders' Rights: 2002; Classification: (Knight Garden or Bloeiende Klisters).

Description: Usually 3–4 bright orange, star-shaped blooms 4.25 in. (11 cm) diameter, 5 in. (13 cm) long, with narrow, exquisitely veined, pointed tepals and a bright yellow and emerald green throat per scape 14–19.5 in. (35–49 cm) tall and 1.5–2 in. (4–5 cm) circumference from 6.75–10.75 in. (17–27 cm) circumference bulbs.

Largest size bulbs measuring 10.75 in. (27 cm) circumference produce up to 3 scapes. They are surrounded by up to 4 principal offsets, each 6.75–8 in. (17–20 cm) circumference and surrounded by 2–6 slightly smaller offsets 4–4.5 in. (10–12 cm) circumference, which in turn are surrounded by 7–14 tiny offsets only 1.5–4 in. (4–10 cm) circumference, in ever widening circles making a cluster of 17–20 bulbs.

Bulbs measuring 6.75–8 in. (17–20 cm) circumference produce up to 2 scapes while smallest size bulblets produce only leaves. The speed of growth of newly planted bulbs was amazing. After only 24–36 hours narrow green spathe leaves with hints of pinkish brown had emerged, and 18 days later some scapes bloomed. Further scapes with subtle shades of pinkish brown towards the base followed, resulting in 5–9 scapes per cluster and a succession of exquisite blooms, each remaining fresh for around 10 days. The entire spectacle lasted around 6 weeks.

After all flowering had finished in mid April 2003, foliage development became even more vigorous. Largest size bulbs produced 8–12 slightly silky green leaves which became darker and slightly tougher during the summer and reached 12–24 in. (55–60 cm) tall and 1.1 in. (2.9 cm) wide. Smallest offsets produced 2–4 leaves which reached up to 12 in. (30 cm) tall and up to 0.9 in. (2.3 cm) wide. Larger offsets produced 4–7 leaves of intermediate proportions.

By August 2003, each of my five 10 in. (25 cm) pots containing a cluster of 'Supreme Garden' bulbs resembled miniature forests. Bulbs were obscured by thick tufts of luxuriant leaves which made delightful fan shapes that looked even more beautiful when interspersed among pots of Cybister and Trumpet hybrids having leaves edged and tipped with shades of chocolate brown or purple.

Hippeastrum 'Supreme Garden' was launched in London on 16 February 2003. Visitors were enthralled by the beauty and delicacy of the blooms and were keen to obtain some bulbs of this most wonderful plant.

Salmon-flowered Modern Hybrid

'Veneto'

Breeder: Hadeco (Pty) Ltd (South Africa): Plant Breeders' Right; 1999; Classification: Sonatini.

Description: Usually 4–6 delicate, salmon-pink blooms 3 in. (7.5 cm) diameter per scape 20 in. (50 cm) tall with a yellow-green center. Usually 1 scape from 5.5–6.5 in. (14–16 cm) circumference, 2 from 8–9.5 in. (20–24 cm) circumference and 3 from 9.5–10.5 in. (24–26 cm) maximum circumference bulbs.

Comment: Several bulbs of 'Veneto' make a wonderful table display when planted in a large pot, blooming 6–7 weeks after planting with most foliage appearing after flowering has finished. Although my plant of 'Veneto' flowered without difficulty in the first year after I purchased it, in subsequent years only slender, glossy green leaves have appeared, unlike some other small-flowering South African hybrids, which have readily produced new shoots each year.

White Modern Hybrid

'Amputo'

Breeder: F. Meyer (United States); Plant Breeders' Rights: 1999: Classification: Trumpet.

Description: Usually 3–4 elegant, snow-white Trumpets 5.5 in. (14 cm) long, 4 in. (10 cm) diameter per scape 12–16 in. (30–40 cm) tall which become even whiter with delightful, gently undulating edges as they mature. The exquisite venation and frosting on the inner side of the tepals along with the snow-white filaments and style leading to the lime green throat are particularly endearing features of this plant. Apart from the lowermost and narrowest tepal 0.75 in. (2 cm) diameter, other tepals are similar in size, ranging from 1.25 in. (3 cm) to 1.4 in. (3.5 cm) at the widest part. A single scape usually appears from 9.5 in. (24 cm) circumference, spherical-shape bulbs, followed by 7–9 silky, matt-green leaves. Since it has not proved possible to obtain larger 'Amputo' bulbs, it is not possible to verify the circumference required to produce 2 or 3 scapes. The cylindrical-shaped seed capsules are supported by unusually thick pedicels which become even broader and longer 2–3 days after fertilization has occurred, reaching 2.5 in. (6 cm) long. 'Amputo' is also cultivated as a cut flower with scapes reaching 24–27 in. (60–70 cm) tall. Such a length is possible when bulbs remain in the ground throughout the year and are not lifted in the autumn and dried off (Plate 6-20).

Green Modern Hybrid

'Emerald'

Breeder: F. Meyer (United States); Plant Breeders' Rights: 1999; Classification: Cybister.

Description: Usually 4–6 delicate, pale green, frilly edged blooms 4 in. (10 cm) diameter per scape 18–20 in. (45–50 cm) tall speckled with myriads of vermilion red dots and a fine red picotee. The slender, pale green scapes and long-lasting blooms which emerge from tall slender, bright green spathe leaves 2.5–2.75 in. (6–6.5 cm) long make 'Emerald' a wonderful cut flower. Prodigious quantities of nectar are produced. Foliage develops after flowering. Usually 1 scape from 9.5 in. (24 cm) circumference and 2 from 11 in. (28 cm) circumference bulbs (Plate 6-21).

Bicolored Modern Hybrids

'Chico'

Breeder: F. Meyer (United States); Plant Breeders' Rights: 2002; Classification: Cybister.

Description: Usually 4–5 chocolate-brown and pale green, wispy blooms per scape 16–18 in. (40–45 cm) tall. The width of individual tepals ranged from only 0.5 in. (1 cm) to 0.08 in. (0.2 cm) with a width of 4.5 in. (12 cm) across the upper tepal pair narrowing to only 3.5 in. (9 cm) across the lower pair. Tiny glossy, chocolate-brown pedicels 1 in. (2.5 cm) long and wine-red, unusually stout, robust scapes which became a dull green towards the top, enhanced the overall effect. Usually 2 scapes from 10 in. (25 cm) circumference, flat-shaped bulbs. Usually 7 weeks from planting to flowering. Individual flowers remain fresh for 7–9 days. Tough, dull-green, matt upright foliage, which reaches 12–16 in. (30–40 cm) tall and 1 in. (2.5 cm) wide with attractive purplish tinges on both sides, develops several weeks after flowering. The exotic blooms and relatively short scapes make 'Chico' an ideal pot plant, particularly when the bases of the scapes are decorated with luxuriant, glossy foliage (Plate 6-22).

'Cyber Queen'

Breeder: Penning Breeding B.V. (The Netherlands); Plant Breeders' Rights: 2002; Classification: Cybister.

Description: Usually 2–4 cream and pale pink, wispy blooms 4.25–4.5 in. (11–12 cm) diameter per scape 20–27 in. (50–70 cm) tall with pale green pedicels and attractive brown-green ovaries. Initially the flowers are more green than cream but gradually they become whiter. Usually 2 green-gray scapes with reddish brown shades towards the base from 11–12 in. (28–30 cm) circumference and 3, occasionally 4, from 13–14.25 in. (33–36 cm) circumference bulbs. Up to 9 slender green leaves 27 in. (70 cm) tall with attractive reddish-brown shades toward the base develop after flowering. 'Cyber Queen' is slower growing compared to some other cybisters, taking 8–9 weeks from planting to flowering (Plate 6-26).

'Grandeur'

Breeder: F. Meyer (United States); Plant Breeders' Rights: 2003; Classification: Gracilis Group.

Description: Usually 4 red and white star-shaped blooms 5 in. (13 cm) diameter per scape 14 in. (35 cm) tall on a bright green background. As the flowers mature the 3 upper tepals reflex at the tips making 'Grandeur' appear even more dramatic. The exquisite venation, skilful blending of different shades of red with white and the overall shape show a slight resemblance to 'Jaguar' (see Chapter 4). Up to 7 green, matt, silky, upright leaves 1.5 in. (3.5 cm) wide at the time of flowering enhance the plant's appearance still further (Plate 6-24).

'Jungle Star'

Breeder: J. L. Doran (United States); Date of Registration: 1997; Classification: 'Papilio'; Parentage: *H. cybister* and *H. papilio.*

Description: Usually 4–5 burgundy and pale green blooms 4.25 in. (11 cm) diameter per scape 24–30 in. (60–75 cm) tall. Usually 3, occasionally 4, robust scapes develop from 12.5–14.25 in. (32–36 cm) circumference bulbs which bear more resemblance to some large-flowering hybrids. Prodigious quantities of nectar ooze slowly down the sensuously, upward-curving filaments. The plump, sharply pointed buds bear resemblance to the head of an exotic bird. Foliage develops after flowering.

'Lima'

Breeder: F. Meyer (United States); Plant Breeders' Rights: 2001; Classification: Cybister; Parentage: *H. cybister* and *H. papilio.*

Description: Usually 2–4 burgundy and pale green blooms 2.75–4.5 in. (6.5–12 cm) diameter per scape 14–24 in. (35–60 cm) tall. The 3 uppermost tepals of this delicate, fragile, slow-rooting hybrid are predominantly ox-blood red, the lower 3 mainly pale green. Usually 1 gray scape from 8+ in. (20+ cm) circumference bulbs. Vase life is 4–5 days per flower. Slender, mid-green foliage with an initial slightly silky texture develops after flowering. 'Lima' is prone to fungal attack; the bulb sometimes rots before the foliage appears. However, since repotting my bulbs into the Kew mix, root and foliage growth have been excellent, and by September 2003 my plants had developed 7–9 mature leaves which spread out, creating delightful fan shapes (Plate 6-23).

'Ruby Meyer'

Breeder: F. Meyer (United States); Plant Breeders' Rights: 2001; Classification: Cybister.

Description: Usually 4–5 ruby-red, wispy blooms 3.5 in. (9 cm) diameter per scape 12–16 in. (30–40 cm) tall which look similar to *Sprekelia formosissima.* A pale yellow central stripe is particularly dominant on the three uppermost 0.6–0.7 in. (1.6–1.8 cm) wide tepals which reflex at the tips when mature. The lowermost, narrower 0.4–0.5 in. (0.9–1 cm) tepals are mainly red. Other distinguishing features are the delicate pale pink filaments which become yellow-green towards the throat; pale green style; pale pink stigma; reddish brown scapes; stubby 0.4–0.7 in. (1.5–2 cm) long, light brown pedicels and glossy, olive-green ovaries. Slender, silky, dark green foliage 0.75 in. (2 cm) wide, edged and tinged with chocolate-brown, usually develops long after flowering has finished. Usually 6–7 weeks from planting to flowering when bulbs are planted mid to late winter (end January–early February). Unlike many other Cybisters, 'Ruby Meyer' has a short vase life of only 4–5 days. Bulbs are prone to fungal attack but after repotting into the Kew mix, many new roots quickly developed which filled the pot after only 6 weeks. Eight new leaves emerged and developed simultaneously during summer and early autumn 2003 (Plate 6-25).

Chapter 7

Doubles

Doubles are a recent development when compared with more than 200 years of breeding large singles. Although dating from the 1930s, doubles only became generally available during the 1990s. By the beginning of the 21st century more than 30 Australian, Dutch, Japanese and South African doubles had entered commercial production, some easier to obtain than others. Dutch and South African developments continued to focus upon large-flowering doubles while Japanese breeders also created smaller flowering, shorter hybrids, adding a new and exciting dimension to the doubles' portfolio.

Reactions towards doubles have been mixed. In the United States they quickly proved popular, but in Great Britain gardeners reacted cautiously. Expressions of disdain and disapproval contrasted with the infectious enthusiasm which greeted the introduction of elegant, floriferous smaller flowering types.

Although breeding doubles takes longer than breeding singles, cultivation is the same as for other hippeastrums with most plants flowering 6–8 weeks after planting. Scape and foliage production and development and the plant's overall dimensions are similar to that of many large- and small-flowering singles.

Chapter 7 explores the development and characteristics of double hippeastrums and the contributions of American, Dutch, Japanese and South African breeders. Further details are given in Chapter 8.

Features of Doubles

Distinguishing features of doubles are the increased number of tepals and the lack, or reduced number, of reproductive organs.

Floral Development

In 1979, W. R. Latapie, a U.S. breeder and grower, devised a classification system for doubles based on the number of tepals per flower: 9 to 11—semidouble, 12 to 17—double, 18 or more—superdouble. His proposal, together with characteristics relating to scape length, was endorsed by the Executive Committee of the American Amaryllis Society and subsequently implemented.

Since obtaining my first double in 1994, I have cultivated almost all commercially available Dutch, Japanese and South African doubles in the National Plant Collection of *Hippeastrum*. It has been fascinating to observe the seemingly endless permutations and inconsistencies regarding the number, shape, size and organization of tepals, not only among different hybrids, but also among flowers on the same and different scapes of the same hybrid.

Unlike singles which have 6 tepals per flower, most doubles have 12–17 tepals organized into 2 or more layers, each comprising 6 tepals. Some, such as *Hippeastrum* 'Jewel' and *H.* 'Razzmatazz', tend to be more semidouble than true double with a single outer layer and a few misshapen fragmentary inner portions clustered to form a corona. They are therefore considered semidoubles. Some South African and Dutch creations, such as the creamy white *H.* 'Alfresco' (Plate 7-7), have a third layer, as well as a few fragmentary pieces in the center and are regarded as triples, although this classification has not been officially recognized.

Consistency of doubleness also varies among hybrids. Research by John Deme (Kinston, United States) in the 1970s discovered temperatures of 90°F (32°C) affected doubleness of some hybrids; some reverted to singles but became double the following year. Reliability also varies between hybrids and within the same hybrid group. *Hippeastrum* 'Red Peacock' and *H.* 'Aphrodite' regularly produce fully double blooms from one season to the next with little variation in the number of tepals among individual flowers. *Hippeastrum* 'Andes', *H.* 'Jewel', *H.* 'Pasadena' and *H.* 'Salmon Peacock' are more unpredictable. Individual plants produce single, semidouble and fully double blooms on the same or adjacent scapes of the same plant and also vary in their degree of doubleness from one season to the next.

Some doubles, such as *Hippeastrum* 'Blossom Peacock', *H.* 'Flaming Peacock' and *H.* 'Promise' have exquisitely proportioned and immaculately sculptured blooms with tepals similar in size and shape and positioned so precisely that the blooms look more like an elaborate geometrical drawing. Others, such as *H.* 'Fanfare' (Plate 7-4) and *H.* 'Joker' (Plate 7-14), are more loosely constructed; tepals sometimes appear to be flung together haphazardly, creating a slightly comical appearance. In some doubles, tepals sit on top of each other, in others they overlap to a greater or lesser extent. They may be long, slender and pointed (*H.* 'Jewel'); broader and slightly pointed with gently undulating edges (*H.* 'Dancing Queen', Plate 7-13; *H.* 'Rainbow') or broad and round with large 10–12 in. (25–30 cm) diameter, peony-shaped blooms which are almost as large as dinner plates (*H.* 'Nymph'). Some hybrids have short tepal tubes while others are longer with smaller, delicate 6–6.5 in. (15–16 cm) diameter trumpet-, star-, oval- or triangular-shaped flowers. Textures vary; *H.* 'Mary Lou' has particularly thick, rounded tepals which sparkle in the sunlight, and *H.* 'Fanfare' and *H.* 'Unique' have such thin, delicate, pointed tepals with a satinlike complexion that they bruise easily when touched.

Reproductive Organs

While many doubles are sterile some, such as *Hippeastrum* 'Double Record' and *H.* 'Blossom Peacock', may have the usual complement or a reduced number of stamens, although not all may produce pollen. Normal stamens are sometimes combined with filaments which lack anthers. Flowers with viable pollen may be used as pollen parents. More often, stamens are converted into misshapen fragments, known as petaloid stamens, which are usually found towards the center of the flower, sometimes hidden among normal and/or misshapen tepals. Petaloid stamens come in various shapes and sizes and vary in number among individual flowers on the same and different plants of the same cultivar, as well as among different cultivars. Some flowers have none, others have up to 10 such structures while 2–6 petaloid stamens per flower are typical. Filaments are usually shortened, thickened, often twisted and embedded within these colored fragments. Anthers are often distorted, smaller than normal, produce little or no pollen and are usually completely or partially embedded in the petaloid structure. Petaloid stamens may be obscured by colored, often distorted and misshapen fragments which lack filaments and anthers and are found mainly towards or in the center of the flower. These are essentially distorted and misshapen tepals and are generally referred to as petaloids. Their presence makes pollination difficult, if not impossible, without human intervention.

The presence of petaloids and petaloid stamens can make some flowers look messy and detract from their beauty. Some flowers combine normal and petaloid stamens.

The proportion of tepals to petaloids and petaloid stamens varies. Some flowers lack all inner fragmentary portions and look magnificent. Others have several such portions which tend to stick together, forming a corona. As the flower matures, the portions move apart slightly, revealing some to be petaloid stamens (Plate 7-8)

The style is often absent, or else thickened, distorted and sometimes twisted. The stigma may have only 1 or 2 prongs instead of the usual 3, and it may lack an ovary, in which case the plant cannot be used as the seed parent. For many years, large Dutch white singles have been used as seed parents for the breeding of doubles.

North American Doubles

Breeding doubles proved attractive to a few American hippeastrum enthusiasts during the early to mid 20th century after M. Albert Wagner discovered *Hippeastrum equestre* f. *albertii* in Havana (Cuba) around 1866 (Plate 2-7). This fully scarlet-orange double form has 2 medium 6.5 in. (16 cm) diameter blooms per scape 12 in. (30 cm) or more tall. Each flower has 30–40 pointed, wispy tepals which remain fresh for 8 days in temperatures of 90°F (30°C). American and Dutch singles provided breeders with seed parents for their experiments, resulting in monocolored and bicolored semidouble and fully double hybrids by the 1930s. Dutch growers were so impressed by some of these early hybrids that they purchased bulbs for their own use. Subsequently, a few entered commercial production and are still available today.

During the 1930s, Captain J. J. McCann (Florida) crossed *Hippeastrum equestre* f. *albertii* with single-flowered Florida Mead hybrids, bred by Theodore L. Mead at the beginning of the 20th century. Mead hybrids were mainly of the Reginae type and came in 6 main colors. They were characterized by their short to medium tepal tubes. Unlike the European-bred Reginae and Leopoldii hybrids, the Mead group was able to be field grown in Florida, providing the soil pH was regulated and correct nutrient levels maintained. McCann's efforts resulted in various colored offspring. Only 6 were doubles, of which only *H.* 'Mary McCann', a delicate pink with white veins, and *H.* 'Madira Bickel', a solid brick-red with ruffled edges, were retained. Both lacked stigmas but produced pollen which was used to create subsequent generations. Although McCann's second-generation (F_2) hybrids lacked the vigor of the first generation (F_1), they were more vigorous than *H. equestre* f. *albertii* and most had 4 blooms per scape which McCann described as distinctive and strangely handsome. Out of all the F_2 hybrids, only *H.* 'Helen Hull' was outstanding. A vigorous grower, it multiplied easily and had brilliant orange-red blooms which measured up to 9.5 in. (24 cm) diameter. *Hippeastrum* 'Helen Hull' inspired John Deme to commence a doubles breeding program in 1970s. Remarkable F_3 hybrids of McCann's program included *H.* 'Edlena' (pink and white) and *H.* 'Captain McCann' (scarlet-orange).

During the 1970s, Charles D. Cothran (California) experimented using doubles such as *Hippeastrum* 'Helen Hull' and *H. equestre* f. *albertii* with white Dutch singles such as *H.* 'Maria Goretti' and pollen obtained from John Doran's 2R5 double to create new hybrids. Success was mixed, but in 1978–1979 all the flowering doubles produced pollen which was placed on large reds (for example, *H.* 'Beautiful Lady', *H.* 'Nostalgia', *H.* 'Queen of Night', *H.* 'Violetta'), as well as some of Cothran's own deep reds to create large, dark red doubles. Thanks to advice, encouragement, seed and bulbs received from Doran during the 1970s and early 1980s, Cothran raised *H.* 'Double Beauty' (1974), a vigorous, evergreen double with 4–5 white and pink-veined 9.5 in. (24 cm) diameter blooms with a red picotee per 18.5 in. (46 cm) tall scape. It bloomed irregularly and produced little pollen. Cothran used pollen from *H.* 'Double Beauty' with large-flowering Dutch hybrids to produce further doubles. He also contributed to the early development of the smaller flowering double using pollen from *H. equestre* f. *albertii* to produce 2 small red hybrids with 4.25 in. (11 cm) diameter blooms. Other doubles included a medium-flowering white which involved a white sibling of *H.* 'Double Beauty' and pollen of *H.* 'Double Beauty'.

John W. Deme's (California) fascination with doubles began during his employment as a grower with Park Seed Company (Greenwood, South Carolina) in the mid 1960s. During this time he noticed *Hippeastrum* 'Helen Hull' which he crossed with *H.* 'Park's Apricot'. All hybrids with 6 or more tepals were retained. Advice and pollen received from Doran in the early 1970s enabled Deme to begin breeding his own doubles. Around 50% were singles, at least 25% were semidouble and, of the remaining 20–25%, only 10% were true doubles. Having discovered some doubles reverted to singles in high temperatures, Deme focused his attention on creating hybrids which retained their doubleness, whether grown outside or in greenhouses. By 1982 he had achieved this goal.

Deme aimed to create flat, well-proportioned, two-toned hybrids with 15 or more tepals. During the 1970s and 1980s he created a portfolio of medium-flowering 6–6.5 in. (15–16 cm) hybrids. Some had red or orange-red flowers (*Hippeastrum* 'Judy', H. 'Louis Parajos'), orange-red and white (*H.* 'Lynn'), red and white (*H.* 'Kristy', *H.* 'Fanny White', *H.* 'Surprise'), salmon (*H.* 'Delbert Howard', *H.* 'Yock'), salmon and white (*H.* 'Double Salmon'), light pink with white veins (*H.* 'Judy Weston'), white with red blotching ('Janet Nestor'), picotee with pink flushes (*H.* 'Matilda Parajos'), and some were almost pure white. Some were evergreen and vigorous, producing up to 6 scapes per year, each 16.25–24 in. (41–60 cm) tall with 4–6 blooms and 15–21 tepals per bloom. Some flowered almost any month of the year; others flowered in spring, summer or winter. Deme regarded *H.* 'Judy Weston' as his best early double and used it as a pollen parent to create further doubles. This hybrid has now been registered by the International Cultivar Registration Authority (ICRA), granted Plant Breeders' Rights and today is sold under the name of *H.* 'Lady Jane'. *Hippeastrum* 'Double Record' and *H.* 'Pasadena' were the first doubles to become widely available in Europe and the United States in the mid 1990s.

Mystery continues to surround the breeder of *Hippeastrum* 'Double Record' and *H.* 'Pasadena'. The ICRA records Deme as the breeder of both hybrids, but Deme remains uncertain as to whether this is correct. *Hippeastrum* 'Double Record' is definitely my favorite with its gorgeous pink and white, long-lasting, frilly edged blooms which have a delightful pink edging and bright yellow and green throat. Compared to *H.* 'Lady Jane' and *H.* 'Pasadena', *H.* 'Double Record' is consistently double and sometimes produces 6 normal stamens and sometimes a 1- or 2-pronged stigma.

Hippeastrum 'Lady Jane' has proved particularly inconsistent in flower shape and color. Some plants have salmon-pink blooms; others almost orange. Over the years, I have observed many different tepal arrangements resulting in some blooms having almost round faces while others are diamond shaped. Like several of the Japanese doubles, *H.* 'Lady Jane' has long, thick, pale green pedicels resulting in drooping of the weighty blooms. Unlike the more floriferous, longer-lasting *H.* 'Pasadena' and *H.* 'Double Record' which regularly produce 5 or 6 flowers per scape, *H.* 'Lady Jane' usually has only 2 or 3 blooms and a vase life of only 4 or 5 days when fully mature. Although the first two flowers usually open within 2 or 3 days of each other, there is sometimes a significant delay of the third flower, which sometimes fails to reach maturity.

Most 10 in. (25 cm) circumference bulbs of Deme's double hybrids produce 1 scape and 2 flowers. Larger 10.5–11 in. (26–28 cm) circumference bulbs usually produce 2–3 scapes, each having 3–4 blooms. Still larger bulbs sometimes produce 5–6 blooms per scape and reach a maximum circumference of 13 in. (33 cm) after 3–5 years with 18.5–24 in. (46–60 cm) tall scapes. Up to 12 leaves per year develop in shades of green and reach up to 24 in. (60 cm) long and 3 in. (7.5 cm) wide. Some doubles display foliage at the time of flowering while others develop leaves after flowering.

Another characteristic of Deme's doubles is that most of them have 4–6 blooms 2–8 in. (5–20 cm) diameter per scape with 6–8 in. (15–20 cm) diameter being the usual size. Usually 15–25 tepals are arranged in 3 or 4 layers. Deme's ideal double was flat when viewed from the side, having evenly distributed tepals and horizontal, well-proportioned blooms which did not droop and no petaloid stamens in the center. Some doubles have thick, waxen, rounded tepals and exquisite veining; others have thinner, pointed tepals with frilly edges and up to 6 petaloid structures per flower. A vase life of 8–10 days per flower is usual, with some flowers remaining fresh for up to 14 days.

John L. Doran's (California) contribution to hippeastrums focused around collecting, distributing and breeding the species he collected from expeditions to South America in the 1960s and 1970s. His visit to the Caribbean islands in the 1960s led to the discovery of various double forms of *Hippeastrum equestre* and a white picotee which showed signs of doubleness. All proved instrumental in producing seed which resulted in *H.* 'Double Beauty', the hybrid which played a key role in some of Cothran's 1970s doubles. A later crossing, resulting in a 7–8 in. (18–20 cm) diameter, picotee-type double which had 25 tepals and petaloids, was registered by Marcia Wilson as *H.* 'Confetti'.

Hilda and Walter Latapie's (Louisiana) interest in hippeastrums spanned almost half a century. One of their ambitions was to create a pure white double. In the early 1960s they crossed *Hippeastrum* 'Captain McCann' with *H.* 'Maria Goretti' as the seed parent, resulting in a range of colors which included an almost pure-white double. This medium 6 in. (15 cm) diameter white hybrid with faint cherry-red streaks on each side of the midrib was named *H.* 'Hilda Latapie' (1969). The broad, frilly edged tepals were organized into 3 layers. No stigma was visible, but 3 stamens were clustered around the center of the green throat. Further crossings were made using *H.* 'Hilda Latapie' with *H.* 'Maria Goretti' to create a pure white devoid of any traces of red. Pollen from the best whites was also used on pastel-colored singles to create delightful rose, salmon, red and white striped doubles.

Hippeastrum 'White Nymph' (1980) is generally regarded as the first large pure-white double. More pure whites followed. *Hippeastrum* 'Michele Latapie' (1982) was red and white striped, slightly fragrant with 3 horizontal 6–7 in. (15–18 cm) diameter blooms per 16.25 in. (41 cm) tall scape. *Hippeastrum* 'Lynn Latapie' was a vigorous hybrid which multiplied easily and had fragrant, crepe-textured, white blooms.

In May 1982, Walter and Hilda Latapie were awarded the Herbert Medal for their work in creating the pure white double.

Australian Doubles

At one time the only doubles available to Australian gardeners were of South African, Japanese or Dutch origin. By 2002, up to 10 Australian-bred doubles in various shades of pink and red had been identified by Maguire's Hippeastrum Farm for possible commercialization. Among these was the delightful pale pink *Hippeastrum* 'Boysenberry Swirl' (Plate 7-1) with peony-shaped, fully double and semi-double blooms and up to 8 petaloids and petaloid stamens which projected forwards, forming a corona. Maguire's doubles produce 2–4 blooms, 5–7.25 in. (13–18.5 cm) diameter per scape 12.5–22 in. (32–55 cm) tall. Foliage develops before or after flowering, depending on the cultivar. Mature leaves reach 12–20 in. (32.5–50 cm) tall and 1.4–2.5 in. (3.5–6 cm) broad with 2 scapes from 8+ in. (20+ cm) circumference bulbs. Most flowers have 12 or more tepals with several petaloids or petaloid stamens, some of which produced varying amounts of pollen. A distorted stigma is sometimes present.

Maguire aims to expand his range of doubles still further and produce a portfolio of well-proportioned, compact doubles in a wide range of colors. Considering his preference for pink, it is possible that several will turn out to be various shades of pink. If his doubles turn out to be as magnificent as his large singles, Australian gardeners are in for a wonderful treat. Unfortunately export regulations and prohibitively high transport costs have made it impossible to obtain Maguire's cultivars for the National Plant

Collection of *Hippeastrum*. Instead, I have had to be content with photographs, computer images and descriptions supplied by Richard Maguire.

Japanese Doubles

Japanese developments are dominated by Isamu Miyake of Miyake Nursery (Chiba-Kon) who began breeding doubles after reading an article about John Deme's work in *Plant Life* (1972). The first Japanese double became available in the early 1990s and more than 10 semi and fully double hybrids have since entered commercial production.

Like many of the large-flowering Dutch singles, most 13.5–14.25 in. (34–36 cm) circumference bulbs of doubles produce 3 scapes in the first year after purchase. Some reach a maximum 14.5–15 in. (37–38 cm) circumference after 4–5 years. Scape length varies from 12 to 27 in. (30–70 cm) with 8–14 leaves per year in various shades of green and reaching up to 22.5 in. (57 cm) long and 3 in. (7.5 cm) wide. Some leaves have a smooth, slightly silky texture (*Hippeastrum* 'Jewel') while others are tough and leathery (*H.* 'Red Peacock'). A few hybrids, such as *H.* 'Red Peacock' and *H.* 'Flaming Peacock', display foliage at the time of flowering, but most bulbs develop foliage after flowering.

Root development varies according to the cultivar. Some British and American gardeners have reported difficulties with *Hippeastrum* 'Blossom Peacock', *H.* 'Red Peacock' and *H.* 'White Peacock': the bulbs fail to develop roots until long after flowering has finished. *Hippeastrum* 'Andes' and *H.* 'Allure' have also proved problematic resulting in pathetic 6–9 in. (15–23 cm) high, rubbery scapes and small, poorly developed and pigmented blooms. No disease or damage was evident on any part of the bulbs, but the lack of roots not only contributed to patchy growth but also resulted in the plant collapsing at the slightest breeze or knock. Having experimented with various potting mixes since 1994, I suspect that such poor growth was partly due to the lack of aeration. I have since transferred all my bulbs into the Kew mix (see Chapter 9), with the most encouraging results. Significant root growth took place during summer 2002, throughout the autumn and even during the cool period, followed by the emergence of fresh scapes, magnificent blooms and luxuriant new foliage in spring.

Most double hybrids produce 3–6, occasionally 7–8 fully double, semi-double or single blooms per scape in shades of bright orange-red

(*Hippeastrum* 'Red Peacock'), cherry red (*H.* 'Red Charm'), salmon-pink (*H.* 'Andes', *H.* 'Lady Jane'), cream (*H.* 'Jewel') and snow-white (*H.* 'White Peacock'). Individual blooms measure 6–9 in. (15–23 cm) diameter. Some hybrids, such as *H.* 'Rainbow, often produce only 3 blooms per scape. Some of Miyake's finest doubles combine white with a delicate red or pink picotee (*H.* 'Allure', *H.* 'Aphrodite', *H.* 'Rainbow') with individual tepals having pink blushes; red and white (*H.* 'Flaming Peacock') or pink and white (*H.* 'Blossom Peacock', *H.* 'Mary Lou').

A feature of some doubles is the wide gap of 7–10 days between the maturing of pairs of flowers, with the second or third pair sometimes failing to complete development. Instead, the tiny florets turn cream and finally brown before withering. Most plants bloom after 6–8 weeks with individual flowers remaining fresh for 7–10 days.

A few doubles have up to 25 tepals per flower, but 15–17 tepals is typical. *Hippeastrum* 'Andes' and *H.* 'Jewel' are often more semidouble than true double with an outer layer of 6 tepals and an incomplete second layer. A swathe of *H.* 'Jewel' hybrids looked magnificent as part of the *Hippeastrum* display in the Princess of Wales Conservatory, Royal Botanic Gardens, Kew (1999). Many visitors detected a slight perfume, similar to a daffodil, emanating from the waxy, 6 in. (15 cm) trumpet blooms which were often mistaken for lilies. Of the many *H.* 'Jewel' plants cultivated specially for the display, less than 10 produced fully double blooms, the majority being semidouble or single. With its bright yellow-green throat lined with a ring of red dots and the corona of fragmentary pieces, *H.* 'Jewel' remains one of my favorite medium-flowering doubles.

Three of my favorite large-flowering Japanese doubles are the floriferous and well-proportioned *Hippeastrum* 'Mary Lou', *H.* 'Blossom Peacock' and *H.* 'Flaming Peacock'. The pink pigments of the first two hybrids and the red of *H.* 'Flaming Peacock' intensified considerably when the plants were cultivated under 600-watt sodium lights. *Hippeastrum* 'Mary Lou' also featured in the Kew display and after 48 hours of being exposed to the early April sun, the thick, frosted tepals became suffused with delightful shades of pink and looked marvelous among swathes of *H.* 'Amigo' (see Chapter 3). Some *Hippeastrum* 'Mary Lou' flowers were more double than others; several had only 6 tepals while others had 15–17 tepals.

Of all Miyake's doubles, *Hippeastrum* 'Blossom Peacock' proved particularly popular with British gardeners. Its consistently double, immaculately proportioned, slightly fragrant star-shaped blooms which adorned a 10 ft.

(3.3 m) high pyramid, provoked considerable favorable comment from visitors to my Hippeastrum Celebration in April 2000.

In March 2002 I obtained bulbs of *Hippeastrum* 'Flaming Peacock', Miyake's latest creation to become available in Europe. Unlike some other doubles, the three pairs of immaculately sculptured and poised blooms opened in quick succession with an interval of only 2–3 days between each pair. The result was a glorious halo of blooms which remained fresh for 3 or 4 days before the first pair began to wilt. All my plants of *H.* 'Flaming Peacock' produced 7–9 mature, upright, robust, dark green leaves at the time of flowering which enhanced the overall effect. It was interesting to note the variation in the proportion of red to white and the various shades of red among individual blooms on the same and different scapes on the same and different plants, in spite of all plants being cultivated under identical environmental conditions in spring 2003 (Plates 7-9, 7-10).

Miyake's breeding program has subsequently focused on small and medium, easy-to-grow spring-flowering doubles which flower after 3 years from small 6 in. (15 cm) circumference bulbs (Plate 7-2). Bulbs reach a maximum size of 9.5 in. (24 cm) circumference after 4–5 years and produced short 8–16 in. (20–40 cm), slender 1.75–2.5 in. (4.5–6 cm) circumference scapes. Each scape bears usually 3–5 dainty, medium size 4.5–6 in. (12–16 cm) diameter blooms which flower 4–6 weeks after planting. The individual flowers remain fresh for 7–10 days. Larger bulbs produce up to 3 scapes with glossy green foliage present at the time of flowering; the leaves reached 12–24 in. (30–60 cm) tall and 1.25–2 in. (3–5 cm) wide when mature. Between 8 and 11 leaves emerge each year. Miyake anticipates the smaller flowering double with its shorter scapes will prove popular in Japanese homes where space is a premium.

For some time Miyake has been interested to produce large-flowered, fragrant doubles. Although it has proved possible to create mildly fragrant doubles, such as *Hippeastrum* 'Blossom Peacock' and *H.* 'Jewel', it is proving harder to create hybrids with a stronger perfume. Efforts continue to improve the level of fragrance. Without doubt, a well-proportioned, fragrant Japanese double would be a great attraction for some gardeners.

Miyake has also created large-flowering doubles with different toned blooms which appear simultaneously on separate scapes. Initially, such differences were thought to be due to some flowers fading, but research showed some hybrids naturally produced scapes with different toned blooms (Plate 7-3). This fascinating development has already generated interest among some British hippeastrum enthusiasts who are keen to obtain bulbs for their own collections.

Dutch Doubles

Dutch developments are dominated by Penning Breeding B.V. and T. van Nieuwkerk Amaryllis B.V. Between them they have created the majority of Dutch doubles available today with many more planned for the future. Particularly interesting are Penning's *Hippeastrum* 'Promise' with its rounded, exquisitely sculptured, red and white blooms; *H.* 'Salmon Peacock' with its delightful semidouble or fully double salmon blooms and *H.* 'Dancing Queen', with its majestic, weighty red and white-striped blooms.

By the beginning of the 21st century Nieuwkerk Amaryllis B.V. had launched a large red and white double: *Hippeastrum* 'Double Queen', similar to Penning's *H.* 'Dancing Queen'. *Hippeastrum* 'Chianti' was Nieuwkerk's first sunset orange double to become available; its face looked like a sunflower with slightly upward-facing blooms. Nieuwkerk's Nymph hybrids were particularly interesting. *Hippeastrum* 'Nymph' (1965) has white and pink, peony-shaped blooms and was closely followed by *H.* 'Red Nymph', *H.* 'Pink Nymph' and *H.* 'White Nymph'.

South African Doubles

Since the late 1980s, around 12 monocolored and bicolored hybrids in shades of red (*Hippeastrum* 'Fanfare', *H.* 'Ragtime'), pink (*H.* 'Rozetta'), white (*H.* 'Alfresco', *H.* 'Snow White'), red and white (*H.* 'Joker', *H.* 'Razzmatazz', *H.* 'Rio') and white and pink (*H.* 'Fluffy Ruffles', *H.* 'My Favourite') have become commercially available, although the South African double remains elusive in Great Britain. Like the other hybrids from Hadeco (see Chapters 3 and 4), the doubles are easy to cultivate, usually blooming after 6–7 weeks, although *H.* 'Joker' is particularly fast-growing, sometimes flowering after only 14 days. Flower count ranges from 3 to 8 blooms 4.25–8.5 in. (11–22 cm) diameter per scape 10–20 in. (25–50 cm) tall. Some doubles produce plenty of upright luxuriant green foliage at the time of flowering, creating an attractive bushy effect.

Of all Hadeco large-flowering doubles exhibited at my display of South African hybrids at the Royal Horticultural Society London Show in November 1999, *Hippeastrum* 'Ragtime', with its short, stout scapes which resembled mini tree trunks and fully double, orient-red, upward-facing blooms, proved very popular. The plant's appearance was enhanced by the presence of mature, upright foliage with tips which reached the top of the scapes. Unlike the looser constructed, floppy, untidy blooms of *H.* 'Snow White', flowers of *H.* 'Ragtime' retained their horizontal position, enabling the plant's beauty to be fully appreciated.

Hadeco was the first company to launch small- and medium-flowering doubles beginning with *Hippeastrum* 'Alfresco' (white), *H.* 'Joker' (maroon and white) and *H.* 'Fanfare' (bright red) which became available towards the close of the 20th century. Each had distinctive characteristics and highlighted the diversity already available among the various hybrids. At the beginning of the 21st century, the company had scaled down its doubles' program to make way for other developments which included smaller flowering hybrids.

Future for Double Hippeastrums

Doubles remain relatively unknown in Great Britain but never fail to arouse considerable interest when exhibited at shows and festivals. Their limited availability and high price mean they still have novelty value and remain exclusive. In the mid 1990s, any double was considered acceptable, provided it was sufficiently double. Today, other traits, such as bulb and root growth, length and firmness of scapes, scape and flower production are becoming more important. Only the best bulbs will enter commercial production and survive.

For an explanation of the classification categories used in the descriptions that follow and for details of hybrid registration or the granting of Plant Breeders' Rights, see the Appendix.

Red Doubles

'Fanfare'

Breeder: Hadeco (Pty) Ltd (South Africa); Launched: 1998; Classification: Sonata Double.

Description: Usually 7–8 bright red, wispy, frilly edged blooms 4.5 in. (11 cm) diameter per scape 12 in. (30 cm) tall. Usually 6–9 true tepals with several inner fragmentary pieces. Fast growing, usually flowering 4–5 weeks after planting. Usually 2 scapes from 8.5–9.5 in. (22–24 cm) circumference and usually 3 from 11–12 in. (28–30 cm) maximum circumference bulbs. Ideal for multiple plantings in a large pot (Plate 7-4).

'Ragtime'

Breeder: Hadeco (Pty) Ltd (South Africa); Launched: 1998; Classification: Symphony Double.

Description: Usually 3–4 fully double, upward-facing, orient-red blooms 7–8.5 in. (18–22 cm) diameter per scape 12 in. (30 cm) tall. Usually 6–12 tepals and 2–7 petaloids or petaloid stamens per flower. Usually 1 scape from 8.5–9.5 in. (22–24 cm) circumference and 2 from 12–13 in. (30–33 cm) maximum circumference bulbs. Plenty of upright foliage at the time of flowering creates a wonderful bushy effect.

'Red Charm'

Breeder: Miyake Nursery (Japan); Plant Breeders' Rights: 1999; Classification: (Medium Double).

Description: Usually 4–6 cherry-red blooms 6–6.5 in. (15–16 cm) diameter per scape 18 in. (45 cm) tall. Often only 6–7 true tepals and 5–6 petaloids or petaloid stamens. Normal and distorted stigmas are sometimes present. All foliage develops several weeks after flowering. Usually 6–8 weeks from planting to flowering. Usually 2 scapes from 11–12 in. (28–30 cm) circumference and 3 from 12–13 in. (30–33 cm) circumference bulbs.

'Red Nymph'

Breeder: T. van Nieuwkerk Amaryllis B.V. (The Netherlands); Classification: (Large Double).

Description: Usually 4 bright red blooms 10–12 in. (25–30 cm) diameter per scape 16–18 in. (40–45 cm) tall. Usually 15–18 broad, white-tipped tepals per flower and 1–3 petaloids.

'Red Peacock'

Breeder: Miyake Nursery (Japan); Plant Breeders' Rights: 1996; Classification: (Large Double).

Description: Usually 4–6 upward-facing, bright red blooms 6.5–6.75 in. (16–17 cm) diameter per scape 14–22 in. (35–55 cm) tall. A thin white streak runs down the length of some tepals leading to thickened white tepal tips which are the remnants of filaments. Normal stamens and a stigma are rarely present. Usually 13–19 tepals and up to 6 petaloids per flower. A particularly robust hybrid with usually 2 stout scapes from 12–13 in. (30–33 cm) circumference or 3 from 13.5–15 in. (34–38 cm) circumference bulbs. Mature, dark green foliage may be present at the time of flowering (Plate 7-5).

Pink Doubles

'Pink Nymph'

Breeder: T. van Nieuwkerk Amaryllis B.V. (The Netherlands); Classification: (Large Double).

Description: Usually 4 deep pink blooms 8.5–10 in. (22–25 cm) diameter per scape 16–18 in. (40–45 cm) tall. Several petaloid stamens are present as white streaks along the length or at the tip of some tepals with a cluster of fragmentary pieces towards the center of the flower.

'Rozetta'

Breeder: Hadeco (Pty) Ltd (South Africa); Plant Breeders' Rights: 1998; Classification: Symphony Double.

Description: Usually 4–6 rose and white streaked, horizontal, loosely constructed, often irregularly shaped and messy blooms 7.5–8.5 in. (19–22 cm) diameter per scape 12–16 in. (30–40 cm) tall. Scapes are particularly thick and blooms have an attractive green center. Usually 8–12 tepals and up to 7 petaloids or petaloid stamens per flower. Usually 1 scape from 8.5–9.5 in. (22–24 cm) circumference or 2 from 11–12 in. (28–30 cm) circumference bulbs. Bulbs reach a maximum size of 12–13 in. (30–33 cm) circumference.

Orange-Salmon Doubles

'Chianti'

Breeder: T. van Nieuwkerk Amaryllis B.V. (The Netherlands); Classification: (Large Double).

Description: Usually 4 sunset-orange blooms with a hint of white 8–8.5 in. (20–22 cm) diameter per scape 16–18 in. (40–45 cm) tall.

'Unique'

Breeder: Kwekersvereniging Amaryl (The Netherlands); Plant Breeders' Rights: 1992; Classification: (Midi Double).

Description: Usually 5–6 bright orange wispy blooms 6–6.5 in. (15–16 cm) diameter per scape 16–18 in. (40–45 cm) tall. This delicate and unusual hybrid with cream stripes typically has 10–12 tepals and 3–6 petaloids or petaloid stamens per flower. Usually 2 scapes from 11–12 in. (28–30 cm) circumference or 3 from 12–13 in. (30–33 cm) circumference bulbs. By 2003 'Unique' had failed to become popular with British gardeners.

Salmon Pink Doubles

'Andes'

Breeder: Miyake Nursery (Japan); Plant Breeders' Rights: 1995; Classification: (Large Double).

Description: Usually 3–4 salmon-pink blooms 6.5–7 in. (16–18 cm) diameter per scape 12–15 in. (30–38 cm) tall. Flowers vary in shape, color and doubleness, with up to 16 tepals and 11 petaloids or petaloid stamens per flower. Usually 2 scapes from 12–13 in. (30–33 cm) circumference, sometimes 3 from 13–13.5 in. (33–34 cm) circumference bulbs. Due to rooting difficulties and susceptibility to rotting, 'Andes' has never become widely available and may be discontinued in the future.

'Lady Jane'

Breeder: John W. Deme (United States); Plant Breeders' Rights: 1995; Classification: (Large Double).

Description: Usually 2–3 (occasionally 4) salmon-pink or orange-pink blooms 6.5–8 in. (16–20 cm) diameter per scape 12–22 in. (30–55 cm) tall with white and darker orange stripes. Usually 15–18 tepals and 3–5 petaloids or petaloid stamens per flower. The long 3.25–3.5 in. (8–9 cm) pedicels often result in slight drooping of the weighty blooms. Usually 2 scapes from 13 in. (33 cm) circumference or 3 from 13–14 in. (33–35 cm) circumference bulbs. Formerly 'Judy Weston'.

'Salmon Peacock'

Breeder: Penning Breeding B.V. (The Netherlands); Plant Breeders' Rights: 1999; Classification: (Large Double).

Description: Usually 4–6 usually semi-double, upward-facing, salmon blooms 6–8 in. (15–20 cm) diameter per scape 12–16 in. (30–40 cm) tall. Usually 9–10 tepals and up to 10 petaloids or petaloid stamens per flower are combined with particularly thick, robust, pale green scapes. A stigma is sometimes present. The presence of luxuriant foliage at the time of flowering creates a magical effect, making this hybrid an ideal pot plant. Usually 5 weeks from planting to flowering. Usually 2 scapes from 11–12 in. (28–30 cm) circumference or 3 from 14.25–15 in. (36–38 cm) circumference bulbs (Plate 7-6).

White Doubles

'Alfresco'

Breeder: Hadeco (Pty) Ltd (South Africa); Plant Breeders' Rights: 1999; Classification: Sonata Double.

Description: Usually 5–8 cream, peony-shaped blooms 6 in. (15 cm) diameter per scape 12–18 in. (30–45 cm) tall with a delightful yellow-green heart. The weighty triple blooms with 18 or more tepals are arranged into 3–4 layers and droop slightly. A few petaloids may be present towards the center of the flower. Foliage develops mainly after flowering. Usually 5–6 weeks from planting to flowering and usually 2 scapes from 8–8.5 in. (20–22 cm) circumference and 3 from 11–12 in. (28–30 cm) circumference bulbs (Plate 7-7).

'Jewel'

Breeder: Miyake Nursery (Japan); Plant Breeders' Rights: 1992; Classification: (Midi, Semi Double).

Description: Usually 2–4 cream, slightly fragrant, semi-double, waxen, narrow, pointed, trumpet-shaped blooms 6–6.5 in. (15–16 cm) diameter per scape 14–20 in. (35–50 cm) tall. Occasionally flowers are fully double or single, but more often semi-double with 6 tepals and a corona comprising up to 6 petaloids or petaloid stamens. A distorted stigma is sometimes present. The yellowish-green throat is lined with a ring of dark red dots.

Up to 15 dark green leaves with a matt finish remain fresh for around 10 months (including the cool period) and reach a maximum of 19.5–22 in. (49–55 cm) long and 1 in. (2.5 cm) wide with a central keel. Usually 2 scapes from 12–13 in. (30–33 cm) circumference and 3 from 12.5–13.5 in. (32–34 cm) circumference bulbs (Plate 7-8).

Mature 'Jewel' bulbs show a propensity to split into two following flowering, each segment having 5–7 leaves. Nine months later, after having begun to divide at the neck, each half had become a separate bulb, joined only at the basal plate (Plate 8-9). Following an 8-week cool period, each half put forward new scapes and new foliage, the old foliage showing no signs of dying back. By September 2003, each half had developed 7–9 mature leaves.

'My Favourite'

Breeder: Hadeco (Pty) Ltd (South Africa); Launched: 1998; Classification: Symphony Double.

Description: 4–5 snow white, fully double blooms 9.5 in. (24 cm) diameter per scape 16 in. (40 cm) tall with reddish brown streaks on a white background. Usually 12–18, undulating, frilly edged tepals and up to 7 petaloids or petaloid stamens per flower.

'Snow White'

Breeder: Hadeco (Pty) Ltd (South Africa); Launched: 1998; Classification: Symphony Double.

Description: Usually 3–4 loosely constructed, snow-white, messy blooms, 6–7 in. (16–18 cm) diameter per scape 16–20 in. (40–50 cm) tall. Usually 11–19, irregular, pointed, undulating, frilly edged tepals which reflex at the tips and up to 7 petaloids per flower. Most foliage develops after flowering. Usually 5–6 weeks from planting to flowering. Usually 1 scape from 8–8.5 in. (20–22 cm) circumference and 2 from 12–12.5 in. (30–32 cm) circumference bulbs.

'White Nymph'

Breeder: T. van Nieuwkerk Amaryllis B.V. (The Netherlands); Plant Breeders' Rights: 2002; Classification: (Large Double).

Description: Usually 4 snow-white, frilly edged blooms with a bright green throat, 8.5–10 in. (22–25 cm) diameter per scape 16–18 in. (40–45 cm) tall. Both petaloid stamens and normal stamens are sometimes present towards the center of the flower.

'White Peacock'

Breeder: Miyake Nursery (Japan); Plant Breeders' Rights: 1997; Classification: (Large Double).

Description: Usually 4–6 snow-white, horizontal or slightly upward-facing blooms 8–8.5 in. (20–22 cm) diameter per scape 8–12 in. (20–30 cm) tall. Often 11–15 pointed tepals and 4–6 petaloids or petaloid stamens per flower. The flowers become whiter with age and produce little pollen. A stigma is usually absent. A gap of up to 7 days between the maturing of individual pairs of flowers is normal and the final pair sometimes fails to reach maturity and withers. The very short, stout scapes distinguish this hybrid from others in the Peacock Group and sometimes make the blooms appear slightly disproportionate. Foliage develops after flowering has finished. Usually 7–8 weeks from planting to flowering.

White and Red, Red and White or Orange and White Doubles

'Allure'

Breeder: Miyake Nursery (Japan); Plant Breeders' Rights: 1995; Classification: (Large Double).

Description: Usually 4 white and orange-red, slightly drooping blooms 7.5 in. (19 cm) diameter per scape 18 in. (45 cm) tall with a thin red picotee and white central band along the length of each tepal. Up to 19, curved, wavy edged tepals and 5 petaloids or petaloid stamens per flower. Individual flowers have shown a remarkable variation in the degree of doubleness, shape and shade of orange-red. The proportion of orange-red to white also varies.

'Dancing Queen'

Breeder: Penning Breeding B.V. (The Netherlands); Plant Breeders' Rights: 1998; Classification: (Large Double).

Description: Usually 3–4 broad, red and white striped, loosely constructed, frilly edged, dramatic blooms 8–8.5 in. (20–22 cm) diameter per scape 20–22.5 in. (50–57 cm) tall. Usually 12–14 tepals reach 1.5–3 in. (4–7.5 cm) wide with several petaloid stamens per flower. Normal stamens and a normal or distorted stigma are also sometimes present. The thick, 1.9 in. (5.0 cm) long pedicles are often unable to sustain the very weighty blooms which droop soon after opening. Usually 5–6 weeks from planting to flowering. Usually 2 scapes from 10.5–11 in. (26–28 cm) circumference and 3 from 13.5–14.25 in. (34–36 cm) circumference bulbs (Plate 7-13).

'Double Queen'

Breeder: T. van Nieuwkerk Amaryllis B.V. (The Netherlands); Plant Breeders' Rights: 1999; Classification: (Midi Double).

Description: Usually 4 orange and white striped, medium-flowering compact blooms 6 in. (15 cm) diameter per scape 12 in. (30 cm) tall.

'Elvas'

Breeder: Stapoflor, Lda (The Netherlands); Plant Breeders' Rights: 1999; Classification: (Midi Double).

Description: Usually 3–4 exquisite, snow-white, rounded blooms 5–6 in. (13–15 cm) diameter per scape 12–16 in. (30–40 cm) tall with a fine, red picotee. Usually 15 tepals and 2–3 petaloids or petaloid stamens per flower. Foliage develops after flowering. Usually 7–8 weeks from planting to flowering.

'Flaming Peacock'

Breeder: Miyake Nursery (Japan); Plant Breeders' Rights: 2002; Classification: Large Double.

Description: Usually 6 exquisitely proportioned, red and white 6.75 in. (17 cm) diameter per scape 16–20 in. (40–50 cm) tall. Flowers vary considerably in the proportion of white to red from one season to the next. Usually 15 tepals and few petaloids or petaloid stamens per flower. Up to 9 broad, upright leaves 24 in. (60 cm) tall are usually present at the time of flowering creating a marvelous full effect. Usually 7–8 weeks from planting to flowering. Usually 2 scapes from 12 in. (30 cm) circumference and 3 from 13.5–14.25 in. (34–36 cm) circumference bulbs (Plates 7-9, 7-10).

'Fluffy Ruffles'

Breeder: Hadeco (Pty) Ltd (South Africa); Launched: 1998; Classification: Symphony Double.

Description: Usually 4–5 snow-white blooms 8.25 in. (21 cm) diameter per scape 9.5 in. (24 cm) tall with feathery red stripes on the inside of the 3 upper tepals. Usually 4–5 weeks from planting to flowering. Usually 1 scape from 8.5–9.5 in. (22–24 cm) circumference and 2 from 11–12 in. (28–30 cm) circumference bulbs.

'Joker'

Breeder: Hadeco (Pty) Ltd, (South Africa), Plant Breeders' Rights: 1999; Classification: Sonata Double.

Description: Usually 4–5 maroon and white blooms 4.5 in. (12 cm) diameter per scape 8–12 in. (20–30 cm) tall with a fine red picotee. A very fast growing hybrid, sometimes flowering after only 10–14 days but normally after 3–4 weeks. New shoots appear after 6 weeks at 55°F (13°C). Foliage develops after flowering. Usually 1 scape from 8.5–9.5 in. (22–24 cm) circumference and 2, sometimes 3, from 10.5 to 11 in. (26–28 cm) circumference bulbs (Plate 7-14).

'Pasadena'

Breeder: John W. Deme (United States) (?); Plant Breeders' Rights: 1995; Classification: (Midi Double).

Description: Usually 4–6 scarlet blooms 5.75–6 in. (14–16 cm) diameter per scape 25.5–33.5 in. (65–85 cm) tall with a white, central star. A ring of red dots lines the base of the yellowish lime green throat. Usually 6–12 tepals and up to 7 petaloids or petaloid stamens per flower. Small amounts of pollen are sometimes produced from normal or embedded anthers. Occasionally a stigma is present. The 2 in. (5 cm) long pedicels result in a slight drooping of the flowers. Usually 2 scapes from 12–12.5 in. (30–32 cm) circumference and 3 from 12.5–13.5 in. (32–34 cm) circumference bulbs. Foliage usually develops after flowering.

'Philadelphia'

Breeder: Fa. G. van Staalduinen (The Netherlands); Plant Breeders' Rights: 1998; Classification: Small Double (Midi Double).

Description: Usually 3–4 white, rounded blooms 6 in. (15 cm) diameter per scape 14–16 in. (35–40 cm) tall with brownish-reddish streaks. Several petaloids or petaloid stamens are usually present. This hybrid has proved particularly easy to cultivate in Great Britain with many gardeners regularly achieving two flowering periods each year.

'Promise'

Breeder: Penning Breeding B.V. (The Netherlands); Plant Breeders' Rights: 2002; Classification: (Large Double).

Description: Usually 4 exquisitely proportioned and sculptured, bright red and white, fully double blooms 7–8 in. (18–20 cm) diameter per scape 14–18 in. (35–45 cm) tall. The broad, slightly pointed tepals have a thick central white stripe surrounded with delightful feathery venation. Up to 8 luxuriant green, upright leaves 10–12 in. (25–30 cm) tall, 1.5 in. (4 cm) wide with inward curving margins enhance the appearance of this beautiful hybrid. Usually 7 weeks from planting to flowering. Mostly 2 scapes from 10.5–11 in. (26–28 cm) circumference and 3 from 13.5–14.25 in. (34–36 cm) circumference bulbs (Plate 8-4).

'Rainbow'

Breeder: Miyake Nursery (Japan); Plant Breeders' Rights: 1992; Classification: (Large Double).

Description: Usually 2–5 snow-white and red blooms 8–8.5 in. (20–22 cm) diameter per scape 18–25.5 in. (45–65 cm) tall with a pencil-thin red picotee and delightful bright green throat. Up to 17 tepals and 4 petaloids or petaloid stamens per flower. The 3–3.25 in. (7–8 cm) long pedicels often result in drooping of the weighty blooms. Tiny, apple-green, sharply pointed florets often emerge prematurely from the spathe leaves with a mere hint of the fine red picotee and take up to 10 days to attain their final shape, size and color. Usually 7 weeks from planting to flowering. Usually 2 scapes from 12–12.5 in. (30–32 cm) circumference and 3 from 13.5–14.25 in. (34–36 cm) circumference bulbs.

'Razzmatazz'

Breeder: Hadeco (Pty) Ltd (South Africa); Date of Registration: 1997; Classification: Symphony Semi-Double.

Description: Usually 4–5 bright red, dramatic, exquisitely veined red and white, slightly frilly edged blooms 7–8 in. (18–20 cm) diameter per scape 10–14 in. (25–35 cm) tall. Usually 6–9 tepals and a corona of 4–6 petaloids or petaloid stamens per flower. A broad central white streak runs the length of each normal tepal. Foliage is usually present at the time of flowering. Usually 4–5 weeks from planting to flowering. Usually 1 scape from 8–8.5 in. (20–22 cm) circumference and 2 from 11–12 in. (28–30 cm) circumference bulbs.

'Rio'

Breeder: Hadeco (Pty) Ltd (South Africa); Available: 1999; Classification: 'Symphony' Double.

Description: Usually 4 broad, sharply pointed, frilly edged, rose-red and white blooms 8 in. (20 cm) diameter per scape 10 in. (25 cm) tall. Usually 12–13 tepals and 4–6 petaloid stamens or structures per flower. Mature leaves are usually present at the time of flowering. Usually 4–5 weeks from planting to flowering. Usually 1 scape from 9.5–10.5 in. (24–26 cm) circumference and 2 from 12–12.5 in. (30–32 cm) circumference bulbs.

White and Pink or Pink and White Doubles

'Aphrodite'

Breeder: Miyake Nursery (Japan); Date of Registration: 1994; Classification: (Large Double).

Description: Usually 5–6 white and pale pink blooms 8.25–9 in. (21–23 cm) diameter per scape 14–18 in. (35–45 cm) tall edged with a darker pink. Usually 13–17, broad, pointed tepals and 3–10 petaloids or petaloid stamens per flower. Small quantities of pollen are usually produced. There is often a gap of 7–10 days between the opening of individual pairs of flowers which often droop from the 3.5 in. (9 cm) long pedicels. Usually 8 weeks from planting to flowering. Usually 2 scapes from 12–12.5 in. (30–32 cm) circumference and 3 from 13.5–14.5 in. (34–36 cm) circumference bulbs (Plate 7-11).

'Blossom Peacock'

Breeder: Miyake Nursery (Japan); Plant Breeders' Rights: 1997; Classification: (Large Double).

Description: Usually 5–6 well-proportioned pink and white, slightly fragrant blooms 6.75–7 in. (17–18 cm) diameter per scape 18–22 in. (45–55 cm) tall. Usually 15–18 tepals and up to 2 petaloid stamens or structures as well as normal stamens. Usually 7–8 weeks from planting to flowering. Usually 2 scapes from 12–12.5 in. (30–32 cm) circumference and 3 from 12.5–13.5 in. (32–34 cm) circumference bulbs. Suitable for mass plantings in flower beds.

'Double Record'

Breeder: John W. Deme (United States) (?); Plant Breeders' Rights: 1990; Classification: (Midi Double).

Description: Usually 5–6, pale pink and white, frilly edged, long-lasting, pointed-tipped blooms 4.75–6.5 in. (12.5–16 cm) diameter per scape 14–18 in. (35–45 cm) tall with a red picotee and yellow-green throat lined with a ring of red dots. Usually 9–15 tepals and 2–4 petaloid stamens/structures. Normal stamens and a normal or distorted stigma may also be present. Usually 2 scapes from 12–12.5 in. (30–32 cm) circumference, usually 3 from 12–13 in. (32–34 cm) circumference bulbs. Foliage develops after flowering. The International Cultivar Registration Authority indicates that Deme is the breeder but doubt exists as to whether this is correct.

'Mary Lou'

Breeder: Miyake Nursery (Japan); Plant Breeders' Rights: 1992; Classification: (Large Double).

Description: Usually 4–6 cream and pale pink, semi or fully double blooms 8.25–8.5 in. (21–22 cm) diameter per scape 18–22 in. (45–55 cm) tall which glisten in the sunlight. Usually 6–17, broad, rounded, waxen-like tepals and up to 10 petaloids or petaloid stamens per flower. Semi double blooms with 7–11 tepals often have a corona of up to 10 petaloids or petaloid stamens. Foliage usually develops after flowering. Usually 7–8 weeks from planting to flowering. Usually 2 scapes from 12–12.5 in. (30–32 cm) circumference and 3 from 12.5–13.5 in. (32–34 cm) circumference bulbs.

'Nymph'

Breeder: T. van Nieuwkerk Amaryllis B.V. (The Netherlands); Plant Breeders' Rights: 1995; Classification: (Large Double).

Description: Usually 4 compact, cream, peony-shaped blooms 8.5–10 in. (22–25 cm) diameter per scape 14–18 in. (35–45 cm) tall with stripes of soft pink-brown. Up to 14 tepals per flower with several petaloids or petaloid stamens per flower (Plate 7-12). Normal stamens are sometimes also present. This hybrid is cultivated as a cut flower and looks magnificent in large formal arrangements when decorated with luxuriant foliage and other ornaments (Plate 7-12).

Chapter 8
Structure and Development

Whether grown from seed, offset, chip or twin scale, some Hippeastrum bulbs may reach 20 in. (50 cm) circumference in less than 3 years, produce up to 20 blooms each year and live for 15–20 years, even longer in some cases. The capacity for such development is truly wonderful. But regardless of the type of hippeastrum—its bulb size, floriferousness or longevity—it is important to understand the plant's structure and the processes involved in its development. Such understanding enables a fuller appreciation of hippeastrums and their requirement for successful cultivation. Chapter 8 describes the structure and development of modern hybrids from seed to mature bulb.

Bulb Structure and Development

Stage 1—Seedling to Bulblet

Although most mature bulbs which are sold today are the result of vegetative, or asexual reproduction, all new hippeastrums begin life as a seed. Within a few days of sowing freshly harvested seed, germination takes place. The first root may be visible after only 24–48 hours, but 4–14 days is typical. A few days later a small leaf appears, a miniature version of a mature leaf, closely followed by a second small leaf 2–3 weeks later. After 14–16 weeks, 3 or 4, occasionally 5, small leaves will have developed. Providing environmental conditions remain favorable, further leaves will develop until 9 have been produced. This stage may last for up to 12 months and will depend on many factors including cultural conditions.

Formation of the bulb begins at a very early stage. Within a month of sowing seed, a tiny bulb has already formed consisting of a shortened flattened stem. Fleshy modified leaves develop on top of this shortened stem and comprise the major part of the bulb. The modified leaves, together with the flattened stem, serve as storage organs, containing reserves of carbohydrates which help sustain the plant. Even when the true leaves have died, the fleshy bases continue to provide sustenance for the plant until they are exhausted and have become brown and papery. They will eventually peel off or decompose in the soil. Underneath the flattened stem is a disc known as the basal plate from which roots develop.

Slowly the bulb acquires its distinctive shape, enabling it to be identified from the bulbs of other hybrids. Some bulbs, such as that of Hippeastrum 'Tango', have slender necks composed of residual leaf bases with gently sloping shoulders and sleek, pear- or oval-shaped bodies (Plate 8-1). Others have broad, tall or short necks with flat, spherical bodies (Plate 8-2), and sometimes the neck is barely visible. Some bulbs have a symmetrical shape while others are irregular and may appear lopsided (Plate 8-3). Offsets usually have a flat side towards the main bulb. The protective outer papery layers of some hippeastrums display attractive shades of brown, pink and cream which, when removed, reveal the creamy white fleshy leaf bases underneath.

Unlike the outer leaf bases of most hybrids which become dry and papery after 2–3 months of active growth, those of *Hippeastrum* 'Germa' and some Brazilian-bred hybrids remain intact, tough and crispy for more than 12 months.

Stage 2—Mature Bulb

After a bulb develops 9 leaves, the first inflorescence is initiated which frequently aborts. Reasons for this remain inconclusive; probably it is due to insufficient food reserves to sustain the development of the florets.

Blaauw (1931), Hayashi and Suzuki (1970) and Rees (1972) discovered that, following the aborted inflorescence, a branching system is established comprising a series of units (or sympodia). Each unit is made up of 4 leaves and an inflorescence. As a new leaf emerges, a new bulb layer is formed. The first 3 leaves of each unit have a circular base, the fourth and youngest leaf is semisheathing. Following the initiation of the inflorescence which develops within the axil of the fourth leaf, the unit is complete. At the same time, a new lateral growing point is initiated on the side of the apex away from the last leaf. As this new point continues to grow, the first leaf of the next unit appears on the same side as the previous inflorescence. Three more leaves develop followed by another inflorescence and the pattern continues. Many bulbous plants with a branched structure produce only one new bulb unit each year, unlike hippeastrums which produce several units. A healthy, mature bulb contains around 6 units.

Contrary to popular belief, *Hippeastrum* hybrids are evergreen and do not require a resting period. Providing the bulb remains healthy and conditions remain favorable, new leaves and inflorescences are initiated throughout the year (although leaf emergence is more rapid in summer), thereby maintaining a state of equilibrium between emerged and unemerged growth. Hayashi and Suzuki (1970) found the most favorable day/night temperatures to be 73/64°F (23/18°C). Higher temperatures of 82/73°F (28/23°C) promoted foliage initiation (5–6 leaves) but inhibited floral development. The amount or quality of daylight did not affect flower or leaf initiation, but after emerging from the bulb, scape, floral and foliage quality were adversely affected by poor lighting.

When grown from seed, the time for a hybrid bulb to reach maturity and be capable of producing 2–3 scapes and 8–18 leaves each year varies considerably. It may be as short as 2 growing seasons of 8–9 months each when grown under commercial conditions, but up to 6 years when grown at home where light conditions are often less than ideal. Up to 3% of some large-flowering Dutch hybrid bulbs grown from seed or twin scaling may reach 14 in. (36 cm) circumference after only 14 months of continuous growth! After a third season's growth, bulbs should reach their maximum size which ranges from 4 to 20 in. (10–50 cm) circumference, depending on the cultivar.

Bulb Weight and Circumference

Research by Rees (1972) and Doorduin (1990) showed little increase in fresh weight and a slight decrease in dry bulb weight during the winter as foliage development was reduced. Within 7–14 days of lifting, commercially cultivated bulbs will have shrunk a size, for example, from 13.5–14.25 in. (34–36 cm) to 12.5–13.5 in. (32–34 cm) circumference, as moisture is removed, resulting in an increase in dry matter content. About 4.5 in. (12 cm) of leaf base circumference is lost from the outside of the bulb as leaf bases become papery and finally peel off. Providing environmental and cultural conditions remain favorable throughout periods of rapid growth, such losses are replaced by a similar amount from within the bulb, but this can sometimes prove difficult in noncommercial environments.

During winter, new leaves and inflorescences are initiated within the bulb, but no bulb expansion takes place as development is at the expense of food materials stored in the leaf bases. The bulb's circumference continues to decrease during winter. As light and temperature begin to improve in the spring and throughout the summer, new roots and foliage develop, food manufacture increases, dry bulb weight decreases and fresh weight increases as the bulb expands in girth.

Considerable shrinkage often occurs when newly purchased bulbs (usually new season's stock, but occasionally old stock harvested 12 or more months previously) are planted in late autumn and winter. Substantial food reserves are utilized to sustain the development of the rapidly emerging scape(s). These may prove insufficient, particularly when several scapes emerge simultaneously or in close succession, each bearing 4–8 blooms. The situation is exacerbated when there are few or no roots, no foliage and poor lighting. The effects are even more pronounced in old, dry bulbs.

Despite regular feeding throughout spring to early autumn with a balanced fertilizer containing trace elements, it may prove difficult, if not impossible, to reverse bulb shrinkage in some home situations. This is partly due to unfavorable light conditions during most months of the year in some Northern Hemisphere countries. Some bulbs may be reduced to a shell after flowering and may fail to recover sufficiently to bloom again. Major improvements in bulb growth occur when plants are given lighting from 600-watt sodium lights combined with the Kew mix and an intensive feeding regime (see Chapter 9).

Relationship Between Bulb Circumference, Flower Type and Scape Production

Table 8-1 shows the number of scapes which can be expected from Dutch and South African hybrids across a range of bulb sizes in the first year after purchase. Smaller flowering types with blooms less than 6.5 in. (16 cm) diameter generally produce more scapes from smaller bulbs compared with larger flowering hybrids. Irrespective of flower size, larger bulbs of all hybrid types generally produce more scapes in the first year after purchase. The bulbs, together with foliage and flowers, increase until the maximum size is reached for a particular cultivar.

Depending on their stage of growth at the time of lifting and subsequent bulb preparation, 2 or 3, occasionally 4 scapes may develop simultaneously or in close succession with a gap of 7–14 days or less between the appearance of each scape (see Chapter 10 for ideal timings). Under conducive cultural and environmental conditions, and providing the plant remains in optimal health, 1 or 2 additional scapes may appear during late summer or early autumn. This often happens after 4–6 weeks at 45–59°F (12–15°C) followed by a return to warmer conditions of 70–86°F (21–30°C). While 4 scapes may be possible in the first season as a result of growers' practices, a maximum of 3 scapes is the norm in subsequent years.

Root Structure, Development and Production

Research by Rimbach (1929) and De Hertogh and Tilley (1991) identified 2 root types—basal, contracting (also referred to as contractile) roots which originated from the basal plate, and thinner, secondary branching roots which grew laterally from the basal roots (Plate 11-13). These branching roots have hairs which increase the absorptive surface to take up water and essential nutrients from the soil for healthy growth.

Basal roots anchor the bulb firmly and, by contracting, pull the bulb down into the soil, essential for 36 in. (90 cm) tall, heavy plants. Large, healthy, mature bulbs may develop up to 70 new basal roots in a year and these may reach 24 in. (60 cm) long. They often coil snakelike around the inside of the pot forming a dense mass and some may appear on the surface where they look like mini drain pipes. Providing roots remain healthy and undisturbed and receive sufficient moisture throughout the year, they can survive for up to a year, possibly longer.

Root development is cultivar specific and is influenced by cultural conditions and the presence of pest and diseases. Some freshly purchased bulbs produce new roots within a few weeks following planting; others are much slower, producing few roots or none until several weeks or months later. The lack of roots makes plants liable to topple at the slightest knock causing serious damage to inflorescences and foliage. Although some plants may develop normal length scapes and blooms with few or no roots, they are more often stunted and rubbery with smaller, underdeveloped and poorly pigmented blooms. Poor root development which persists during the summer can have a major adverse effect upon bulb, foliage and future

Table 8-1. Relationship between scape production, bulb circumference and flower diameter of modern Dutch and South African hybrids.

Origin	Flower type and diameter in inches (cm)	Bulb circumference in inches (cm) and number of scapes: 1 scape	2 scapes	3 scapes
Dutch hybrids	Large: 6.5 in. (16 cm) and over	6.5–8 in. (16–20 cm)	Usually 10.5–11 in. (26–28 cm), 11–12 in. (28–30 cm) and over	Usually 12 in. (30 cm) and over
	Medium: 4.5–6.5 in. (12–16 cm)	5.75–7 in. (14–18 cm)	Usually 9.5–10.5 in. (24–26 cm) and over	Usually 11–12 in. (28–30 cm) and over
	Small: 4–4.5 in. (10–12 cm)	5.75–6.5 in. (14–16 cm)	Usually 8–9.5 in. (20–24 cm) and over	Usually 10–11 in. (25–28 cm) and over
South African hybrids	Symphony: 6.5 in. (16 cm) and over	Usually 7–9.5 in. (18–24 cm)	Usually 10.5–13.5 in. (26–34 cm)	Usually 12 in. (30 cm) and over
	Sonata: 4.0–6.5 in. (10–16 cm)	Usually 7–9.5 in. (18–24 cm)	Usually 9.5–11 in. (24–28 cm)	Usually 11–12 in. (28–30 cm)
	Sonatini[a]: 2.5–4.0 in. (6–10 cm)	Usually 5.75–6 in. (14–16 cm)	Usually 7–8 in. (18–20 cm)	Usually 9.5 in. (24 cm)

[a] Maximum diameter for Sonatini cut flowers under development by Andre Barnhoorn is 3.5 in. (9 cm).

Sources: Dutch—Marko Penning, Penning Breeding B.V., Honselersdijk, The Netherlands. South African—Floris Barnhoorn, Hadeco (Pty) Ltd, Maraisburg, South Africa.

inflorescence development. It is therefore important to identify the cause as early as possible and take appropriate remedial action.

Scape Development

All aspects of the hollow scape (that is, height, circumference, color and texture) are cultivar specific and are influenced by environment and cultivation practices. After emerging from the bulb, scapes elongate rapidly by up to 2 in. (5 cm) a day when cultivated at 70–77°F (21–25°C), until the maximum length is reached (see Chapters 3–7 for details of individual cultivars).

Many small- and medium-flowering singles and doubles, such as *Hippeastrum* 'Emerald', *H.* 'Fanfare', *H.* 'Germa', *H.* 'Pamela' and *H.* 'Salmon Pearl', have slender scapes of 1.5–2 in. (4–5 cm) circumference. Others, such as *H.* 'Calimero', *H.* 'Carina', *H.* 'Fairytale' and *H.* 'Moviestar', have broader 2.75–3 in. (7–7.75 cm) circumference scapes which reach 20–30 in. (50–75 cm) tall. Some Japanese Super Mini and South African Sonatini hybrids have particularly short 6–8.5 in. (15–22 cm) slender scapes.

Some Dutch and Japanese large-flowering singles and doubles have much taller scapes reaching 24–36 in. (60–90 cm) and 3.5–4 in. (9–10 cm) circumference while 16–22 in. (40–55 cm) is typical for those grown under optimal conditions. A few, such as *Hippeastrum* 'White Peacock' and *H.* 'Angelique', have unusually short, broad 3.25–4 in. (8–10 cm) circumference scapes which resemble mini tree trunks and may appear disproportionate to their spectacular blooms. Several Dutch and American Cybisters reach 30 in. (75 cm) tall.

Scapes usually come in various shades of green. Several smaller flowering cultivars such as *Hippeastrum* 'Calimero' and *H.* 'Toledo' have attractive shades of pink-brown to pink-red which are particularly prominent at the base. Others have purple-red (*H.* 'Flamengo', *H.* 'Reggae'), wine-red (*H.* 'Chico'), purple-green (*H.* 'Rapido', *H.* 'Starlet'), purple-brown (*H.* 'Charisma'), green-gray (*H.* 'Cyber Queen', *H.* 'Merengue'), gray-brown (*H.* 'Tango'), gray-purple (*H.* 'Tinto') or brown scapes (*H.* 'Bianca', *H.* 'White Equester III', *H.* 'Yellow Goddess'). Some retain their color along the entire length of the scape while others revert to green as they become longer. Some Japanese hybrids have spotted or variegated scapes (Plate 6-5).

When the scape reaches a certain height, flowers start to develop. Following fertilization, the scape remains rigid until the capsules have ripened and the seeds are released. Then it becomes limp, soft and weak, wrinkled and drained of its former color, eventually collapsing and becoming dry and papery, at which point it can be easily removed from the neck of the bulb. If fertilization does not take place, the scape may collapse 1–3 days after the final bloom has withered or up to a month later.

Leaf and Flower Initiation

Research by Joop Doorduin (1990) at the Glasshouse Crops Research Station, Naaldwijk (The Netherlands) using *Hippeastrum* 'Red Lion' and

H. 'Apple Blossom' bulbs revealed 4 leaves and an inflorescence to be initiated every 11.5 and 13 weeks respectively. During a 52-week period *H.* 'Red Lion' bulbs produced 16–18 leaves compared with *H.* 14–16 for *H.* 'Apple Blossom'. On average 3.75 and 4.25 buds were initiated respectively, indicating that when bulbs are grown over a long period, there is a relationship between the numbers of emerging leaves and buds. These results supported the earlier findings of Blaauw (1931), Hayashi and Suzuki (1971) and Rees (1972). Based on the above figures, it would appear that a new leaf is initiated every 20–23 days.

The Naaldwijk experiments also showed that bud initiation was not influenced directly by light intensity. Even when plants were grown under poor light conditions, initiation and development of leaves and inflorescences continued, providing the bulb had sufficient food reserves. Rees (1972) demonstrated that a leaf took 3–8 months to emerge from the bulb, growth being faster during the summer, compared with 11–14 months for an inflorescence. After 4–6 weeks, the leaf reached its maximum length. Flowers usually bloomed 3–5 weeks after emerging from the bulb, but some cultivars, such as *Hippeastrum* 'Germa' and *H.* 'Picotee', were slower.

The 11.5–13 week gap between the initiation of each group of leaves resulted in each bulb unit being at a different stage of development. Leaves 1–8 of the oldest, outermost units (1 and 2) had died back, leaving only the leaf bases. Bases of the first unit had become dry and papery, all nutrients having been exhausted several weeks or months previously. Some may have

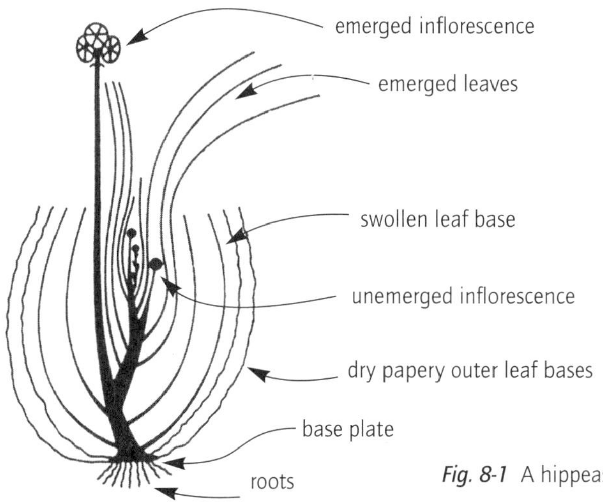

Fig. 8-1 A hippeastrum bulb with only leaf bases

disintegrated and become detached from the bulb. Leaves 9–16 of units 3 and 4 had emerged from the bulb, while leaves 17–24 of units 5 and 6 were yet to emerge.

Figure 8-1 is a diagrammatic representation of a hippeastrum bulb which has only leaf bases. Emerged parts are shown much reduced and the base plate is extended to show the bulb parts (Rees 1972).

Although a mature, healthy bulb usually contains 4 inflorescences, the 7–14 months required after initiation for one inflorescence to reach a minimum 0.75 in. (20 mm) long before emerging from the neck of the bulb means that a maximum of 3 scapes are possible in a 52-week period (see Table 8-2). The considerable variation in the speed of growth of the inflorescence is both cultivar specific and influenced by environmental conditions (for example, higher temperatures result in faster growth rates). Since an inflorescence takes longer to develop than do leaves, the first inflorescence to emerge each year appears alongside leaves which were initiated later but have already emerged from the neck of the bulb. This results in a gap of one bulb unit between the emerged inflorescence and leaves and gives the appearance that the inflorescence is lateral to the leaf tuft.

Table 8-2. Relationship between initiation, emergence and flowering of inflorescences.

Initiation (every 11.5-13 weeks) 2002	Emergence (after 11-14 months)* 2002-2003	Flowering (after 3-8 weeks)* 2002-2004
1 January 2002	End November 2002 to end February 2003	3rd week December 2002 to end April 2003
1 April 2002	End February 2003 to end May 2003	3rd week March 2003 to end July 2003
1 July 2002	End May 2003 to end August 2003	3rd week June 2003 to end October 2003
1 October 2002	End August 2003 to end November 2003	3rd week September 2003 to end January 2004

*The number of months for the scape to emerge and for newly planted bulbs to flower will be influenced by many factors including the plant's genetic make-up, preparation given prior to planting and environmental conditions. It is possible that some scapes will emerge in less than 11 months, while some bulbs will not flower for up to 10 weeks following emergence of the scape.

CHAPTER 8

Leaf Development

Crops of 3–4 leaves appear at regular intervals throughout the year when bulbs are kept in continuous growth. The leaves grow vigorously, up to 2 in. (5 cm) a day, until they reach their maximum size which is genetically determined and influenced by cultural and environmental conditions. Some large- and small-flowering hybrid leaves reach 39 in. (100 cm) long but typically are 18–24 in. (45–60 cm). Width varies from only 0.5 in. (1 cm) for some Cybisters to up to 3.5 in. (9 cm) for some large-flowering types when measured at the widest part of the leaf. Although some smaller flowering cultivars have narrower leaves, they may reach as tall as some larger flowering hybrids (*Hippeastrum* 'Amalfi', *H.* 'Calimero', *H.* 'Cyber Queen', *H.* 'Tango', *H.* 'Toledo'). The gap of only 2–4 days which may separate the development of individual leaves following their emergence from the bulb gives the impression of a cluster of leaves appearing and developing almost simultaneously. In summer, 12 or more mature leaves may be present.

As temperatures drop and daily light intervals are reduced, new leaf development is reduced. Oldest leaves turn buttercup yellow and orange before collapsing and dying. By mid to late autumn, the balance shifts between old and new foliage: more older leaves remain, resulting in a slight reduction in the total number of leaves present. During winter, a few new leaves may emerge and, together with the remaining older leaves, ensure that the plant remains in leaf throughout the year.

Leaf shape may be linear or lorate with sharply pointed or more rounded tips. Some cultivars have thick, leathery leaves with pronounced parallel venation and a distinct keel on the underside of the leaf extending the full length. With their sharply sloping sides, such leaves look more like long narrow boats. Other cultivars have thinner, flatter leaves with less visible veins. Leaves may spread out to create attractive fan shapes or remain upright. Some make grand sweeping gestures and hang over the edges of the container while others, such as *Hippeastrum* 'Salmon Peacock', flex backwards or forwards, looking more like snakes' heads.

Leaf color varies from pale to dark green, and a few Japanese hippeastrums are attractively variegated with green and cream stripes (Plate 6-5). Some cultivars have leaves tipped and edged purple, red or chestnut-brown with similar coloring on the under side, towards the base of the leaf. Leaves of some Klister hybrids (Plate 6-14) have attractive shades of brown along leaf margins and at the tips. When cultivated at particularly high temperatures of 77–86°F (25–30°C) and under high light intensities, some leaves acquire hues of chocolate brown which soon disappear when light levels and temperatures return to typical levels. As leaves age and as lighting improves, some leaves lose their glossy, silky or satin texture and become a darker, duller green, leathery and matt.

Flower Structure and Development

The hippeastrum inflorescence is distinctive in appearance, as well as in construction, comprising an umbel of 2–10 showy blooms, each connected to the top of the scape by a pedicel. By the beginning of the 21st century, flowers in shades of red (blackcurrant to orange red), carmine rose to apple blossom pink, orange, salmon, creamy yellow, pale green, cream and snow white had become available. Flower shapes and sizes vary; some are circular (Plate 3-2), others triangular (Plate 3-6), star-shaped (Plate 3-10), orchid-shaped (Plate 4-15), Cybister (Plates 6-16, 6-18, 6-19, 6-21 to 6-23, and 6-25) or trumpet-shaped (Plates 6-1, 6-20). Some are monocolored, others combine 2 or more colors to produce stunning effects (Plates 4-11, 4-13, 4-15, 6-18). A prominent trait of many species is a bright green throat. Some flowers have exquisite venation and elaborate patterns which include streaks or stripes (Plates 3-5, 3-13), spots or speckles (Plate 6-21) and/or colored edgings (Plates 3-10, 4-9). The flowers of *Hippeastrum* 'Angelique', *H.* 'Green Star', *H.* 'Sydney' and *H.* 'Tangellino', among others, have a wonderful silver frosting on the inner and/or outer side of the tepals as if studded with tiny diamonds. Individual flowers range from less than 2.5 in. (6 cm) to 12 in. (30 cm) diameter.

Flower Production

Most older, large-flowering Dutch and South African singles produce 4 blooms per scape, but an increasing number of hybrids developed since 1980 have 5 or 6 and occasionally 7or 8 blooms per scape. Many small- and medium-flowering Dutch and South African hybrids have 5 or 6 flowers per scape (*Hippeastrum* 'Charisma', *H.* 'Fairytale', *H.* 'Floris Hekker', *H.* 'Moviestar', *H.* 'Top Choice') and some are even more floriferous with up to 10 blooms per scape. Doubles may have 2–4 flowers per scape, as in *H.* 'Lady Jane', or be more floriferous, as in *H.* 'Alfresco', *H.* 'Aphrodite', *H.* 'Flaming

Peacock' and *H.* 'Red Peacock' which regularly produce 5 or 6 blooms per scape. Sometimes scapes have an odd number of blooms (*H.* 'Desert Dawn'). This is possibly due to a genetic abnormality or a failure of the flower to complete its development while still within the bulb, due to harvesting at a crucial stage in the flower's development.

Floral Initiation and Development

Blaauw (1931) divided the process of floral initiation and development into 11 stages. After the formation of 4 leaves in stage 1, initiation of the flower parts begins stage 2. Spathe leaves which enclose and protect the florets are then formed (stages 3 and 4), their size, shape and color being cultivar specific. Some are long, slender and a bright, glossy green, while others are broader, shorter with a duller complexion. Some display attractive shades of pink-red or brown when cultivated under high light intensities. Some disintegrate, turning brown and papery before the florets attain their final size and shape. Others remain fresh and upright throughout the life of the flower. It is particularly important that the spathe leaves remain green and fresh for those sold as cut flowers.

Floral development begins in stages 5 and 6. A thin creamy, leaflike bract develops in the axil of each flower. Some bracts remain erect during the flower's natural vase life, others collapse and lay limp (Plate 7-13) while still others become shriveled and papery soon after the flower opens. Bulbs flowering for the first time invariably produce a single pair of flowers, only larger bulbs produce 2, sometimes 3, occasionally 4 and rarely 5 pairs (that is, 10 flowers); the final number is cultivar specific.

Outer and inner tepal rings are initiated in stages 7 and 8 respectively and comprise the perianth made up of 6 tepals. The lower portion of each tepal is fused into a tube which varies in length and width. Some hybrids have short, broad tubes less than 1.5 in. (4 cm) long with flat, wide-open blooms and almost regularly shaped tepals, which may be broad, rounded and heavily imbricated. Others have long, slender tubes with tiny, pointed, frilly edged tepals which overlap for 25–40% of their length (Plate 7-1) and are sometimes mistaken for lilies. Tepal tips reflex to a greater or lesser extent, creating a more rounded appearance which enables the throat to be seen more clearly (Plate 4-4). Innumerable permutations lay between these extremes as a result of over 100 years of commercial breeding. Flowers exhibit bilateral symmetry whereby a line can be drawn through the middle of the uppermost to the lowermost tepal, cutting it into equal halves.

While some hybrids have tepals of similar shapes and sizes, distinct differences can be observed among the tepals of many hybrids. The uppermost tepal is usually the largest and broadest, followed by the slightly smaller, narrower, upper and lower tepal pairs. The lowermost tepal, sometimes referred to as the "beard" tepal, is usually the longest, narrowest and most pointed, an example being *Hippeastrum* 'Salmon Pearl' in which the uppermost tepal measures 1.5 in. (4 cm) diameter and 3 in. (7.5 cm) long while the beard tepal is 0.75 in. (2 cm) diameter and 3.5 in. (9 cm) long. Cybisters have even narrower tepals; those of *H.* 'Chico' range from only 0.08 to 0.5 in. (0.2 to 1 cm) diameter.

Some large-flowering hybrids, such as *Hippeastrum* 'Design', develop tepaloids, or small earlike appendages which protrude either side of the upper tepal pair but may also be present on the lowermost tepal. Bristles may also be present at the base of the throat.

The male reproductive organs develop in the next two stages. Outer and inner whorls of stamens are initiated in stages 9 and 10 respectively, each stamen comprising a long filament, culminating in the pollen-bearing anther. So far, it has proved impossible to determine exactly at which stage in the development of the anther the pollen grains are formed. Cytogenetic studies by Read at the Jodrell Laboratories, Royal Botanic Gardens, Kew, in 2002 showed meiosis has already occurred and pollen grains developed by the time the florets emerge from the bulb.

The formation of the female reproductive organs in stage 11 completes the early development of the flower. The tripartite or capitate stigma has a long style leading to the inferior ovary which is connected to the scape via the pedicel. The tripartite ovary comprises 3 carpels fused together, forming 3 chambers, each containing numerous ovules displaying axial placentation (in which the margins of the carpels grow inwards towards the center of the ovary forming 3 distinct locules). The fruit is a 3-valved capsule containing numerous black, flattened or compressed seeds (Plates 8-6 to 8-8 inclusive).

Research by Dutch growers in the 1970s showed the interval from stages 10 to 11 may be only 7–14 days, making it crucial to establish the stage buds have reached, prior to harvesting, to ensure maximum flowering of the crop.

Floral Maturity

Some inflorescences fail to complete their development and thus abort before emerging from the bulb. Research by Doorduin (1990) showed that the oldest and outermost inflorescences are always the first to abort, their flattened, brown, tissuelike remains sandwiched among the leaf bases. Some abort at a very early stage while others almost reach the neck of the bulb. Possible reasons for abortion include disease or too high temperatures during storage or growth, resulting in the plant competing for water, nutrition and hormones.

Stage 11 flower buds and inflorescences which have reached 0.75–1 in. (2–2.5 cm) long at the time of lifting, or before the commencement of the cool period, will emerge after a suitable period of storage and be capable of reaching maturity and flowering, usually 3–8 weeks after planting. Those which have reached stage 10 or less at lifting will not develop any further. Further elongation will occur during the cool period. While flowering is not usually a problem for the first floret of the umbel, other florets may not be so advanced and may therefore fail to complete their development. Others fail to reach maturity possibly due to the lack of food reserves within the bulb. This is evident with some large, floriferous doubles, including *Hippeastrum* 'Aphrodite', *H.* 'Red Peacock' and *H.* 'White Peacock' and some small-flowering singles with a high flower count, such as *H.* 'Rapido' and *H.* 'Top Choice'. The final 2 or 3 florets may fail to expand and instead turn brown or cream before dying.

Little floral development appears to take place during emergence and subsequent elongation of the scape from the bulb, but once the scape has reached its maximum length, attention is diverted to further development of the florets. Floral expansion is rapid. The spathe leaves split, revealing a cluster of upright, immature blooms, usually lacking their final color and shape (Plate 8-4). In some cases, florets are so large they force the spathe leaves to split much earlier while the scape is actively growing. Sometimes the spathe leaves are poorly aligned, so that by the time they emerge from the neck of the bulb, the immature florets are already visible.

A gap of 1–4 days usually separates the maturing of each pair of flowers while an interval of up to 10 days is possible with some large-flowering doubles, such as *Hippeastrum* 'Aphrodite', *H.* 'Red Peacock' and *H.* 'White Peacock'. Depending on this gap, air temperature and the plant's natural vase life, it is sometimes possible for all 3 pairs of flowers to be open simultaneously and remain fresh for 1–2 days, creating a magical halo of blooms before the first and oldest pair begins to wilt.

Pigmentation

Apart from red florets which are well pigmented by the time they emerge from the spathe leaves (Plate 8-5), little pigmentation is evident in many pastel-colored hybrids until the blooms have attained their final size and shape. As the flowers mature and particularly when cultivated under high light intensities, pigments become much brighter and veining more pronounced. The red, orange, pink and white contrast becomes more vivid in striped hybrids, and creams often become snow white. When hippeastrums were placed outside in weak February sunlight for around 4 hours in South East England, floral pigments intensified considerably. As lighting improved during late spring and summer, the flowers acquired deeper hues, the deepest colored pinks, reds and oranges being obtained when plants bloomed outside in late summer or early autumn.

Flower color appears to be partly influenced by the plant's rate of transpiration, soil pH and nutrient balance. As light and temperatures improve and with low humidity, good ventilation and robust root development, pigments intensify. Plants cultivated under poor lighting and high humidity with lower transpiration rates produce paler blooms. Research at the Glasshouse Crops Research Station, Naaldwijk (The Netherlands), showed ideal electro conductivity levels (EC) to be 1.82 milli Siemens (mS). Higher levels (2.5–3.0 mS) resulted in more intense pigments lending credibility to the possible role played by fertilizers in influencing color intensity (see Table 9-4).

Nectar and Fragrance

Some American Cybisters produce prodigious amounts of nectar which slowly oozes along the filaments and lays suspended just below the anthers. Among these are *Hippeastrum* 'Chico', *H.* 'Emerald', *H.* 'Flamengo', *H.* 'Jungle Star', *H.* 'La Paz', *H.* 'Lima', *H.* 'Merengue', *H.* 'Reggae' and *H.* 'Tango'. Most hippeastrum hybrids lack fragrance, although some breeders are endeavoring to breed perfumed hybrids (see Chapters 6 and 7 for details).

Pedicel Development

Pedicels vary in length and width among different hybrids as well as among individual pairs of flowers. Some South African and Dutch hybrids have short 0.25–0.5 in. (0.5–1 cm), stubby pedicels which prevent the flower from moving into the horizontal position, forcing them to remain upright. This feature characterizes plants infested with the tarsonemid mite. Other hybrids have long 3.5–4 in. (9–10 cm), slender or thick pedicels, which may result in the drooping of particularly heavy blooms (*Hippeastrum* 'Aphrodite', *H.* 'Dancing Queen'). Pedicels are usually green but some smaller flowering hybrids have attractive glossy, red-brown ones (*H.* 'White Equester III'), pale brown (*H.* 'Merengue') or bright red (*H.* 'Charisma').

Following their emergence from the spathe leaves, florets expand rapidly. The first pair usually moves from the vertical into the horizontal position 2–4 days later. Hybrids with particularly heavy blooms, such as *Hippeastrum* 'Aphrodite' and *H.* 'Dancing Queen', may droop long before they have fully expanded. Other flowers are slower and take up to 10 days before they begin to open. After a further 24–48 hours, the first pair is usually fully open.

Floral Decay

Observing the process of floral decay is fascinating and as incredible as the development and maturing of a new floret. Flowers which have not been pollinated usually take around 14 days to decay, while fertilized ovules will result in the flower starting to wilt within 24 hours, accompanied by a gradual draining of color from the tepals and a gradual disintegration of the flower. Tepals become duller and thinner and their edges curl inward or outward. Flowers become ragged and soggy. If left undisturbed, they come to resemble fragments of tissue paper (Plate 8-6). Finally the flowers too disintegrate, leaving the remnants of the reproductive organs with drops of nectar sometimes suspended on the withered filaments.

Bulb Preparation, the Cool Period

Foliage and inflorescence development may be halted at any time by lifting and drying the bulb for 7–14 days at 73–80°F (23–27°C), the exact temperature and timing varying according to growers' cultivation practices. A period of storage, also known as the cool period, at 55°F (13°C) for ideally 8–10 weeks (but as few as 6 for some smaller flowering hybrids such as *Hippeastrum* 'Salmon Pearl'), is then required to resume growth and for further scape elongation prior to emerging from the bulb. Although foliage and inflorescence initiation is continuous under favorable conditions, failure to give bulbs the cool period either after lifting or in their pots will adversely affect the appearance of next season's inflorescences. Flowering may be delayed by several weeks or months; scape production may be reduced due to scape abortion having taken place within the bulb and, in some cases, plants will fail to bloom and will produce only leaves.

Following the cool period, usually 2, sometimes 3 scapes from large mature bulbs will appear simultaneously or consecutively within 2 or 3 days after planting. In some cases, sprouting has occurred within 4–6 hours of bringing the plant back into the warmth, although 3–14 days is typical. A gap of 10–12 days between the appearance of the first and second scapes results in a succession of blooms lasting several weeks, a situation which growers consider to be ideal. Some cultivars are naturally slower growing and, despite having been given the appropriate preparation, may not sprout until 3–8 weeks after planting. It is possible for 12–18 flowers to be fully open simultaneously when all 3 scapes have developed simultaneously (Plates 4-12, 4-15).

Lowering the temperature to 41°F (5°C) delays sprouting by several weeks or months without damaging the plant. It also prevents the inflorescence from drying out. Some smaller flowering cultivars sprout after only 6 weeks at 55°F (13°C), making extended storage impossible. Most hybrids can be successfully stored at 41°F for 3 months after 8–10 weeks at 55°F without incurring any damage, and many large-flowering hybrids can be safely stored for 6–8 months at this lower temperature without problems. Some small-flowering varieties, however, such as *Hippeastrum* 'Pamela' and *H.* 'Calimero', will not flower after more than 6–7 months at 41°F due to drying out or aging of the bud. The breeder of *H.* 'Calimero' has found that the longer bulbs are stored at 55°F, the shorter time they are able to be stored at 41°F before flowering difficulties are encountered.

Some hybrids which have been stored for 14–16 weeks at 55°F have difficulty rooting, resulting in scapes which are shorter than normal and flowers which are smaller than normal. Depending on the variety and quality of the bulb, 9–10 months of storage at 41°F can also adversely affect scape length and flower quality.

Freshly harvested bulbs which have received insufficient preparation may take up to 6 weeks, sometimes longer, before a shoot appears. After 4 more weeks, a second scape may emerge. Such delays are due to scapes not having elongated sufficiently to emerge soon after planting. A third scape may follow during the summer or early autumn.

Sexual Reproduction

Even before the flowers have fully opened, the anthers may have already split, releasing prodigious amounts of pollen in different shades of yellow from creamy to buttercup. The stigma takes longer to mature. Initially the 3 lobes are tightly entwined and the style hangs downwards, away from the anthers (Plates 3-5, 3-12). After 2–3 days, the style is fully extended and curves upwards (Plates 3-2, 3-11, 4-10). The now fully expanded, sticky, mature, stigmatic lobes are covered with tiny hairs, ready to receive the pollen grains and provide nourishment for the growth of the pollen tubes. The positioning of the reproductive organs and the delay in ripening of the stigma ensure that, without intervention by insects, birds or humans, self-pollination is unlikely to occur.

Pollination is easy to accomplish using a small camel-hair brush or pipe cleaner to transfer pollen from the anthers onto the stigma. If the flower continues to remain fresh after pollination, then it is unlikely that fertilization has occurred. Fresh pollen should be applied 24–48 hours later. Although two flowers of one of my plants of *Hippeastrum* 'Amputo' plants were successfully pollinated, the third flower showed no signs of wilting after 4 days. I applied fresh pollen and within 24 hours the flower began to wilt. Three days later, fertilization appeared to have been successful from the rapidly expanded pedicel and swelling of the carpels.

Further swelling occurs during the next 3–5 weeks to accommodate the developing seeds within the locules (Plate 8-7). The ripening fruit, a capsule, varies in shape, color and size according to the cultivar. The capsules of *Hippeastrum* 'Moviestar' are a glossy midgreen while those of *H.* 'Charisma' are initially darker with shades of dark brown and bottle-green markings separating each carpel. Four weeks later, they have become a matt, lighter green. In some hybrids, the capsules become bulbous from an early stage while others remained squat and cylindrical for the first 2–3 weeks before becoming bulbous. Some hybrids, such as *H.* 'Amputo', have unusually long, almost oblong capsules. Although the thickness of individual pedicles of an umbel is similar, lengths may vary considerably. Two pedicels on a scape of one of my *H.* 'Moviestar' bulbs reached 2.5 in. (6 cm) long within 2 weeks following fertilization while a third pedicel reached 4.25 in. (11 cm).

After 5–6 weeks, the outer wall of the glossy, taut, sputniklike capsule begins to shrink and becomes a matt, dull green. Wrinkles and yellowing appear before the capsule finally turns a straw color. Between 7 and 14 days later the fruit dehisces revealing each chamber crammed full of neatly stacked black, discoid or D-shaped seeds, each surrounded by a thin, papery dark brown band, similar in texture to tissue paper (Plate 8-8). Some capsules may contain up to 90 seeds but between 30 and 60 seeds are typical, although not all of them may be viable. Unfertilized ovules remain as tiny, dark brown-black tissuelike fragments; some embryos may have begun to develop but failed to reach maturity.

After exposure to the air for 24–48 hours, the seeds will have dried. Some may have fallen to the ground, assisted by air currents. Usually 7–10 days after the capsule has split, the pedicels and scape begin to wither, their role now accomplished.

Offset Production and Development

Production of offsets around the rim of the basal plate (called bulblets) and in the axils of the fleshy leaf bases (called bulbils) of the main bulb are another way of ensuring the plant's survival. Bulbils become obvious when they reach a certain size and a bump can be seen beneath the surface. As the bulbil grows, the bump becomes larger. As new leaf bases are initiated and outermost ones become depleted of food reserves, the bump becomes more noticeable. Finally, as the outer leaf bases become dry and papery and peel off, the bulbil is fully exposed (Plate 9-3).

Some cultivars, such as *Hippeastrum* 'Germa', *H.* 'Lemon Lime' and *H.* 'Yellow Goddess', produce offsets from an early age even before the parent bulb has reached maturity. Others start reproducing much later, and some may produce very few offsets during their lifetime.

Some North American hybrids such as *Hippeastrum* 'Pink Floyd' and *H.* 'Tango' produce both bulbils and bulblets. Up to 20 slender, needle-shaped offsets have been found attached to the basal plate on some mature bulbs of *H.* 'Tango' at different stages of development, and up to 10 offsets within the outer papery layers of a 7.5 in. (19 cm) circumference bulb of *H.* 'Pink Floyd'.

The development of many bulblets around the base of the parent bulb can make lifting difficult and prove detrimental to the parent. The parent bulb may shrink and develop little new foliage, while the bulblet continues to expand, producing robust, disproportionately tall foliage, all the while utilizing the reserves of the parent. Appearance of foliage indicates that the bulblet has developed roots and therefore can be detached and potted up separately, allowing the parent bulb to recover.

Some bulbils may develop 3–4 leaves while encased within the fleshy leaf bases of the parent bulb. Sufficient light may penetrate to enable photosynthesis to take place. When leaves emerge, development proceeds even faster, the offset sometimes appearing to compete with its parent resulting in particularly well-developed foliage from the offset but little or no foliage development from the parent bulb.

Hybrids such as *Hippeastrum* 'Germa' and *H.* 'Jewel' have a tendency to divide into 2 identical bulbs after flowering has finished, each half remaining attached at the basal plate. Several of my bulbs of *H.* 'Jewel' split 2–3 months after flowering in spring 2002 and, 9 months later, apart from being joined at the base, both bulbs were functioning independently (Plate 8-9). Each bulb put forward 5–7 leaves in February 2003, which were followed 4–5 weeks later by scapes. Apart from sharing a common basal plate, both bulbs were independent and developed around 30 basal roots each. They were subsequently detached, and the cut surfaces dusted with sulfur as a precautionary measure against fungal attack. Both bulbs quickly became re-established and in May 2003 further leaves emerged.

Conclusion

Observing the development of a large, mature bulb from a tiny seed or offset is a wonderful and fascinating experience which is enhanced still further by developing an understanding of the plant's physiology and its cultural requirements.

Chapter 9

Growers' Guide to Cultivating Better Hippeastrums

Cultivating a hippeastrum is quick, easy and great fun. The sight of fresh, plump shoots and luxuriant green foliage which emerge a few days or weeks after planting newly purchased bulbs is wondrous. (It will even flower in the dark, in a box, plastic bag or on a table without any soil or water.) Even more marvelous are the brilliant blooms which usually appear 3–6 weeks after the shoot has emerged. Providing the plant remains healthy and is given appropriate care and attention throughout the year, there is no reason why it should not continue to produce spectacular blooms for many years.

Hippeastrum hybrids naturally bloom in spring (March–May in the Northern Hemisphere, October–November in the Southern Hemisphere). However, by altering the start and end dates of the cool period, it is possible to extend the flowering period so that plants bloom at almost any time during the year (see Table 8-2).

In the Northern Hemisphere, hippeastrums are superb indoor pot plants and cut flowers, ideal for many domestic and commercial environments including shopping and leisure centers, hospitals and nursing homes, hotel and office reception areas, restaurants and cathedrals. They make marvelous bedding plants for large greenhouse displays in parks and botanic gardens. In warmer, frost-free climates, they make wonderful patio and outdoor bedding plants, providing great swathes of color in mass plantings in municipal parks and gardens (Plate 9-1).

This chapter describes, step-by-step, how to successfully cultivate and flower hippeastrum hybrids and the Brazilian species *Hippeastrum papilio.* Instructions are not given for other species as they are not widely available, and many of them have specific requirements that make them unsuitable for home cultivation.

Current Situation

More than 100 American, Dutch, Japanese and South African hybrids are currently available, but few outlets offer more than a handful each autumn. Large singles dominate annual assortments with well-established favorites such as *Hippeastrum* 'Apple Blossom' (pink and white), *H.* 'Minerva' (red and white striped) and *H.* 'Red Lion' (red) decking many supermarket and garden center shelves each autumn. Many British retailers appear reluctant to expand their range to include the latest large-flowering singles and doubles. They are even more hesitant to offer the delicate and exotic smaller flowering types. Garden center chains, wholesalers and some mail-order companies offer a much wider selection, including some of the more exotic singles and doubles.

Bulb size and quality

Bulbs vary considerably in size and quality. Some are so small and shriveled that one has to doubt if they have reached flowering size. Others are larger, measuring 14.25–16 in. (36–40 cm) circumference and producing up to 3, occasionally 4 scapes in the first year after purchase, each scape bearing 4–6 and occasionally 8 blooms. Most Dutch and Japanese cultivars sold in British supermarkets and high street retail outlets measure 10.5–11 in. (26–28 cm) circumference, although some are even smaller at 9.5–10.5 in. (24–26 cm) circumference. An increasing number of modern large-flowered Dutch hybrids are capable of producing 2 scapes from this size, but many of the older varieties produce only a single scape and a few, none at all. Most large-flowering South African hybrids will produce 2 scapes from 12–12.5 in. (30–32 cm) circumference or slightly smaller bulbs.

Bulbs sold loose in garden centers or specialist nurseries and those available from mail-order companies are usually larger, ranging from 12–12.5 in. (30–32 cm) circumference to 15–16 in. (38–40 cm) circumference. Smallest size bulbs will normally produce a minimum of 2 scapes in the first year of purchase, while those measuring 13.5–14.25 in. (34–36 cm) and larger will usually produce 3 and occasionally, 4 scapes. Larger bulbs not only produce more scapes and flowers, but the plant's overall dimensions will be larger.

Quality ranges from excellent to very poor. Some bulbs may have completely rotted by the time they are purchased or planted. Others may be leftover from the previous season's harvest and likely to produce plants of inferior quality.

Cultural information

Most people have little difficulty in getting their bulb to flower in the first season but find it much harder to achieve repeat flowering. The following season, the plant may produce ample quantities of luxuriant foliage which can reach 36 in. (90 cm) tall, but no flowers. This lack of success can be attributed, in no small part, to the inadequate and often inaccurate cultural information supplied with the bulb and lack of advice available at the time of purchase. It is not uncommon for inexperienced gardeners to assume hippeastrums are annuals or similar to hyacinths and thus discard plants outside the backdoor after flowering.

Packaging and labeling

Hippeastrum packaging has undergone major changes since the mid 1990s. Increasingly, bulbs are pre-packaged in brightly colored, cardboard cartons, decorated with pictures of the plant in flower and often accompanied by brief, inadequate and sometimes incorrect cultural information. A plastic or ceramic pot and a small bag of inferior compost may also be supplied. Pots are usually too shallow and ceramic pots often lack drainage holes. The combination of the oversize box and absence of padding may lead to bruising and cause serious damage to the bulbs. Some bulbs are already planted in a medium which may become compacted and lack sufficient aeration for long-term, healthy growth. The incorrect name "amaryllis" is often emblazoned on the box, thus perpetuating the confusion between *Amaryllis* and *Hippeastrum*.

Bulbs sold in garden centers, specialist nurseries, supermarkets, open-air markets and by mail order may also be offered loose. They are frequently offered under a generic name such as "Large Red." In the absence of a picture or any other information, it is impossible to know which of the several reds now available (*Hippeastrum* 'Ferrari', *H.* 'Liberty', *H.* 'Parma', *H.* 'Red Sensation', *H.* 'Roma', *H.* 'Royal Velvet') is being sold. The problem is further compounded when customers remove loose bulbs from open containers to examine them, only to replace them in the wrong box. This is particularly frustrating for those gardeners seeking a particular cultivar to add to their collection. Cultural information is seldom supplied and upon purchase, bulbs are usually placed in a paper bag.

Some mail-order companies offer customers a choice of packaging—paper bags or gift boxes. However, in Great Britain, this is an exception. Most companies package the bulbs in paper bags with or without any protective wood or paper shavings. They are then placed in an outer carton prior to dispatch. Cultural information is sometimes included but its accuracy is questionable. Some pre-packaged gift-boxed bulbs are completely covered with wood shavings providing first-class protection during transport. Others are placed in oversize boxes with little or no protective material. They may arrive badly bruised with broken flower shoots and torn leaves.

Storage conditions

Conditions in shops, nurseries and garden centers vary. Bulbs may be stored in cold, damp conditions which, in the worst cases, may lead to the death of the bulb by fungal attack. Bulbs may be bruised as a result of careless handling. Bulbs and roots may be coated with blue-green Penicillium mold which usually disappears after 24 hours when bulbs are placed in a warm, dry place. Temperatures are frequently too high in shops and garden centers, resulting in premature sprouting, distorted scapes and, in some cases, flowering of the plant while still in the box or tray! This often happens with hybrids which naturally sprout after 6–8 weeks or those which have already received 8–10 weeks of preparation (cool period) and are keen to grow.

Prepare to Grow Better Hippeastrums

By following the guidelines given here, you too should be able to achieve prize-winning blooms and repeated success year after year. While hippeastrum can be made to flower in most months of the year depending on the timing of the cool period and the health of your bulb, this would require you to have several bulbs and the facilities to provide different temperatures for various plants simultaneously. This is likely to prove difficult, particularly during the warmer months of the year.

Select a Top Quality Bulb

If you require a particular cultivar, purchase your bulbs from a reputable mail-order company or specialist nursery as their reputation depends on their selling top quality bulbs under the registered name. Whatever hippeastrum you wish to grow, it is best to select the largest size bulb available for that hybrid. Regardless of type, the bigger the bulb, the more scapes and blooms you can expect from it in the first year after purchase. However, it is not possible to guarantee the number of scapes a particular hybrid will produce either in the first season after purchase or in subsequent years, since scape production depends on many factors including the bulb's state of health, preparation the bulb has received prior to purchase and planting and environmental and cultural conditions after planting.

Even if and when the bulb eventually reaches its maximum size, 3 scapes are usually the maximum number possible each year. It is unlikely pot-grown bulbs cultivated at home will reach 20 in. (50 cm), which is the maximum size for some hybrids, due to the environmental conditions both within and outside the pot. Suppliers' catalogs should give the bulb's circumference and indicate the number of scapes and flowers which can be expected in the first year after purchase. If they do not, then it is worth inquiring so you are not disappointed.

Take time to select your bulb, as its performance will be influenced by its size and its condition. Make sure it is firm and dry, with no sign of bruising (often around or below the neck or towards the base), mold, fungus (*Fusarium oxysporum* or *Stagonospora curtisii*) (often around and underneath the bulb and on the roots) or insects lurking beneath the dry papery outer layers (Plate 11-1). Having been sold rotting or rotten bulbs, I speak from experience when I say that it is essential to examine your bulb thoroughly before purchase. While a bulb might appear healthy from the outside, closer examination of it may reveal significant rotting among the fleshy layers, usually around the neck base. The bulb should be covered with several brown, almost black, thin, papery outer layers. Some may have already become detached, others may be about to do so—this is normal. Some retailers may have already removed any outer layers which had showed signs of damage or disease. A few red, pink or other colored dots or patches may be visible on the outer leaf bases. These may be superficial and insignificant, providing the fleshy layers immediately underneath are white and free from any markings or blemishes which could signify fungal and/or insect attack. Some hybrids are genetically disposed to "blistering" where fluid accumulates under the skin. This can lead to infection and subsequent rotting beneath the outer layers. The best advice is not to purchase the bulb if any part of it feels damp, soft or even worse, soggy.

Make sure the disc underneath the bulb is dry, intact and free from signs of basal rot and/or small punctures which could indicate insect damage. There may be a few white, fleshy basal roots, but more often they are shriveled and dead. Some bulbs may have had their roots removed. Select a bulb with as many fleshy, healthy roots as possible.

Some hybrids are particularly fast-growing and the bulbs may have even begun sprouting. If the bulb has been stored in the dark, any growth is likely to be creamy white but after 24–48 hours of exposure to the light, it will have started to turn green. Examine any emerged scapes or leaves for signs of damage. Make sure they are free from brown or red dots, patches, streaks, stripes or scarring.

Select the Correct Size of Pot

Hippeastrums require a deep pot to allow sufficient room for root development and to provide anchorage. A gap of 1 in. (2.5 cm) between the outside of the bulb and the pot's rim is recommended to allow for future growth and facilitate watering. It is important that the pot is not over-large so the roots fail to reach the bottom and fill the pot. Ideally, the plant should become pot-bound within 6–8 weeks but this is unlikely where bulbs produce few or no roots until after flowering. If the pot is too large, depending on the potting mix, the soil may become sour or remain too moist, resulting in poor aeration and root decay.

Potted bulbs from The Netherlands are often crammed into containers filled with nutritionally weak coir that are far too small and shallow. It is therefore recommended that you repot the plant after it has finished flowering into a larger, deeper pot to give more room for root development and provide greater stability for the plant. The plant will benefit considerably from being transferred to a more nutrient-rich mix such as the Kew potting mix. A particular problem when plants are planted in 100% coir are the clouds of fungus gnats that soon develop, swirling around and above the pot and compost.

Small- or medium-flowering cultivars look wonderful when three bulbs are planted in a large pot. The Klisters look absolutely spectacular when 5 or 6 clumps are planted in a large terracotta pot, creating a miniature garden of blooms lasting several weeks. Table 9-1 lists recommended pot sizes for single and multiple plantings of different size bulbs.

Select the Best Mix

Since the 1800s many growing media have been devised for pot plant cultivation. They differ mainly in their use and ratio of organic to nonorganic matter, as well as the materials required to create a free-draining, well-aerated

Table 9-1. Selecting the correct size pot.

Bulb circumference for 1 bulb per pot	Pot size
9.5–11 in. (24–28 cm)	5 in. (13 cm)
11–12 in. (28–30 cm)	6 in. (15 cm)
12–13.5 in. (30–34 cm)	7 in. (18 cm)
13.5–15 in. (34–38 cm)	8 in. (20 cm)
15 in. (38 cm) and over	10.5 in. (26 cm)[a]
Bulb circumference for 3 bulbs per pot	**Pot size**
5.5–6 in. (14–16 cm)	4.75 in. (12.5 cm)
6.5–7 in. (16–18 cm)	6 in. (15 cm)
7–8 in. (18–20 cm)	7 in. (18 cm)
8–9.5 in. (20–24 cm) and over	8 in. (20 cm)[a]
Klisters	**Pot size**
1 Klister[b]	9.5–10.5 in. (24–26 cm)
5 Klisters[b,c]	15–18.5 in. (38–46 cm)

[a] May be larger, depending on bulb size.
[b] Comprises a parent bulb of 8–10.5 in. (20–26 cm) circumference with up to 6 mature offsets 5.75–7 in. (14–18 cm) circumference attached. Several much smaller immature offsets may also be attached around the base of the parent bulb.
[c] Plant 4 towards the edge of the pot, the 5th in the center.

mix and fertilizer products. By the 1960s, breeders found soil-based mixes containing rotted garden composts and manures to be inappropriate for successful cultivation. They were not only nutritionally weak, but decomposed, resulting in poor aeration and subsequent root rotting. They were also considered a possible source of contamination. Bulbs had to be repotted, causing root disturbance, and took time to settle and become re-established.

The essential ingredients for successful *Hippeastrum* cultivation are a moisture-retentive compost with excellent drainage properties and a high organic content. The compost must remain well aerated at all times and not become compacted, as this may lead to water logging and rotting of the roots and basal plate. Some breeders and growers recommend mixes of peat, sand and well-rotted organic matter in equal proportions, others use 50 percent peat and 50 percent sand or 60 percent coarse peat and 40 percent perlite. Some recommend a sandy loam with added grit. The combinations are numerous. I have tried many different mixes since 1994 with varying degrees of success. Although initial growth was good, peat and grit mixes degraded and compacted after 4–6 months, resulting in poor aeration and subsequent rotting of the roots and basal plate leading to plant death in severe cases.

Over the years, reactions have been mixed regarding the use of perlite. Some professional breeders do not recommend it as it has been found to cause a leaf and root "burn" reaction due to its high fluoride content in some cases. It can become easily waterlogged and, when dried out, tends to float to the top of the soil and blow away.

The Kew mix

A new mix prepared by the Royal Botanic Gardens, Kew (RBG Kew), in 1999 has already proved particularly successful for cultivating *Hippeastrum* and is recommended. It consists of 10% loam, 45% coir and 45% Sylvafibre®, (chipped and composted forestry waste, mostly bark and twigs from commercial East Anglian forests in Great Britain). The mix creates an excellent moisture-retentive, free-draining compost.

In the absence of the recommended ingredients, substitutes can be used. For the loam, any proprietary loam-based compost will do, such as John Innes No. 1 in Great Britain. The coir compares favorably with peat. It retains water and maintains aeration, unlike peat where water fills the spaces between the particles, resulting in poor aeration and waterlogging. Kew likens coir particles to tiny sponges which soak up the water and leave air spaces between them. In the absence of coir, sphagnum peat moss may be used. The third ingredient, Sylvafibre, "contains lots of comparatively large, durable fibers" which "trap the fine particles of loam to keep them well distributed through the mix and generally preserve structure and drainage when the compost is in the pot" (*Kew Magazine*, autumn 2002). The fibers also absorb and release nutrients to the plant as required. An alternative to Sylvafibre is propagating bark (5 ml) or composted bark.

It is essential to add to this basic mix a well-balanced, slow-release fertilizer containing trace elements including magnesium oxide (MgO). Kew uses a liquid feed with a nitrogen–phosphorus–potassium (N–P–K) ratio of 15–11–13, adding 0.21 oz. for each gallon (1.5 g per liter) of mix. Kew then adds 2 parts magnesium oxide and trace elements to this fertilizer. When coir is used in the mix, Kew also adds mineral kieserite (hydrated magnesium sulfate) at the time of planting at the rate of 0.07 oz. per gallon (0.5 g per liter) to preserve the balance between magnesium and potassium and to avoid magnesium deficiency.

Kew recommends adding about 10% Seramis®, (expanded, baked, inert clay granules, pH neutral) to the mix to improve aeration and drainage further, thereby allowing a free supply of air through the soil and preventing water logging. Seramis does not compact or degrade under any conditions. Each granule is capable of absorbing more than its weight in water which is released to the plant as required.

A balanced liquid feed containing trace elements and magnesium oxide is applied with every watering from after 6 weeks of growth until the beginning of the cool period. It may be necessary to adjust the concentration to ensure that levels recommended by the manufacturer over a given time period are not exceeded.

Other mixes

Other successful potting mixes have been developed by professional and amateur breeders and growers. Five of them are mentioned here. Some ingredients in these mixes are more appropriate to particular environments, and some will not be available (or indeed appropriate) in certain situations.

John Bryan (California, United States) uses a mix with two main ingredients: 75% loamy soil (having at least 5% organic content) and 25% well-rotted compost. If necessary, he adds sharp sand to improve drainage. Plants growing in this medium receive weekly feedings of an organic, balanced liquid fertilizer at half strength. At the other end of the United States, J. W. Deme (North Carolina) combines 51–68% fine ground pine bark, 16% coarse sand, and, to improve drainage, 16% perlite. To his mix he adds 2.5 lb. (1.1 kg) slow-release fertilizer. For every bushel (44 liters) of mix, he adds trace minerals and 2.5 lb. of dolomite limestone.

The National Botanical Research Institute, Lucknow (India), mixes equal parts of sandy loam, leaf mold, and decayed organic manure. For every cubic foot (28 liters) of this mix, 1 oz. (28 g) bone meal is added. Plants growing in this medium receive fortnightly feedings with a balanced liquid manure (that is, an oil cake or any animal manure) and 0.24 oz. of superphosphate of lime for every gallon of liquid manure (1.75 g per liter).

In Japan, Miyake Nursery (Chiba-kon) combines 70–80% free-draining, well-aerated compost with 20–30% well-rotted rice chaffs. In South Africa, Justin Bowles (Port Elizabeth) uses 12.5% well-rotted manure, 25% compost, 25% river sand, 12.5% red bush soil (clay), and 25% black bush soil. No doubt other mixes can and are being used by successful growers elsewhere.

Feeding

Hippeastrum hybrids have high nutrient requirements and require regular feeding when actively growing to ensure healthy, robust roots, scapes, flowers and leaves. Some Dutch and South African growers do not feed container-grown hippeastrums until flowering has finished. They then advocate using an N–P–K feed with a high potassium content but do not recommend adding trace elements. Such advice is contrary to Dutch cultivation practices. For example, the Research Station for Floriculture and Glasshouse Vegetables, Naaldwijk (The Netherlands) recommends that water used for commercially grown bulbs have a pH of 6.5 and an electroconductivity (EC) of 0.8 milli Siemens per cm. Furthermore, for each liter of water, they recommend the following:

Trace mineral content	
Iron	7 micromols
Manganese	0.8 micromol
Zinc	1 micromol
Boron	7 micromols
Copper	0.8 micromol
Anions (-)	
Nitrogen	2.5 millimols
Chlorine	less than 1 millimol
Sulfur	1.5 millimols
Bicarbonate	0.5 millimol
Phosphorus	0.15 millimol
Cations (+)	
Ammonium	0.1 millimol
Potassium	1.3 millimols
Sodium	less than 1 millimol
Calcium	1.5 millimols
Magnesium	1 millimol

Concentration and frequency of feeding is heavily influenced by the initial composition of the compost and the characteristics of the individual hybrid, including its growth rate and stage of development. Some mixes have low nutritional levels, requiring the addition of a well-balanced, slow-release fertilizer containing trace elements at the time of planting. Further supplements may also be required in some cases to ensure sufficient nutrients are available to the plant during its first few weeks of growth. Regular applications of a balanced liquid feed containing trace elements will become particularly important after flowering if the plant is to stand any chance of regaining its former size and condition, quite apart from producing high quality blooms the following season.

It is important to avoid the peak and trough effect which can occur when feeding at full strength is followed by water only. The initial boost to nutrient levels may be followed by deficiencies as subsequent watering leaches any residual nutrients from the soil. Kew recommends including a liquid feeding with EVERY watering to ensure that nutrient levels remain constant, allowing for adjustments as necessary so that manufacturers' recommended concentrations are not exceeded. If in doubt, it is better to underfeed rather than overfeed, as nutrient levels can always be increased if discovered to be low. Avoid feeding during the hottest part of the day—early morning or evening is recommended—and ensure the medium is moist before applying any liquid feed to avoid leaf and/or root burn.

A recommended feeding formula

For a decade I have tried many different feeding formulas. The following recipe has produced excellent results on all hybrid groups and *Hippeastrum papilio* and is recommended for robust, healthy plants. Dissolve 3 pinches of the formula in 4 qts. (1 liter) of tepid tap water and apply weekly from spring through autumn until the commencement of the cool period. The relatively low nitrogen and high potassium content of the formula, together with excellent lighting from 600-watt sodium lights, have resulted in outstanding leaf quality (foliage growth is particularly robust and leathery). The liquid feed can also be applied as a foliar feed. Except for the first three ingredients (nitrogen, phosphorus, and potassium), all the ingredients are soluble in water.

Macronutrients	
Nitrogen	14.0%
Phosphorous	10.0%
Potassium	27.0%
Magnesium oxide	2.5%
Calcium oxide	2.0%
Sulfur trioxide	11.0%
Trace elements	
Boron	0.0120%
Copper	0.0055%
Iron	0.0400%
Manganese	0.0200%
Molybdenum	0.0016%
Zinc	0.0055%

Watering

The importance of developing a sound watering program cannot be overemphasized. Each year many hippeastrums are damaged or killed by overwatering and being grown in unsuitable potting mixes having poor drainage qualities. After the initial watering, always allow the top 2 in. (5 cm) of soil to dry out before rewatering thoroughly with tepid tap water or uncontaminated rainwater which has been allowed to stand at room temperature. Tepid water is recommended to help maintain soil temperature as near to 70–72°F (21–22°C) as possible, apart from during the cool period.

Contrary to popular belief, the plant must only be watered from the top, NEVER from the bottom since roots that stand in water are likely to rot. As soon as the water comes through into the saucer, tip it away. Care must be taken to avoid getting water over any part of the bulb. Any browning of the leaf tips, particularly during the winter, may be due to an overdry environment but also to insufficient light and nutrients. A fine misting is recommended to increase the humidity.

After planting and watering newly purchased bulbs, it is important to keep the soil just moist until a shoot and/or leaves have reached 2–3.25 in. (5–8 cm). Doing this encourages new roots to develop which are essential for successful growth. As growth becomes more active and temperatures rise, more frequent watering is required, the exact amount varying from plant to plant, according to its stage of development and environmental conditions. Ultimately, best watering practice will be developed not only by following these guidelines, but by gaining an intimate understanding of each plant. Most hippeastrums in the National Plant Collection of *Hippeastrum* are watered every 5–7 days from spring to early autumn, but in July and August 2003, it became necessary to water the plant every 2 or 3 days as temperatures rose to 37°F (100°C) in mid August. Plants were misted twice daily and remained in excellent condition throughout the unprecedented hot weather. Only time will tell if the exceptionally high temperatures have adversely effected floral developments taking place within the bulbs.

Lighting

Many hippeastrums originate from areas of high ultraviolet levels. Accordingly, plants require plenty of light throughout the year for healthy, robust growth. A combination of low lighting and high temperatures during late autumn and winter is likely to result in excessively tall 30–36 in. (75–90 cm) soft, weak scapes and foliage which collapse easily and frequently split at the base. Flower color is intensified when plants are grown under good lighting and low humidity. Therefore, if possible, plant newly purchased bulbs in late winter (at the end of February in the Northern Hemisphere) when light quality is beginning to improve. If this is not possible, then grow your plant at a slightly lower temperature of 61–64°F (16–18°C). Although this lower temperature will result in slower growth, scapes and foliage will be more robust and less likely to collapse.

Unidirectional light, from a window, for example, will result in scapes becoming twisted. Turn pots 45° each day to keep plants growing straight.

Temperatures and the Cool Period

During active growth, hippeastrums thrive in temperatures of 70–81°F (21–27°C) by day, 61–64°F (16–18°C) by night and a soil temperature of 68–72°F (20–22°C). Dutch bulb and cut flower growers prefer an air temperature of at least 59–63°F (15–17°C) and a soil temperature of 72–73°F (22–23°C) as some cultivars may bloom prematurely at slightly lower soil temperatures of 68°F (20°C).

Because hippeastrums are evergreen, they do NOT require a resting period and, contrary to popular belief, they should not be dried off but kept in continuous growth. However, a period of cooler temperatures, known as the cool period, is essential for repeat flowering. The differences in quality and growth rates of new scapes and leaves following the cool period were significant between plants cultivated throughout the year and those dried off the previous autumn. The constant availability of moisture and the lack of root disturbance resulted in firmer, denser bulbs which produced stronger scapes, each bearing magnificent, well-proportioned flowers simultaneously with 5–7 mature, luxuriant leaves, creating a delightful bushy effect.

It is not uncommon for a hippeastrum to flower twice a year—spring and summer (March–May and mid August–early November in Northern Hemisphere countries). Some Brazilian-bred hybrids flower even later in December. Some gardeners in the Inner and Outer Hebrides and Northern Isles, Scotland, have reported a second flowering period at the end November–early January after a late spring flowering (May–June). This slightly later flowering compared to hippeastrums cultivated in England may be due to a difference in latitude. Irrespective of when the plant flowers for a second or third time in a 12-month period, it is recommended to delay the cool period by up to 3 months to encourage the building up of the bulb and the development of new foliage following flowering. However, depending on when flowering occurred, significant new foliage development may prove difficult during late autumn or winter months in Northern Hemisphere countries when light is particularly poor and growth rates naturally decrease. This problem can be easily overcome by using 600-watt sodium lights suspended from the ceiling for 12–14 hours per day, prior to commencing the cool period.

Plant Hygiene

Hippeastrums are susceptible to attack from a range of pests and diseases whether grown indoors, outside or under glass. Regular plant inspections are recommended so that actual or potential problems can be dealt with at the earliest possible stage, thereby increasing the plant's chances of making a full and speedy recovery. It is particularly important to watch for fungal attack (often around the neck or shoulders), mealybug (around the neck of the bulb and on the leaves) and aphids (on the underside of the leaves if growing the plants under glass or outside).

Take action immediately after isolating all infected plants and apply the appropriate treatment, sterilizing all cutting implements prior to and after use, to avoid transmitting infection to healthy plants. Furthermore, it is advisable to wear protective clothing such as a long gown or laboratory coat, full length apron and thin surgical gloves when handling diseased or potentially infected material; when propagating by chipping, twin scaling or notching; when recommended by the chemical manufacturer; and when cuts or abrasions are on any parts of your hands or wrists.

Always remove and dispose of dead, decaying or damaged material including soggy or decomposing leaf bases and collapsed scapes and foliage. It is advisable to remove crispy and/or papery layers from around the neck of the bulb since these are popular hiding places for pests, such as the tarsonemid mite, which can kill the plant if allowed to multiply. Each day I spend a few minutes removing these crispy and/or papery layers, making sure the necks remain clean and firm. Such attention has avoided many problems. Keep plant surfaces clean and free from plant or soil debris. Ensure that there is adequate space between pots, making sure leaves and pots do not touch as these provide instant bridges for unwanted insects.

Indoor Pot Cultivation for Cooler Climates

The best time to purchase bulbs in the Northern Hemisphere is October–January. Go to a reputable supplier. Most bulbs sold in retail outlets and by mail order have been cultivated in The Netherlands. Those harvested in July or August may not have been adequately prepared by the time you purchase them. Storage requirements and recommended planting dates may be given on pre-packaged types. If not, then store your bulb in a dark, dry place at 55°F (13°C) until ready for planting. As a precautionary measure against rotting, dust the bulb with green or yellow sulfur prior to storing it and examine it regularly to ensure it remains healthy. If the bulb has already received 8–10 weeks at this temperature (preferably 10 weeks), further storage should be at 41°F (5°C). Bulbs from Brazil and South Africa will have already received the full preparation and should be planted by the end of October so that they bloom for Christmas.

Any bulbs which have begun to sprout should be planted immediately or stored at 41°F (5°C) to stop further sprouting. Otherwise, the best time to plant newly purchased bulbs is at the end of February. A list of the best planting times in the Northern Hemisphere for selected bulbs follows:

H. 'Amputo'	1 February
H. 'Chico'	1 February
H. 'Emerald'	1 February
H. 'Flamengo'	1 February
H. 'Germa'	1–14 February
H. 'Grandeur'	1 February
H. 'La Paz'	1 February
H. 'Lima'	1 February
H. 'Merengue'	1 February
H. papilio	1–31 December
H. 'Pink Floyd'	1 February
H. 'Reggae'	1 February
H. 'Ruby Meyer'	1 February
H. 'Tango'	15 January

Planting Bulbs

If the bulb has any basal roots, they may be shriveled. If so hydrate them for 12–24 hours before planting by resting the base of the bulb on top of a jar filled with tepid tap water (Plate 9-2). Allow the roots to enter the water but make sure that the base of the bulb does NOT become wet. After soaking, drain to remove excess moisture. Any dead roots can be readily identified and after soaking will come away easily from the basal plate (Plate 9-3). They may have already become detached while soaking. Hydrating the roots will enable the plant to begin taking up water at an earlier stage which will aid the plant's development.

Some authorities recommend soaking the bulb (including any live roots) in a systemic fungicide for 20 minutes as a precautionary measure against fungal attack immediately prior to planting. After soaking, drain well to remove any excess liquid and pat dry; the bulb is then ready for planting. Any new and existing bulbs to the National Plant Collection of *Hippeastrum* which show evidence of fungal attack are always treated prior to planting as a precautionary measure. Bulbs showing no signs of damage are not given this treatment. Some experts have questioned the advantages of using a systemic fungicide at this stage, since experience has shown that it can weaken the bulb. However, they advise using a fungicide treatment at the first sign of fungal attack.

Referring to Table 9-1 for appropriate pot sizes for different size bulbs, prepare the potting mix. The Kew mix is particularly recommended. Fill the bottom of the pot with the mix and, holding the bulb in one hand with the roots hanging downwards and the bulb's shoulders level with the rim of the pot (Plate 9-4), gradually add compost, firming as you go, until two thirds of the bulb is covered. The top third of the bulb should remain exposed. Some mixes have better drainage qualities than others. If in doubt about the mix you are using, place crocks or pieces of broken pottery in the bottom of the pot to further aid drainage.

If the bulb has no roots, put some mix into the pot, firming as you go and form a mound in the center of the mix. Sit the bulb on top of the mound (Plate 9-5) and gradually add more compost until two thirds of the bulb is covered.

Water in well, following the guidelines given elsewhere in this text, and place the plant in a warm, lighted and well-ventilated place, but free from drafts (Plate 9-6). A shelf above a warm radiator or a sunny windowsill is ideal for plants being grown in the Northern Hemisphere.

Caring for Bulbs in Spring from Planting to Flowering

When growing most hippeastrums, keep the compost just moist until a shoot appears. Then begin to water more liberally as growth becomes more vigorous, always using tepid water. A few hybrids are more delicate and susceptible to rotting. These are listed on page 194. It is advisable not to water these plants after the initial watering until a shoot is visible. However, it is important that the potting mix is not allowed to dry out completely.

When to start feeding most hippeastrums will depend on the composition of the potting mix and the individual cultivar. If a slow-release fertilizer has been incorporated into the compost, additional feeding should not be necessary until 6 weeks after growth has commenced. In most cases this will coincide with flowering having partially, or completely finished. Bulbs planted in mixes having a low nutritional level may benefit from feeding once the shoot has reached 2 in. (5 cm) high. Recommended concentrations, pH, electro-conductivity (EC) and nutrient levels are given elsewhere in this chapter.

The exceptions to these general guidelines are the delicate hippeastrums listed on page 194. Delay feeding these until roots have developed and foliage growth has become vigorous.

Once feeding has begun, continue to feed plants with every watering, adjusting the concentration as necessary to ensure levels recommended by the manufacturer and those given on page 190 are not exceeded.

Give plants as much direct light as possible, but avoid exposing foliage to the sun's hottest rays as this may cause leaf scorch. Hybrids with particularly tall scapes and large, weighty blooms are best secured with a cane and tie when they reach 18 in. (45 cm) to prevent them from possible collapse. This is particularly important if plants are being grown under poor lighting. As the flowers begin to open, move the plants to a cooler place at 61°F (16°C) if possible, to prolong flower life. Allow the flowers to decay naturally or else remove them. If possible, allow scapes to die back naturally after the flowers have decayed so that nutrients can return to the bulbs. Once the scapes have collapsed and withered, they can be easily removed.

Caring for Bulbs in Summer

Water more liberally in summer as root and foliage growth becomes more vigorous and as temperatures rise. Never let the soil dry out and do not remove the leaves unless they are diseased. Continue using a balanced liquid feed with trace elements throughout the summer and early autumn, applying with every watering and adjusting as necessary to ensure that manufacturers' recommended concentrations are not exceeded.

Although the plant may stand outside after all danger of frost has passed, severe damage may occur if plants are exposed to torrential rain, hail stones, high winds and sharp fluctuations in day and night temperatures. These conditions can occur in Great Britain during the summer and may also occur in other Northern and Southern Hemisphere countries. Slug and snail damage may also prove extensive and, in some cases, may prove fatal. In the absence of a conservatory or greenhouse and suitable outdoor conditions, it is recommended to keep the plants inside. If growing the plants in a greenhouse, ensure that temperatures do not exceed 86°F (30°C) and that the atmosphere does not become too dry since this will encourage pests. Shading may be required to prevent leaf scorch.

New foliage will develop throughout the summer and early autumn and will become tougher and darker with age and as lighting improves. Do not be tempted to remove the leaves unless they are diseased or damaged.

Caring for Bulbs in the Cool Period

As the quantity and quality of light becomes poorer (mid-October in the Northern Hemisphere), it is appropriate to commence the cool period. Move the plants to a cool, well-lit place and maintain a temperature of 55°F (13°C) for a minimum of 8, preferably 10 weeks. In South West England, it may not be possible to reduce temperatures sufficiently to begin the cool period until November or December. It is also advisable to delay the cool period by up to 3 months after an autumn or early winter second flowering. In such cases, continue to feed and water the plant and commence the cool period once temperatures can be reliably maintained at 55°F.

Advice regarding *Hippeastrum papilio* varies. Some breeders give 12–14 weeks (October–February) at 45–46°F (7–8°C) while others recommend either 6–8 weeks maximum at 55°F (13°C) or 10 weeks at 45–48°F (7–9°C). Bulbs planted at the beginning of December after receiving 8 weeks at 55°F (13°C) have flowered at the beginning of January.

Do not feed hippeastrums during the cool period, but do keep the soil moist so that the roots do not dry out. The exact frequency and amount of water will depend on the environmental conditions and the level of internal and external growth. Every 10–14 days is often sufficient. Plants will benefit considerably by being left undisturbed and having their roots kept moist. Several new leaves may emerge during this period and a few old ones may die back, but generally growth will be much slower from November–February. It is recommended that leaves be allowed to die back naturally; they can then easily be removed. Examination of my plants at the end of the cool period has revealed the development of many new basal roots during the cool period as well as the preservation of older, mature roots.

The exceptions to these guidelines are *Hippeastrum papilio* and the delicate hybrids list on page 194. Do not water these until the cool period has ended. Reportedly, *H.* 'Germa' may benefit from being given a longer cool period and already excellent results have been obtained when bulbs are planted early February–end March following 14–16 weeks at 55°F (13°C).

Caring for Bulbs after the Cool Period

To bring bulbs back into the warmth after the cool period, remove any remaining old leaves by cutting them diagonally 4 in. (10 cm) above the nose of the bulb using a sterilized knife. The stumps will decay quickly, often becoming soggy, and are best removed. Do not remove any newly emerged leaves. Inspect the plant thoroughly to make sure that no pests are lurking in or around the neck of the bulb and that bulbs remain free from fungal infection. If you notice anything suspicious, take appropriate action immediately.

It is recommended that the top 2 in. (5 cm) of mix be removed and replaced with a fresh supply of the same mix. Annual repotting is not necessary and plants develop a much stronger root system if left undisturbed for 2–3 years between repotting. However, if the soil is exhausted and/or the plant has outgrown its pot, then now is the time to repot, as disturbance to the bulb and the roots will be minimal.

At the end of January 2003, immediately prior to the ending of the cool period, I repotted the entire National Plant Collection of *Hippeastrum* into the Kew mix and was delighted to see how quickly the plants reestablished. Within 3–7 days of being repotted, many had already put forward new foliage and in some cases, new flowering shoots had already emerged. Certainly, the presence of up to 40 live basal roots and an extensive network of smaller branching roots contributed to the plants' quick recovery and subsequent vigorous growth.

If flowering is preferred in April or May, then it may be possible to extend the cool period for a further 4–8 weeks by lowering the temperature to 41°F (5°C) to prevent the bulb from sprouting.

After topping-up or repotting mature plants and offsets, return them to 70°F (21°C) and grow in exactly the same way as in the first year. The sight of fresh new foliage and shoots emerging within 3–21 days after just 8 weeks at 55°F (13°C) is truly wondrous. While most hybrids will produce flowering shoots after only 8 weeks at these lower temperatures, 10, even 12 weeks is preferable, particularly for most large-flowering singles and doubles if flowering is required within 6–7 weeks. Experience has shown that when large-flowering types receive only 8 weeks at 55°F (13°C), it may be up to 6 weeks before a flowering shoot emerges from the neck of the bulb. Some bulbs put forth 2 new scapes simultaneously, others a single scape followed by a second 3–4 weeks later. A few put forward 3 scapes in close succession. The Meyer hybrids and other small- and medium-flowering hybrids are the quickest to sprout, closely followed by the larger flowering hybrids, and result in a glorious display of blooms accompanied by luxuriant foliage lasting almost 12 weeks.

Repotting offsets

Hippeastrum papilio and some hybrids produce many offsets. When the container becomes overcrowded, separate rooted offsets and pot up separately at the end of the cool period. Do this prior to returning mother and daughter bulbs to the warmth.

Outdoor Cultivation for Warmer Climates

Cultivating hippeastrums has become an increasingly popular pastime in Australia, Canada, Greece, Italy, New Zealand, North America, South Africa and Spain. Plants may bloom twice each year in spring and late summer. In frost-free areas, the plant can be grown outside year-round, either in containers or in the open soil, but in areas where nighttime frosts are likely, plants are best brought inside. You may need to protect your plants from torrential rain, hailstones and strong winds which can sometimes prove fatal.

Many of the principles for successful cultivation and flowering which have been described earlier apply irrespective of whether the plant is cultivated indoors, outside, in pots or flowerbeds. However, modifications may be needed to reflect environmental, climatic and geographical differences, as well as product availability and the presence of particular pests and diseases.

Zones 10 and 11 in North America

Along the Gulf Coast of the southern United States, in southern Florida and in USDA climate zones 10 and 11 (includes Southern California and Hawaii), hippeastrums can be found growing outdoors in open borders in light shade. In cooler areas they are mostly grown as container plants that can easily be brought indoors if frost is expected. *Hippeastrum* 'Apple Blossom' has proved to be one of the hardiest hybrid hippeastrums and grows well in gardens along the Gulf Coast, Southern California, Florida and Hawaii.

Hippeastrums thrive when cultivated in a moisture-retentive loam that is high in organic matter. Shading will be necessary to protect plants from the sun's strongest rays. Along the Gulf Coast they can overwinter in the soil and will survive even if the soil is made crusty by frost. However, they will not tolerate soil that is frozen below the surface. In marginal areas, a covering of mulch is recommended. High temperatures during the day do not seem to bother hippeastrums, but at no time should they be without moisture when in growth. Cold and wet conditions should be avoided at all times so as to avoid fungal attack.

American horticulturists recommend planting bulbs in loam having a high organic content with 20–25% well-rotted compost and a pH of 6–6.8. Sharp sand should be added, if necessary, to improve drainage. A weekly application of a half-strength, organic, balanced liquid feed is recommended when foliage growth is active, but care must be taken not to feed too heavily or else the bulbs may rot. Excellent drainage becomes even more important when feeding. Viral diseases can prove problematic when plants are grown outdoors. Hippeastrum mosaic virus (HMV) and aphid attack are particularly common.

Conclusion

Like many other exotic plants, hippeastrums have specific requirements which must be satisfied for successful long-term cultivation. The sight of their spectacular blooms each year is a wonderful reward for all the time and effort spent on caring for them.

Chapter 10
Commercial Breeding and Production

Each year many gardeners visit shops, garden centers, nurseries and wholesale outlets, scour through bulb catalogs and visit Web sites, eagerly seeking the latest hippeastrum introductions to add to their collections. Few understand the processes involved in creating and bringing a new hybrid into commercial production.

This chapter reviews current breeding criteria, practices and techniques of leading Australian, Dutch, Israeli and South African hippeastrum breeders and growers for dry bulb, pot plant and cut flower production and describes the procedures involved in registering a new hybrid and obtaining Plant Breeders' Rights. Breeders and growers develop methods to suit their own requirements and those of the company. Practices are continually being refined to reflect latest technologies and to satisfy exporters and retailers' stringent demands. While principals remain the same, irrespective of environment and climate, specific techniques and methods are influenced by geography and climate, as well as human and economic resources and constraints.

A Model for Breeding Hippeastrums

It takes around 7–9 years from the initial crossing to a new hippeastrum becoming commercially available. Only a small fraction of several hundred crosses made each year enter commercial production; some have a short life span as they fail to live up to breeders' and growers' expectations and others may not prove to be as popular as originally forecast. The processes involved in creating a new hippeastrum under Dutch glasshouse conditions are described in Table 10-1. Applicable in 2002, this model may have since been modified and can only be regarded as a starting point for understanding the breeding process.

Table 10-1. A Dutch breeder's model from initial crossing to third (final) selection.

Month/Year	Length	Activity
January–March 2000	3 months	Potential parents are selected for desired characteristics and cross-pollinated to produce seeds.
May–August 2000	3 months	Seeds are either sown in beds of seedling compost or stored at 68°F (20°C) at 60–70% humidity until planting. Equal periods with and without light are given following planting. • Soil temperature is maintained at 72–73°F (22–23°C) • Air temperature is maintained at 59–81°F (15–27°C) depending on the outside temperature and light intensity. Ideal temperature is 64–68°F (18–20°C). • Ideally relative humidity level is more than 60%.
August 2000–July 2001	12 months	Seedlings are transplanted and grown continuously under the following conditions. • Soil temperature is maintained in summer at 75°F (24°C), in winter at 72–73°F (22–23°C). • Air temperature is maintained in summer at 68–77°F (20–25°C) during the day and at 63°F (17°C) during the night. In the winter, day temperature is maintained at 61–64°F (16–18°C), although on sunny days, it may reach 72–73°F (22–23°C); night temperature is maintained at 61°F (16°C). Specially constructed transparent shading is used to conserve heat during the winter months and to reduce energy costs. • Relative humidity levels can reach 50–60% in summer, 90% in winter. The ideal level is 70–80%. During the summer, plants are sprayed to increase humidity levels, if necessary. • Light levels are 20 lux in winter, 70–90 lux in summer (1 milliwatt = 1 kilo lux). The ideal light level is 40–50 lux. When levels rise above 50 lux, shading is used to prevent the temperature in the greenhouse from becoming too hot. • Watering in summer occurs 2–3 times per week for 8–10 minutes per session, which equals 1–2 quarts per 10 square feet (1–2 liters per square meter) daily. In winter, watering occurs

Table 10-1 *(continued)*

Month/Year	Length	Activity
		every 8–12 days. Frequencies vary according to the outside temperature, light and soil type. Sandy soils require more frequent watering and plants grown from large bulbs will need more water than bulblets. The amount of water per plant also varies according to plant density. Surface water obtained from ditches, waterways or small lakes around the greenhouse is used but rain water is preferred since nutrient contamination and salt levels are lower. Water temperatures range from 73°F (23°C) in summer to 41°F (5°C) in winter.
		• A complete liquid feed is applied with every watering. Soil analysis is carried out every 2–3 months followed by any necessary adjustments to ensure levels remain as close as possible to those recommended elsewhere in the book.
		• Carbon dioxide (CO_2) is maintained at 600–700 ppm (parts per million) in the air and is administered either via the heating system or through long plastic tubes on the surface of the soil throughout the day when the plants are actively growing resulting in thicker leaf bases and larger bulbs.
		• Note that most Dutch breeders do not transplant the seedlings at this stage but grow them continuously for 6 months until November. They are then lifted, dried, sorted and replanted the following January.
July–September 2001	3 months	Mature bulbs are lifted and dried for 10–14 days at 77–86°F (25–30°C) to reduce the bulb water content by 10–15%. (Some breeders start lifting in August and even later).
		• Next the bulbs are given a hot water treatment for 80 minutes at 118°F (48°C) or for 120 minutes at 115°F (46°C), depending on the bulb's condition.
		• The bulbs are then dried for 2–4 days at 77–86°F (25–30°C) to remove excess moisture.
		• Finally the bulbs are stored at 55°F (13°C) for a minimum of 8 weeks although 10 weeks is preferable.

Table 10-1 *(continued)*

Month/Year	Length	Activity
October – December 2001	3 months	Up to 10% of bulbs are replanted from October to December, the exact time depending on when the bulbs were lifted, the rest are discarded. • Most large-flowering types will have reached 8–15 in. (20–38 cm) circumference, and around 2.5% of bulbs reach 14.25 in. (36 cm) circumference after only 19 months of growth. • Average bulb size is 9.5–10.5 in. (24–26 cm) circumference. Some breeders will discard smaller bulbs unless they are small-flowering types. In most cases, bulbs less than 7 in. (18 cm) circumference will be discarded, with the exception of those bred from species which naturally flower from tiny bulbs. All breeders have their own criteria.
December 2001– April 2002	5 months	Bulbs flower for the first time in December 2001–April 2002, the exact time depending on when they were planted and cultivar.
April – October 2002	6 months	After flowering, selected seedlings are cultivated to enable bulbs to increase, thus enabling more twin scales to be obtained. The cultivation time may be as long as 11 months, for bulbs that first flowered in December 2001, or as short as 6 months, for bulbs that first flowered in April 2002.
November 2002 – January 2003	3 months	At the end of October 2002, selected bulbs are twin scaled and incubated for 10–12 weeks at 81–82°F (27–28°C).
February– September 2003	8 months	First growing season. Healthy twin scales are transplanted and grown for 8 months. By October, the bulblets will have reached 2.5–8 in. (6–20cm) depending on the cultivar.
October 2003	1 month	Small bulbs are lifted and dried for 10–14 days at 77–86°F (25–30°C). • Next the bulblets are given a hot water treatment at 118°F (48°C) for 80 minutes or 115°F (46°C) for 90 minutes. • The bulblets are then dried for 3–4 days. • Finally the bulblets are stored at 55°F (13°C) and 80–85% humidity for 2–4 weeks.

Table 10-1 *(continued)*

Month/Year	Length	Activity
		• Note that some breeders store for longer and will commence the second growing season in January 2004 and keep the bulbs growing until October 2004.
November 2003–	8 months	Second growing season. Bulblets are July 2004 replanted and cultivated for 8 months. By July 2004 they will have reached 7–14.25 in. (18–36 cm).
August–October 2004	3 months	Mature bulbs are lifted. • Next the bulbs are given a hot water treatment for 120 minutes at 115 F (46°C). • They are then stored for 10–12 weeks at 55°F (13°C).
November 2004	1 month	The stored bulbs are replanted.
December 2004–January 2005	2 months	Second selection. Flowering occurs and once again, bulbs are selected to go forward to the third and usually final selection stage. This time 5–15% of bulbs are selected.
January 2005–November 2007	35 months	The cycle is then repeated (see December 2001–November 2004).
December 2007–January 2008	2 months	Third selection. The bulbs flower for the third time and the final selection takes place although some may be grown for a further 2 seasons before a final decision is taken. For those that are selected, commercial arrangements are discussed and finalized with growers. Applications are made to register the successful bulbs and some are put forward for granting National or European Plant Breeders' Rights.

CHAPTER 10

Breeding Criteria

Breeders monitor, assess and evaluate every bulb over a period of several years against criteria which include bulb, scape, flower, leaf and offset production and development; consistency and reliability of growth and performance; vase life; and resistance to pests and diseases. Some characteristics apply specifically to bulbs grown for pot plant or cut flower production, others apply irrespective of end use. For example, breeders place particular emphasis on shape and presentation of the buds for bulbs cultivated as cut flowers: they should be elegant and well-proportioned and display plenty of color at the time of harvesting. For pot plant sales, breeders consider scape and leaf length to be critical. Some retailers regard leaves at the time of flowering as essential. Dutch breeders regard a leaf length of 6–12 in. (15–30 cm) to be ideal while South African breeders consider 10 in. (25 cm) to be desirable with leaf tips reaching the lowermost part of the flower bud.

Bulb and Root Development

Quick and easy-to-grow hippeastrums are desired which produce the maximum number of scapes and flowers per scape in the shortest time and from the smallest bulbs. Some breeders are already breeding multiscape, small-flowering hybrids which produce up to 10 blooms per scape from bulbs no bigger than a golf ball. Although it is possible for up to 3% of some Dutch, large-flowering hippeastrum bulbs to reach 14.25 in. (36 cm) circumference after only 14 months of continuous growth, most large-flowering Dutch and Japanese hybrids reach 9.5–10.5 in. (24–26 cm) after this period.

Some small-flowering Dutch hybrid bulbs reach proportions similar to some large singles and doubles with a circumference of 17.5–18.5 in. (44–46 cm) after 3 seasons of growth. Hadeco's Sonata and Sonatini bulbs are smaller; *Hippeastrum* 'Amico' and *H.* 'Top Choice' do not exceed 10.5–11 in. (26–28 cm) circumference, and some are even smaller than this. Japanese Super Mini bulbs do not grow beyond 4 in. (10 cm) circumference but still produce up to 3 scapes, each with 3–5 blooms.

Regardless of type and flower size, bulbs should reach maturity and bloom after 2 growing seasons of 8–9 months each. At the end of the first growing season, Dutch breeders aim for an average bulb size of 5.75–6.5 in. (14–16 cm) circumference with 80–90% of the bulbs reaching over 4–4.5 in.

(10–12 cm) circumference, the latter size being the minimum to obtain a 9.5 in. (24 cm) circumference bulb at the end of the second growing season. A bulb that measures 4.5–5.5 in. (12–14 cm) circumference at the beginning of the second season should, at the end of 8–9 months' growth, reach 11–12 in. (28–30 cm) circumference for large- and medium-flowering hippeastrums, slightly smaller for smaller flowering types. Hadeco aims to create bulbs no larger than the size of a golf ball with 3 scapes; each having 7–8 dainty blooms.

The ability of the bulb to recover after flowering and then produce leaves and further buds for several years is particularly important to the cut flower grower who expects to use the same bulbs for 3–4 years or more before discarding them. Flat (spherical) bulbs with wide shoulders are generally preferred to oval bulbs since they have a larger circumference and hence command a higher price.

Although vigorous root development is important for optimum plant growth and performance, some breeders pay greater attention to it than others. Most Dutch breeders are more concerned with floral developments, since it is expected that many consumers will discard their plants after flowering and purchase fresh bulbs each year.

Bulbs should store well without rotting or sprouting during the preparation, or cool period. Some bulbs rot easily before or after flowering. This problem is sometimes exacerbated by growers' watering practices in which bulbs are given more water than is necessary to stimulate growth, resulting in large, soft, watery bulbs with a propensity to rot easily. The role of temperature in the rotting process is yet to be investigated.

The number of days from planting to flowering depends on the plant's genetic constitution, preparation given prior to purchase and environmental and cultural conditions after planting. Four weeks from planting to flowering is considered particularly fast, 5–6 desirable and 7 weeks acceptable for pot plants. Breeders consider 8 weeks acceptable for cut flower production to allow sufficient time for the scape to elongate. Most large Australian, Dutch, Japanese and South African singles and doubles take 4–8 weeks from planting to flowering when grown at 68–70°F (20–21°C). Smaller flowering Dutch and South African hybrids are often quicker, blooming after 3–5 weeks. Some American and Dutch Cybisters are slower, taking up to 9 weeks before flowering. Pot plants take, on average, 30 days from planting to marketing, although this varies with the cultivar and the retailer's requirements for the plant to have reached a particular stage in its development prior to sale.

Scape Production and Development

Mature bulbs for bare bulb or pot plant sales should produce a minimum of 2 scapes which ideally appear simultaneously or consecutively with a maximum interval of 7–14 days between each scape. Pot plants should show 2 scapes at the time of purchase. Occasionally, a third may appear at the same time from larger bulbs but more often, up to 7 months later.

Usually 2, sometimes 3 and occasionally 4 scapes from large 11–14 in. (28–36 cm) circumference Dutch bulbs will appear simultaneously or consecutively within 2 or 3 days and sometimes within 4–6 hours of planting! This pattern of development can prove problematic when several inflorescences reach maturity at the same time making it difficult for individual flowers to open out properly. Growers consider a gap of 10–12 days between the appearance of the first and second scapes to be ideal since this will result in a succession of blooms lasting several weeks.

Most older, large-flowering Dutch hybrids did not produce 2 scapes until bulbs reached 11–12 in. (28–30 cm) or 12–12.5 in. (30–32 cm) circumference, compared to an increasing number of large singles which produce 2 scapes from 10.5–11 in. (26–28 cm) circumference bulbs. Dutch breeders aim to reduce bulb circumference even further so that large-, medium- and small-flowering hippeastrums produce 2 scapes from 8.5–10.5 in. (22–26 cm) circumference bulbs and higher planting densities can be achieved. Although it is possible for some large Dutch cultivars to bloom from 5.5 in. (14 cm) circumference bulbs, such small bulbs will only produce a single scape and a single pair of flowers. Some small-flowering Japanese hybrids flower from 3.25 in. (8 cm) circumference bulbs while 4.5–6.5 in. (12–16 cm), 5.5–7 in. (14–18 cm) and 6–8 in. (16–20 cm) circumference bulbs are typical minimum sizes for modern small-, medium- and large-flowering Dutch hybrids respectively.

Scapes must be firm, robust and proportional to flower size. Some Dutch and South African breeders are creating hippeastrums for pot plant sales with shorter, more robust scapes which do not require staking and therefore are less prone to collapse. Dutch breeders consider 14–18 in. (35–45 cm) to be the ideal scape length with a minimum length of 12 in. (30 cm) and a maximum length of 20 in. (50 cm). South African breeders have always preferred shorter scapes, considering 12 in. (30 cm) to be ideal. Some breeders consider 20 in. (50 cm) scapes to be too tall for very small-flowering types, particularly when foliage is absent at the time of flowering.

Cut flower breeders aim for 27 in. (70 cm) scapes from freshly planted bulbs in their first year of production but 24 in. (60 cm) is also acceptable. Even taller 33–36 in. (85–90 cm) scapes can be expected from those bulbs in subsequent years if they are not lifted but remain in the soil; such tall scapes are due possibly to lack of root disturbance which occurs after lifting. Growers who lift their bulbs annually prefer a scape length of 27–31 in. (70–80 cm). Scapes of smaller flowering hippeastrums may reach 24–27 in. (60–70 cm).

Flower Development, Presentation and Production

South African breeders prefer large, flat, open, upward-facing blooms, while Dutch breeders, until recently, have preferred large, rounded forms. Attitudes among some Dutch breeders are slowly changing, resulting in more distinctive flower shapes, patterns and color combinations. Flowers should have 6 well-proportioned tepals with uniform pigmentation; the tepals should retain their color and not fade with age.

Bulbs bred for pot plant and cut flower sales should produce a minimum of 4 blooms per scape. A maximum of 6 flowers per scape is appropriate for large-flowered bulbs and just 4 for exceptionally large singles and doubles so that individual flowers have sufficient space to open fully. Dutch and South African breeders aim to augment the flower count for small-flowering hippeastrums. An increasing number reliably produce 6–8 blooms and a few 9—10 blooms per scape. As few as 3 or 4 flowers per scape is considered acceptable for Bloeiende Klisters in view of the multiple scapes which ensure a continuous supply of delicate blooms for many weeks.

Leaf Development

Fan-shaped leaves are attractive, but upright foliage is generally favored by breeders and growers since vertical leaves dry quicker after watering, reducing the incidence of fungal attack. Management of greenhouse-cultivated bulbs with upright, rather than spreading leaves, is easier as they do not obstruct the narrow paths between plots. In South Africa, upright leaves are less likely to be damaged by hail stones which can be a major problem.

Offset Production

Breeders regard 1 or 2 offsets as ideal, enabling stocks to be maintained without the need to twin scale. High offset production may cause difficulties (see Chapter 8).

Consistent Growth and Reliable Performance

These aspects are particularly important for the cut flower grower who seeks to cultivate individual mature bulbs for 4–6 years. Plants should bloom each year and produce a minimum of 4 well-proportioned blooms per scape, each flower having 6 tepals.

Vase Life

Vase life refers to the number of days an umbel remains fresh—from the first to the last flower. A minimum vase life of 10 days per was considered standard until the beginning of the 21st century. Fourteen days at 68–72°F (20–22°C) is now becoming the norm for some Dutch and South African hippeastrums enabling them to compete with other popular cut flowers. A vase life of 7–8 days per bloom is regarded as acceptable, 10–12 days as good and 14 days even better.

Resistance to *Fusarium oxysporum* and *Stagonospora curtisii*

Some breeders are devoting attention to resolving the problem of bulbs rotting during storage, or before or after flowering, while others concentrate upon improving flowers, since most consumers are only interested in the flowers and neglect or discard the bulbs after flowering.

Preparing for Commercial Production

Breeders' Open Days

Dutch breeders organize open days, usually in March and April, to display their latest developments. A committee comprising bulb and cut flower growers, wholesalers, exporters, sales representatives, researchers and other interested parties is invited to comment upon second and third selections using information prepared by the breeder. Following the third and usually final selection, data is analyzed and commercial decisions taken. The decision to commercialize a new hippeastrum may be taken after the second flowering for particularly promising plants, but in other cases, a fourth selection will be necessary before a decision can be made.

Propagating a New Hippeastrum

After a new hippeastrum is selected, it is propagated by chipping and twin scaling. Once stocks have reached 100–1000 bulbs, commercial production can begin. Within only 2 years of twin scaling, stocks will have reached 30,000–40,000 bulbs. Promising hybrids may become commercially available within 4–5 years following the final selection. Others may undergo several years of testing, resulting in larger stocks; these will be available for sale after only 2 years following the decision to commercialize. Some growers start with 1000–3000 bulbs to test the market's response before expanding production, while others begin with larger quantities.

Breeders establish their own policies regarding selling their stock and they negotiate with growers to secure the best deal. Some breeders sell their entire stock of mature and immature bulbs to growers who propagate the bulbs, while others choose to propagate the bulbs themselves and then sell the 1-year-old bulblets to growers. In some cases, breeders sell large, mature bulbs to the grower who undertakes all the propagation.

Some breeders sell their entire stock, including eventual breeding rights, for a certain price. Thus they derive profits from the outset, with all future profits belonging to the grower. Other breeders who are also commercial growers keep their new varieties partly or totally for themselves, at least during the first year of commercial production.

Exclusivity

Some breeders may pursue exclusive rights for hippeastrums with special characteristics, such as a distinctive shape, unusual pattern or color combinations. Growers place bids to grow and propagate the bulbs for an initial period of 4–5 years, paying all monies directly to the breeder. The contract may be renewed at the end of the period or additional growers may become involved.

Regular red, white or striped cultivars are unlikely to be exclusively sold, since it is in the breeder's interests for these to be grown by as many growers as possible so as to obtain maximum sales. Stock may be divided into 2 or 3 portions and sold to several growers. Some Dutch groups have sufficient capacity to grow their new developments.

Full details of the processes involved in obtaining Plant Breeders' Rights can be found elsewhere in this book.

Commercial Production Practices

At the beginning of the 21st century, commercial bulb, pot plant and cut flower production for domestic and international sales were dominated by Brazil, Israel, South Africa and The Netherlands. Smaller quantities were grown in Australia and Japan. Table 10-2 highlights the environmental and geographical differences; variations in practices and techniques of commercially produced and propagated bare bulbs, pot plants and cut flowers cultivated in Australia, Brazil, Israel, The Netherlands and South Africa.

Bulb Preparation—Cool Period

Annual lifting enables bulbs to be sorted and graded, diseased or damaged bulbs to be discarded, and bulblets to be removed from the parent bulb. By August, the foliage of bulbs cultivated in the Northern Hemisphere has become long, sometimes untidy. Since the bulbs have now reached the required size for sale and the function of the leaves to manufacture food has therefore been completed, they can be removed without detriment to the bulb. Their removal also makes packing and transporting easier and improves the bulb's aesthetic appeal.

Although research has shown most bulbs require a minimum of 8 and preferably 10 weeks at 55°F (13°C) for scapes to emerge within a few days after replanting, possible temperatures may range from 48–64°F (9–18°C). Six weeks at 55°F (13°C) has proved sufficient for bulbs cultivated at 64–66°F (18–19°C). Some Dutch-grown bulbs harvested in July or August may not have received any preparation at the time of export due to pressure exerted by exporters, wholesalers and retailers upon growers to lift the bulbs in time for them to reach the shops by early October, ready for pre-Christmas sales. In such cases, preparation will be given during transportation and in subsequent storage so that bulbs harvested in July should have completed their preparation by mid-October. However it is possible that not all bulbs will have received 8–10 weeks preparation at the time of sale.

Due to the earlier harvesting of hippeastrums grown in Brazil, Israel and South Africa, bulbs receive the full 8–10 weeks preparation at 55°F (13°C) prior to, during and/or following export to Europe, Japan, Scandinavia and the United States. Extended storage is then given at 41–48°F (5–9°C) until the bulbs are ready to be potted up for pot plant sales or to be dispatched to their final destination. Some bulbs given several months of extended storage may experience problems (see Chapter 8 for details).

Bulbs harvested in September or October may have already received 4–6 weeks of preparation in the soil as temperatures naturally fall and will therefore only require a further 4–6 weeks at 55°F (13°C). It is crucial that growers inform exporters and wholesalers of any preparation the bulbs have already received, so they can be given any remaining preparation after their arrival, to ensure flowering soon after planting.

Storing bulbs at higher temperatures results in less foliage at the time of flowering. This can be particularly useful to growers who wish to avoid excessive leaf growth when cultivating hybrids which naturally produce plenty of foliage at the time of flowering.

Cut flower growers do not lift their bulbs each autumn, but give the cool period in the soil. Although this enables the plant's root system to be preserved, resulting in taller scapes the following season, flowering is more uneven compared to bulbs stored in tightly controlled environments. The ease with which flowering can be manipulated means it is now possible to have hybrids in flower for most months of the year.

Conclusion

Growers are continually required to make difficult decisions as new hybrids become available. Understanding customers' requirements will become increasingly important as awareness and knowledge of hippeastrums increase. Enthusiasts are likely to demand higher quality bulbs and improved pre- and post-sales service as they acquire greater knowledge and experience of growing hippeastrums. Competition among breeders and growers will intensify and, ultimately, only the most resourceful and imaginative companies will survive.

Table 10-2. Commercial bulb cultivation and production.

	Australia	Brazil	Israel	The Netherlands	South Africa
Markets	Home only.	Home: ca. 13%. Overseas: 87% (mainly Europe and South Africa).	Home: ca. 5%. Overseas: ca. 95% (mainly Great Britain, Germany, The Netherlands, Scandinavia and United States [70%]).	Home and overseas (mainly Australia, Europe, Japan, Scandinavia, New Zealand and United States).	Home: ca. 3%. Overseas: ca. 97% (mainly Australia, Europe, Iceland, Japan, Scandinavia, New Zealand and United States).
2001–2002 sales volume	Ca. 15,000 bulbs. Over 50% imported from The Netherlands.[a]	Ca. 4 million bulbs. Many exported for pot plant sales.[b]	Ca. 2 million dry bulbs including 200,000 pot plants, 100,000 stems for home sales only.[c]	Ca. 10 million dry bulbs including 1.6 million pot plants (figures include bulbs may imported from Brazil and Israel). Ca. 90 million stems.[d]	Several million bulbs exported yearly to Japan for the November gift season. Over 3 million pot plants sold in Scandinavia at Christmas.[e]
End use	Pot plant and garden bedding plant.	Pot plant for inside and outside the home, garden plant bedding in frost-free climates.	Pot plant, cut flower and garden bedding plant in private gardens.	Pot plant for inside and outside the home, cut flower and garden bedding plant in frost-free climates.	Pot plant for inside and outside the home, garden bedding plant in frost-free climates.
Most popular hybrid types	Large single. Increasing interest in doubles.	Large single. Increasing interest in smaller flowering hippeastrums.	Large single.	Large single. Increasing interest in Japanese doubles and smaller flowering hippeastrums.	Large single, doubles and smaller flowering hippeastrums.

Table 10-2 *(continued)*

	Australia	Brazil	Israel	The Netherlands	South Africa
Leading growers	2 growers: D. Rix and Maguire's Hippeastrum Farm.	2 growers: Brasbonitas and Andreas J. C. Boersen.	6 growers including Jordan River Bulbs and Saad-Assaf Nurseries.	Numerous, with separate growers of dry bulbs and cut flowers.	Dominated by Hadeco (Pty) Ltd.
Breeding and cultivation locations and environment	In fields in Queensland, 434 miles (700 km) south of the Tropic of Capricorn.	In fields 93 miles (150 km) west of Sao Paulo.	In glasshouses in Jordan Valley and south west.	In glasshouses mainly around 's-Gravenzande and near the coast	In fields 31–37 miles (50–60 km) northwest of Johannesburg at 3936–5248 ft. (1200–1600 m) above sea level.
Summer temperatures	Day: 86–100°F . (30–38°C) Night: 57–68°F (14–20°C).	Day: 95°F (35°C). Night: 77°F (25°C).	Day: 77–95°F (25-35°C). Night: 68–77°F (20–25°C).	Day: 68–77°F (20-25°C). Night: 63°F (17°C).	Day: 82°F (28°C). Night: 68°F (20°C).
Winter temperatures	Day: 68–75°F (20–24°C). Night: 39–54°F (4–12°C).	Day: 77°F (25°C). Night: 41–59°F (5–15°C).	Day: 59–77°F (15–25°C). Night: 50–59°F (10–15°C).	Day: 61–64°F (16–18°C) Night: 61°F (16°C)	Day: 66°F (19°C). Night: 50°F (10°C).
Rainfall	Total: ca. 59 in. (1500 mm) per year. Summer and autumn: ca. 43 in. (1100 mm) but periodically —8 in. (200 mm) may fall over 5 days, followed by a dry	Total: 63 in. (1600 mm) per year. Summer: 47 in. (1200 mm). Winter: 16 in. (400 mm).	Total: 47 in. (1200 mm) per year. Summer: 12 in. (300 mm). Winter: 35 in. (890 mm). Only drip irrigation system used.	Summer: water 2–3 times per week for 8–10 minutes per session, equaling ca. 1–2 qts. per 10 sq. ft. (1–2 liters per sq meter). Winter: water every 8–12 days.	Total: 29 in. (740 mm) per year. Summer: 28 in. (720 mm). Winter: 0.8 in. (20 mm).

Table 10-2 *(continued)*

	Australia	Brazil	Israel	The Netherlands	South Africa
Rainfall continued	period for 3–5 weeks. Winter and spring: ca. 16 in. (400 mm). Overhead sprinklers used in spring and early summer.				
Relative humidity	Summer: 60–70%. Winter: 50–60%.	Summer: 60–80%. Winter: 30–50%.	Year-round: 60–80%.	Summer: 50-60%. Winter: 90%. Ideal: 70–80%.	Unknown.
Growing media	Red volcanic loam to sandy loam; pine bark used as a mulch. pH: 5.5–6.0. EC: 0.6 mS/cm.	Clay. Balanced liquid feed with trace elements administered during the growing period. pH: 5.5–6.0.	Peat or cocoa peat. pH: 6.0–7.0. EC: 1.8–2.2 mS/cm.	Sandy loam. Balanced feed and trace elements with every watering. Regular soil analysis. pH: 6.5. EC: 0.8 mS/cm.	Sandy loam enriched with cow, chicken, or pig manure prior to planting. Additional feeding as required. pH: 6.0–6.8.
Natural flowering period	September–November	September–October	April–May	March–May	September–October
Prepared or forced bulb flowering period	Not applicable.	Pot plants and dry bulbs: October–April.	Pot plants and dry bulbs: October–April.	Pot plants and dry bulbs: October–May. Cut flowers: October–April.	Pot plants and dry bulbs: October–April.

Table 10-2 *(continued)*

	Australia	Brazil	Israel	The Netherlands	South Africa
Harvesting of mature bulbs	September. September.	April–June.	June–July.	August–October and later.	May–June.
Bulb circumference at fattest part after 2 growing seasons	8–12 in. (20–30 cm).	9.5–14.25 in. . (24–36 cm)	9.5–12 in. (24–30 cm), but as small as 8 in. (20 cm) and as large as 16 in. (40 cm).	11–13 in. (28–12.5 cm), but as small as 9.5 in. (24 cm) and as large as 14.25 in. (36 cm).	7–12 in. (18–30 cm).
Problems	Mealybug, slugs, snails, rusts.	*Botrytis*, *Fusarium oxysporum*, *Stagonospora curtisii*, thrips.	Aphids, snails.	*Fusarium oxysporum*, *Stagonospora curtisii*, mites, nematodes, thrips.	Lily borer beetle.
Propagating	Offsets, twin scaling.	Twin scaling.	Twin scaling.	Twin scaling, chipping, offsets.	Twin scaling, notching.

[a] Source: Richard Maguire, Maguire's Hippeastrum Farm, Queensland.

[b] Source: Kebol, Hillegom.

[c] Source: Agrexco Agricultural Export Company.

[d] Source: Verenigde Bloemenveilingen Nederland (VBN) United Flower Auctions of the Netherlands.

[e] Source: Hadeco, Maraisburg.

Chapter 11

Propagation

Propagating hippeastrums is exciting. With the exception of sterile (aseptic) tissue culture techniques, which are more appropriate to the professional breeder and geneticist, all others may be performed successfully in most home environments.

New hybrids may result from cross pollination and propagating by seed. As parentage become more complex, it is possible for some progeny to show little resemblance to their parents; for example, flowers may be semi or fully double, even though both parents had single flowers. This unpredictability, coupled with the long time (up to 6 years) it takes a bulb to reach maturity and flower when cultivated in a home environment, limits the usefulness of propagating from seed to the professional breeder and the enthusiastic, amateur gardener. Propagating from offsets is quicker; bulbs usually reach maturity and flower in 3–4 years, the exact time depending on the cultivar, environment and cultural conditions.

Rapid multiplication techniques such as twin scaling, chipping and notching enable growers to produce several million bulbs each year for dry bulb, pot plant and cut flower sales. Chapter 11 explores a range of methods from the professional and amateur breeder's and grower's perspectives, followed by step-by-step instructions for each technique.

Commercial Propagation Methods

Commercial breeders and growers rely primarily on three techniques, twin scaling, chipping and notching.

Chipping and Twin Scaling

Twin scaling is the most widely used propagation technique by commercial breeders and growers. Chipping is also used for building up stocks of new cultivars from small initial quantities. Both methods have advantages and disadvantages so depending on the desired outcome, the breeder or grower will select the most appropriate method.

Best time to chip and twin scale

Although bulbs are best chipped or twin scaled 10 weeks after harvesting, equally high success rates have been obtained 6 months after harvesting. An 80% success rate is even possible after 8 or 9 months and good results have also been obtained after only 4–6 weeks of storage at 55°F (13°C).

What size bulb to use

Healthy bulbs measuring 11–12.5 in. (28–32 cm) circumference are the most commonly used sizes for chipping and twin scaling. Larger bulbs up to 16 in. (40 cm) circumference or much smaller bulbs may also be used. Bulbs measuring less than 7 in. (18 cm) circumference are cut into 12 or 16 segments and usually left as chips. If the basal plate is particularly large, each chip may be cut into 2 twin scales, however, this is not generally recommended. Using small bulbs which have not yet flowered makes it impossible to check for uniformity, as those chipped for 3 years in a row will have never flowered. Twin scaling mature bulbs which have previously flowered enables those which do not come true to type to be discarded.

Bulblet production rate

The basal plate plays a key role in bulblet development. While larger circumference bulbs generally produce more chips or twin scales, some bulbs have relatively small basal plates resulting in fewer chips and/or twin scales. Bulbs measuring 11–12 in. (28–30 cm) and 16 in. (40 cm) circumference will generally produce 54–60 and 72–80 twin scales respectively—the exact number varying according to the cultivar. A 12–12.5 in. (30–32 cm) circumference bulb will usually be cut into 14–16 equal pieces. Each piece is then cut into 3 or 4, sometimes 5 twin scales, depending on the size of the basal plate and the number of scales. Inner and outer leaf bases are used but sometimes the outer leaf bases are too dry and are therefore unsuitable. Larger bulblets are usually obtained from more vigorous, outer bases.

Bulblets may develop just above the basal plate on one or both outer surfaces, as well as, or instead of, in between the scales. One bulblet per twin scale is the norm, but thicker twin scales may produce 2 or 3 bulblets and up to 8 in some cases. Some produce none.

The net percentage rate of healthy bulblets per 100 twin scales after 10–12 weeks of incubation at 81–82°F (27–28°C) varies from as little as 20 to 120%. Based on an average 80% success rate and a multiplication factor of 1.8–2.0, around 43–48 healthy bulblets can be expected from a 12 in. (30 cm) circumference bulb. Some varieties have a 100% success rate, producing 60 bulblets per bulb. Success factors include the size and number of initiated inflorescences inside the bulb, temperature and humidity levels during storage, moisture levels of the medium (Seramis or vermiculite) and the twin scale's propensity to rot during incubation. Rotting is usually a result of *Penicillium* species developing in conditions where ventilation is inadequate and the medium too moist. Because *Fusarium oxysporum* may also cause serious problems, it is advisable to dip the scales in a solution of systemic fungicide prior to incubation.

Chipping large bulbs yields fewer but larger bulblets than twin scaling. Generally, one chip is obtained per 0.5 in. (1 cm), that is, 28 chips from an 11 in. (28 cm) circumference bulb, but this requires technical skill and a sharp knife. Chips used for twin scaling are generally twice as large as chips used for chipping, that is, 1 chip per 0.75 in. (2 cm) yielding 14 chips from an 11 in. (28 cm) circumference bulb. However since it is possible to obtain 2, 3 and even 4 twin scales per chip, up to 56 healthy bulblets could result from this size bulb based on a 100% success rate. If only 2 twin scales per chip are obtained and the rate of healthy bulblets is reduced, the final number of bulblets which reach maturity could be the same as those obtained from chipping.

Chipping small bulbs can result in a higher multiplication factor compared to twin scaling an 11–12 in. (28–30 cm) circumference bulb (40–60 bulblets at the end of 2 growing seasons). For example, at the end of the first growing season (8–9 months), bulbs grown from bulblets will have reached 3.25–6.5 in. (8–16 cm) circumference, 4.5 in. (12 cm) circumference being the average. Chipping a 4.5 in. (12 cm) bulb will yield 10 chips, each producing one bulblet. After 8–9 months of growth, the resulting small bulbs are chipped, each resulting in up to 10 chips, each producing one bulblet. After 2 growing seasons, a multiplication factor of up to 100 will have resulted.

Incubating chips and twin scales

Chipping and twin scaling are carried out from April to July in the Southern Hemisphere and from June to October or even later in the Northern Hemisphere. The timing depends on when the bulbs are harvested and prepared and on the schedules of breeders and growers.

Dutch and Israeli growers place the chips and twin scales in plastic or 3.25in. (8 cm) high wired boxes or flat trays containing vermiculite moistened with tap water. Around 34 pints (17 liters) of water are added to 200 pints (100 liters) of vermiculite, the exact proportions varying according to individual growers' cultivation practices and relative humidity levels during storage, ideally 80–95%. Some breeders incubate the twin scales using equal portions of sand and peat with usually one layer of twin scales per tray, sometimes two. Twin scales are incubated in the dark for 10–12 weeks at 72–86°F (22–30°C), the exact temperature varying according to individual breeder's and grower's requirements.

Chips and twin scales are susceptible to fungal infections, particularly when incubated in moistened vermiculite. To avoid this problem, the Royal Botanic Gardens, Kew, uses Seramis as an alternative. The unique properties of Seramis allow moisture levels to be precisely controlled, thereby eliminating rotting (see Chapter 9 for details).

First growing season

After 10–12 weeks, the twin scales or chips are transplanted into compost which may be loam-based with or without added pig, cow or chicken manures or loam-free (perlite or coir). A soil temperature of 72°F (22°C) is maintained throughout the growing season. Most breeders and growers administer a balanced liquid feed containing trace elements at regular intervals throughout the first growing season once leaf growth has become vigorous.

After 9–10 months of growth, bulblets will have reached 2.5–10.5 in. (6–26 cm) circumference, depending on the cultivar. After lifting, the bulblets are prepared and given hot water treatment as a precautionary measure and to eradicate any pests and diseases present within the bulb. The bulbs are then dried again and replanted. Full details of the hot water treatment are given in Chapter 12.

Second growing season

After a second growing period of 8–10 months, most bulbs will have reached 8.5–14.25 in. (22–36 cm) circumference depending on cultivar, and planting and harvesting dates. Greenhouse-cultivated Dutch bulbs planted in January and harvested in September–October will be larger than those planted in November and harvested the following July, because July, August and September are particularly good months for hippeastrum development. A 10.5–11 in. (26–28 cm) circumference bulb grown in 9 months will produce more scapes, on average, than the same size bulb grown in 7 months.

Smaller flowering Dutch, Japanese and South African hippeastrums naturally produce 2–3 scapes from smaller bulbs and will have reached a correspondingly smaller size by the end of the second growing season. Most Israeli-cultivated bulbs will have reached 9.5–12 in. (24–30 cm) circumference, compared to the slightly larger Dutch-cultivated bulbs which will have reached 11–12.5 in. (28–32 cm) circumference at the end of the second growing season. After harvesting, mature bulbs are dried for 7–10 days at 73–81°F (23–27°C) then graded and stored, prior to export.

Notching

Notching or basal cutting is used by Indian and South African breeders in addition to, or as an alternative to, twin scaling. Research undertaken at the Plant Propagation and Floriculture Laboratory, National Botanical Research Institute, Lucknow (India), in the late 1970s by V. N. Gupta and M. A. Kher found notching to be quick, safe, effective and reliable. Only basic equipment was required, making it possible for amateur gardeners to carry out the technique in a home environment. The best time for notching was in the third week of January resulting in the greatest number of bulblets—an increase of 1860% from 16 notches. As the number of notches and bulblets increased, so the size and weight of bulblets decreased from 1 to 0.5 in. (2.5 to 1 cm) circumference and from 0.7 to 0.2 oz (21.25 to 5.65 gm) respectively. Most cultivars reached maturity and flowered 2–3 years after transplanting but some took longer, depending on the cultivar, environmental and cultural conditions such as temperature, lighting and nutrition.

Step-by-step Propagation Techniques

Details of four propagation techniques are described here: propagating from seed, chips and twin scales, offsets and notching.

Propagating from Seed

Although growing from seed is the slowest method, it is the most fascinating, particularly when a new hybrid comes into flower for the very first time. Most hybrids readily self-pollinate and cross-pollinate with other hybrids, producing ample quantities of seed. Details of pollination and seed development are given in Chapter 8.

Collecting and storing pollen

When cross-pollination is required, the pollen parent may not always be available, making it necessary to collect and store pollen. Pfeiffer (1936) discovered pollen stored at 50°F (10°C) with less than 50% humidity retained a germination rate of 50–75% for 5 months. If pollen is to be kept for longer, it should be frozen.

To collect and store pollen you will need either gelatin capsules (size 00 or 000) or glass or plastic vials, a pair of forceps, an airtight jar or other container and a desiccant such as anhydrous calcium silicate. Sold as silica gel in Great Britain and Drierite® in the United States, calcium silicate absorbs moisture contained within the pollen grains. When dehydrated, the desiccant is bright blue, changing to pink when saturated.

Use the forceps to remove the ripened anther and place it in a capsule. Label with the name and collection date. Place the pollen-filled capsule in an airtight container containing desiccant. Add more desiccant until the capsule is covered, then seal the container. If storing pollen in a vial, first line the bottom of the vial with desiccant, then add the ripened anther. Add more desiccant and seal, placing the vial in an airtight container containing more desiccant.

Whether storing in gelatin capsules or in plastic or glass vials, it is important to allow the pollen-filled capsules or vials to stand at room temperature for 24 hours before freezing or storing in a refrigerator. During this period, moisture from the pollen grains will be absorbed, resulting in crystals turning pink. Replace with fresh blue crystals. It is recommended to examine the capsules or vials every 3–4 days and replace the old desiccant as necessary as further moisture may be absorbed.

Storing seeds

Research by W. J. Carpenter and E. R. Ostmark (Department of Ornamental Horticulture, IFAS, University of Florida, United States) in the mid 1980s showed freshly harvested seeds to have the highest germination rates. Even after 12 months of storage at 11% or 52% relative humidity at either 41°F (5°C) or 59°F (15°C) with 6 or 12% seed moisture, seeds retained a germination rate of 86–93%, compared to 68–70% after only 6 months when seeds were stored at 77°F (25°C) and 95°F (35°C) at the same relative humidity.

If the seeds will not be sown immediately, dry them for 24–48 hours. Discard any which do not have a hard, raised central portion (the seed). Place the seeds in an airtight container containing desiccant and store at 41–59°F (5–15°C). Check the seeds every 2–3 weeks to ensure they remain healthy. Replace saturated desiccant with fresh as necessary.

Best time for sowing seeds

The best time to sow seeds in the Northern Hemisphere is March–April so that seedlings have plenty of time to become established before the winter. Seeds sown in May–July should also make good progress before the autumn. Freshly harvested seeds can be sown and grown in water or Seramis for the first few weeks. A high success rate has been obtained using either.

Growing seed in water (0-4 weeks)

Fill a clean, glass jar three-quarters full of uncontaminated, tepid tap water. Sprinkle the seeds on top, making sure there is space between each seed. Place the jar in a light, warm place at 70°F (21°C). A heated propagator, warm conservatory, sunny windowsill or shelf above a warm radiator are ideal. Ensure the jar remains free from algae by cleaning with a mild detergent after carefully removing the seedlings. Then refill with fresh, tepid tap water and replace the seedlings. Some may sink to the bottom and continue growing in the water.

Ensure the seedlings remain free from mold. Discard any moldy seedlings, clean the jar as described previously, refilling with fresh, tepid tap water, then replace the seedlings. After 4 weeks, remove seedlings with 1 or 2 roots and leaves. The leaves should be around 1.5–2 in. (4–5 cm) long or longer. Pot up into 3 in. (7.5 cm) pots using the Kew mix or a suitable alternative. Slower-growing seedlings should remain in water until they have reached this stage of growth.

The advantages of growing hippeastrums in water are fourfold. First, problems associated with drying-out and contracting soil-borne diseases are avoided. Drying out can be a serious problem in hot weather, sometimes leading to the death of the plant. Second, mold or other disease can be detected and action taken at an early stage, avoiding other seedlings becoming contaminated. Third, only healthy plants are grown on. Last, minimal disturbance and damage are caused to the plant's delicate organs, essential if scientific studies are being carried out.

Growing seed in Seramis (0–12 weeks)

Research at the Royal Botanic Gardens, Kew (RBG, Kew), has found planting and growing seeds in Seramis for the first 12–14 weeks to be successful. The process is as follows. Fill a 3 in. (7.5 cm) pot with Seramis leaving the top 0.5 in. (1 cm) clear, then soak and drain the pot. Sow the seeds just below the surface before putting the pot in a clear, plastic bag and sealing it with a tie. Place the bag in a light, warm place at 70°F (21°C). Further watering is not needed until growth becomes vigorous. As the leaves develop, split open the bag and begin feeding weekly with a complete liquid feed containing trace elements. After 12–14 weeks, transplant the seedlings into the Kew mix.

Growing hippeastrum seed in Seramis has several advantages. First, the sterile environment prevents contamination by air- and soil-borne organisms since everything is sealed inside the bag. Second, potentially fatal consequences of overwatering are avoided due to the unique properties of Seramis. Last, only healthy plants with an established root structure and foliage are potted up and grown on.

Potting up (4–12 weeks)

When the seedlings are ready for potting up, fill a 3 in. (7.5 cm) pot with a free-draining, well-aerated, moisture-retentive mix and then moisten it. The Kew mix is recommended. Make a small hole in the compost using a dibber, place the seedling's root in the hole, and fill up with further mix. Place the pot in a light warm place. A soil temperature of 70°F (21°C) and an air temperature of 70–77°F (21–25°C) are recommended. Avoid exposing seedlings to the sun's fiercest rays as they may cause leaf scorch. Some shading may be needed to protect the plant during the summer. Keep the compost moist and fertilize weekly with a balanced liquid feed containing trace elements throughout spring, summer and early autumn.

Seedlings are best grown continuously for the first two winters. However, if the leaves die back, then reduce the amount of water and cease feeding the plant, but do not allow the soil to dry out. Resume feeding when new growth becomes vigorous, which is usually end February or early March in Great Britain. After the second winter, give the seedlings a cool period (see

Chapter 9). As the bulbs grow, repot into larger pots using fresh mix. Always use as deep a pot as possible.

Propagating from Offsets

In most cases, the presence of an offset on a bulb is first observed when leaves appear during the summer, either from within the parent bulb or towards the rim of the pot, around the base of the bulb (Plate 9-3). Further leaves and roots develop during the summer, increasing in size as offset girth increases. Some offsets may have already become detached while others remain attached to the main bulb.

Robust foliage development is usually a good indicator that the offset has developed its own roots and can be detached and potted up separately. The best time to repot is at the end of the cool period (mid-January to mid-March in the Northern Hemisphere; June–August in the Southern Hemisphere) when disturbance to the parent bulb and offset is minimal. If the offset appears to be developing at the expense of the parent, both bulbs will benefit by earlier repotting.

To separate the offset from the parent plant, hold the latter firmly in one hand. Gently disentangle the roots of the two bulbs with the other hand while washing the roots under tepid tap water. Try not to get the basal plate wet. Remove any dead or damaged roots from the parent and offset bulbs. The offset may have already become detached from the parent bulb. If not, gently detach it now; it should come away quite easily. Take care not to tear any roots.

After separating the bulbs, pat all the roots dry using absorbent paper to remove excess water. Dry the basal plate and the rest of the bulb thoroughly; a hair dryer may be useful to assist with this. If any damage is suspected or visible, dip the bulbs in a systemic fungicidal solution for 20 minutes.

Depending on the size of the offsets, either pot them up separately or plant several together in a large, deep pot. Depth is particularly important to enable robust root development. The Kew mix is particularly recommended. Water in well and place the pot in a light warm place. A temperature of 70°F (21°C) is ideal. Keep the soil moist and feed weekly during spring, summer and early autumn with a complete feed containing trace elements. Do not give the offset a cool period in the first winter but keep growing it at 70°F (21°C). Thereafter, treat the offset in the same way as mature bulbs. Repot when necessary.

Propagating from Chips and Twin Scales

Before beginning either technique, assemble the following equipment and materials in three groups as indicated:

Group 1

Protective covers for work surfaces, such as plastic sheets or newspaper

Protective clothing such as lab coat, long plastic apron and thin surgical gloves

Large cutting board for chipping and twin scaling

Sharp knife, scalpel or razor blades for cutting the bulbs

Glass jars or plastic containers for sterilizing knives

Alcohol burner or gas flame

Cloths or cotton buds for sterilizing bulbs

Cloths for wiping down surfaces

Surgical spirit for sterilizing work surfaces and equipment

Healthy bulbs 12–12.5 in. (30–32 cm) circumference or larger

Group 2

Bowls for soaking chips or twin scales

Strainer or sieve

Clock with timer

Measuring jug

Systemic fungicide or green or yellow sulfur for damaged bulbs

Clean water (distilled, if possible)

Group 3

10 × 7 in. (25 × 18 cm) clear polyethylene bags and ties for chips or twin scales

Plant labels

Permanent pen or pencil

Measuring jug

Seramis (vermiculite as alternative)

Heated propagator or warm airing cupboard; 81–86°F (27–30°C) is an ideal temperature

Dark covering for propagator

With the supplies in hand, ensure all work surfaces and equipment are thoroughly cleaned using surgical spirit. Then cover work surfaces to protect them from possible spillage. Sterilize knives by flaming and dipping in surgical spirit before use. Cover any cuts and abrasions, particularly on the hands and wrists, before putting on surgical gloves. Always discard and replace punctured gloves with a fresh pair immediately. Wear protective clothing at all times to safeguard against possible chemical damage to eyes and skin. Always read manufacturers' instructions and any other precautionary advice before preparing, using and disposing of chemicals, and follow instructions exactly.

Next, prepare a systemic fungicidal solution for dipping chips, twin scales, notched bulbs. Set it aside and prepare the bags for incubating the chips and twin scales. Place Seramis into a bowl and dampen thoroughly with water (preferably distilled) before half-filling the polyethylene bags. If Seramis is unavailable, vermiculite may be used instead: add 1 part distilled water to 8 parts vermiculite.

Heat the propagator to 81–86°F (27–30°C) or prepare some space in the airing cupboard. Finally, prepare a label for each bag with the hybrid's name and date of chipping or twin scaling.

Stage 1—chipping and twin scaling

Begin by selecting a large, firm, healthy bulb (Plate 11-1). First remove the bulb's neck, leaving a flat surface (Plate 11-2), then remove the roots, cutting as close as possible to the basal plate and taking care not to damage the basal plate (Plate 11-3). Remove the brown, papery outer layers until a clean, white bulb remains. Sterilize the surface of the bulb, including the cut nose, using cotton buds or a clean cloth dipped in surgical sprit (Plate 11-4). Place the bulb, nose down, on the cutting board. Holding the bulb firmly in one hand and, using a sharp knife (sterilized), cut the bulb vertically into halves, quarters, eighths (Plate 11-5) and, if possible, sixteenths. WARNING: Great care is required when cutting the bulb as it can become very slippery. Each segment (chip) must have a piece of basal plate attached. Remove and discard any scapes and leaves within the bulb. No further cutting is required if chipping is being undertaken. Now go to Stage 2.

If, however, you are undertaking twin scaling, a few additional steps are needed before moving into Stage 2. Starting from the outside, carefully peel away the 2 outermost scales from one of the segments (chips). Using a scalpel or sharp blade, make a vertical cut through the basal plate, separating the 2 scales from the rest of the segment (Plate 11-6). It is essential that both scales remain attached to the basal plate. You now have your first twin scale (Plate 11-7). Place it in a polyethylene bag immediately to prevent it from drying out and possible airborne contamination. Working towards the center of the bulb segment, prepare further twin scales in exactly the same way, placing each one in the polyethylene bag. Innermost scales are very small and all the basal plate may have been used up on the other twin scales. In this case discard the innermost fragments and proceed to the next segment. When all segments have been twin scaled, proceed to Stage 2.

Stage 2—Dipping, bagging and incubating chips and twin scales

Immerse the chips or twin scales in a systemic fungicide for 30 minutes to protect them from fungal attack (Plate 11-8). Remove the chips or twin scales and drain thoroughly to remove excess moisture. If no systemic fungicide is available, dust the chips or twin scales with green or yellow sulfur.

Place the chips or twin scales into the polyethylene bags containing dampened Seramis or vermiculite. Shake the bags gently to ensure the chips and twin scales are completely covered with Seramis or vermiculite. Dampened Seramis may also be placed directly into the propagator tray and the chips or twin scales buried in it. This method avoids using polyethylene bags and makes examination of the chips and twin scales easier.

Place a prepared label in each bag or in the propagator (Plate 11-9) and inflate the plastic bags to ensure an adequate air supply. Secure firmly with a tie (Plate 11-10). Place the inflated bags upright in the heated propagator, allowing space between each bag. Do not place bags on top of each other.

After replacing the propagator cover, place a dark blanket or other suitable covering over the propagator to ensure no light penetrates (Plate 11-11). Bags may also be placed with the ties uppermost on a tray and incubated in the airing cupboard. Maintain a temperature of 81–84°F (27–29°C), 24 hours a day for up to 12 weeks. The amount of time spent in the propagator or airing cupboard will vary according to bulblet development.

Stage 3—Early growth of bulbils from chipping and twin scaling

Inspect the bags regularly to ensure there is adequate air supply and moisture. It is preferable to start off with slightly lower moisture levels, adding water as necessary during the incubation period, rather than having to improve the ventilation to get rid of fungal problems. Re-inflate the bags as required and ensure there is sufficient moisture in the bags to avoid the developing bulbils becoming desiccated.

If any rotting is observed, remove and discard the affected chip or twin scale immediately. Transfer all remaining healthy chips and twin scales to clean bags containing fresh moistened Seramis or vermiculite. To date, I have not encountered any rotting when using Seramis. Twin scales and chips will naturally decay and disintegrate as nutrients are utilized by the developing bulbils; therefore remove and discard any decaying material as necessary.

Within 2–4 weeks, one or more bulbils may have begun to develop on the twin scales. More may appear during the next few weeks. Development tends to be slower with chipping. In some cases, 5–8 bulbils have begun to develop after 21 days on twin scales and early signs of bulbil development are also visible within 28 days.

After 8–9 weeks, some twin scales may have disintegrated and a root(s) and a leaf or leaves may be visible on some bulbils. It is recommended to pot up bulbils which have reached this stage so that further development can continue unimpeded.

Stage 4—Potting up

By week 12, one or more bulbils will have developed on the chips and twin scales (Plate 11-12). Some may have developed 1–2 leaves and roots. Chips and twin scales may be potted up individually into 3 in. (7.5 cm) pots or several into a large pot. Excellent drainage is essential at all times.

Fill the pot with a light porous mix; the Kew mix is recommended. Place the chips or twin scales on top of the mix, lightly covering them with more mix. Depending on the position and stage of bulbil development, ensure any leaves and the top third of large bulbils are exposed. Water the pot using tepid tap water.

Chips and twin scales which have not yet developed leaves can be potted up and placed in a polyethylene bag. Seal the bags to prevent moisture loss and possible contamination from fungal or bacterial spores. Split open the bags as the foliage develops. Feed weekly with a balanced liquid feed containing trace elements when leaf development becomes vigorous.

From now on, excellent ventilation and adequate moisture are essential at all times to prevent the bulbils from drying out. Maintain a soil temperature of 70–72°F (21–22°C). A shelf above a warm radiator, a sunny windowsill or a heated propagator is ideal with an air temperature of 70–77°F

(21–25°C) for the first 2 years. Do not expose the leaves to the sun's fiercest rays as they are easily scorched.

After 2 years, treat the bulbils in the same way as mature bulbs. Repot into larger pots as necessary (Plate 11-13).

Propagating by Notching

Begin by assembling the following equipment and materials in three groups as indicated:

Group 1

Protective covers for work surfaces, such as plastic sheets or newspaper
Protective clothing such as lab coat, long plastic apron and thin surgical gloves
Large cutting board for notching
Sharp knife, scalpel or razor blades for cutting the bulbs
Alcohol burner or gas flame
Cloths for wiping down surfaces
Surgical spirit for sterilizing work surfaces and equipment
Moist sphagnum moss
Healthy bulbs 12–12.5 in. (30–32 cm) circumference or larger

Group 2

Bowls for soaking notched bulbs
Measuring jug
Strainer or sieve
Clock with timer
Systemic fungicide or green or yellow sulfur for damaged bulbs
Clean water (distilled, if possible)

Group 3

7 in. (18 cm) pots and plant saucers
Kew mix
Labels
Permanent pen or pencil

With the supplies in hand, ensure all work surfaces and equipment are thoroughly cleaned using surgical spirit. Then cover work surfaces to protect them from possible spillage. Sterilize knives by flaming and dipping in surgical spirit before use. Cover any cuts and abrasions, particularly on the hands and wrists, before putting on surgical gloves. Always discard and replace punctured gloves with a fresh pair immediately. Wear protective clothing at all times to safeguard against possible chemical damage to eyes and skin. Always read manufacturers' instructions and any other precautionary advice before preparing, using and disposing of chemicals, and follow instructions exactly.

Next, prepare a systemic fungicidal solution for dipping notched bulbs. Also prepare the Kew mix and one label per pot.

Notching technique

Select a large healthy bulb which has been growing throughout the previous summer and autumn. Wash thoroughly under running tepid tap water. Avoid wetting the neck if possible. Pat dry using absorbent paper. Place the bulb on a cutting board on its side. Using a sharp knife, cut back the roots to about 1 in. (2.5 cm) from the basal plate. Remove all leaves by cutting level with the neck of the bulb. Holding the bulb firmly in one hand, with the other make a series of cuts through the basal plate, dividing the bulb into halves, quarters, eighths and sixteenths. The cuts must ONLY extend up to two-thirds of the length of the bulb so that the segments remain attached at the top. No further cutting is required. WARNING: Great care is required when cutting the bulb as it can become very slippery.

Immerse the notched bulb in systemic fungicide for 5 minutes to prevent rotting. Remove and strain it, then wrap it in moist sphagnum moss to prevent the bulb from drying out. If no systemic fungicide is available, dust the cut surfaces of the notched bulb with green or yellow sulfur.

Place some Kew mix in the bottom of a 7 in. (18 cm) pot and bury the bulb in the compost, leaving the neck exposed. Place the pot in a light, warm place and maintain a soil temperature of 70–72°F (21–22°C). A shelf above a warm radiator, sunny windowsill or heated propagator is ideal with an air temperature of 70–77°F (21–25°C). Water lightly with tepid tap water, keeping the compost moist at all times.

As new foliage develops, increase watering. Maintain an air temperature of 70–77°F (21–25°C) for the first year. Treat the bulblets as mature bulbs in the second year and give the 10–12 week cool period as described in

Chapter 9. Repot into larger pots as the bulblets increase in size. The parent bulb will wither and die.

Conclusion

Propagating hippeastrums is well worth trying. Although it takes several years for bulbs to reach maturity and flower, the pleasure to be derived from caring for and observing the plants as they develop is well worth the wait.

Chapter 12

Pests and Diseases

Hippeastrums are susceptible to attack by a range of pests and diseases. Some problems occur irrespective of geographical and environmental location while others are limited to specific areas. In many cases, the likelihood of damage or disorders occurring can be significantly reduced and sometimes eliminated by ensuring that only freshly harvested, disease-free bulbs are purchased and that correct horticultural practices are followed. Legislation (national and international) has resulted in many chemicals being withdrawn from use. This trend is likely to increase, making good husbandry even more necessary.

Some gardeners have developed their own remedies to solve particular problems with varying degrees of success. Some of these remedies have limited application and, since not officially endorsed, they are omitted from this chapter. Local horticultural societies and gardening clubs may be able to suggest local treatments which have proved effective. Biological controls have proved effective for some problems at the Royal Botanic Gardens, Kew, where they are used as part of an integrated pest control program involving chemicals, to achieve the most effective control; however, they may be inappropriate for minor infestations and inadequate for major outbreaks. Sometimes there is no alternative to using chemicals if an endangered species or unusual hybrid is to survive. An accurate assessment of the problem is therefore essential to enable the most appropriate strategy to be devised and implemented.

Some treatments require special precautions and equipment and may be unsuitable for certain environments. The hot water treatment which is widely used by professional breeders and growers to control thrips, mites and nematodes within the bulbs requires an insulated thermostatically controlled container which could be constructed for home use. A recipe devised for use by amateur gardeners at home will be given in this chapter.

Chapter 12 focuses on problems which can affect *Hippeastrum* hybrids cultivated in greenhouses as well as indoors or outdoors in the Northern and Southern Hemispheres. Due to the seriousness of the tarsonemid mite which can result in the entire destruction of a crop or valuable collection, in-depth information is given on this particular pest. Signs and symptoms of the principal pests and diseases are described and diagnoses given. Chemical, non-chemical and biological treatments are suggested where these exist. Further information regarding the conditions listed in Tables 12-1 and 12-3 can be found in specialized texts. Those which I have found to be particularly helpful are listed at the end of this chapter.

Pests

Many pests damage hippeastrum at various stages in its development, the most common being ants, aphids, bulb flies, caterpillars, eelworms, grasshoppers, mites, scale insects, slugs, snails and thrips. Some appear to cause only minor damage; others weaken the plant, making it more vulnerable to secondary infections. Some may have a devastating effect which can prove fatal. Damage is often most severe in spring and summer when growth is most active. Some pests thrive under hot and dry (glasshouse red spider mite) or hot and humid (glasshouse thrips) conditions and will attack plants grown in the Northern and Southern Hemispheres. Some do not confine their activities to plants grown outdoors but will also attack those cultivated in glasshouses and in the home. Some, such as the eastern Lubber grasshopper confine their attack to plants cultivated outside in specific parts of North America.

Several pests cause red staining on roots, leaf bases, scapes, spathe leaves, flowers and foliage in the form of speckles, spots, streaks, stripes or scarring. The latter are particularly noticeable along scape and leaf margins and may result in severe and unsightly distortions and severe weakening of affected areas. Since reddening is due to the pigment anthocyanin, even the slightest damage will result in tissue staining. It is therefore essential to distinguish whether the reddening is due to mechanical damage or some other factor.

Some pests restrict feeding to the inner leaf bases (large and small narcissus bulb flies); others attack both inner and outer leaf bases (tarsonemid mite), while others, such as slugs and snails, attack almost any part of the plant above or beneath the ground. Red streaking and scarring may already be apparent as scapes and leaves emerge from the bulb neck, often indicative of a tarsonemid mite infestation. The stem eelworm, also known as bulb eelworm, attacks roots, causing serious damage and poor, stunted growth of scapes and foliage. In other cases, dissecting the bulb will confirm the diagnosis.

Diagnosing the Problem

Table 12-1 details the signs and symptoms associated with a range of diseases which affect plants grown in the Northern and Southern Hemispheres. A diagnosis is then given with details of possible treatments where these are known to exist. Use the table as your starting point and then, if necessary, consult a specialized text for further information and seek advice from your local garden center or agricultural agent regarding appropriate and available treatments.

Tarsonemid Mite (*Steneotarsonemus laticeps*)

Although barely invisible to the naked eye, the tarsonemid mite, also known as bulb scale mite, can cause extensive damage which may prove fatal and, unless diagnosed at an early stage, can result in the total destruction of a crop or collection. By the time the bright orange-red streaks, stripes and scars are visible, infestation is severe and bulbs should be destroyed immediately. If cultivating plants indoors, any remaining healthy plants should be isolated immediately and all known and possible mite-infested areas thoroughly cleaned and disinfected. Depending on if and where bulbs had been stored prior to planting and where the plants were being cultivated, this may necessitate disinfecting cupboards, steam-cleaning carpets and washing or dry cleaning curtains and other furnishings. Once deprived of their food source, the mites will quickly die, but if cultivating the plants in the home, it is advisable not to reintroduce existing or fresh bulbs for 6 months until you are sure that all traces of the mites have been eradicated.

Mites are active between 50 and 68°F (10–20°C) becoming motionless at 38°F (3.5°C), at which temperature eggs will cease to hatch. Mites will be killed at temperatures over 100°F (38°C). They dislike light, cold and dry conditions and therefore damage can be reduced during the bulb's preparation or cool period by lowering the temperature, decreasing humidity levels and maintaining good lighting. Damage appears to be less during dry summers.

Table 12-1. Pests of hippeastrums.

Affected areas, growing locations and time of year	Signs and symptoms	Cause of symptoms	Possible reasons for occurrence and suggested treatments
Site: Upper and underside of leaf, often hiding in the curled up margins. **Location:** Greenhouse and outside. **Time of year:** Any, mainly March–October for greenhouse plants and for plants grown outdoors in the Northern Hemisphere.	Honeydew deposits which encourage the development of sooty molds on foliage, punctured foliage, distorted new growth and general weakening of the plant. Greenhouse plants are mainly affected in spring and summer as aphids enter through the vents.	Aphids (commonly referred to as greenfly or blackfly)	Commence treatment immediately as damage can be devastating. **Chemical controls:** Systemic or non-systemic organic and inorganic insecticides and insecticidal soaps. **Biological controls:** Parasitic wasp (*Aphidius colemani*) and aphid midge (*Aphidoletes aphidimyza*).
Site: Bulb interior. **Location:** Greenhouse and outside. **Time of year:** Any. Damage becomes visible during spring and summer.	Bulbs may appear normal from the outside but give way when pressed, revealing rotting tissue. Yellow, weak foliage may be distorted. Eventual death of the plant.	Large narcissus bulb fly (*Merodon equestris*)	Treat bulbs with a persistent insecticide before or at the time of planting as a precautionary measure. Destroy suspect or damaged bulbs immediately. Apply hot water treatment.
Site: Bulb. **Location:** Greenhouse and outside. **Time of year:** Any.	Bulbs may appear normal from the outside but give way when pressed, revealing rotting tissue. Weak, distorted foliage. Eventual death of the plant.	Small narcissus flies or lesser bulb flies (*Eumerus tuberculatus*, *E. strigatus*)	Bulbs already weakened by large narcissus fly, fungi, mites, or nematodes or those damaged by slugs are liable to be attacked. Destroy damaged material immediately, identify the main reason for the damage and treat appropriately.

Table 12-1 *(continued)*

Affected areas, growing locations and time of year	Signs and symptoms	Cause of symptoms	Possible reasons for occurrence and suggested treatments
Site: In and above the compost around the pot and around the plant generally. **Location:** Greenhouse, indoors and outside. **Time of year:** Any.	Mainly a nuisance factor. Attracted to soil and potting media with a high organic content.	Fungus gnats (often known as mushroom or sciarid flies)	Often as a result of poor plant husbandry, particularly under- or over-watering. **Chemical controls:** Systemic insecticide sprays and drenches. **Biological control:** A predatory mite, *Hypoaspis miles.* **Other controls:** Apply 0.5 in. (1 cm) of sand or grit on top of the compost to help deter egg-laying adults. Yellow sticky traps are effective against adult flies in greenhouses.
Site: Outer papery leaf bases. **Location:** Greenhouse and outdoors. **Time of year:** Any.	Red spots, usually confined to outer leaf bases. Usually only on the innermost leaf bases when the bulb is decomposing.	Bulb mite (*Rhizoglyphus echinopus*)	Usually an indication of other pests or diseases present and/or rotting material. Obtain bulbs from a reputable supplier and destroy all damaged material. Apply hot water treatment.
Site: Inner and outer leaf bases, scapes, foliage, spathe leaves and flowers. **Location:** Greenhouse and indoors.	Bright orange-red spots on outer leaf bases. A severe infestation will result in all leaf bases being red. Red streaks and stripes along the length	Bulb scale mite, also known as tarsonemid mite (*Steneotarsonemus laticeps*)	Isolate or destroy affected plants as soon as signs of mite infestation are noticed. **Chemical controls:** No effective chemical controls

Table 12-1 ***(continued)***

Affected areas, growing locations and time of year	Signs and symptoms	Cause of symptoms	Possible reasons for occurrence and suggested treatments
Time of year: Any. *continued*	of leaves and scapes with a toothed pattern on leaf margins and scarring on scape margins. Foliage is brittle, puckered and often curled at the edges. Scapes are soft, rubbery, severely stunted and liable to collapse. Spathe leaf contours may be thickly edged with orange-red and florets may be entirely red. Underdeveloped pedicels result in flowers remaining upright. Poorly developed, smaller than normal flowers are limp, often shriveled, fail to openly properly, have patchy pigmentation and remain upright. Secondary infections may follow, such as bulb scale mite and the fungus *Fusarium oxysporum*, leading to bulb decomposition and plant death.		are available to the amateur gardener. Professional breeders and growers widely use hot water treatment to eradicate the mites.

Table 12-1 ***(continued)***

Affected areas, growing locations and time of year	Signs and symptoms	Cause of symptoms	Possible reasons for occurrence and suggested treatments
Site: Leaves, buds, flowers. **Location:** Greenhouse and indoors. **Time of year:** Any, but mainly summer to early autumn.	Light speckling followed by red staining on the leaves as damage becomes extensive. Mites, eggs, egg shells and mite molt skins may be present on the underside of the leaves. Severe weakening of foliage in major infestations, leading to plant death unless controlled.	Glasshouse red spider mite (also known as the two-spotted spider mite) (*Tetranychus urticae*) and, in Japan, Kanazawa spider mite (*Tetranychus kanzawai*)	Often as a result of overcrowding, over dry and too hot atmosphere. Destroy infested plants immediately and improve cultural conditions. Mist with water twice daily to increase humidity levels and lower the temperature. **Chemical controls:** Effectiveness varies. Some are ineffective because the pest has developed resistance. **Biological controls:** The predatory mite *Phytoseiulus persimilis* may be introduced at an early stage as soon as the mites are observed. *Amblyseius californicus* works well in drier conditions.
Site: Roots. **Location:** Greenhouse. **Time of year:** Any.	Reddening of roots resulting in root death, stunted foliage and flowers.	Stem eelworm, also known as bulb eelworm (*Ditylenchus dipsaci*)	Chemical controls: No effective chemical controls are available to the amateur gardener. The hot water treatment is recommended.

Table 12-1 ***(continued)***

Affected areas, growing locations and time of year	Signs and symptoms	Cause of symptoms	Possible reasons for occurrence and suggested treatments
Site: Leaves, flowers and buds. **Location:** Glasshouse, indoors and outside. **Time of year:** Any.	Red staining and localized red and brown globules of liquid from feeding thrips resulting in general weakening of the plant.	Glasshouse thrips (*Heliothrips haemorrhoidalis*, *H. setosus*, *H. mouton*, *H. tabaci* (also known as thunder flies because of the increased presence of some species of thrips during humid weather)	Often due to poor cultural conditions, resulting from under-watering and over-heating. **Chemical controls:** Organic and inorganic insecticide sprays.**Biological control:** The predatory mite *Amblyseius cucumeris* is appropriate for glasshouse cultivation if introduced before a damaging infestation has developed.
Site: Undersides of leaves. **Location:** Greenhouse. **Time of year:** Any.	Honeydew deposits and often sooty molds are visible on leaf surfaces. Damage can be extensive and out of proportion to the number of insects, resulting in severe weakening of the plant.	Soft scale insect *(Coccus hesperidum)*	**Chemical controls:** Contact and systemic insecticide treatments. Fatty acids may also prove effective. **Biological control:** Parasitic wasp *Metaphycus helvolus* may be appropriate for certain circumstances, particularly at high light intensities.
Site: Bulb neck, leaves, scapes. **Location:** Greenhouse and indoors. **Time of year:** Any.	White woolly wax on leaves and often around the bulb neck Nymphs can often be seen around the leaves causing red staining, fouling of plant	Mealybug (*Trionymus lounsburyi*)	**Chemical controls:** Contact insecticides. Fatty acids may also prove effective. **Biological control:** Australian predatory ladybird,

Table 12-1 ***(continued)***

Affected areas, growing locations and time of year	Signs and symptoms	Cause of symptoms	Possible reasons for occurrence and suggested treatments
	surfaces with honeydew and sooty molds. General weakening of the plant.		*Cryptolaemus montrouzieri*, may prove effective in controlling major greenhouse infestations, but it should be noted that chemical controls are harmful to the predator.
Site: Bulbs, scapes, foliage spathe leaves, flowers, seed capsules. **Location:** Greenhouse and outside. **Time of year:** Any but particularly on warm humid evenings in spring, summer and autumn.	Devouring of plant tissues, particularly during damp evenings and nights. A slimy trail is often visible around the plant, soil and pot.	Field slug (*Deroceras reticulatum*, syn. *Agriolimax reticulatus*); garden slug (*Arion hortensis*); black slug (*A. ater*); keeled slugs (*Milax* spp.); garden snail (*Helix aspersa*); strawberry snail (*Trichia striolata*, syn. *Hygromia striolata*); banded snails (*Cepaea nemoralis*, *C. hortensis*)	**Chemical controls:** Slug pellets may prove effective for short periods. Repeat applications may be necessary. Note that some pellets are harmful to domestic and wild animals and birds. **Alternative controls:** Various, including eggshells, grapefruit skins, grit placed on the surface of the soil around the base of the plant to deter attack. Beer traps can be most effective in trapping slugs. **Biological control:** A drench of nematode *Phasmarhabditis hermaphrodita* may prove effective for slugs only, particularly in small areas. Effects may be limited if the soil is too dry or too wet or when

Table 12-1 *(continued)*

Affected areas, growing locations and time of year	Signs and symptoms	Cause of symptoms	Possible reasons for occurrence and suggested treatments
			soil temperatures are below 41°F (5°C).
Site: Foliage. **Location:** Outdoors. **Time of year:** Any.	Devouring of foliage.	Spanish moth or convict caterpillar (*Xanthopastis timais*)in the USA and Brazil; *Glottula heterocampa* in Brazil; *Brithys crini* (syn. *Glottula dominica*), *Noctua dominica* and *Calogramma festiva* in Australia, Taiwan and some Far East locations	Seek advice from your local agricultural agent.
Site: Bulb neck. **Location:** Outside. **Time of year:** Any.	Colonies of ants around bulbs infested with mealybug.	Ants	Seek advice from your local agricultural agent.
Site: Foliage and exposed bulbs **Location:** Outside. **Time of year:** Any.	Devouring of bulbs and foliage.	Eastern lubber grasshopper (*Romalea microptera*) in the USA	Seek advice from your local agricultural agent.
Site: Roots, bulbs and foliage. **Location:** Greenhouse and outside. **Time of year:** Any.	Devouring of decaying organic material which may include roots.	Sowbugs, also known as pill bug and roly-poly in USA or woodlice in Great Britain. Commonest species are	Seek advice from your local agricultural agent. Destroy plant debris and clear up piles of unwashed pots, seed

Table 12-1 *(continued)*

Affected areas, growing locations and time of year	Signs and symptoms	Cause of symptoms	Possible reasons for occurrence and suggested treatments
		Oniscus asellus, *Porcellio scaber* and *Armadillidium vulgare*).	trays, piles of rubble, rotting wood and other possible breeding sites. **Chemical controls:** Contact insecticides. **Other controls:** Boiling water.
Site: Flowers. **Location:** Outside. **Time of year:** Midsummer.	Devouring of flowers.	Blister beetle (*Epicauta strigosa*) in Florida (USA)	Seek advice from your local agricultural agent.
Site: Bulb interior. **Location:** Outside. **Time of year:** Any.	Eventual disintegration of the bulb.	Weevil (*Brachycerus* sp.) in Africa and parts of Europe.	No effective treatment is available.

The hot water treatment

The hot water treatment is the only known effective method for eradicating a range of pests including the tarsonemid mite. The temperature applied and the duration of the treatment is critical to the success of the operation. Fluctuating temperatures may allow some pests to survive or may cause damage to the bulbs. The temperature used to kill the pests is very close to that which is harmful to the plant so that there is little margin for error. To maintain the correct temperature it is necessary to have a thermostatically controlled heating unit and an insulated tank to hold the water and the bulbs.

Healthy and damaged bulbs in the National Plant Collection of *Hippeastrum* have been successfully treated using the procedure described in this chapter. Most bulbs flowered the following season following the cool period and some showed an increase in offset production, a side effect of the treatment.

Development of the hot water treatment

Earliest reports of hot water treatment date from 1908 to 1938 when Saunders, Blattiny, Smith and Wilson carried out experiments to assess its effectiveness from temperatures of 104–125°F (40–52°C) for 10–90 minutes. Wilson investigated the effects of rapid and slow cooling of the bulbs after treatment and discovered that bulbs which were allowed to cool naturally after treatment produced more vigorous growth and flowered earlier. Pollen viability and ovule development were unaffected by treatment at 110°F (43°C). Experiments by Blattiny in the 1930s showed mite infestations were reduced from 46% to 13% following treatment and storage in a dry atmosphere.

Research carried out at the Glasshouse Crops Research Station, Naaldwijk (The Netherlands), in the 1990s found treating at 115°F (46°C) for 60–180 minutes to be effective for mature bulbs and bulblets. Timings varied according to the size and condition of the bulbs—healthy mature bulbs were immersed for 120 minutes, bulblets for 60 minutes. Unhealthy bulbs and bulblets were treated for a further 60 minutes. If bulbs were treated for 180 minutes at 115°F (46°C) little floral damage occurred but pollen failed to develop properly. Healthy bulbs and bulblets may also be immersed together for 90 minutes at 115°F (46°C).

Achieving the correct temperature and timing

Timing of the hot water treatment is crucial. If bulbs are treated after 10–12 weeks at 55°F (13°C), they are more vulnerable to floral damage and therefore commercial breeders and growers administer the treatment immediately after lifting and drying. Dutch breeders treat small bulbs and those being used for propagation shortly before replanting or twin scaling to be certain of eliminating any infestation present in the bulbs during storage. They consider treating at 117–118°F (47–48°C) for 120 minutes to be appropriate for killing mites and thrips, but the higher temperature is more likely to cause floral damage to unemerged buds. Dutch growers only treat bulblets which have completed their first growing season; they do not treat mature bulbs scheduled for export, since florets inside the bulb can easily be damaged.

It is essential that a temperature of 115°F (46°C) penetrates the bulb's core to ensure all mites and insects are killed. Ideally, breeders and growers would prepare a schedule for each bulb, taking into account its condition, age, size and any other relevant factors. However, time and resource constraints make this unrealistic, particularly when thousands of bulbs have to be treated within a very short time. Compromises are inevitable resulting in bulb and floral damage in some cases due to over or under treatment. Table 12-2 details the procedures currently used by Dutch, Israeli and South African commercial breeders and growers. A simpler method is available for amateur growers.

Hot water treatment for amateur gardeners

Assemble the following equipment and materials:

Protective covers for work surfaces, such as plastic sheets or newspaper
Protective clothing such as lab coat, long plastic apron and thin surgical gloves
Equipment for heating the water
Large board for bulb preparation
Plastic trays for drying the bulbs
Fan for drying bulbs (may not be necessary)
Sharp knives
Glass jar or plastic container for sterilizing knives
Clock with timer

Net bags and ties
Aluminum plant labels and waterproof marker
Cloths for wiping down surfaces
Bulbs
Clean water
Surgical spirit for sterilizing knives and work surfaces
Absorbent paper for drying bulbs (may not be necessary)
Systemic fungicide (may not be necessary)

Method

With the supplies in hand, ensure all work surfaces and equipment are thoroughly cleaned using surgical spirit. Then cover work surfaces to protect them from possible spillage. Sterilize knives by flaming and dipping in surgical spirit before use. Cover any cuts and abrasions, particularly on the hands and wrists, before putting on surgical gloves. Always discard and replace punctured gloves with a fresh pair immediately. Wear protective clothing at all times to safeguard against possible chemical damage to eyes and skin. Always read manufacturers' instructions and any other precautionary advice before preparing, using and disposing of chemicals, and follow instructions exactly.

Next, prepare plant labels using a waterproof marker pen. Take bulbs and bulblets from pots and remove foliage 4 in. (10 cm) above the neck by making a slant cut. Wash bulbs and bulblets under tepid tap water, removing any rotting leaf bases, debris from the basal plate and dead roots. Try not to get the bulb's neck wet.

If the basal plate is more than 0.5 in. (1 cm) thick or shows any signs of damage, then remove a sliver of it. The basal plate can be a popular hiding place for a range of insects which can cause serious damage and sometimes prove fatal. Very thick basal plates may also impede new root growth.

After cleaning the bulbs and bulblets, stand each one on its base at an angle of 30° on a tray, ensuring excellent ventilation at all times. Dry for 7–10 days at 77–81°F (25–27°C). It is essential that the neck of the bulb and all cut leaf surfaces be dry within 24 hours to avoid fungal infection and rotting. A fan may help with drying. If these instructions are carried out correctly and if drying conditions are good, it is not necessary to pat bulbs dry using absorbent paper, prior to positioning them on a tray.

If you are in any doubt about the efficiency of the drying conditions or if

Table 12-2. Hot water treatment procedures used by Brazilian, Dutch, Israeli and South African breeders and growers.

Activity	Brazil	The Netherlands	Israel	South Africa
1. Lift and dry bulbs	June–July, for 10 days at 81°F (27°C), then store at 77°F (25°C).	October–November, for 7–14 days at 77–86°F (25–30°C).	September, for 28 days at 86°F (30°C).	July, for 7–10 days at 77–81°F (25–27°C).
2. Hot water treatment[a]	60 mins. at 115°F (46°C)	Usually 120 mins. at 115°F (46°C) for mature bulbs; 60 mins. at 115°F (46°C) for small bulbs less than 8 in. (20 cm) circumference. Bulbs to be used for twin scaling or chipping (large and small) or small bulbs to be replanted and grown for a second season may be treated at 117–118°F (47–48°C) for 120 mins. since survival of the flower buds is not important.	90–150 mins. at 110°F (43.5°C)	60 mins. at 115°F (46°C) for healthy bulbs; 120 mins. at 115°F (46°C) for unhealthy bulbs
3. Dry bulbs after treatment	June–July, for 2 days at 81°F (27°C)	November, for 2–4 days at 77–86°F (25–30°C)	Bulbs are not dried but planted immediately	July, for 4–5 days at 77–81°F (25–27°C).
4. Replant bulbs	August–September	November–December	September–November	October after 8–12 weeks storage at 55°F (13°C)

[a]It should be emphasized that while the duration and temperature required for drying the bulbs before and after the hot water treatment are not critical, the temperature and duration of the hot water treatment itself needs to be adhered to precisely so as to avoid damaging or killing the bulbs.

you suspect the bulbs to be damaged in some way, it is advisable to dip them in a systemic fungicide for 30 minutes prior to drying. After dipping, gently pat dry using absorbent paper to remove as much moisture as possible, particularly from the neck region, basal plate and roots.

Once the bulbs have been thoroughly dried they are ready for hot water treatment. Healthy and unhealthy bulbs are best treated separately. If you have several different cultivars, place each cultivar in a net bag, add a prepared label and then secure with a plastic tie. Place mature and immature bulbs in separate bags so they can be removed easily and quickly from the water after the appropriate time. Make sure the bulbs have sufficient room in the bags so that they do not knock against each other and become damaged. They must also be completely surrounded by hot water. It is also advisable to check before starting that water can easily penetrate the bags.

Heat and maintain water at 115°F (46°C). Before placing the bulbs into the water, check the temperature. Gently lower the bulbs into the water until they are completely immersed. They may float to the surface and therefore you may need to use weights to ensure the bags and bulbs remain below the surface for the duration of the treatment. Set the timer and treat as follows:

healthy bulbs for 120 minutes
healthy bulblets for 60 minutes
unhealthy bulbs for 180 minutes
unhealthy bulblets for 120 minutes

Check the temperature periodically during treatment to ensure it remains at 115°F (46°C).

After treatment, gently remove the bulbs and bulblets from the hot water. They will be much heavier and dripping water. Carefully take them out of their bags and remove excess water from the necks and basal plate using absorbent paper. Stand each bulb or bulblet on its base at an angle of 30° on a tray, ensuring excellent ventilation at all times. Although professional breeders and growers dry the bulbs for 3–4 days following treatment, this may prove insufficient in a home situation. It is essential that bulbs are dried thoroughly before commencing the cool period to avoid rotting. If in doubt, it is better to dry them for a few days longer—up to 10 days will not harm the bulbs.

After drying, place the bulbs in a dark, cool and dry place at 55°F (13°C) for 8–10 weeks prior to replanting (also known as the cool period). Always ensure there is good ventilation and inspect the bulbs every 7–10 days to ensure they remain in optimum health. It may be possible to extend the cool period for some hybrids before replanting (see Chapter 8 for details).

Diseases

Hippeastrums are susceptible to fungal attack from *Stagonospora curtisii* (also known as red spot, fire or narcissus leaf scorch), *Fusarium oxysporum* (basal rot), *Phytophthora nicotianae* (phytophthora rot), *Botrytis cinerea* and ***Penicillium*** species (blue mold rots). Full details of these conditions are given in Table 12-3. Further information can be found in specialized texts.

Hippeastrums are also susceptible to attack from hippeastrum mosaic virus (HMV), cucumber mosaic virus (CMV), tomato spotted wilt virus (TSWV) and tobacco mosaic virus (TMV). Aphids transmit HMV and CMV at any time of the year. Signs of HMV are light and dark green stripes on leaf margins or a mosaic pattern. Yellow rings and stripes and spots on the surface of the leaf indicate CMV. There is no cure for either virus and affected plants are best destroyed immediately. TSWV is transmitted by thrips causing yellowing or white spots on the leaves which may have formed pale patches. Leaves turn yellow and die and there is general weakening of the plant. TMV results in stunted plants with distorted leaves having necrotic spots.

Table 12-3. Diseases of hippeastrums.

Affected areas, growing locations and time of year	Signs and symptoms	Cause of symptoms	Possible reasons for occurrence and suggested treatments
Site: Leaf bases—particularly around the bulb neck; also scapes, spathe leaves and leaves. **Location:** Greenhouse, indoors and outside. **Time of year:** Any, but particularly in cool, damp conditions.	Red spots or blotches may become long cankers with red borders and brown or gray centers. Scarring on scapes, contours and tips of spathe leaves can result in unsightly distortion and disfigurement. Weakened scapes are liable to snap. Although the condition looks unsightly and weakens the plant, it is not fatal.	Fire, also known as red blotch, red fire, red spot (*Stagonospora curtisii*)	1. Only purchase bulbs from a reputable supplier. 2. Select only healthy bulbs and store them so they stay healthy. 3. Maintain correct environmental and cultural conditions (potting mixes, soil and air temperatures, humidity, watering practices). 4. Avoid splashing from rain as this can lead to healthy tissues becoming infected. 5. Avoid overcrowding and allow sufficient space between plants. 6. Ensure cut surfaces are dried within 24 hours and treat with a fungicide as a precautionary measure. 7. Isolate affected plants immediately and treat with a systemic fungicide prior to planting/replanting in sterilized soil or potting mix.

Table 12-3 *(continued)*

Affected areas, growing locations and time of year	Signs and symptoms	Cause of symptoms	Possible reasons for occurrence and suggested treatments
Site: Outer and inner leaf bases, around and below neck and nose of bulb, basal plate, roots, soil. **Location:** Greenhouse, indoors and outside. **Time of year:** Any, but particularly in cool, damp conditions.	Soft, dark brown-black patches. Stunted, weak scapes collapse easily; rotted roots become detached from the plant; general weakening of the plant. In severe cases the basal plate will be completely rotten and the bulb reduced to a soggy, slimy mess. A pungent odor may emanate from the soil.	Basal rot (*Fusarium oxysporum*)	1. Select only healthy bulbs and store them so they stay healthy. 2. Maintain correct environmental and cultural conditions (potting mixes, soil and air temperatures, humidity, watering practices). 3. Discard infected bulbs immediately unless damage is slight and bulb rescue is possible. 4. If damage is minor, discard infected material and treat with a systemic fungicide before repotting in a sterilized pot with fresh mix.
Site: Roots. **Location:** Greenhouse, indoors and outside. **Time of year:** Any.	Stunted growth.	Phytophthora rot (*Phytophthora nicotianae*)	No chemical treatments are available. 1. Only purchase bulbs from a reputable supplier. 2. Maintain correct environmental and cultural conditions (potting mixes, soil and air temperatures, humidity, watering practices). 3. Discard infected bulbs immediately unless damage is slight and bulb rescue is possible.

Table 12-3 *(continued)*

Affected areas, growing locations and time of year	Signs and symptoms	Cause of symptoms	Possible reasons for occurrence and suggested treatments
Site: Bulb leaf bases, roots. **Location:** Pre-packaged and loose bulbs purchased from wholesale, retail outlets and via mail-order companies. **Time of year:** Mainly October–January in Northern Hemisphere. Prior to and after purchase, prior to and following hot water treatment.	Gray fluffy mold. In severe cases, the bulb will be soggy and have rotted completely.	Gray mold (*Botrytis cinerea*)	Mild, wet, humid environment favors development of this mold. 1. Only purchase bulbs from a reputable supplier. 2. Always handle the bulb with care to avoid mechanical damage, such as bruising, which could result in other infections. 3. Store only healthy bulbs. 4. Dust with green or yellow sulfur powder as a precautionary measure prior to storing. 5. Store bulbs in a cool, dry environment. 6. Ensure excellent ventilation at all times. 7. Avoid over crowding of bulbs during storage. 8. Inspect regularly to ensure bulbs remain free from mold. 9. Only plant bulbs free from disease.

Table 12-3 *(continued)*

Affected areas, growing locations and time of year	Signs and symptoms	Cause of symptoms	Possible reasons for occurrence and suggested treatments
Site: Bulb leaf bases, roots, twin scales, chips. **Location:** Pre-packaged and loose bulbs purchased from wholesale, retail outlets and via mail-order companies; plastic bags containing twin scales or chips; drying place for bulbs prior to and after carrying out hot water treatment. **Time of year:** Mainly October–January in Northern Hemisphere. Prior to and after purchasing bulbs; prior to and following hot water treatment; during incubation of the twin scales or chips.	Blue-green mold. Weak stunted growth and possible flower abortion arising from planting infected bulbs. Soggy, rotten twin scales/chips.	Blue mold rot (*Penicillium* sp.)	Damp, cold conditions favor the development of this bulb rot. Refer to advice given above for *Botrytis cinerea* Maintain correct environmental conditions for incubating twin scales or chips and for drying bulbs prior to and after the hot water treatment respectively. Use Seramis for early growth of bulblets from twin scaling and chipping.

Conclusion

Several excellent illustrated texts are available which give further information on the conditions described previously. I have found the following publications to be particularly helpful.

Alford, D. V. 1995. *A Colour Atlas of Pests of Ornamental Trees, Shrubs and Flowers.* London: Manson Publishing.

Bradley, S. 2003. *What's Wrong with My Plant?* London: Hamlyn.

British Crop Protection Council. 1990. *Plant Protection in the Garden.* London: British Crop Protection Council.

Buczacki, S., and K. Harris. 2000. *Pests, Diseases and Disorders of Garden Plants.* London: Harper Collins.

Greenwood, P., and A. Halstead. 1997. *The RHS Pests and Diseases.* London: Dorling Kindersley.

Strider, D. L., ed. 1985. *Diseases of Floral Crops*, vol. 1. New York: Praeger Publishers.

While the range of potential problems may appear daunting, many of these rarely occur when growing hippeastrums indoors, providing only top quality bulbs are purchased from reputable suppliers; correct horticultural practices are implemented and adhered to and the highest standards of hygiene are maintained at all times.

Appendix

Further Information on the Hybrid Lists in Chapters 3 to 7

Most hybrids described in the lists at the ends of Chapters 3–7 inclusive are featured in the National Plant Collection of *Hippeastrum*. The descriptions are based on information supplied by breeders, growers and registration authorities and my experience of having cultivated the plants for several years. It has not been possible to obtain bulbs of many of the latest Nieuwkerk Amaryllis hybrids and therefore details are limited to information supplied by the breeder. In most chapters the plant descriptions are grouped by flower color and are arranged alphabetically together with the following information, where available:

Name and nationality of breeder
Date of granting of Plant Breeders' Rights, registration, launch or sales availability
Classification (for example, large single, double, Gracilis, Cybister, Sonatini)
Physical description and any unusual features

In a few cases it has not proved possible to ascertain the name of the breeder and, in some cases, the accuracy of published information is also questionable.

Plant Breeders' Rights

As breeders develop distinctive groups with a high novelty value, more cultivars are being submitted for granting of national and/or European Plant Breeders' Rights. Some Dutch breeders apply to The Board for Plant Breeders' Rights (Raad voor het Kwekersrecht), Wageningen (The Netherlands), which is the Dutch statutory registration authority, while others choose to apply to the Community Plant Variety Office (CPVO), Angers (France), for European Plant Breeders' Rights.

The International Union for the Protection of New Varieties of Plants (Union Internationale pour la Protection des Obtentions Végétales [UPOV]) in Geneva gives guidance and principles which are interpreted by individual countries or groups of countries into national legislation. The procedures involved in obtaining Plant Breeders' Rights in other countries such as Israel, South Africa and the United States may be different from the Dutch or European system. Some countries are still in the process of developing their own legislation in order to be able to join UPOV.

As defined in the 1991 Act of the UPOV Convention, granting of Plant Breeders' Rights not only gives the breeder the exclusive right to exploit the variety, but also to varieties that are very close in appearance and those which are essentially derived from the protected variety. If a mutation of a protected variety is discovered or developed by someone other than the breeder, although Plant Breeders' Rights may be awarded, commercialization will not be permitted unless permission from the holder of the rights of the original variety is given. If permission is not forthcoming, granting of Plant Breeders' Rights for the mutation may have no commercial value.

Obtaining Plant Breeders' Rights

The breeder completes 2 forms about the variety, giving information about its parentage, flower and foliage type and color, end use (cut flower or pot plant) and a statement confirming no bulbs or bulblets have been sold prior to 1 year before the date of application in the country of the application, or 4 years before the date of application in countries other than that of the application. This is submitted to the Council for Plant Breeders' Rights.

The breeder is sent a confirmation note acknowledging receipt of the forms and another form requesting the proposed name (denomination) of the new cultivar. Application details together with the proposed name are published in the Council's monthly magazine following completion of all appropriate checks and receipt of the application trial fees. All application decisions are subsequently published in this publication. Applications for granting of European Plant Breeders' Rights are published on the Community Plant Variety Office (CPVO) Web site.

Any objections to the proposed name must be received within 3 months of publication. If none are received, the name becomes official.

In the meantime, the Council requests 20 flowering-size bulbs of the proposed cultivar to grow for testing in December–January. Dutch breeders applying for National or European Breeders' Rights are directed to the comprehensive guidance issued by UPOV (identical to that given by the CPVO) which relates to the health and storage of the bulbs prior to testing; conditions under which the tests will be carried out; methods and observations; grouping of varieties by flower type, size and color; and plant characteristics such as flower color, shape and size of leaf and scape. The breeder is also required to indicate the shape of the petaloid staminodes (regular or irregular) in the case of doubles. The Netherlands is responsible for conducting both national and European trials. Further details on these aspects can be found in the "General Introduction to the Examination of Distinctness, Uniformity and Stability and the Development of Harmonized Descriptions of New Varieties of Plants" (TG/1/3) and in a series of papers covering specific topics relating to the testing procedure, published by UPOV and available from their Web site.

The test is normally conducted for one growing period in which a special panel, appointed by the Council and including some growers and other hippeastrum specialists, will judge the variety, if there remains a need to compare the variety with other known varieties. The panel does not make a decision on distinctness, uniformity and stability (DUS), such aspects being the responsibility of the examiner(s) of the testing station and the permanent expert of the Board of Plant Breeders' Rights. The final decision rests with the Board which receives recommendations from the examiner(s) by way of its permanent expert. If distinctness or uniformity cannot be sufficiently established in one growing period, the test may be extended for a second growing period.

Distinctness means that the variety *must be clearly distinguishable* by one or more important characteristics from any other variety whose existence is a matter of common knowledge. *Uniformity* means that, subject to the variation that may be expected from the particular features of its mode of propagation, the variety *must be sufficiently uniform. Stability* means that, subject to the variation that may be expected from the particular features of its mode of propagation, the variety *must be stable in its essential characteristics*. UPOV also issues the following definition concerning the naming of the plant: "The variety must be given a denomination enabling it to be identified; the denomination must not be liable to mislead or to cause confusion as to the characteristics, value or identity of the new variety or the identity of the breeder."

When all criteria are met, Plant Breeders' Rights are granted. A fee of €129.78 is charged in the first year, rising to €454.23 in the 5th and subsequent years in respect of Dutch Plant Breeders' Rights and €300 rising to €500 in the 4th and subsequent years for European Plant Breeders' Rights. (Fees were correct as of October 2002 but may have since changed.) The entire process usually takes between 6 and 24 months to complete, depending on the date of application. In some cases, the Council may decide that further testing is needed.

To date, none of the Australian hybrids bred by Maguire's Hippeastrum Farm have been submitted to any authority for granting of Plant Breeders' Rights. Some hybrids are rejected because they do not fulfil the stringent requirements laid down by the authorities.

Registering Hippeastrum Hybrids

Breeders wishing to register their new cultivar with the American Amaryllis Society prior to 1990 had to complete a form supplying details about the plant including flower type, height, number of flowers per scape, flower depth and diameter, color, flowering time and plant habit (deciduous or evergreen). Flower names had to confirm to criteria laid down by the International Code of Nomenclature for Cultivated Plants (ICNCP) 1961 or later editions.

Today, all applications for the registration of new hybrids, except in The Netherlands, are required to complete a form and supply a color photograph of the cultivar. In The Netherlands only, the breeder is also required to cultivate 6 bulbs for one, sometimes 2 seasons, and to complete an application form with color photograph for the Royal General Bulbgrowers' Association (KAVB), for scrutiny and assessment. The plants are assessed by a panel of experts for distinctness, uniformity and stability. A description is prepared and published, only if the plant satisfies all 3 criteria.

The breeder is then invited to suggest a suitable name that must accord with the ICNCP, as well as the rules laid down by Plant Breeders' Rights. Once the name has been agreed, details of the newly registered cultivar are published on the KAVB Web site (www.kavb.nl) and in the KAVB journal. Ideally, the entire registration process takes less than 12 months, but if any problems are discovered with the plants or the name, it can take much longer.

Although registration of a new cultivar is, in theory, voluntary, there is a greater incentive in The Netherlands for the breeder to register his/her new cultivars since the Dutch Bulb Inspection Service (Bloembollenkeuringsdienst [BKD]), a semi-governmental organization, now requires cultivars to be registered with the KAVB before granting a license to the grower for export.

Classifying Hippeastrum Hybrids

The development of *Hippeastrum* classification originated in 1934. Reginae and Leopoldii categories were devised and adopted by the American Amaryllis Society (AAS) to reflect the most common large-flowering hybrid types at that time. By 1953, a total of 9 categories had been devised to encompass the new forms which had subsequently been developed. The AAS remained the international registration authority for all new hybrids until 1989.

Until 1989, the American Amaryllis Society defined the following categories of hippeastrum.

Division 1 Cultivated Wild *Hippeastrum*. All cultivated species as they were known in the wild, including subspecies, varieta and forma.

Division 2 Long Trumpet Hybrids. Hybrids having long 4.25–5.25 in. (11–13.5 cm) tepal tubes with distinctly drooping pedicels and trumpet-shaped flowers. Some were mistaken for lilies. The influence of *Hippeastrum reticulatum H. immaculatum*, *H. tucumanum* and *H. viridiflorum* were apparent in the shape of the flowers.

Division 3 Belladonna Hybrids. Tepal tubes and flowers were shorter than those of Division 2. Pedicels were relatively long and the variously shaped flowers sometimes drooped. These plants showed the influence of species having an informal flower structure, such as *Hippeastrum equestre* and *H. striatum*.

Division 4 Reginae Hybrids. Tepal tubes were short. The length of the flower when viewed sideways, not including the ovary, measured 4 in. (10 cm) or more and the moderately open-faced flowers could be drooping, horizontal, or slightly upright showing the influence of *Hippeastrum correiense* and *H. reginae*. The pedicels were usually shorter than those in Divisions 2 and 3. Two overlapping subdivisions were recognized. **Division 4a Markedly Imbricated Type:** Individual tepals overlapped for about 75% or more of their length and had rounded, rarely pointed tepal tips. **Division 4b Less Imbricated Type:** Individual tepals overlapped for less than 75% of their length with rounded, sometimes pointed tepal tips.

Division 5 Leopoldii Hybrids. Similar to Division 4, except the flowers were wide open, often flat and held horizontally showing the influence of *Hippeastrum leopoldii* and *H. pardinum*. The length of the flower when viewed sideways was less than 4 in. (10 cm). Two subdivisions were recognized. **Division 5a Markedly Imbricated Type:** Individual tepals overlapped for almost their entire length and had rounded tips. **Division 5b Less Imbricated Type:** Similar to Division 5a, except there was less overlapping among individual tepals and tips were either rounded or slightly pointed.

Division 6 Orchid-Flowering Hybrids. Tepals were not arranged or shaped according to the usual *Hippeastrum* flower pattern. They could be twisted or extremely reflexed and showed the influence of *H. calyptratum*, *H. cybister* and *H. maracasum*.

Division 7 Double Hybrids. All semidouble and fully double hybrids.

Division 8 Miniature Hybrids. Although the variously shaped flowers were smaller than those with taller scapes (Reginae and Leopoldii type), they were still a good size. Hybrids showed the influence of *Hippeastrum espiritense*, *H. reticulatum* and *H. traubii*.

Division 9 Unclassified Hybrids. All hybrids which did not belong in any other division.

Following discussions with the American Amaryllis Society, the Royal General Bulbgrowers' Association (KAVB) of Hillegom (The Netherlands), a non-statutory registration authority and the Dutch National Cultivar Registration Authority, was appointed the International Cultivar Registration Authority (ICRA) for the registration of all Hippeastrum cultivars on 1 September 1990 by the International Society for Horticultural Science (ISHS).

Although early South African Hadeco hybrids were classified according to the American classification system, the company has since developed its own system founded upon classical music terminology—Solo, Sonatini, Sonata and Symphony—which they insist on retaining. Recently they have added Butterfly and Trumpet categories. Japanese breeders have also developed their own terminology including included Mini and Super Mini to describe their small and dainty hybrids.

By the late 1990s, an increasing number of hybrids were being classified by the ICRA only as small- or large-flowering, resulting in some incorrect classifications and ignoring the considerable differences in flower shape and other physical characteristics existing among the various hybrid groups. This was a particular problem for those hippeastrums which were neither large or small, such as *Hippeastrum* 'Floris Hekker'. While *H.* 'Floris Hekker' is a Midi hybrid, the Dutch registration authority has insisted on classifying it as a Leopoldii hybrid. Some large-flowering hippeastrums continued to be classified as Leopoldii or Reginae hybrids but no further categorization was made within each of these two groups. In the absence of corrections having been made by the ICRA, the correct classification is given in the descriptions in brackets.

By 2001, several new American and Dutch hybrid groups had become commercially available which did not fit into any of the existing categories. Breeders devised their own categories which included Cybisters, Trumpets and Klisters, which only exacerbated an already increasingly messy and confused situation.

The Royal General Bulbgrowers' Association (KAVB) initiated discussions in 2001 with Dutch and South African bulb and cut flower breeders, growers, exporters and wholesalers to develop a coherent and appropriate internationally accepted classification system for all existing and new hybrid groups. By summer 2003, significant progress had been made with the development of a new system to embrace both conventional-shaped large-, medium- and small-flowering singles and doubles and the new hybrid groups. At the time of writing, further work was being undertaken by the KAVB to ensure the proposed system would be accepted and used by breeders and growers of *Hippeastrum* worldwide. Only after international consultation had taken place, would it be possible for full details of the new classification to be released.

According to information supplied by Johan van Scheepen, senior taxonomist and senior registrar of the International Cultivar Registration Authority, several hybrids do not appear to have been classified. Among these are hybrids currently in the process of being granted Plant Breeders' Rights and/or being registered. Some are unlikely to be registered due to a variety of reasons and therefore no official record exists other than those maintained by the breeder and/or grower and the National Plant Collection Holder of *Hippeastrum*. In all such cases, I have assigned a classification (unofficial) based on my experience of growing the plant and following discussions with the breeder. This classification is given in brackets in the descriptions.

None of the Australian hybrids have been submitted to any authority for registration and no official classification has been assigned to these hybrids.

Background to Hybrid Descriptions

Average flower sizes and scape lengths are given, the majority from my experience of having cultivated the plants. It should be noted that all plants in the National Plant Collection of *Hippeastrum* are cultivated under 600-watt sodium lights throughout the year, apart from during the winter when temperatures are lowered to 48–55°F (9–13°C) for 10–12 weeks (also known as the cool period) resulting in shorter scapes compared to hippeastrums cultivated under poor lighting. Some bulbs may produce significantly shorter scapes and sometimes smaller than normal blooms in their first season following purchase. This may be due to disease such as the tarsonemid mite, lack of roots or some other damage sustained either before or after lifting. Providing the plant remains in optimum health and is given the correct environmental and cultural conditions, there is no reason why plants should not produce normal size scapes and blooms in subsequent years.

Occasionally an individual flower may have a different number of tepals, stamens and stigmas. Providing this only affects individual flowers, this is likely to be due to some abnormality which occurred during the early stages of development. Subsequent flowers are likely to be normal. Only if all flowers on all scapes are significantly different is it possible that a mutation has occurred.

While many newly purchased hippeastrums develop little or foliage until flowering has finished, potted plants kept in growth and watered throughout the cool period usually produce 3–7 leaves prior to or simultaneously with the scapes with up to 18 leaves per year.

Glossary

acuminate sharply pointed with slightly concave sides

acute sharply pointed with slightly convex sides

anatropous completely inverted

anion a negatively charged atom

anther a sac at the end of the filament which bears pollen; part of the male reproductive organ

apex the tip of a shoot or leaf

asexual reproduction any method of reproduction which does not involve the fusion of male and female cells

axil the angle between two of the bulb's leaf bases or between the scape and a pedicel

bacterium (pl. bacteria) a single-celled microscopic organism lacking a nucleus and chlorophyll but having a cell wall; beneficial and harmful types exist

basal plate the disc underneath the bulb from which roots develop

biological control a method of controlling pests which uses natural predators, parasites and pathogens

boron a micronutrient essential for development of the pollen tube after pollination

bract a thin, green, leaflike structure arising below a flower or inflorescence

branching roots secondary roots which develop lateral to the basal roots and increase a plant's ability to absorb water and nutrients from the soil

bulbil a small bulb which develops within the leaf bases of the bulb

bulblet a small bulb which develops around the rim of the basal plate

capitate used to describe a stigma having a knoblike end

capsule a dry dehiscent fruit which develops from three carpels fused together

carpel a female reproductive unit comprising ovary and ovules

cation a positively charged atom

chipping a propagation technique in which a bulb is cut vertically into series of segments or chips

chromosome a threadlike structure in the cell nucleus containing DNA

clone a genetically identical individual arising from asexual reproduction or propagation

coir coconut husk fiber; used in some potting mixes as a peat substitute
colchicine a chemical used to produce plants with more than the usual number of chromosomes
contractile a contracting root which pulls the bulb down into the soil, positioning it correctly and providing anchorage
corona a crownlike ring of petaloids or petaloid stamens towards the center of a flower
cross-pollination the transfer of pollen from one flower to another
cultivar a cultivated hybrid
DNA deoxyribonucleic acid; the carrier of hereditary material in all organisms
deciduous shedding leaves annually at the end of the growing season
dehisce to split
desiccant a moisture-absorbing agent used in the storage of pollen and seed
diploid having 2 basic sets of chromosomes ($2n = 22$); a characteristic of many *Hippeastrum* species
elongation the process of increasing in length or stretching
embryo the rudimentary plant within the seed
embryo culture the process of developing an embryo in the laboratory
epiphytic growing on a host but remaining independent
evergreen retaining leaves throughout the year
F_1 hybrid a first-generation hybrid created by crossing 2 species
fertilization the union of male and female sex cells to produce a fertilized egg cell
filament a stalk which bears the anther at its tip; part of the male reproductive organ
floret an immature flower
floriferous bearing many flowers
fruit the ripened ovary of a seed plant
fungicide a chemical used to kill or control fungus
fungus a plant lacking chlorophyll and feeding on living plant tissue and decaying organic material
germination a process beginning with the uptake of water by the seed and ending with the production of the first leaf
glaucous having a whitish, bluish or grayish bloom
hot water treatment a technique used by commercial bulb breeders and growers to eradicate harmful insects using hot water
humus decomposing material formed by the action of bacteria and fungi

hybrid the offspring of crossing two or more species

hysteranthous developing leaves after flowers, as is true for *Amaryllis belladonna*

imbricated used to describe overlapping tepals

in vitro literally "in glass"; the culture of plant tissue in glass or plastic containers

inferior ovary an ovary lying beneath the insertion of the floral parts into the tepal tube; a characteristic of *Hippeastrum*

inflorescence a flower-bearing shoot

insecticide a chemical used to control or kill insects

keel a ridge running lengthwise down the center of the underside of the leaf; giving a boatlike appearance

linear long and narrow

loam a well-balanced fertile soil containing sand, clay and humus

lobe a partially divided portion as in the *Hippeastrum* stigma which has 3 lobes

locule the space inside the ovary containing ovules

lorate strap-shaped

macronutrient an element required in relatively large quantities for plant growth

meristem culture a propagation technique carried out in a laboratory using actively dividing cells found in tips of roots and shoots to create new plants

micronutrient an element required in very small quantities for plant growth

mutation a freak individual arising spontaneously

nectar a sweet, sugary substance secreted by some flowers to attract pollinators

nitrogen a macronutrient and ingredient of N–P–K fertilizers

notching a propagation technique in which a series of cuts or notches is made through the basal plate of a bulb

nutrient a substance required for growth and taken up by plant roots from the soil

oblanceolate spear shaped

offset a small bulb arising from the mother bulb

organic referring to matter derived from or consisting of living organisms such as animal waste (manure); containing carbon

ovary the part of the female reproductive unit which develops into a fruit following fertilization

ovule an unfertilized seed

peat partially decomposed organic matter, usually derived from mosses or sedges; found in boggy areas

pedicel the stalk connecting an individual flower to the scape

perennial a plant which survives and reproduces for several years

perianth a collective term for the outer (sepals) and inner (petals) whorls of a flower

perlite volcanic rock used in some potting mixes to improve soil aeration

petal inner colored layer of the flower; attractive to pollinators

petaloid petal-like; used of stamens or staminodes which have been converted into misshapen fragments; a feature of double hippeastrums

pH a measure of the acidity or alkalinity

phosphorus a macronutrient needed for healthy root development; a component of N–P–K fertilizers

photosynthesis the process by which plants use carbon dioxide, water, sunlight and chlorophyll to produce carbohydrates

physiology the study of internal plant processes including respiration, reproduction and nutrition

picotee a colored edging on a flower; also a flower of one basic color with an edging of another color

pistil the female reproductive organ comprising stigma, style and ovary

pollen tube a threadlike structure which develops from a germinating pollen grain and transports the male reproductive cell to the ovule

pollen grain one of the granular spores in the anther containing the male reproductive cells required for sexual reproduction

pollination the act of transferring pollen grains from the anther to the stigma

pollinator the agent responsible for pollination, such as a moth or bird

potassium a macronutrient essential for protein synthesis, osmosis and operation of stomata; a component of N–P–K fertilizers

progeny offspring

propagation the act of increasing a hybrid or species by sexual or asexual reproduction

reproduction the process by which plants produce offspring from asexual or sexual methods

relative humidity the degree of water vapor saturation in the atmosphere

sap the fluid that circulates in a plant's vascular system

scape a leafless stem bearing flowers

seed a fertilized ovule arising from sexual reproduction

sepals the outer colored portion of the flower

Seramis® non-degradable, inert clay particles used to improve soil aeration by controlling the release of moisture to the plant, also used as a growing medium for chips and twin scales

sexual reproduction the fusion of male and female reproduction cells to create a new individual

spathe leaf a green, leaflike structure which encloses and protect the florets

stamen the male reproductive organ comprising filament and anther

stigma the tip of the female reproductive organ which receives the ripened pollen grains

style a long cylindrical structure in the female reproductive organ culminating in the stigma

systemic used of a pesticide that is taken up and transported throughout the plant

taxonomy the science of naming and classifying of plants

tepal a colored segment of the flower, part of the perianth

tepal tube a tube of variable length and width formed by the fusion of the lower portion of the tepals

tepaloids earlike appendages which develop on either side of the tepals

tetraploid having 4 basic sets of chromosomes ($4n = 44$); a feature of most large-flowering single *Hippeastrum* hybrids

tissue culture a method of propagation which involves isolating cells from an organism cultured on a medium

trace element a micronutrient

transpiration the act of losing water by evaporation from leaves and other parts of the plant

trifid deeply divided into three parts; used to describe a type of stigma in *Hippeastrum*

tripartite divided into three parts; used to describe the *Hippeastrum* ovary

triploid having 3 basic sets of chromosomes ($3n = 33$); usually the result of crossing a tetraploid with a diploid; often sterile

tunicate covered with concentric layers, like an onion

twin scaling a propagation technique in which a bulb is cut into a series of twin scales, each with a piece of basal plate attached

umbel a cluster of blooms at the top of the scape

undulating wavy; used to describe the edge of *Hippeastrum* tepals

vegetative propagation asexual propagation

venation an arrangement or pattern of veins

vermiculite sterile, expanded mica used in potting mixes and as a growing medium for chipping and twin scaling

Bibliography

Alders, G. 1950. Hybrid amaryllis—Van Meeuwen Superiora and Graceful clones. *Plant Life* 6: 109–111.

Alford, D. V. 1995. *A Colour Atlas of Pests of Ornamental Trees, Shrubs and Flowers.* London: Manson Publishing.

Amaryllis in the north. 1894. *Gardeners' Chronicle* 15: 441.

Arroyo, S. 1982. The chromosomes of *Hippeastrum*, *Amaryllis* and *Phycella* (Amaryllideae). *Kew Bulletin* 37: 211–216.

Ayres, A., ed. 1990. *The Gardening Which? Guide to Gardening Without Chemicals.* London: Consumers' Association and Hodder and Stoughton.

Bagust, H. 1994. *The Gardener's Dictionary of Horticultural Terms.* London: Cassell Publishers.

Baker, J. G. 1878a. A new key to the genera of Amaryllidaceae. *Journal of Botany* 7: 161–169.

Baker, J. G. 1878b. An enumeration and classification of the species of *Hippeastrum. Journal of Botany* 16: 79–85.

Baker, J. G. 1888. *Handbook of the Amaryllideae, Including the Alstroemerieae and Agaveae.* London: George Bell and Sons.

Barnhoorn, F. 1991. Cultivars of *Hippeastrum*: Their evolution from the past and their development for the future. *Herbertia* 47 (1–2): 76–79.

Beckham, E. M. 1991. Hybridizing double *Hippeastrum* (*Amaryllis*). *Herbertia* 47 (1–2): 56–57.

Beckwith, D. S. 1964. Growing amaryllids in north Georgia. *Plant Life* 20: 81–83.

Bell, W. D. 1977. More potentials in *Amaryllis* breeding. *Plant Life* 33: 65–67.

Blaauw, A. H. 1931. Formation and periodicity of the organs in *Hippeastrum hybridum. Laboratoroium voor Plantephysiologisch Onderzoek Wageningen, Mededeling* 32: 1–91.

Blossfeld, H. 1966. Notes on *Worsleya. Plant Life* 22: 15–22.

Blossfeld, H. 1970. Two Brazilian *Amaryllis* species. *Plant Life* 26: 58–62.

Blossfeld, H. 1973a. *Amaryllis calyptrata* Ker-Gawler. *Plant Life* 29: 30–34.

Blossfeld, H. 1973b. Breeding for yellow *Amaryllis* hybrids. *Plant Life* 29: 56–58.

Blossfeld, H. 1976. *Amaryllis calyptrata. Plant Life* 32: 41–44.

Bonavia, E. 1908. Hippeastrums as cut flowers. *Gardeners' Chronicle* 43: 318.

Bose, T. K., B . K. Jana, and T. P. Mukhopadhyay. 1980. Effects of growth regulators on growth and flowering in *Hippeastrum hybridum* Hort. *Scientia Horticulture* 12: 195–200.

Bowes, B. G. 1997. *A Colour Atlas of Plant Structure.* London: Manson Publishing.

Bowes, B. G. 1999. *A Colour Atlas of Plant Propagation and Conservation.* London: Manson Publishing.

Bradley, S. 2003. *What's Wrong with My Plant?* London: Hamlyn.

Brett, R. 1999. Perfect chips for finer flowers. *Kew Friends Magazine* (spring): 39–40.

Bryan, J. 2002. *Bulbs.* Rev. ed. Portland, Oregon: Timber Press.

Buchmann, F. 1970. Hybridizing with *Amaryllis* species—1969. *Plant Life* 26: 108–111.

Buczacki, S., and K. Harris. 2000. *Pests, Diseases and Disorders of Garden Plants.* London: HarperCollins.

C. R. Fielder, V.M.H.: Obituary. 1947. *Gardeners' Chronicle* 121: 35.

Cage, J. M. 1975. Breeding and culture of *Amaryllis. Plant Life* 31: 65–72.

Cage, J. M. 1977. Pot culture of *Amaryllis aglaiae. Plant Life* 33: 78–79.

Cage, J. M. 1980. End of a breeding project. *Plant Life* 36: 79–81.

Calderón, J. C. 1975. Contribution to Peruvian Amaryllidaceae. *Plant Life* 31: 2–32.

Calderón, J. C. 1984. The Peruvian species of the genus *Amaryllis* (Amaryllidaceae). *Herbertia* 40: 112–134.

Callaway, D. J., and M. B. Callaway, eds. 2000. *Breeding Ornamental Plants.* Portland, Oregon: Timber Press.

Campbell, N. A. 1990. *Biology.* San Francisco, California: Benjamin Cummings Publishing Company.

Cárdenas, M. 1972. New Bolivian *Amaryllis* species. *Plant Life* 28: 48–55.

Carpenter, W. J., and E. R. Ostmark. 1988. Moisture content, freezing, and storage conditions influence germination of *Amaryllis* seeds. *HortScience* 23 (6): 1072–1074.

Castillo, J. A. 1987. Notes on the cultivation of South American bulbous plants. *Herbertia* 43 (2): 2–11.

Castillo, J. A. 1991. *Hippeastrum* in the wild in Argentina. *Herbertia* 47 (1–2): 103–114.

Chapman, H. J. 1907 Seedling hippeastrums at Oakwood, Wylam. *Gardeners' Chronicle* 41: 199.

Cothran, C. D. 1979. Yellow-flowered and other *Amaryllis* hybrids in genetics and breeding. *Plant Life* 35: 61–65.

Cothran, C. D. 1980a. Charles Dewitt Cothran—An autobiography. *Plant Life* 36: 10–19.

Cothran, C. D. 1980b. The quest for large yellow-flowering hybrid *Amaryllis*. *Plant Life* 36: 19–22.

Cothran, C. D. 1981a. Continuing quest for large yellow-flowering *Amaryllis*. *Plant Life* 37: 110–111.

Cothran, C. D. 1981b. The Miyake hybrid amaryllis. *Plant Life* 37: 111–113.

Cothran, C. D. 1982. The continuing pursuit of yellow. *Plant Life* 38: 61–63.

Cothran, C. D. 1984. Large yellow *Amaryllis* hybrids. *Herbertia* 40: 105–111.

Cothran, C. D. 1985. Quest for large, yellow hippeastrums. *Herbertia* 41: 34–36.

Coutts, J. 1914. Hippeastrums. *Gardeners' Chronicle* 56: 145–146.

Craft, D. D. 1979. *Amaryllis evansiae*. *Plant Life* 35: 109–111.

Crochet, C. J., and Mrs. J. S. Barry. 1964. Growing *Amaryllis* in pots. *Plant Life* 20: 80–81.

Dandy, J. E., and F. R. Fosberg. 1954. The type of *Amaryllis belladonna* Linnaeus. *Taxon* 3: 231–232.

Datta, S. K., and V. N. Gupta. 2000. *Hippeastrum*: An excellent bulbous plant, at National Botanical Research Institute, Lucknow, India. *Applied Botany Abstracts* 20 (3): 248–260.

De Hertogh, A. A. 1994. *Home Forcing of Potted Amaryllis (Hippeastrum)* Horticulture Information Leaflet 529. North Carolina Cooperative Extensive Service: North Carolina State University College of Agriculture and Life Sciences.

De Hertogh, A., ed. 1996. *Holland Bulb Forcer's Guide*. Lisse, The Netherlands: International Flower Bulb Center and Dutch Bulb Exporters Association.

De Hertogh, A., and M. Le Nard, eds. 1993. *The Physiology of Flower Bulbs*. Elsevier: London.

De Hertogh A. A., and M. Tilley. 1991. Planting medium effects on forced Swaziland- and Dutch-grown *Hippeastrum* hybrids. *HortScience* 26 (9): 1168–1170.

Decker, D. 1964. Growing amaryllids and other seedlings on water. *Plant Life* 20: 104–108.

Deme, J. W. 1978. Breeding double *Amaryllis*. *Plant Life* 34: 102–103.

Deme, J. W. 1980. Double *Amaryllis* update. *Plant Life* 36: 94.

Deme, J. W. 1981. Double *Amaryllis*—Summer 1981. *Plant Life* 37: 65–66.

Desmond, R. 1995. *The History of the Royal Botanic Gardens Kew*. London: Harvill Press.

Diener, R. 1933–1934. The Diener hybrid *Amaryllis*. *American Amaryllis Society Year-Book* 1: 67.

Doorduin, J. C. 1990. Growth and development of *Hippeastrum* grown in glasshouses. *Acta Horticulturae* 266: 123–131.

Doran, J. L. 1969. Notes by an amateur collector. *Plant Life* 25: 37–40.

Doran, J. L. 1970a. Collecting South American amaryllids (1964–1968). *Plant Life* 26: 49–56.

Doran, J. L. 1970b. Some cultural requirements of *Amaryllis* species. *Plant Life* 26: 89–91.

Doran, J. L. 1972a. John Leonard Doran—An autobiography. *Plant Life* 28: 6–8.

Doran, J. L. 1972b. Exploring for amaryllids in South America 1969–1970. *Plant Life* 28: 8–17.

Doran, J. L. 1972c. Some cultural requirements of *Amaryllis* species. *Plant Life* 28: 89–91.

Doran, J. L. 1976. *Amaryllis* species and their hybrids. *Plant Life* 32: 39–41.

Doran, J. L. 1991. *Hippeastrum* (*Amaryllis*) growing. *Herbertia* 47 (1–2): 138–144.

Douglas, I. 1906. The *Hippeastrum*. *Gardeners' Chronicle* 43: 177–178.

Douglas, J. 1908. The *Hippeastrum*. *Gardeners' Chronicle* 43: 145–146.

Early, W. 1892. Hippeastrums for greenhouse culture. *Gardeners' Chronicle* 12: 535.

Edwin Hill: Obituary. 1904. *Gardeners' Chronicle* 35: 255.

Elderkin, S. 2003. Miss Read's passion. *Saturday Telegraph* (Gardening): 1 February.

Fesmire, V. R. 1970. The attractive Miniature *Amaryllis*. *Plant Life* 26: 105–108.

Fielder, C. R. 1914–1915. The cultivation of Hippeastrums. *Journal of the Royal Horticultural Society* 40: 35–39.

Flint, G. J., and G. R. Hanks. 1982. Twin scaling and chipping—virus-free bulbs in bulk. *The Grower* (4 February), supplement: 7, 9–10.

Floral Committee, 19 April 1904. 1904–1906. *Journal of the Royal Horticultural Society* (*Proceedings of the Royal Horticultural Society*) 29: 64–65.

Floral Committee, 3 April 1906. 1907. *Journal of the Royal Horticultural Society* (*Proceedings of the Royal Horticultural Society*) 32: 114–115.

Florists' flowers: Garden varieties of *Hippeastrum*. 1910. *Gardeners' Chronicle* 47: 326.

Glover, W. 1985. Australian *Hippeastrum* hybridization. *Herbertia* 41: 31–34.

Goedert, R. D. 1961. Comments on the 1959–1960 *Amaryllis* season. *Plant Life* 17: 129–134.

Goedert, R. D. 1962. 1960–1961 *Amaryllis* season—hybrids and species. *Plant Life* 18: 132–139.

Goedert, R. D. 1963. 1961–1962 *Amaryllis* season. *Plant Life* 19: 118–127.

Goedert, R. D. 1964. 1962–1963 *Amaryllis* season. *Plant Life* 20: 93–101.

Goedert, R. D. 1965. 1963–1964 *Amaryllis* season. *Plant Life* 21: 119–129.

Goedert, R. D. 1966. 1964–1965 *Amaryllis* season. *Plant Life* 22: 82–94.

Goedert, R. D. 1967. 1965–1966 *Amaryllis* season. *Plant Life* 23: 132–140.

Goedert, R. D. 1968. 1966–1967 *Amaryllis* season. *Plant Life* 24: 103–111.

Goedert, R. D. 1970. *Amaryllis* season 1969. *Plant Life* 26: 153–161.

Greenwood, P., and A. Halstead. 1997. *The RHS Pests and Diseases*. London: Dorling Kindersley.

Griffiths, M. 1994. *Index of Garden Plants*. London: MacMillan.

Gunn, S. 2002. Cycles of sustenance. *Kew Magazine* (autumn): 18–21.

Gupta, V. N., and M. A. Kher. 1983. Rapid multiplication of *Hippeastrum* bulbs by notching. *Indian Journal of Horticulture* 40 (192): 98–101.

Gupta, V. N., and M. A. Kher. 1987. Improved techniques for growing *Amaryllis*. *Indian Journal of Horticulture* 33 (1): 12–14.

Gurr, S. J., and J. Peach. 1995. Blue genes. *The Garden* 120 (Part 5): 287–289.

Guthrie, D. 1991. Growing hippeastrums. *Herbertia* 47 (1–2): 118–121.

Hadeco (Pty) Ltd. 1999. *Hippeastrum Datapak*. Maraisburg, South Africa.

Halevy, A. H., and A. M. Kofranek. 1984. Prevention of stem base splitting in cut *Hippeastrum* flowers. *HortScience* 19 (1): 113–114.

Hanger, F. 1953. Hippeastrums today and tomorrow. *Gardening Illustrated* 70 (3): 68.

Hanks, G. R. 1986. The effect of temperature and duration of incubation on twin-scale propagation of *Narcissus* and other bulbs. *Crop Research* (Hort. Res.) 25: 143–152.

Hanks, G. R., and S. Phillips. 1982. Twin-scaling. *Growers' Bulletin* 6. Littlehampton, United Kingdom: Glasshouse Crops Research Institute.

Hartman, H. T., D. E. Kester, and F. T. Davies Jr. 1990. *Plant Propagation, Principles and Practices.* 5th ed. Englewood Cliffs, New Jersey: Prentice Hall.

Hayashi, I. 1974. Studies on the growth and flowering of *Hippeastrum hybridum.* Part 3, The effects of day length to the growth and flower bud development. *Bulletin of the Kanagawa Horticultural Experiment Station* 22: 116–119.

Hayashi, I., and M. Suzuki. 1970. Studies on the growth and flowering of *Hippeastrum hybridum.* Part 1, Effects of temperature to the growth of young seedlings and bulbs. Part 2, Growth and flowering in outdoor culture and effects of autumnal temperature to the growth. *Bulletin of the Kanagawa Horticultural Experiment Station* 18: 171–188.

Hayward, W. 1933–1934. The Mead strain of the Nehrling hybrid amaryllis. *American Amaryllis Society Year-Book* 1: 62–63.

Hayward, W. 1948. Hybrid *Amaryllis* improvement. *Herbertia* 15: 63–67.

Hayward, W. 1950. *Amaryllis* of tomorrow. *Plant Life* 6: 97–104.

Hayward, W. 1959. Simon Adrianus de Graaff to Peter Barr, 1890. *Plant Life* 15: 10–15.

Heaton, I. W. 1933. The Heaton hybrid *Amaryllis. American Amaryllis Society Year-Book* 1: 66–67.

Herbert, W. 1821. Preliminary treatise. Appendix to Vol. 7 of the *Botanical Register* and *Botanical Magazine.* London: James Ridgeway and Sons.

Herbert, W. 1837. *Amaryllidaceae.* London: James Ridgeway and Sons.

Hippeastrum ackermannii or *acramannii* (plant notes). 1918. *Gardeners' Chronicle* 63: 63.

Hippeastrum 'Calypso'. 1910. *Gardeners' Chronicle* 47: 290.

Hippeastrum 'Mrs Carl Jay'. 1907. *Gardeners' Chronicle* 41: 424.

Hippeastrum pardinum (plant notes). 1909. *Gardeners' Chronicle* 45: 242.

Hippeastrum reticulatum. 1918. *Gardeners' Chronicle* 65: 127.

Hippeastrums. 1914. *Gardeners' Chronicle* 56: 145.

Hippeastrums. 1918. *Gardeners' Chronicle* 63: 63.

Hippeastrums (amaryllis) at Tring Park. 1906. *Gardeners' Chronicle* 39: 90.

Hippeastrums at Bridge Hall. 1934. *Gardeners' Chronicle* 96: 89.

Hippeastrums at Chelsea. 1910. *Gardeners' Chronicle* 47: 259–260.

Hippeastrums for greenhouse culture. 1892. *Gardeners' Chronicle* 12: 535.

Howard, F. H. 1937. The Howard and Smith hybrid *Amaryllis* strain. *Herbertia* 4: 189–190.

Huang, C. W., H. Okubo, and S. Uemoto. 1990a. Importance of two scales in propagating *Hippeastrum* hybridum by twin scaling. *Scientia Horticulturae* 42: 141–150.

Huang, C. W., H. Okubo, and S. Uemoto. 1990b. Comparison of bulblet formation from twin scales and single scales in *Hippeastrum hybridum* cultured *in vitro*. *Scientia Horticulturae* 42: 151–160.

Huxley, A. 1974. *Plant and Planet*. London: Allen Lane.

Huxley, A., and M. Griffiths, eds. 1992. *The New Royal Horticultural Society Dictionary of Gardening*. Vols. 1 and 2. London: MacMillan.

In Memoriam—Fred J. Buchmann, 1913–1971. 1972. *Plant Life* 28: 19.

Jackson, J. 2000. Flower power. *Password* (Cranfield University Alumni) (Summer): 18–19.

Kawa, L., and A. A. De Hertogh. 1992. Root physiology of ornamental flowering bulbs. *Horticultural Reviews* 14: 57–88.

Ker, J. B. 1804. *Amaryllis belladonna* (a) belladonna lily. *Botanical Magazine* 9: tab. 733.

Komoriya, S. 1991. Breeding of *Hippeastrum* in Japan. *Herbertia* 47 (1–2): 131–136.

Krelage, E. H. 1938. Amaryllid culture in Holland. *Herbertia* 5: 5–60.

Krelage, E. H., and Sons. 1896. *General Catalogue for 1896—Second Part* (490B). Haarlem: The Netherlands.

Krelage, E. H., and Sons. 1906. *General Catalogue for 1906*. Haarlem: The Netherlands.

Larsson, J., and L. Larsson. 1991. Notes on *Hippeastrum* culture. *Herbertia* 47 (1–2): 64–65.

Lassanyi, E. 1991. How to plant and care for *Hippeastrum. Herbertia* 47 (1–2): 115–117.

Latapie, W. R. 1966. New double white double hybrid *Amaryllis. Plant Life* 22: 47–49.

Latapie, W. R. 1980. Suggested standards for judging double *Amaryllis. Plant Life* 36: 41.

Latapie, W. R. 1982a. Walter Ralph Latapie—An autobiography. *Plant Life* 38: 10–12.

Latapie, W. R. 1982b. Breeding hybrid *Amaryllis*—A rewarding experience. *Plant Life* 38: 14–19.

Late B. S. Williams, The. 1890. *Gardeners' Chronicle* 18: 19.

Leeuwen, A. J. M. van. 1986. Grondkoeling werkt gunstig bij *Amaryllis. Vakblad voor de Bloemisterij* 41 (24): 36–37.

Leeuwen, A. J. M. van, and J. C. M. Buschman. 1991. The *Hippeastrum* as a cut flower. *Herbertia* 47 (1–2): 93–102.

L'Heritier, C. L. 1788. *Sertum anglicum.* Paris: Didcot.

Linnaeus, C. 1738. *Hortus Cliffortianus.* Amsterdam.

Linnaeus, C. 1759. *Systema Naturae.* Ed. 10, 2. Stockholm: Salvius.

Linnaeus. C. 1762. *Species Plantarum.* Ed. 2. Stockholm: Salvius.

Linnaeus. C. 1775. *Plantae surinamenses.* Uppsala: Edmann.

Ludwig and Company. 1951–1969. *Hippeastrum* catalogs 1, 4, 6, 8, 9 10, 14, 15 and 19. Hillegom, The Netherlands.

Luyten, I. 1935. Propagation (vegetative propagation of hippeastrums). *American Amaryllis Society Year-Book* 2: 115–122.

MacDaniels, L. H., and A. J. Eames. 1925. *An Introduction to Plant Anatomy.* London: McGraw-Hill Book Company.

Manning, R. H. 1980. Amaryllid culture in Minnesota. *Plant Life* 36: 113–115.

Mathew, B. 1999. Secret of the Knights Star. *Kew Friends Magazine* (spring): 34–37.

McCann, J. J. 1937. New double hybrid amaryllis. *Herbertia* 4: 185–186.

McCann, E. J. 1950. McCann double amaryllis. *Plant Life* 6: 107–108.

Mead, T. L. 1935. Theodore L. Mead—An autobiography. *American Amaryllis Society Year-Book* 2: 11–22.

Meerow, A. W., T. K. Broschat, and M. E. Kane. 1991. *Hippeastrum* breeding at the University of Florida. *Herbertia* 47 (1–2): 4–10.

Meerow, A. W., J. van Scheepen and Julie H. A. Dutilh. 1997. Transfers from *Amaryllis* Linnaeus to *Hippeastrum* Herbert (Amaryllidaceae). *Taxon* 46: 15–19.

Mertzweiller, J. K. 1973. *Amaryllis* breeding—1972 report. *Plant Life* 29: 61–66.

Mii, M., T. Mori, and N. Iwase. 1974. Organ formation from the excised bulb scales of *Hippeastrum hybridum in vitro. Journal of Horticultural Science.* 49: 241–244.

Miyake, I. 1979. Breeding hybrid amaryllis with 6–8 flowers per umbel. *Plant Life* 34: 73–75.

Miyake, I. 1991. Observation of an hippeastrum breeding program. *Herbertia* 47 (1–2): 73–75.

Moore, H. E. 1963. *Amaryllis* and *Hippeastrum. Baileya* 11: 15–16.

Moore, W. C. 1979. *Diseases of Bulbs.* Rev. by A. A. Brunt, D. Price and A. R. Rees. London: Ministry of Agriculture, Fisheries and Food.

Mr James Douglas, V.M.H. 1909. *Journal of Horticulture and Home Farmer* 58: 198–200.

Narain, P. 1974. Summary—Hybridization and polyploidy in relation to *Amaryllis* species and cultivars. *Plant Life* 30: 94–96.

Narain, P. 1982. *Amaryllis* hybrids. *Plant Life* 38: 72–78.

Narain, P. 1983. *Amaryllis* hybrids II. *Plant Life* 39: 84–92.

Narain, P. 1985. A sectional chimera in hybrid *Hippeastrum. Herbertia* 41: 43–46.

Narain, P. 1987. *Hippeastrum* hybrids. *Herbertia* 43: 25–27.

Narain, P. 1991. *Hippeastrum* hybrids. *Herbertia* 47: 72.

Narain, P., and T. N. Khoshoo. 1968. Cytogenetic survey of amaryllis cultivars. *Journal of Cytology and Genetics* 3: 41–45.

Narain, P., and T. N. Khoshoo. 1977. Origin and evolution of garden amaryllis. *Indian Journal of Horticulture* 34: 80–85.

Nehrling, H. 1907. Hippeastrums in America. *Gardeners' Chronicle* 42: 241–242, 258.

Nehrling, H. 1909. *Die Amaryllis oder Rittersterne (Hippeastrum).* Berlin: Verlagsbuchhandlung Paul Parey.

North Mymms, Hatfield. 1900. *Gardeners' Chronicle* 28: 254–255.

Obituary: B. S. Williams. 1890. *Gardeners' Chronicle* 17: 801.

Pfeiffer, N. E. 1936. Storage of pollen of hybrid *Amaryllis. Herbertia* 3: 103–104.

Pickard, N. 1957. Evaluation of Dutch hybrid *Amaryllis. Plant Life* 13: 110–111.

Pickard, A. C. 1964. Golden rules for growing hybrid *Amaryllis. Plant Life* 20: 101–103.

Pope, J. 1895. English *Amaryllis* at Haarlem. *Gardeners' Chronicle* 17: 432–433.

Prakash, S. 1981. Pollination mechanism and hybridizations in *Amaryllis. Plant Life* 37: 114–118.

R. Wilson Ker, V.M.H.: Obituary. 1910. *Gardeners' Chronicle* 47: 306.

Ravenna, P. F. 1970. Contributions to South American *Amaryllidaceae* III. *Plant Life* 26: 73–85.

Ravenna, P. F. 1971. Contributions to South American *Amaryllidaceae* IV. *Plant Life* 27: 61–89.

Ravenna, P. F. 1981. Contributions to South American *Amaryllidaceae* VII. *Plant Life* 37: 57–66.

Read, V. M. 1998a. Blooming bold. *The Garden* 123 (10): 734–737.

Read, V. M. 1998b. Seed germination and early growth of *Hippeastrum* species and hybrids in water. *Herbertia* 53: 116–119.

Read, V. M. 1998c. How to grow better hippeastrums. *Herbertia* 53: 195–198.

Read, V. M. 1998d. Kew hippeastrum festival. *The London Group of the NCCPG Plant Heritage Conservation Newsletter* 59: 13–14.

Read, V. M. 1999a. *Hippeastrum* 'Germa'—hybrid with an uncertain future. *Plant Heritage* 6 (1): 18–23.

Read, V. M. 1999b. *Hippeastrum* hybridisation developments. *Herbertia* 54: 84–109.

Read, V. M. 1999c. Developments in *Hippeastrum* hybridisation 1799–1999. *National Council for the Conservation of Plants and Gardens [NCCPG], National Plant Collections Directory 2000*: 39–44, 50–52.

Read, V. M. 1999d. Hippeastrum adventures in 1999. *The London Group of the NCCPG Plant Heritage Conservation Newsletter* 63: 7–9.

Read, V. M. 2000a. *Hippeastrum* hybridisation developments, part 1. *Amaryllids (Nerine and Amaryllid Society)* January: 2–17.

Read, V. M. 2000b. *Hippeastrum* hybridisation developments, part 2. *Amaryllids (Nerine and Amaryllid Society)* April–May: 1–15.

Read, V. M. 2000c. *Hippeastrum* hybridisation developments, part 3. *Amaryllids (Nerine and Amaryllid Society)* July–August: 8–19.

Read, V. M. 2000d. NCCPG national collection. *Professional Gardener* 89: 39–43.

Read, V. M. 2001a. How to grow better hippeastrums. *Professional Gardener* 90: 38-40

Read, V. M. 2001b. Latest developments in *Hippeastrum* breeding. *Professional Gardener* 92: 32–33.

Read, V. M. 2001c. Latest developments in *Hippeastrum* breeding—The Fred Meyer hybrids, part 2. *Professional Gardener* 93: 29–31.

Read, V. M. 2001d. The perils of having a National Collection in a flat! *The London Group of the NCCPG Plant Heritage Conservation Newsletter* 68: 4–10.

Redoute, P. J. 1982. *Lilies and Related Flowers*. London: Michael Joseph.

Rees, A. R. 1972. *The Growth of Bulbs*. London: Academic Press.

Rees, A. R. 1989. Evaluation of the geophytic habit and its physiological advantages. *Herbertia* 45: 104–110.

Registration of new *Amaryllis* clones, 1964. 1965. *Plant Life* 21: 97–100.

Registration of new *Amaryllis* clones, 1969. 1970. *Plant Life* 26: 70–71.

Registration of new *Amaryllis* clones, 1974. 1975. *Plant Life* 31: 36.

Registration of new *Amaryllis* clones, 1978. 1979. *Plant Life* 34: 91–93.

Registration of new *Amaryllis* clones, 1979. 1980. *Plant Life (General Edition)* 36: 128.

Registration of new *Amaryllis* clones, 1980. 1981. *Plant Life* 37: 108.

Registration of new *Amaryllis* clones, 1981. 1982. *Plant Life* 38: 58.

Registration of new *Amaryllis* clones, 1983. 1984. *Herbertia* 40: 94–95.

Reynolds, J., and J. Tampion. 1983. *Double Flowers: A Scientific Study*. London: Pembridge Press.

Rice, E. G., and R. H. Compton. 1950. *Wild Flowers of the Cape of Good Hope*. Kirstenbosch, Newlands, South Africa: Botanical Society of South Africa.

Rimbach, A. 1929. Die Verbreitung der Wurzelverkurzung in Pflanzenreich. *Deut. Bot. Ges.* 47: 22–31.

Rix, D. V. 1991. *Worsleya rayneri. Herbertia* 47 (1–2): 66.

Royal Horticultural Society. 1956. *Dictionary of Gardening: A Practical and Scientific Encyclopaedia of Horticulture*. Vols. 1 and 2. Ed. Fred J. Chittenden. Oxford: Clarendon Press.

Royal Horticultural Society. 1997. *Bulbs*. London: Dorling Kindersley.

Rudometkin, M. 1991. Instinct in the development of *Hippeastrum. Herbertia* 47 (1–2): 68–70.

Ruppel, C. G. 1970. May–June 1969 collection trips. *Plant Life (Amaryllis Year Book)* 26: 56–58.

Scavia, J. 1959. *Amaryllis* breeding notes. *Plant Life* 15: 81–82.

Schauenberg, P. 1965. *The Bulb Book.* London: Frederick Warne and Company.

Sealy, J. R. 1939. *Amaryllis* and *Hippeastrum. Bulletin Miscellaneous Information Kew* 54: 49–68.

Sherwood, S. 2001. *A Passions for Plants.* London: Cassell.

Smith, B. D. 1968. Notes on *Worsleya rayneri* (blue amaryllis). *Plant Life* 24: 98–100.

Stearn, W. 1990. *Flower Artists of Kew.* London: Herbert Press.

Stearn, W. 1992. *Botanical Latin.* 4th ed. Portland, Oregon: Timber Press.

Stone, W. 1934. In Memoriam—Henry Nehrling 1853–1929. *American Amaryllis Society Year-Book* 1: 7–10.

Street, A. 2001. Closing the show. *The Garden* 126 (9): 712–715.

Strider, D. L., ed. 1985. *Diseases of Floral Crops*, vol. 1. New York: Praeger Publishers.

Strout, E. B. 1951. The blue amaryllis—*Worsleya rayneri. Plant Life* 7: 123–130.

Stuurman, J. R., ed. 1980. *The Alphabetical List of Amaryllis (Hippeastrum) Cultivars in Cultivation in The Netherlands.* Hillegom, Netherlands: Royal General Bulbgrowers' Association (KAVB).

Sugden, A. 1992. *Botany Handbook.* Harlow: Longman Group UK.

Theodore L. Mead. 1935. *American Amaryllis Society Year-Book* 2: 11–22.

Thornburgh, R. G. 1957. Hybrid *Amaryllis*—The potted queen. *Plant Life* 13: 111–118.

Tjaden, W. 1981a. *Amaryllis belladonna* Linnaeus—An up-to-date summary. *Plant Life* 37: 21–26.

Tjaden, W. 1981b. *Amaryllis belladonna* Linnaeus (*Species Plantarum* 293, 1753). *Taxon* 30: 294–298.

Tombolato, A. F. C., V. Bovi, L. A., F. Matthes and C. Azevedo. 1991. Breeding new varieties of *Hippeastrum* with Brazilian native species. *Herbertia* 47 (1–2): 88–92.

Traub, H. P. 1935. Propagation of amaryllids by stem cuttage. *American Amaryllis Society Year-Book* 2: 123–126.

Traub, H. P. 1954. Typification of *Amaryllis belladonna* Linnaeus (1753). *Taxon* 3: 102–111.

Traub, H. P. 1958. *The Amaryllis Manual.* New York: MacMillan.

Traub, H. P. 1970. *An Introduction to Herbert's "Amaryllidaceae, etc." 1837, and Related Works.* Lehre: Verlag von Cramer.

Traub, H. P. 1974. *Amaryllis Leopoldii* T. Moor, emend. *Plant Life* 30: 81–83.

Traub, H. P. 1980a. A Sherlock Holmes of biological nomenclature. *Plant Life* 36: 25–26.

Traub, H. P. 1980b. The subgenera of the genus *Amaryllis* Linnaeus. *Plant Life* 36: 43–45.

Traub, H. P. 1983. The lectotypification of *Amaryllis belladonna* Linnaeus (1753). *Taxon* 32: 243.

Traub, Hamilton P., W. R. Ballard, W. D. Morton Jr., E. F. Authement, comp. 1964. *Catalog of Hybrid Amaryllis Cultivars 1799 to Dec. 31, 1963.* Supplement to *Plant Life (Journal of the American Amaryllis Society).*

Traub, H. P., and H. N. Moldenke. 1949. *Amaryllidaceae: Tribe Amarylleae.* Stanford, California: American Plant Life Society.

Traub, H. P., and I. S. Nelson. 1958. *Amaryllis evansiae. Plant Life* 14: 29–30.

Troughton, J., and L. A. Donaldson. 1972. *Probing Plant Structure.* London: Chapman and Hall.

Turner, D. H. 1979. A step-by-step guide to twin scale propagation. *The Grower* (10 May): 35–37.

Uphof, J. C. Th. 1938. The history of nomenclature—*Amaryllis belladonna* (Linnaeus) Herbert and *Hippeastrum* Herbert. *Herbertia* 5: 101–109.

Uphof, J. C. Th. 1939. Critical review of Sealy's "*Amaryllis* and *Hippeastrum.*" *Herbertia* 6: 163–166.

Union Internationale pour la Protection des Obtentions Végétales (UPOV). 2001. *Guidelines for the Conduct of Tests for Distinctness, Uniformity and Stability TG/181/3.* Geneva, Switzerland: UPOV.

Union Internationale pour la Protection des Obtentions Végétales. 2002. *General Introduction to the Examination of Distinctness, Uniformity and Stability and the Development of Harmonized Descriptions of New Varieties of Plants TG/1/3* (UPOV). Geneva, Switzerland: UPOV.

Veitch, H. 1980. The *Hippeastrum (Amaryllis). Journal of the Royal Horticultural Society* 12 (1890): 243–258.

Veitch, J. 1906. *Hortus Veitchii: A History of the Rise and Progress of the Nurseries of Messrs James Veitch and Sons, Together with an Account of the Botanical Collectors and Hybridists Employed by Them and a List of the Most Remarkable of Their Introductions.* London: James Veitch and Sons.

Veitch Nursery, James. 1888, 1890, 1891 *Catalogues of Hyacinths and other Bulbous Plants.* London: Chelsea.

Vijverberg, A. J. 1981. Growing amaryllis. *Grower Guide* 23. London: Grower Books.

Wiel, T. van der. 1999. Twee vormen van Knight garden *Hippeastrum* goed in beeld. *Vakerk* (13 March): 11.

Wiel, T. van der. 2000. *Hippeastrum* Easter Festival zorgt voor productreputatie. *Vakerk* 17: 44–45.

Williams, P. H. 1970. An aquatic *Amaryllis* species from Argentina. *Plant Life* 26: 65–67.

Wilson, G. F. 1939. *Amaryllis* pests. *Journal of the Royal Horticultural Society* 64: 318–326.

Wilson, M. C. 1981. *Amaryllis* hybrids of J. L. Doran in genetics and breeding. *Plant Life* 37: 109.

Worsley, A. 1896. *The Genus* Hippeastrum [= *Amaryllis*]. London.

Worsley, A. 1929. *Hippeastrum procerum. Gardeners' Chronicle* 85: 377–379.

Worsley, A. 1931. Hardier hippeastrums. *Gardeners' Chronicle* 90: 414.

Worsley, A. 1933. Hybridization in Amarylleae. *American Amaryllis Society Year-Book* 1: 52–60.

Worsley, A. 1935. Hybridization in Amarylleae. *American Amaryllis Society Year-Book* 2: 52–60.

Worsley, A. 1936. Life and career of Arthington Worsley—An autobiography. *Herbertia* 3: 10–19.

Yanagawa, T., and Y Sakanishi. 1977. Regeneration of bulblets on *Hippeastrum* bulb segments excised from various parts of a parent bulb. *J. Japan. Soc. Hort. Sci.* 46 (2): 250–260.

Ypma, A. 1999. Star of the Knight nieuwe lijn fraaie hippeastrums. *Vakerk* (23 January): 6–9.

Index

Agriom B.V., 100, 103–104
Agronômico Institute at Campinas, 108, 116
×*Amarcrinum memoria-corsii* 'Howardii', 21
×*Amarine tubergenii*, 21; Plate 1.11
Amaryllis, 15–17, 18, 19, 21, 23–25, 26
hybrids, 21
Amaryllis aglaiae. See *H. aglaiae*
Amaryllis atamasco, 15
Amaryllis belladonna, 15–26; Plates 1.1, 1.10
Amaryllis blanda, 18
Amaryllis 'Bloemfontein', 21
Amaryllis equestris. See *Hippeastrum equestre*
Amaryllis formosissima, 15
Amaryllis gigantea. See *Worsleya rayneri*
Amaryllis guttata, 15
Amaryllis 'Jagerfontein', 21
Amaryllis 'Johannesburg', 21, 23
Amaryllis 'Kimberley', 21
Amaryllis longifolia, 15
Amaryllis lutea, 15
Amaryllis orientalis, 15
Amaryllis procera. See *Hippeastrum procerum*
Amaryllis reginae. See *Hippeastrum reginae*
Amaryllis sarniensis, 15
Amaryllis 'Windhoek', 21
Amaryllis zeylanica, 15
Ammocharis, 17
Ardagh, J., 19
Aschamia, 18
asexual propagation, 59, 159, 177–178, 210, 211, 227; Plates 8.1, 9.3. See also chipping; notching; offsets; twin scaling
Australian hybrids. See Maguire, Richard
Authement, E.F., 42
Avon Bulbs, 21, 23

Baker, John Gilbert, 16, 18
Ballard, W.R., 42
Barbados amaryllis. See *Amaryllis belladonna*
Barnhoorn, Andre
Sonatini hybrids, 101, 107, 118, 120–122; Plate 6.15
yellow hybrids, 101; Plate 5.4
Barnhoorn, Floris. See Hadeco (Pty) Ltd
beard tepal, 171
Bell, William D., 98
Belladonna hybrids, 261
belladonna lily. See *Amaryllis belladonna*
Berbee and Sons. See Ludwig and Company
Bloeiende Klisters, 107, 118–120, 122–124, 126, 127, 168, 184, 185
Blossfeld, Harry, 107
blue amaryllis. See *Worsleya rayneri*
Bodnant collection, 41
Boegschoten, H., 81, 82
Boersen, Andreas J.C., 215
Boophone, 17
Bornemann, Georg, 45
Bowles, Justin, 188
Brasbonitas, 215
Brazilian hybrids, 108, 116; Plates 6.2, 6.3
breeders' open days, 210–211

breeding hippeastrums, 201–210
criteria, 206–210
hybrid registration, 260–261
plant breeders' rights, 211–212, 257–260
propagation, 211
Brunsvigia, 17
Bryan, John, 187
bulbils, 177
bulblets, 159–160, 177, 220–223
bulbs
blistering, 183
breeding criteria, 206–207
planting. See cultivation
propagation. See propagation
quality, 180, 182–184
selecting, 182–184; Plate 9.2
size and weight, 161–164, 180
splitting, 150; Plate 8.9
storage, 175, 182, 183–184, 193, 207, 213
structure and development, 159–166, 206–209; Plates 8.1 to 8.3
Burns, Mrs W.H., 45
butterfly amaryllis. See *Hippeastrum papilio*

Cage, John, 98, 100
Calderón, Julio Cesar Vargas, 107
Callicore rosea. See *Amaryllis belladonna*
Cárdenas, Martin, 107
Carpenter, W.J., 224
Chapman, A., 46
Charpentier, Jerry, 98–100
chipping, 159, 211, 219–223, 228–232; Plates 11.1 to 11.5, 11.8 to 11.13
Clivia, 18
Coburgia, 19
color, pigmentation, 173; Plate 8.5
commercial breeding and production, 201–217
plant breeders' rights, 211–212, 257–260
propagation methods, 211, 219–223
cool period, 174–175, 179, 191–192, 197–198, 212–213
Cothran, Charles D.
double hybrids, 137
yellow hybrids, 98, 106, 137
Crineae, 19
Crinum, 18
Crinum erubescens, 24
cultivated wild *Hippeastrum*, 261
cultivation, 179–200
commercial, 201–217
cool period, 174–175, 179, 191–192, 197–198, 212–213
feeding, 188–190, 195–196
harvesting, 212–213
indoor, 193–199
Kew potting mix, 186–187, 198, 226
lighting, 173, 191, 192, 196, 197
outdoor, 199–200
plant care, 195–199
plant hygiene, 192
planting, 194–195; Plates 9.2 to 9.6
pot size, 184, 185–186
potting media, 184–188
potting mix, 184–188
potting up, 226
propagation. See propagation
purchasing bulbs, 182–184
repotting, 198–199
species, 33–34
temperature, 191–192, 196, 197
watering, 190–191, 195–196; Plate 9.6
Cybister hybrids, 107, 108, 111–115, 120, 123–126, 128–131, 165, 168, 194; Plates 6.16 to 6.19, 6.21 to 6.23, 6.26

Dandy, J.E., 19
Datta, S.K., 117
Deleeuw, Harry, Ltd. See Hadeco (Pty) Ltd

Dell collection, 41
Deme, John W., 134, 135, 137–139, 148–149, 153, 187
diseases, 183, 192–193, 235–236, 251–255
  basal rot (*Fusarium oxysporum*), 123, 210, 251, 252, 253
  blue mold rot (*Penicillium* sp.), 255
  fire. See red spot
  fungicide treatment, 194–195
  gray mold (*Botrytis cinerea*), 254
  mosaic viruses, 251
  narcissus leaf scorch. See red spot
  phytophthora rot (*Phytophthora nicotianae*), 251, 253
  red spot (*Stagonospora curtisii*), 33, 210, 251, 252
  resistance, breeding criteria, 210
Donna bella. See *Amaryllis belladonna*
Doran, John Leonard, 107–109, 139
  Papilio hybrid, 108, 109, 130
  Trumpet hybrids, 109, 125
  yellow hybrids, 98, 100, 102–103, 108–110, 137, 139, 160, 177, 178
double flowers, 133–158, 172, 262
  bicolored, 151–157
  orange-salmon, 148
  pink, 147
  red, 145–147
  reproductive organs, 133, 135–136
  salmon, 148–149
  white, 149–151
double hybrids, 262
Douglas, James, 44
Dutch hybrids. See Agriom B.V.; Boegschoten, H.; Geest, D.J. van; Kwekerij den Oudendam B.V.; Kwekersvereniging Amaryl; Ludwig and Company; Meeuwen & Sons, G.C. van; Mense, Jac J.; Meyers-Mense; Nieuwkerk Amaryllis B.V., T. van; Osselton, Cathy; Penning Breeding B.V.; Staalduinen, Fa. G. van; Stapoflor Lda; Warmenhoven, W.S.; Waveren, M. van.
Dutilh, Julie. See Agronômico Institute at Campinas

empress of Brazil. See *Worsleya rayneri*
evergreen, *Hippeastrum* as, 161, 192
exclusivity, 211–212

fertilizers, 173, 188–190, 195–196
Fielder, C.R., 45–46
flowers
  aborted, 172
  breeding criteria, 208
  decay, 115, 174, 196; Plate 8.6
  development, 159–161, 169, 170–173, 208; Plates 8.4, 8.5
  flowering period, 179, 192
  fragrance. See fragrance
  initiation, 165–167, 170–171; Fig. 8.1
  nectar. See nectar
  pigmentation, 173; Plate 8.5
  production, 169–170, 208–209; Plates 4.5, 4.6, 4.10
  repeat flowering, 181, 207
  size, shape, and color, 58, 164, 209; Plate 8.5. See also individual hybrid descriptions in chapters 3-7
  structure, 169–172
  vase life, 49, 85, 104, 106, 117, 121, 210. See also individual hybrid descriptions in chapters 3-7
Fosberg, F.R., 19
fragrance, 110, 143, 173; Plate 7.8
fruit. See reproduction, sexual
fungicide treatment, 194–195
Galaxy hybrids. See Avon Bulbs
Garroway & Sons, 44
Geest, D.J. van, 84
Graaff, de Hybrids, 45

Graaff, Jan de, 44
Graaff, Simon Adrianus de, 44
Gracilis and Gracilis group hybrids, 82–84, 88–89, 92, 93, 95, 130; Plates 4.1, 6.24
green hybrids, 98–100, 107, 118
Gupta, V.N., 117, 223

Habranthus, 18, 29
Hadeco (Pty) Ltd, 144–145, 215
  large single hybrids, 60, 66, 71, 77
  Solo hybrids, 48
  Sonata double hybrids, 48, 145–146, 149, 153, 164, 206; Plates 7.4, 7.7
  Sonata single hybrids, 48, 87, 90, 91, 164, 172, 206
  Sonatini double hybrids, 48, 145, 146, 164, 206
  Sonatini single hybrids, 48, 87–88, 90, 94, 95, 120–122, 127, 164, 206; Plate 4.4
  Symphony double hybrids, 48, 145–147, 150, 153, 155, 164
  Symphony single hybrids, 47, 48, 51, 52, 55, 56, 57, 61, 62, 63, 73, 74, 164
  yellow hybrids, 101
Hennipman, Elbert, 107
Herbert, Dean W., 16–17, 44
Hill, Edwin, 45
Hippeastrum, 15, 17–20, 23, 24–27; Plate 9.1
  species, 29–40
H. ×acramannii, 44
H. ×acramannii 'Pulcherrima', 44
H. 'Agamemnon', 46
H. aglaiae, 31, 32, 34, 97, 98, 100, 108
H. 'Albescens', 45
H. 'Alfresco', 134, 144, 145, 149, 169; Plate 7.7
H. 'Alipur Beauty', 82
H. 'Allure', 141, 142, 151
H. 'Amalfi', 87, 90, 168
H. 'Amazone'; Plate 8.3
H. 'Ambiance', 96; Plate 4.14
H. 'Ambient', 45
H. ambiguum. See *H. elegans* var. *ambiguum*
H. ambiguum var. *tweedianum*, 32, 35, 108, 110
H. 'Amico', 85, 87–88, 206; Plate 4.4
H. 'Amigo', 54, 63, 142; Plate 3.4
H. 'Amputo', 115, 127–128, 176, 194; Plate 6.20
H. 'Andes', 134, 141, 142, 148
H. 'Angelique', 54, 63–64, 165, 169
H. angustifolium, 29, 30
H. anzaldoi, 97
H. 'Aphrodite', 134, 142, 155, 169, 172, 174; Plate 7.11
H. 'Apple Blossom', 46, 47, 52–53, 64, 165–166, 180, 199
H. 'Apricot Beauty', 67
H. 'Athene', 56, 69
H. aulicum, 16, 29–30, 31, 32, 34, 35, 44, 45, 118; Plate 1.4
H. aulicum var. *platypetalum*, 44
H. 'Autumn Beauty', 45
H. 'Baby Star', 93
H. 'Bahia', 110
H. 'Bambino', 87, 88
H. 'Barbara's Magic', 58, 71; Plate 3.10
H. 'Barotse', 55, 64
H. 'Basuto', 52, 60
H. 'Beacon', 53
H. 'Beau Joliat', 84
H. 'Beautiful Lady', 53, 68, 137; Plate 3.7
H. 'Belinda', 49, 50, 60
H. 'Benfica', 50, 60
H. 'Bestseller', 64
H. 'Bianca', 82, 83, 92, 165; Plate 4.1
H. 'Black Beauty', 46

H. 'Black Knight', 46
H. 'Black Prince', 46
H. 'Blossom Peacock', 134, 135, 141–143, 156
H. 'Blushing Bride', 55, 64
H. 'Bold Leader', 52, 60
H. 'Bolero', 64
H. 'Boysenberry Swirl', 140; Plate 7.1
H. brasilianum, 31, 33, 35, 108, 110
H. 'Brevney', 56, 58, 65
H. bukasovii, 31
H. 'Calimero', 86, 88, 165, 168, 175
H. 'Calypso', 46
H. calyptratum, 16, 30–32, 35, 118; Plate 1.5
H. candidum, 108
H. 'Candy Floss', 55, 65; Plate 3.5
H. 'Captain McCann', 139
H. 'Carina', 83, 88, 165
H. 'Carnival', 57, 71
H. 'Charisma', 57, 85, 86, 93–94, 165, 169, 174, 176; Plate 4.9
H. 'Charmeur', 75
H. 'Chianti', 144, 148
H. 'Chico', 111, 112, 114–115, 128–129, 165, 171, 173, 194; Plates 6.22, 8.6
H. 'Chimborazo', 46
H. 'Christmas Gift', 50, 56, 69, 97; Plate 3.9
H. 'Christmas Joy', 84
H. 'Christmas Star', 87, 91
H. 'Clown', 71
H. 'Cocktail', 57, 71
H. 'Confetti', 139
H. 'Constant Comment', 83
H. 'Coquette', 57, 72
H. correiense, 31, 32, 35
H. ×*cramannii*, 44
H. ×*cramannii* 'Pulcherrima', 44
H. 'Crimson King', 45
H. 'Crown Princess of Germany', 45
H. 'Cupido', 90, 129
H. 'Cyber Queen', 120, 129, 165, 168; Plate 6.26
H. cybister, 30–32, 36, 130; Plate 2.3
H. 'Cynthia', 45
H. 'Dancing Queen', 135, 144, 152, 174; Plate 7.13
H. 'Defiance', 45
H. 'Delbert Howard', 138
H. 'Delicate Damsel', 58, 76
H. 'Desert Dawn', 55, 68, 170
H. 'Design', 57, 72, 171; Plate 3.11
H. 'Desire', 68
H. 'Donau', 91
H. 'Double Beauty', 137, 139
H. 'Double Queen', 144, 152
H. 'Double Record', 135, 138, 139, 156
H. 'Double Salmon', 138
H. 'Double Six', 52, 60
H. 'Duke of York', 46
H. 'Dutch Belle', 53, 65
H. 'Dutch Doll', 56
H. elegans, 16, 29, 31, 32, 36; Plate 1.7
H. elegans var. *ambiguum*, 31, 32, 36, 108
H. 'Elvas', 152
H. 'Elvira Aramayo', 53, 65
H. 'Emerald', 111–113, 128, 165, 173, 194; Plate 6.21
H. 'Empress of India', 44
H. 'Eos', 60
H. equestre, 15–16; Plate 1.2. See also *Amaryllis belladonna*
H. equestre f. *albertii*, 136–137; Plate 2.7
H. 'Eurydice', 45
H. evansiae, 30–33, 36, 97, 98, 100, 108
H. 'Exotica', 67
H. 'Exposure', 55, 76
H. 'Fairytale', 85, 86, 94, 165, 169; Plate 4.10

H. 'Fanfare', 135, 144–146, 165; Plate 7.4
H. 'Fanny White', 138
H. 'Faro', 55, 76
H. 'Ferrari', 50, 61, 181
H. 'Field Marshal', 46
H. 'Fire Fly', 83
H. 'Firefly', 86
H. 'Flair', 75
H. 'Flamengo', 111, 112, 124–125, 165, 173, 194; Plate 6.18
H. 'Flaming Peacock', 134, 135, 141–143, 152, 169; Plates 7.9, 7.10
H. 'Flavio', 55, 65
H. 'Floris Hekker', 85, 86, 89, 169; Plate 4.5
H. 'Flower Record', 65, 84
H. 'Fluffy Ruffles', 144, 153
H. fosteri, 17, 30–32, 37, 97, 108
H. fragrantissimum, 31, 33, 37, 108
H. 'Furore', 50, 61
H. 'Germa', 97, 98, 100, 102–103, 108–110, 137, 139, 160, 165, 166, 177, 178, 194, 197; Plate 5.2
H. 'Gracile', 81–82
H. 'Gracile Ballet', 82
H. 'Grand Cru', 50, 61
H. 'Grandeur', 129–130, 194; Plate 6.24
H. 'Graveana', 44
H. 'Green Goddess'. See H. 'Bianca'
H. 'Green Star', 99, 100, 169; Plate 5.1
H. 'Happiness', 57, 72
H. 'Happy Memory', 57, 72
H. 'Harbour Lights', 56, 58, 66
H. 'Helen Hull', 137
H. 'Hercules', 54, 66
H. 'Hermitage', 57, 72
H. 'Hilda Latapie', 140
H. 'Honeymoon', 52, 61
H. 'House of Orange', 84
H. hugoi, 31
H. immaculatum, 31, 32, 37
H. 'Intokazi', 56, 70
H. 'Irish Summer', 100
H. 'Jaguar', 96, 130; Plate 4.15
H. 'Janet Nestor', 138
H. 'Jennifer Jean', 58, 72–73
H. 'Jewel', 134, 135, 141–143, 149–150, 177, 178; Plates 7.8, 8.9
H. 'John Ruskin', 45
H. 'Johnsonii', 41, 44; Plate 3.1
H. 'Joker', 135, 144, 145, 153; Plate 7.14
H. 'Judy', 138
H. 'Judy Weston', 138
H. 'June Maree', 58, 73
H. 'Jungle Star', 108, 109–110, 130, 173
H. 'Kaitlin', 56, 58, 76
H. 'Kristy', 138
H. 'La Paz', 111–112, 123, 173, 194
H. 'Lady Jane', 138, 139, 142, 148–149, 169
H. 'Lambada', 55, 76
H. lapacense, 31, 32, 33, 37, 108, 110
H. 'Las Vegas', 77
H. 'Lemon Lime', 97, 101, 103–104, 177
H. leopoldii, 30–32, 37, 43; Plate 2.1
H. 'Liberty', 50, 51, 61, 181
H. 'Lilac Wonder', 66
H. 'Lima', 110–112, 130, 173, 194; Plate 6.23
H. 'Lime A', 100
H. 'Limone', 97, 101, 104
H. 'Little Sweetheart', 83
H. 'Lothair', 45
H. 'Louis Parajos', 138
H. 'Lovely Garden', 123–124
H. 'Ludwig's Dazzler', 70
H. 'Lynn', 138
H. 'Lynn Latapie', 140
H. 'Madira Bickel', 137
H. 'Maguire's Envy', 56, 58, 70–71
H. 'Mambo', 57, 73

H. 'Mananita', 100
H. mandonii, 33
H. 'Maria Goretti', 97, 137, 139, 140
H. 'Marjory', 46
H. 'Mary Lou', 135, 142, 156
H. 'Mary McCann', 136–137
H. 'Masai', 55, 77
H. 'Matilda Parajos', 138
H. 'Matterhorn', 70
H. 'Melody Lane', 83
H. 'Melpomene', 45
H. 'Mercury', 45
H. 'Merengue', 111–114, 125–126, 165, 173, 174, 194; Plate 6.19
H. 'Merry Christmas', 52, 61
H. 'Michele Latapie', 140
H. 'Midas', 45
H. 'Milady', 55, 66
H. 'Minerva', 57, 73, 180
H. 'Miracle', 52, 62
H. 'Mont Blanc', 54, 56
H. 'Moonlight', 97, 101, 104
H. 'Moviestar', 85, 86, 91–92, 165, 169, 176; Plate 4.6
H. 'Mrs Garfield', 45
H. 'Mrs Lancaster', 82
H. 'Murillo', 46
H. 'My Favourite', 144, 150
H. 'Nagano', 55, 69; Plate 3.8
H. 'Naughty Lady'. See *H.* 'Voodoo'
H. 'Nivalis', 97
H. 'Nostalgia', 137
H. 'Nymph', 135, 144, 157; Plate 7.12
H. 'Oasis', 100
H. 'Orange Sovereign', 53–54, 68
H. 'Pamela', 83, 89, 165, 175
H. papilio, 30–34, 38, 96, 97–99, 110, 130, 179, 194, 197, 199; Plate 2.4
H. pardinum, 30–32, 38, 43, 45, 110; Plate 2.2
H. 'Park's Apricot', 137
H. 'Parma', 50, 62, 181
H. parodii, 30–33, 38, 97, 98, 100, 108
H. 'Pasadena', 134, 138, 153
H. 'Pastel', 100
H. 'Pearl Maiden', 46
H. 'Petticoat', 56
H. 'Philadelphia', 154
H. 'Piccolo', 87, 94–95
H. 'Pico Bello', 87, 91
H. 'Picotee', 56–57, 93, 166
H. 'Picture', 83
H. 'Pink Blossom', 46, 77
H. 'Pink Diamond', 55, 77
H. 'Pink Floyd', 108, 109, 125, 177, 194; Plate 6.1
H. 'Pink Floyd' Plate 9.3
H. 'Pink Impression', 55, 77
H. 'Pink Nymph', 144, 147
H. 'Pink Star', 86, 95; Plate 4.12
H. 'Piquant', 79
H. 'Pixie', 83
H. 'Pizzazz', 57, 73; Plate 3.12
H. 'Prelude', 57, 73
H. 'President', 45
H. 'Pretty Pal', 83
H. procerum. See *Worsleya rayneri*
H. 'Promise', 135, 144, 154; Plate 8.4
H. psittacinum, 16, 30–32, 38, 44, 45; Plate 1.6
H. 'Pygmee', 84
H. 'Queen of Hearts', 55, 77
H. 'Queen of Night', 137
H. 'Queen of the Nile', 56, 58, 78; Plate 3.13
H. 'Ragtime', 144–146
H. 'Rainbow', 135, 142, 154
H. 'Rapido', 85, 86, 89, 134, 165, 172
H. 'Razzle Dazzle', 57, 74
H. 'Razzmatazz', 134, 144, 155

H. 'Red Charm', 142, 146
H. 'Red Lining', 56
H. 'Red Lion', 47, 49–50, 52, 62, 165, 166, 180; Plate 8.5
H. 'Red Man', 83
H. 'Red Nymph', 144, 146
H. 'Red Peacock', 134, 141, 142, 147, 170, 172; Plate 7.5
H. 'Red Riding Hood', 84
H. 'Red Sensation', 50, 62, 181
H. 'Reggae', 111–114, 124, 165–166, 173, 194; Plates 6.16, 8.2
H. reginae, 16, 17, 29–32, 39, 41, 44; Plate 1.3
H. reticulatum, 29, 31, 32, 39, 44; Plate 2.6
H. reticulatum var. *striatifolium*, 32, 82, 110
H. 'Rilona', 53, 69
H. 'Rio', 110, 144, 155
H. 'Robin', 46
H. 'Roma', 50, 62, 181
H. 'Rotterdam', 49, 50, 63
H. 'Royal Ruby', 49
H. 'Royal Velvet', 50–51, 63, 181; Plate 3.3
H. 'Rozetta', 144, 147
H. 'Rubina', 83
H. 'Ruby Meyer', 111–113, 130–131, 194; Plate 6.25
H. rutilum, 33, 81
H. 'Salmon Peacock', 134, 144, 149, 168; Plate 7.6
H. 'Salmon Pearl', 92, 165, 171, 174; Plate 4.7
H. 'Sampa', 110
H. 'San Remo', 78
H. 'Satura', 45
H. 'Scarlet Gem', 45
H. 'Scarlet Globe', 49; Plate 3.2
H. 'Showmaster', 57, 74
H. 'Snow White', 144, 145, 150
H. 'Snowdon', 46
H. solandriflorum. See *H. elegans*
H. 'Solomon', 55, 69
H. 'Sparkling Gem', 83
H. 'Springtime', 55, 66
H. 'Star of Bethlehem', 84
H. 'Stargazer', 57, 74
H. 'Starlet', 85, 86, 95–96, 165; Plate 4.13
H. 'Stein's Glory', 84
H. 'Ster van Holland', 57, 74
H. striatum, 30, 32, 39, 44, 97, 98
H. stylosum, 30–32, 39, 82; Plate 2.5
H. 'Summertime', 55, 66
H. 'Sun Dance', 63
H. 'Supreme Garden', 126–127; Plate 6.14
H. 'Surprise', 138
H. 'Susan', 54, 67
H. 'Swan Lake', 121
H. 'Sydney', 57, 74, 169
H. 'Table Decoration', 83
H. 'Tangellino', 52, 58, 68, 169; Plate 3.6
H. 'Tango', 111–113, 124, 160, 165, 168, 173, 177, 194; Plates 6.17, 8.1
H. 'Telstar', 53, 67
H. 'The Chancellor', 45
H. 'Tinto', 112, 165
H. 'Toledo', 85, 86, 89–90, 165, 168
H. 'Top Choice', 87, 90, 169, 172, 206
H. 'Toronto', 75
H. 'Trendsetter', 55, 78
H. 'Twinkling Star', 83
H. 'Unique', 135, 148
H. 'Veneto', 120, 127
H. 'Vera', 54, 67
H. 'Vienna', 70
H. 'Violetta', 137
H. 'Virgin Queen', 45
H. 'Virginia', 46

H. vittatum, 16, 29–32, 40, 41, 44, 45; Plate 1.8
H. 'Vlammenspel', 75
H. 'Voodoo', 82, 83, 95; Plate 4.11
H. 'Vulcan', 46
H. 'Wedding Dance', 56, 70
H. 'White Christmas', 97
H. 'White Equester III', 93, 165, 174; Plate 4.8
H. 'White Nymph', 140, 144, 151
H. 'White Peacock', 141, 142, 151, 165, 172
H. 'Williamsii', 45
H. 'Windswept', 100
H. 'Wonderland', 54, 78
H. 'Yellow Goddess', 50, 85, 97, 104–105, 118, 165, 177; Plate 5.5
H. 'Yellow Moon', 86, 97, 100, 101, 105–106; Plate 5.3
H. 'Yellow Pioneer', 97, 98–100, 106
H. 'Yock', 138
H. 'Zanzibar', 52, 63
Holford, Lt. Col. George L., 46
Hooker, Joseph D., 17
hot water treatment, 222, 235, 246–251
Houtte, Louis van, 45
humidity, 173
hybrids, 21, 219
  classification, 261–264
  registration, 260–261
  See also breeding hippeastrums
Hymenocallis, 18

Indian hybrids, 116–117
indoor cultivation, 193–199
inflorescence. See flowers

Japanese hybrids, 117–118
Jersey lily. See *Amaryllis belladonna*
Johnson hybrid, 41, 44
Jordan River Bulbs, 215
Ker & Sons, Robert P., 41, 45
Kew potting mix, 186–187, 198, 226
Kher, M.A., 117, 223
Khoshoo, T.N., 117
Klisters. See Bloeiende Klisters
Knight Garden hybrids. See Bloeiende Klisters
Krelage hybrids, 45
Kwekerij den Oudendam B.V., 68
Kwekersvereniging Amaryl, 61, 74, 75, 148

labeling, 181–182
Lais, 18, 19
Lancaster, S.P., 82
large single hybrids, 41–79
  bicolored, 56–57, 71–78
  classification, 48
  flowers, 58
  green, 70–71
  offset production, 59
  orange, 67–68, 75
  pink, 52–56, 63–67, 76–78
  red, 49–52, 60–63
  salmon, 68–69, 75
  scapes and foliage, 58–59
  tricolored, 79
  white, 56, 69–70
Latapie, W.R., 134, 139–140
  leaves, 159–161, 165–169; Fig. 8.1
  breeding criteria, 209
  evergreen nature of *Hippeastrum*, 161, 192
large flowering hybrids, 58–59
Leopoldii hybrids, 43–46, 49, 60–73, 75, 79, 93, 96, 106, 136, 262; Plates 3.3, 3.4, 3.7, 3.8
L'Héritier, Charles, 16
Libon, Joseph, 24

lighting, 173, 191, 192, 196, 197
Lilium longiflorum, 31
Lilium reginae. See *Hippeastrum reginae*
Lindley, John, 17
Linnaeus, Carolus, 15, 16
long Trumpet hybrids, 261
long-styled knight's-star lily. See *Hippeastrum stylosum*
Ludwig and Company, 51, 52–53
  Gracilis and small single hybrids, 82–84, 88, 89, 91, 92, 95, 165; Plate 4.1
  large single hybrids, 46–53, 56, 63–65, 68, 70, 72, 137, 166; Plate 3.7
Lycoris, 29

McCann, J.J., 136–137
Macropodastrum, 18, 19
Maguire, Richard
  double hybrids, 140–141, 215
  large single hybrids, 52, 55–59, 65, 66, 68, 70–73, 76, 78, 215; Plate 3.6
March lily. See *Amaryllis belladonna*
Mead, Theodore L., 136
Meerow, Alan W., 108, 110
Meeuwen & Sons, G.C. van
  large single hybrids, 46, 49–50, 60, 69, 71, 73
  small single hybrids, 82
Mense, Jac J., 54, 56, 61–64, 66, 67, 69, 74, 75, 78, 79
Mexican lily. See *Hippeastrum reginae*
Meyer, Fred, 42, 107, 108, 111, 198
  Cybister hybrids, 111–115, 123–126, 128–131, 194; Plates 6.16 to 6.19, 6.21 to 6.23
  other hybrids, 129–130, 194
  Trumpet hybrids, 115, 127–128, 130; Plate 6.20
Meyers-Mense, 79
Miller, John, 16
mini single hybrids. See Miyake Nursery Ltd
miniature hybrids, 107, 262. See also Gracilis and Gracilis group hybrids; hybrid classification
Miyake Nursery Ltd
  autumn hybrids, 107, 118; Plate 6.7
  compost, 188
  double hybrids, 141–144, 146–156; Plates 7.2, 7.3, 7.5, 7.8
  large green hybrids, 107, 118
  large single hybrids, 117
  medium cut flower single hybrids, 86, 117; Plates 4.2, 4.3
  mini single hybrids, 108, 117; Plate 6.5
  miniature single hybrids, 107
  small single hybrids, 86, 117; Plate 6.4
  super mini single hybrids, 108, 117–118, 165, 206; Plate 6.6
  modern single hybrids, 107–131
Moldenke, Harold. N., 18, 19
Morton, W.D. Jr., 42

naked lady. See *Amaryllis belladonna*
Narain, P., 117
National Botanical Research Institute, Lucknow, 108, 116–117, 187, 223
nectar, 111, 128, 130, 173. See also individual hybrid descriptions in chapter 6
Nerine, 17
netted-veined amaryllis. See *Hippeastrum reticulatum*
Nieuwkerk Amaryllis B.V., T. van
  double hybrids, 144, 146–148, 151, 152, 157
  large single hybrids, 54, 55, 60, 61, 65–67, 72, 74–77, 100
  yellow hybrids, 100, 104
North American hybrids. See Cage, John; Cothran, Charles, D.; Deme, John W.;

Doran, John L.; Latapie, W.R.; McCann, J.J.; Meerow, Alan W.; Meyer, Fred
notching, 219, 223, 232–234

offsets, 159, 177–178, 198–199, 227; Plates 8.1, 9.3
  breeding criteria, 210
Omphalissa, 18, 19
Oporanthus, 17
orchid-flowering hybrids, 262
Osselton, Cathy, 107, 108, 118–120
  Bloeiende Klister hybrids, 107, 118–120, 122–124, 126–127, 168, 184, 185
  Queen of the Knight hybrids, 108, 118, 119; Plates 6.8, 6.13
  Star of the Knight hybrids, 108, 118, 119; Plates 6.8 to 6.12
Ostmark, E.R., 224
outdoor cultivation, 199–200

packaging, 181–182
Pancratium, 18
Papilio hybrid, 108–110, 130, 173
Pearce, Richard William, 43
pedicel development, 173–174
Penning Breeding B.V., 118, 165, 168, 175
  conventional small single hybrids, 93–96, 165, 168, 175
  Cybister hybrids, 120, 129, 165, 168; Plate 6.26
  double hybrids, 135, 144, 149, 152, 154, 168, 174
  large single hybrids, 50, 54–55, 57, 60, 62, 63, 69, 70, 72–74, 76–78, 142, 171; Plates 3.4, 3.11
  medium/midi single hybrids, 86, 89, 91–93, 94, 165, 174, 176
  small flowering hybrids, 86–89
  yellow hybrids, 86, 100, 104–106
Penning Breeding. See Penning Freesia
pests, 192–193, 235–245, 251
  ants, 244
  aphids, 192, 238, 251
  banded snail, 243
  biological control, 235
  black slug, 243
  blackfly, 238
  blister beetle (*Epicauta strigosa*), 245
  bulb eelworm. See stem eelworm
  bulb mite (*Rhizoglyphus echinopus*), 239
  bulb scale mite. See tarsonemid mite
  caterpillars, 244
  eastern Lubber grasshopper (*Romalea microptera*), 236, 244
  field slug, 243
  fungus gnat, 239
  garden slug, 243
  garden snail, 243
  glasshouse red spider mite (*Tetranychus urticae*), 236, 241
  glasshouse thrip (*Heliothrips*), 235, 236, 242
  greenfly, 238
  Kanazawa spider mite (*Tetranychus kanzawai*), 241
  keeled slug, 243
  large narcissus fly, 236, 238
  lesser bulb fly. See small narcissus fly
  mealybug (*Trionymus lounsburyi*), 192, 242–243
  mites, 235, 237, 239, 241
  moths, 244
  mushroom fly. See fungus gnat
  nematodes, 235
  pill bug. See sowbug
  roly-poly. See sowbug
  sciarid fly. See fungus gnat
  small narcissus fly, 236, 238
  soft scale insect (*Coccus hesperidum*), 242
  sowbug, 244

stem eelworm (*Ditylenchus dipsaci*), 241
strawberry snail, 243
tarsonemid mite (*Steneotarsonemus laticeps*), 236, 237, 239–240
thunder fly. See glasshouse thrip
two spotted spider mite. See glasshouse red spider mite
weevil (*Brachycerus*), 245
woodlouse. See sowbug
pH, soil, 173
Phycella, 18, 29
picotee hybrids, 56–57, 85
pigmentation, 173; Plate 8.5
pollination, 176, 219
pollen collection and storage, 224
pot size, 184, 185
potting media, 184–188, 226
propagation, 23–24, 219–234
chipping, 159, 211, 219–223, 228–232; Plates 11.1 to 11.5, 11.8 to 11.13
notching, 219, 223, 232–234
offsets, 159, 177–178, 198–199, 210, 227; Plates 8.1, 9.3
seed, 159–160, 224–227; Plates 1.9, 8.7, 8.8
twin scaling, 159, 161, 210, 211, 219–223, 228–232; Plates 11.1 to 11.11
Pyrolirion, 18

Queen of the Knight. See under Osselton, Cathy

Ravenna, Pedro Felix, 107
Rayner, John F., 24
Reginae hybrids, 43–45, 49, 60, 62, 64, 65, 71, 75, 77, 103–104, 136, 261–262
reproduction
asexual, 59, 159, 177–178, 210, 211, 227; Plates 8.1, 9.3
sexual, 176–177; Plates 1.9, 4.10, 8.6 to 8.8
reproductive organs, 171, 176
Rhodophiala, 18, 29
ripening, 33
Rix, D., 215
roots, 114, 163–164, 183; Plates 9.3, 11.12
breeding criteria, 206–207
hydrating, 194
Rothschild collection, 41, 45
Ruppel, C. Gomez, 107

Saad-Assaf Nurseries, 215
Savage, S., 19
scape, 161, 162–163, 164–165, 175, 191. See also individual hybrid descriptions
breeding criteria, 208–209
large flowering hybrids, 58–59
Sealy, J.R., 19
Sealyana, 19
seeds, 159–160, 219; Plates 1.9, 8.7, 8.8
propagating from, 224–227
storage, 224–225
small and medium single hybrids (conventional), 81–96, 198
bicolored, 85, 93–96
classification, 83–85
orange, 85, 91–92
pink, 85, 90–91, 95–96
red, 82, 85, 87–90, 93–95
salmon, 85, 92–93
Solo hybrids, See Miyake Nursery Ltd
Sonata hybrids. See Hadeco (Pty) Ltd
Sonatini hybrids. See Barnhoorn, Andre; Hadeco (Pty) Ltd
South African hybrids. See Hadeco (Pty) Ltd
Sprague, T.A., 19
Sprekelia, 17
Sprekelia formosissima, 29
Tumbler sprekelia. See *Hippeastrum cybister*

Hippeastrum Sumatra (Amaryllis - Spider Group)

Code: 220879

Hover over to zoom, click to enlarge

Exotic-looking flowers

Exotic-looking flowers of salmon-pink and white. Height 45-60cm. Bulb size 26/28cm. **Buy any 4 Hippeastrums and SAVE £6.00!** Commonly (though incorrectly) known as Amaryllis, these amazing flowers, which originate from the Andes mountain regions of Chile and Peru, make fantastic houseplants that will light up your home in winter and early spring (flowering approx. 8 weeks after planting). And, by following a few easy steps, they should bloom year after year. The many cultivars available have recently been divided into nine groups, and here we are delighted to present our favourites from each of those groups.

1 Bulb

Quantity – 1 +

Add to Basket £8.95

Add to wish list

Culture: Full growing instructions included.

Average Growing Height: 51-60CM

Delivery Guarantee

14 Days

16 Comments

NEWEST FIRST | OLDEST FIRST | BEST | WORST | CONTROVERSIAL

1 2

Jorrocks ...

33 minutes ago

Have you started thinking about Christmas Gifts yet?

Here is an excellent idea for those who enjoy a good crime thriller or are countryside enthusiasts...

The Shrew by Nicholas Gordon

0 2

Report Spam

Mike Nimrod (Thecountryisbad)

44 minutes ago

You CANNOT spot isolate weight loss. If you lose it off your BELLY you will be losing it everywhere - fact.

As a boxer and cyclist neither do a great deal to lose stomach fat - in fact minimal. The ONLY way to do that is with a decent diet AND more importantly RUNNING / JOGGING / SWIMMING. There is no other way unless you are wanting to do lyposuction.

a sauna / Steam room for a couple of hours gets the heary rate up but get out every 15-20 mins and let your heart rate go oback down before going back in.

regaridng organic - have been organic and vegetarian for years and noticed no difference in performance or weight loss. Organic is fine and imo essential for juicing but don't bellieve the hype about needing it in every meal. Besides, most of it is grown hydroponically and rarely sees any natural sunlight - just look at Waitrose's anemic looking organic celery for example and it still costs a bomb.

More

2 0

Report Spam

john mclaren (kiwijock)

1 hour ago

[illegible]

Growing Guide

Amaryllis - How to plant, grow, and enjoy

To Induce Growth: Amaryllis in green pots need only a thorough watering to begin growing. Amaryllis shipped with potting mix require potting. It's also possible to grow Amaryllis in pebbles and water. Watch our head gardener demonstrate simple steps to follow in the videos "How to Pot and Care for Amaryllis" and "Growing Amaryllis in Water."

GROWING AMARYLLIS: These bulbs are prized for their willingness to produce large and colorful blooms indoors in the dead of winter. In Zones 9 and 10, they can also be planted outdoors in full sun and well-drained soil, with the shoulders of the bulbs 1in above the soil. Bulbs planted in the ground generally bloom in late spring or early summer. What follows are instructions for forcing Amaryllis indoors for winter bloom.

POTTING THE BULBS: Amaryllis shipped in bags require potting. Pot bulbs individually in 6–7in pots or group 3 bulbs together in a 10–12in container. Begin by placing a well-drained potting mix in a plastic tub. Slowly add warm water and stir with your hand until the mix is moist but not soggy. Then fill the pot about half full with potting mix, set the bulb on top of the mix and fill in around the bulb with additional mix. Adjust the position of the bulb as needed, so that the top third of the bulb is exposed. The final level of the mix should be about 1/2in below the rim of the pot to allow for watering. Firm the mix and water lightly to settle it around the bulbs. Then follow the instructions under "Pre-bloom Care" below.

PRE-POTTED BULBS: Amaryllis sent already potted need only a thorough watering with lukewarm water to begin growing. Then follow the instructions under "Pre-bloom Care" below. Please note: Prepotted Amaryllis in baskets are shipped with a layer of decorative Spanish moss on top of each pot. With a pair of scissors, snip the rubber band that holds the Spanish moss in place and arrange the moss around the bulb so it looks attractive.

Sainsbury's

PRE-BLOOM CARE OF AMARYLLIS: Place the pot where the temperature remains above 60°F. The warmer the temperature (70–80°F night and day is ideal), the faster the bulb will sprout and grow. Water only when the top inch of the potting mix is dry to the touch. Watering more frequently, particularly just after potting, can cause the bulb to rot. (If the pot is covered with Spanish Moss, lift the moss and pour water directly on the potting mix.) Growth generally begins in 2–8 weeks. Provide ample sunshine (a south-facing window or a sunroom) as soon as the bulb sprouts. Rotate the pot frequently to prevent the flower stalks from leaning toward the light. The flower stalks may require support to keep from toppling; our Amaryllis stakes are ideally suited to this purpose.

REBUILDING THE BULB: After flowering, your bulb is exhausted. If you want flowers next year (many people prefer simply to purchase new bulbs every fall), you must allow it to rebuild itself. After the last bloom fades, cut off the flower stalk 3–5 inches above the bulb, but leave the foliage intact. Put your plant in a sunny window (a south-facing one is best), water when the top inch of the potting mix is dry to the touch, and begin fertilizing with a balanced, water-soluble fertilizer once a month. When the danger of frost has passed in spring, set the pot outdoors in full sun or knock the bulb out of its pot and plant it in the ground in a sunny location. In fall—we often wait until frost blackens the leaves—bring the bulb indoors, cut the foliage off just above the bulb, and store it dry in a cool (55°F), dark place such as a basement for 8–10 weeks. Then pot (or repot) the bulb and water it. Thereafter, keep the potting mix almost dry until new growth emerges, and follow the instructions under "Pre-bloom Care" above.

GROWING AMARYLLIS IN STONES AND WATER: These large bulbs will grow happily and bloom abundantly in nothing more than stones and water. To "plant" your bulb, begin by carefully placing river stones to a depth of about 4 inches in our Hurricane Vase, or 2 inches in the Crackle-glazed Planter. With scissors, trim off any roots on the bulb that are brown and dried, but let the roots that are whitish and fleshy remain. Place the Amaryllis bulb, roots down, on top of the stones, then put the remaining stones around the bulb, leaving the top third of the bulb exposed. Finally, add water until the level reaches just below the base of the bulb but no higher. If the base of the bulb sits in water, it will rot.

After planting, set the container on a sunny windowsill in a room where the temperature remains above 60°F. The warmer the temperature (70–80°F night and day is ideal), the faster the bulb will sprout and grow. Check the water level daily. Add water as needed to keep the level below the base of the bulb. A shoot will emerge from the top of the bulb in 2–8 weeks; you may (or may not) see thick white roots pushing between the stones before then. Rotate the container frequently to prevent the flower stalks from leaning toward the light. After the last blooms fade, we recommend that you dispose of the bulb; Amaryllis grown in water may not perform well in subsequent years. However, if you do wish to continue growing the bulb, follow the instructions given in "Potting the Bulbs" and "Rebuilding the Bulb."

1 0 Report Spam

M Aslam Chohan 1 hour ago

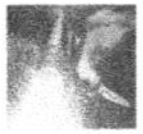

"Eat fresh produce, ...eat organic food where possible. ....Drink lots of water: cut down on alcohol, tea and coffee, with the odd cup of green tea. This will help clear your body of toxins, hydrate you, and speed up your metabolism."
Eat organic food where possible --- where is the scientific evidence for this, the trials and the results in peer reviewed journals.

Clear your body of toxins -- as if the body is not doing this all the time and really eliminating completely the 'toxins' would actually harm the body.

Speed up the metabolism -- just by drinking water, would speed the proceses in the body. (Drinking coffeee has been stated as being good for Asthmatic).

More

2 0 Report Spam

david parsons (blitzy) 1 hour ago

I went down with a muscle spasm three years ago...it changed my life,as i HAD to walk,so not to end up in a wheelchair(at least that's where my mind went)...i lost weight,gained weight and three years later,i still have a PAUNCH,but now have the strength to carry it,therefore leading to more walking...basically,i am told that my whole shape changed...it lead to other things..i have since started writing words to inspire folk..RESURRECTION(a song i wrote) was penned purely to inspire...hopefully it will one day reach mainstream and everyone will have access to a copy..then all that walking..up to 8 miles a day will have been well worth it...one guy who inspired me was an American writer who i met on the net...one of his songs was called "Get back up(HALLELUJAH)and helped me to recover.... and his name...... BRION RIBORN...we have now become good friends..please have a listen to this song or "OPEN EYES"...this guy is amazing and i am and always will be grateful that he has always kept in touch,even during some dark times...this one's for you,my American bro...thanks for helping me GET BACK UP!!!..hope he inspires others..he's well worthy of three and a half minutes of anyone's time...kinda feel a tear or two coming...please tell him,if you like him,where you heard his name first..i owe him this..and tell others about him...

More

4 3 Report Spam

p 1 hour ago

Customers Who Bought This Item Also Bought

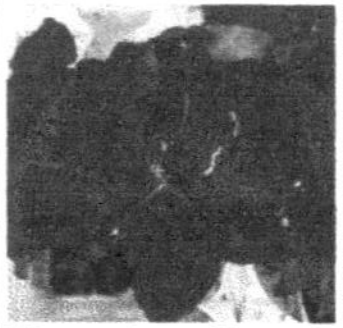

Hippeastrum Cherry Nymph (Amaryllis - Double Colibri Group) More Info £7.95

Hippeastrum Evergreen (Amaryllis - Spider Group) More Info £8.95

Hippeastrum Gervase (Amaryllis - Galaxy Group) More Info £7.95

Review this Product

Recently Viewed Products

More Info

More Info

More Info

Follow us on Facebook | Follow us on Twitter | Sutton's on YouTube | Sutton's blog and forum

Customer Services